LEPER KNIGHTS

The Order of St Lazarus of Jerusalem in
England, *c.*1150–1544

Studies in the History of Medieval Religion

ISSN 0955–2480

General Editor
Christopher Harper-Bill

Previously published titles in the series
are listed at the back of this volume

LEPER KNIGHTS

The Order of St Lazarus of Jerusalem in
England, *c.*1150–1544

David Marcombe

THE BOYDELL PRESS

© David Marcombe 2003

All Rights Reserved. Except as permitted under current legislation
no part of this work may be photocopied, stored in a retrieval system,
published, performed in public, adapted, broadcast,
transmitted, recorded or reproduced in any form or by any means,
without the prior permission of the copyright owner

First published 2003
The Boydell Press, Woodbridge
Reprinted in paperback 2004

ISBN 978 0 85115 893 8 hardback
ISBN 978 1 84383 067 2 paperback

Transferred to digital printing

The Boydell Press is an imprint of Boydell & Brewer Ltd
PO Box 9, Woodbridge, Suffolk IP12 3DF, UK
and of Boydell & Brewer Inc.
668 Mt. Hope Avenue, Rochester NY 14620, USA
website: www.boydellandbrewer.com

A CIP record for this title is available
from the British Library

Library of Congress Catalog Card Number 2002154333

This publication is printed on acid-free paper

Contents

Illustrations

Plates

Tables

Graphs

Maps

Plans

Acknowledgements

It is sobering, and a little humbling, to sit down and write a set of acknowledgements for a book on this scale. Any author who may be seduced by delusions of grandeur at this stage should recall the words of the slave whispering in the ear of the successful general during the Roman Triumph – 'you are but mortal'. Similarly with a book. Though an author takes the credit as the one who puts it all together, he is only as good as the numerous people who have offered help and support during the long hours of its compilation. It is appropriate that these individuals should be thanked and share in the pride rightly felt on the completion of a major undertaking such as this.

The first thing to say is that the book has been a collaborative venture and much of the information in it has been gathered together by what soon came to be known, quite informally, as the Burton Lazars Research Group. Remarkably, all those who were there at the start of our adventure in 1983 are still up and running at the finish – older, if not always wiser. The group comprises Mike and Jenny Allsop, Terry Bourne, Joe and Moira Ecob, and Judy Smithers, all residents of Melton Mowbray or the immediate vicinity. All of them have contributed enthusiastically to the end result. It would be invidious to pick out individuals in such a united and hard-working team, but I am sure the whole group would wish me say a special word of thanks to Terry, whose painstaking work on the charters (not least the Burton Lazars Cartulary) has been second to none.

Though these individuals formed the inner cabinet of what sometimes seemed like some new, undercover order of St Lazarus, they brought with them an outer ring of helpers who were invariably there to offer support when the need arose – Eddie Smithers with his computer skills and Valerie Bourne, always on hand with food and warm drinks! Indeed, working with the Burton Lazars Research Group has been a memorable experience of the sort one enjoys only once in a lifetime. Our scholarly efforts have been enhanced by all manner of social activities and above all we have functioned as a group of friends, a factor that has not only illuminated our academic discoveries but has also enhanced our lives as well. Our thanks to the University of Nottingham's School of Continuing Education for quietly encouraging and supporting our work over such a long period – even though it never fitted into any category devised by educational bureaucrats or accountants. There, perhaps, lies another reason for its success.

Much of our landscape work has depended on access, and owners and occupiers of St Lazarus-related properties have been generous in allowing us to do just about what we wanted. Thanks are due to the late Captain Patrick Drury-Lowe (Locko Park), Major Peter Hutchinson (Choseley Manor), Colin McDowel (Harehope), and Jim Cooil (Tilton). Among the farmers of Burton

Lazars, the Hawleys, Gills and Toulsons have all been accommodating, but a special word of thanks must go to Geoff Child who farms the land on which the preceptory itself is located. Our numerous visits to show around visitors, take photographs and undertake all manner of survey work have been greeted with the same tolerance and good humour. Geoff even doubled up as Burton Lazars churchwarden for some years and therefore had the additional, onerous duty of letting us into the church. We hope that the book answers all of the questions about his bumpy field that he is ever likely to ask!

When it came to analysing these varied historic landscapes, we received help from a number of specialists – Dr Chris Salisbury (watercourses), Fred Hartley (earthworks), and Ann Borrill and Jean Nicholson (flora and fauna). Special thanks must go to Tony Brown of the University of Leicester and his Archaeology Certificate students (among whom were Mike and Jenny Allsop), who mapped the complex Burton Lazars earthworks in the 1980s. Mary Hatton, archaeological warden for Burton Lazars, ensured we had eyes and ears in the local community. Among other things, Mary was instrumental in the discovery of the Burton House stones in 2000, which we were able to record with the permission of Jim and Christine Greaves, at that time owners of the house. The stones were moved, cleaned and recorded by a team of students from the University of Nottingham who all deserve a mention because of their hard work under difficult circumstances – Lesley Redgate, Richard Albery, Ted White, Janet Jackson, Sarah Seaton, Brian Jones, Diana Archer, Colin Pendleton, Margaret Smith, Brian Hodgkinson, Jan Davies, Trevor Lane, Sue Hadcock, Amanda Jennings, David Brown, Maggie Malkin, Dave Pollard, Shona Husband, Sandra Green, Tracey Wormald and Jenny Adams. If these people made up the much needed workforce, the experts who drew the conclusions were Dr Jenny Alexander and Bernard Martin. By their combined skills in archaeology and architecture the lost church of the Lazarites is coming to life once more.

In our quest for documents, the staffs of the various libraries, museums and record offices in which we have worked have been uniformly helpful and supportive. Academic colleagues and local enthusiasts have contributed details from their unpublished research or have assisted with awkward details. In this respect we would like to offer our thanks to the late Revd Philip Hunt, Dr Kenneth Baird, Dr Joan D'Arcy, Barry Alexander, Professor Mark Ormrod, Syd Lusted, Dr Alison McHardy, Dr Ted Connell, Dr Keith Manchester, Dr Charlotte Roberts, Pamela Willis and Julian Roberts. For assistance with details of translation our advisors have been Barbara Panton, Dr Nicholas Bennett, John Wade, Dr Mary Lucas and Irina Feichtl. We are most grateful to them all for the time they have put in on our behalf.

The book has been compiled by a range of people over a surprisingly long period of time, our earliest typescripts being produced more than a decade ago – before the age of the word processor. The following University of Nottingham secretaries helped in this ongoing process – Judy Matsell, the late Catherine Beeston, Margie D'Arcy and Sue Andrews. At some point Rita Poxon came to our rescue with a piece of technical wizardry that made pages of old-fashioned typescript compatible with a computer. Norman Fahy drew the earthwork plan of Man Mill, and all of the other maps and plans were put into publishable form by Dr Anne Tarver whose skill in these matters is a byword among *cognoscenti*. Likewise with Trevor Clayton, our photographer in chief. Though occasional examples of the work of others intrude on these pages, the vast majority of the photographs were taken by Trevor, whose patience and good humour were always exemplary.

A particular word of thanks to those people whose contribution has spilled over into more than one area. Sue Clayton has provided us with organisational skills, information, sandwiches and shadows. Dr Rafäel Hyacinthe has been our link with the order of St Lazarus overseas, and we have enjoyed useful (and convivial) collaborative visits both in this country and in France. Rafäel's selfless sharing of information has filled many gaps – and we hope we have reciprocated sufficiently to provide similar support for his forthcoming book on the history of the order in Europe. Thanks to Rafäel the *entente cordiale* once more flourishes! Kate Holland, like Sue, came into the project in the later stages, but has made a tremendous contribution just when it was needed most. She has assisted with research, taken over the preparation of the typescript, undertaken the picture editing, completed the index and proof-read the final version of the text. This has been hugely time-consuming for someone already leading a frenetic life. Without her help and support the book could not have been completed in the time available. Neither could I have finished it without the tolerance of my partner, Ann. In a house where dining room and study are synonymous, mountains of paper have impeded normal social intercourse for the best part of a year. She will be relieved, at last, to be living with a human being, rather than a leper-obsessed zombie.

Finally, my thanks to the University of Nottingham for providing me with a period of study leave in 2001 to complete the book; to Boydell & Brewer for agreeing to publish it; and to Professor David Loades and Dr Carole Rawcliffe for reading parts of the typescript and offering many helpful and constructively critical comments. Most of these have been incorporated into the final version of the text, though I must emphasise that any surviving errors are my own. A most rewarding project has drawn to a close, not with the sudden death of the author, as occurred under similar circumstances in 1792, but with well-deserved thanks to an unusually long list of people. At last the story of the order of St Lazarus has been told – and I hope a wide readership will enjoy it.

David Marcombe
Newark-upon-Trent
19 October 2001

Abbreviations

Books and calendars are listed as they appear in the Bibliography, unless an editor is specified.

AA	*Archaeologia Aeliana*
AASRP	*Associated Architectural Societies, Reports and Papers*
AC	Alnwick Castle
AN	Archives Nationales
ASV	Archivio Segreto Vaticano
BAR	British Archaeological Reports
BC	Brasenose College, Oxford
BÉFAR	Bibliothèque des Écoles Françaises d'Athènes et de Rome
BL	British Library
BM	British Museum
BN	Bibliothèque Nationale
Bod Lib	Bodleian Library
CA	College of Arms
Cart	Cotton Ms, Nero Cxii
CCA	Canterbury Cathedral Archives
CCC	Corpus Christi College, Cambridge
CLBCL	*Calendar of Letter Books of the City of London* (ed. Sharpe)
CCR	*Calendar of Close Rolls*
CChR	*Calendar of Charter Rolls*
CChanR	*Calendar of Chancery Rolls*
CDS	*Calendar of Documents relating to Scotland* (ed. Bain)
CFR	*Calendar of Fine Rolls*
Cal Inq	*Calendar of Inquisitions*
CLR	*Calendar of Liberate Rolls*
CPR	*Calendar of Patent Rolls*
CPapR	*Calendar of Papal Registers*
CR	*Charter Rolls*
CRO	Cheshire Record Office
CS	Camden Society
CYS	Canterbury and York Society
DAJ	*Derbyshire Archaeological Journal*
DCAD	*Descriptive Catalogue of Ancient Deeds*
DNB	*Dictionary of National Biography*
DRO	Derbyshire Record Office
EETS	Early English Text Society
Farnham	Farnham, *Leicestershire*

FM	Fitzwilliam Museum
GRO	Gloucestershire Record Office
HL	Huntingdon Library
HS	Harleian Society
HMC	Historical Manuscripts Commission
JDANHS	*Journal of the Derbyshire Archaeological and Natural History Society*
LAASRP	*Lincoln Architectural and Archaeological Society Reports and Papers*
LAO	Lincolnshire Archives Office
LCCM	Lincoln City and County Museum
LH	Longleat House
LJRO	Lichfield Joint Record Office
LonRS	London Record Society
LOSJ	Library of the Order of St John of Jerusalem
LP	*Letters and Papers of Henry VIII*
LRO	Leicestershire Record Office
LRS	Lincoln Record Society
MFR	Melton Fieldworkers' Report
MH	Melbourne Hall
MH	*Medical History*
MUOL	McGill University, Osler Library
NRO	Norfolk Record Office
OS	Österreichischen Staatsarchivs
PRO	Public Record Office
PRS	Pipe Roll Society
Rot Chart	*Rotuli Chartarum* (ed. Hardy)
Rot Hund	*Rotuli Hundredorum* (ed. Illingworth and Caley)
Rot Parl	*Rotuli Parliamentorum*
SMR	Sites and Monuments Record
SR	*Statutes of the Realm* (ed. Luders *et al.*)
SRO	Staffordshire Record Office
SRRS	Shropshire Records and Research Service
SS	Selden Society
StS	Staffordshire Studies
SurS	Surtees Society
Taxatio	*Taxatio Ecclesiastica* (ed. Ayscough and Caley)
TLAHS	*Transactions of the Leicestershire Archaeological and Historical Society*
TRHS	*Transactions of the Royal Historical Society*
UNCLH	University of Nottingham, Centre for Local History
UNMD	University of Nottingham, Manuscripts Department
Valor	*Valor Ecclesiasticus* (ed. Caley and Hunter)
VCH	*Victoria County History* (ed. Page *et al.*)
WAM	Westminster Abbey Muniments
YAS	Yorkshire Archaeological Society

Notes on the text

Place-names and surnames have been adjusted and modernised in the interests of consistency, unless the medieval form is obviously distinctive. Spelling too has been modernised for quotations, and Latin, French and German have been translated. New-style dating has been adopted throughout and continental names have been anglicised.

Introduction

When our embryonic Research Group was first talking about compiling a history of the order of St Lazarus in England, I was at first highly sceptical. As a newly appointed lecturer at the University of Nottingham I was already leading a busy life and, logically, the last thing I wanted to become involved with was another project requiring a further input of time, energy and resources. However, on a damp and misty November morning in 1983 I was persuaded to make my first visit to see the earthworks at Burton Lazars, and after that fateful encounter there was no turning back. It was not so much the persuasiveness of my friends that won me over, as the spirit of the place – and after that first visit I freely admit to being hooked. My instincts told me, strongly, that this was a location that had *something* to offer, though what precisely that was was not at that point clear in any of our minds. The site seemed to be calling out for our involvement and attention, leading us into a dark tunnel from which there could be no escape.

Once we got started on the work of unravelling Burton Lazars we soon realised we were not the first to have initiated such enquiries. In 1674 the marquis de Louvois, Louis XIV's minister of war and 'grand vicar-general of Our Lady of Mount Carmel and St Lazarus of Jerusalem', had dispatched an emissary to peruse records in the Tower of London and Westminster Abbey in the hope of uncovering something of the history of the Lazarites in England, but he appears to have returned to France disappointed. A little later, in the eighteenth century, Philip Burton, a lawyer and antiquarian, became preoccupied with the history of Burton Lazars and promised to give his assistance to John Gough Nichols, Leicestershire's principal antiquary, who was writing a history of the county at about the same time. But, alas, fate intervened, and Burton was struck down, literally, while putting the finishing touches to his manuscript in 1792. 'On the morning of the day on which he died . . . he rose, as was his usual custom, at six o'clock, and at five in the afternoon it pleased the Almighty to take him, while the pen was in his hand.'[1] The great work disappeared forever. It is impossible to know if Burton was in possession of material which has now perished – probably not very much, if the truth be known. The order of St Lazarus has never made a major impact on documentary sources, largely because of its exemption from many of the things that generally bring medieval religious orders to the attention of historians. But historians should not be dissuaded from their purpose by the lack of obvious pieces of paper and parchment . . . or by the untimely deaths of their progenitors. Indeed, the Burton Lazars project has proved that when a wide

---

1   J.G. Nichols, *History and Antiquities of Leicestershire*, 2 pt 1 (London, 1795), p. 268.

range of sources is tapped, documentary and archaeological, more information can be pulled together than might ever have seemed possible in the first instance.

If I had been drawn to Burton Lazars by some sense of *genius loci*, an eighteenth-century engraving, reproduced in some of the standard histories of the order, symbolised what many people still believed it stood for. It seemed a reasonable starting point for our research. In it a female personification of the order of St Lazarus stands guard over two prostrate figures, who look sick to the point of decrepitude. The skyline of Jerusalem is in the background, beyond a somewhat uninviting-looking sea. One of the paupers looks up imploringly, with a begging bowl near his outstretched left arm. The noble figure, which is the subject of his attentions, carries a sword in her right hand and a cross and rosary in her left. Her military credentials are further endorsed by her oval shield and the extravagantly plumed classical helmet she wears on her head, and to clarify her identity the insignia of the order hangs conspicuously from her neck. Though her pose is protective, she seems somewhat detached from the plight of the poor, sick people at her feet. This is because her eyes are fixed on higher things, specifically a heraldic achievement in the sky, the arms of Louis, duke of Berry, grand-master of the order (1757–73) and subsequently king of France (1774–92). To leave these royal associations in absolutely no doubt, the lilies of the French royal house shine forth from a sunburst still higher in the heavens, making the whole scene strangely reminiscent of the vision of Constantine or some such highly charged mystical moment.

The engraving makes three clear and basic points about the order as it perceived itself in the eighteenth century – it was noble, charitable and chival-rous – the same 'valiant knighthood of St Lazarus of Jerusalem', perhaps, that we soon began to encounter in the English medieval sources. Yet the more these documents were explored and the more we investigated those mysterious earth-works on site, the greater was our sense of doubt and confusion. Soon we began to wonder if the allegorical figure had feet of clay. The chapters that follow aim to explore the legend of St Lazarus in the context of what little has survived to elucidate its activities in medieval England. It is a story of myth and reality, and the sometimes uncomfortable relationship between the two.

1

Lepers and Knights

> Brother knights and others of the aforesaid hospital have many
> times been horribly killed and their house in Jerusalem and in
> many other places in the Holy Land devastated.
>
> (Charter of John, bishop of Jerusalem, 1323)

Historians of the order

The order of St Lazarus in the Holy Land was the root from which the English
province stemmed, and for this reason some discussion of it is necessary before
the national operation can be properly quantified. This is particularly true for
the years before 1291 when England was merely an adjunct of a much wider
crusading venture and, indeed, for a hundred years after that when traditional
links were still, rather tenuously, being maintained. The order, which still exists
in a modified form in many parts of the world today, has had a long and unusual
historiography with few attempts at impartial evaluation until recently. In 1649
the order in France published its *Mémoires, Regles et Statuts* and in 1772 it
commissioned its first comprehensive history by Sibert.[1] Since then historians
such as Pétiet, Bertrand and Bagdonas have carried on the tradition, and with
the advent of the Internet St Lazarus websites have proliferated, along with
sometimes acrimonious exchanges between members of rival branches of the
order.[2] Although all of these provide useful information, particularly about
post-medieval happenings, there is a marked tendency among these partisans to
approach the sources uncritically and to make use of history to endorse
present-day preoccupations. Even the normally sober *Catholic Encyclopedia* has
commented that 'the historians of the order have done much to obscure the

---

1 *Mémoires, Regles et Statuts, Ceremonies et Privileges des Ordres Militaires de Nostre Dame du
Mont-Carmel et de S. Lazare de Ierusalem* (Lyon, 1649). Reprinted by Les Éditions du Prieuré as *Ordre
Militaire de Notre-Dame et de Saint-Lazare: mémoires, statuts, rituels, 1649* (Rouvray, 1992); G. de
Sibert, *Histoire des Orders Royaux, Hospitaliers-Militaires de Notre Dame du Mont Carmel et de Saint
Lazare de Jerusalem* (Paris, 1772).

2 R. Pétiet, *Contribution à l'Histoire de l'Ordre de Saint-Lazare de Jérusalem en France* (Paris, 1914); P.
Bertrand, 'Ordre de St-Lazare de Jérusalem en Orient', *La Science Historique* (June 1927); P. Bertrand
de la Grassière, *L'Ordre Militaire et Hospitalier de Saint-Lazare de Jérusalem* (Paris, 1960); R. Bagdonas,
The Military and Hospitaller Order of St Lazarus of Jerusalem: its history and work (nd).

question [of its origins] by entangling it with gratuitous pretensions and suspicious documents'.[3]

Among modern historians of the Crusades, Forey has equated the Lazarites with 'the major military orders' because of their exemption from episcopal jurisdiction; yet, on the other hand, Nicholson has swung to the opposite extreme and has alleged that they were 'hardly recognised in Europe as a military order'.[4] To add to the confusion, Gilchrist has suggested that the principal English preceptory at Burton Lazars was taken over by the Hospitallers in 1414 when the houses of the order were confiscated by the crown as 'enemy assets'.[5] When non-specialists have fished in the muddy waters of the order of St Lazarus in this way they have invariably become unstuck. In this context it is fortunate that since the 1980s the work of Shahar, Walker, Barber, Jankrift and Hyacinthe has become available to create a more consistent and balanced picture.[6] Having read these authors, with their contrasting styles and approaches, it does not require much imagination to realise that the order was a strange hybrid with at least three separate, but interrelated, roles. It was at one and the same time knightly, leprous and monastic, sharing certain characteristics with the Hospitallers and others with the Templars. Indeed, it is these unique features that have generally led historians such as Nicholson and Gilchrist to draw the wrong conclusions.

When and why the order developed in this unusual fashion is a more problematical question, complicated by a shortage of documentary and archaeological material for almost all periods before 1500.[7] The issue is also clouded by an attitude which, until recently, has sidelined the history of leprosy as something 'not quite respectable'. Yet to our medieval ancestors the order clearly had a high profile. In fourteenth-century England, when the international brotherhood was already falling apart, people still had a clear view (or so they believed) about how it all began. The brothers of Burton Lazars were part of 'the valiant knighthood of St Lazarus of Jerusalem, founded in the first army of the Christians against the Saracens', an emphatic enough statement in itself to contradict Nicholson's

3   C.G. Herbermann *et al.* (eds), *The Catholic Encyclopedia*, 9 (London, 1910), p. 97.
4   A.J. Forey, 'The Military Order of St Thomas of Acre', *English Historical Review*, 92 (1997), pp. 491–2; H. Nicholson, *Templars, Hospitallers and Teutonic Knights: images of the military orders, 1128–1291* (Leicester, 1993), p. 47; see also pp. 5, 86.
5   R. Gilchrist, *Contemplation and Action: the other monasticism* (London, 1995), p. 67.
6   S. Shahar, 'Des lépreux pas comme les autres. L'ordre de Saint-Lazare dans le royaume latin de Jérusalem', *Revue Historique*, 541 (January–March 1982), pp. 19–41; J. Walker, 'The Patronage of the Templars and the Order of St Lazarus in the Twelfth and Thirteenth Centuries', University of St Andrews, Ph.D. thesis (1990); M. Barber, 'The Order of St Lazarus and the Crusades', *The Catholic Historical Review*, 80, no. 3 (July 1994), pp. 439–56; K.P. Jankrift, *Leprose als Streiter Gottes: institutionalisierung und organisation des ordens vom Heiligen Lazarus zu Jerusalem von seinen anfängen bis zum jahre 1350*, Vita Regularis, 4 (Münster, 1996); K.P. Jankrift, 'Die Leprosenbruderschaft des Heiligen Lazarus zu Jerusalem und ihre Ältesien Statuten', in G. Melville (ed.), *De Ordine Vitae: zu Normvorstellungen, Organisationsformen und Schriftgebrauch im mittelalterlichen Ordenswesen*, Vita Regularis, 1 (Münster, 1996), pp. 341–60; R. Hyacinthe, 'L'Ordre militaire et hospitalier de Saint-Lazare de Jérusalem en Occident: histoire – iconographie – archéologie', University of Paris (Sorbonne), Ph.D thesis (2000); R. Hyacinthe, 'L'Ordre militaire et hospitalier de Saint-Lazare de Jérusalem aux douzième et treizième siècles', in *Utiles est Lapis in Structura: mélanges offerts à Léon Pressouyre*, Comité de Travaux Historiques et Scientifiques (Paris, 2000), pp. 185–93.
7   Jankrift, *Leprose*, pp. 22–7.

Plate 1: Lazarus the beggar, from a seventeenth-century
Bible. As the rich man feasts with his friends, Lazarus lies
rejected at the door, dogs licking hungrily at his sores.

gloomy view of non-awareness.[8] Other documentary sources of the same period
stress that the order was 'founded on lepers', but uniformly fail to explain how or
why this unusual circumstance came about.[9] The emergence of the order in the
Holy Land and its expansion into Europe sheds some light on these complex and
controversial issues.

Who was St Lazarus?

The dedication of the Jerusalem hospital and the subsequent order to St Lazarus
was one of its most enduring hallmarks, yet the precise identity of Lazarus
remains obscure. Literally, Lazarus means 'God is my help' and in the early
church five saints bore this very distinctive name. However, in the context of the
order the possible contenders can be narrowed down to two, both of them
mentioned in the New Testament.[10] First, Lazarus the beggar, the man 'full of

8 CPR, 1345–48, p. 284.
9 CPR, 1292–1301, p. 404.
10 The Book of Saints, compiled by the Benedictine Monks of St Augustine's Abbey, Ramsgate (London,
    1994), p. 339.

Plate 2: 'The Raising of Lazarus' from a *fresco* by Giotto in the Arena
Chapel, Padua, *c.* 1305. The shrouded figure of Lazarus of Bethany
returns to life, much to the amazement of the bystanders.

sores', who is seen as an outcast in this world but who eventually gains his
rightful place in heaven.[11] Lazarus' ailment has traditionally been taken to be
leprosy, and the compelling story of Dives and Lazarus is basically a parable
demonstrating the rewards of the virtuous acceptance of poverty and the
torments that await those wealthy people who fail in their charitable obligations
(Plate 1). Second, Lazarus the brother of Mary and Martha of Bethany who was
raised from the dead by Jesus and who subsequently attended a banquet at the
house of Simon the Leper, reporting back to the assembled company, according
to an apocryphal account, his horrific visions of hell (Plate 2).[12]

Lazarus of Bethany was almost certainly a real person, but beyond the scriptural references nothing for sure is known about him. In the eastern tradition he
and his sisters were set adrift in a leaking boat by the Jews at Jaffa. Making a safe
landfall on Cyprus, Lazarus became bishop of Kition and died there after thirty
years in office, his relics being translated to Constantinople in 890. According to
a less secure western tradition, a rudderless boat carried him and his sisters to
the south of France where he became bishop of Marseilles and was martyred

---

[11] Luke 16: 19–31.
[12] John 11: 5, 41–44; 12: 1–11; Matthew 26: 6–16; Mark 14: 3–11; E. Duffy, *The Stripping of the Altars: traditional religion in England, c. 1400–1580* (Yale, 1992), pp. 340–1.

during the reign of the emperor Domitian (81–96).[13] Virtually all authorities are agreed that this latter story is apocryphal and that inspiration for it probably derived from a fifth-century Lazarus who was consecrated bishop of Aix at Marseilles and subsequently travelled to the Holy Land and back again.[14] In the Middle Ages the cathedral of Autun, in Burgundy, claimed to have the tomb of Lazarus, and though this was destroyed in 1766, two Romanesque figures of Mary and Martha, which once adorned it, still survive.[15] There are several representations of the raising of Lazarus from the Roman period onwards. In the fourteenth century the scene was depicted by Fra Angelico, and Giotto painted it twice in *fresco*, once for the Lower Church, Assisi, and once for the Arena Chapel, Padua.[16] These representations demonstrated that out of death came new life and that, with faith, even the horrors of leprosy could represent a fresh beginning. As a spiritual message this complemented the more practical imperative implicit in the parable of Dives and Lazarus.

Since both of the New Testament Lazaruses have a tangential connection with leprosy, it is difficult to know from which the hospital and order derived their name. Certainly in modern Catholic hagiography the popular image of 'St Lazarus' is Lazarus the beggar and Farmer believes that it was he whom the military order adopted as its patron.[17] Jankrift seems equally convinced that Lazarus of Bethany was the true inspiration.[18] The iconography of the order and the wider hagiographical context suggest less emphatic interpretations. The seal of the hospital in the Holy Land, which might normally be expected to proclaim founding saints, shows on one side a priest holding a crozier and the inscription 'St Lazarus of Jerusalem'; on the other is a leper, holding a clapper and his face covered in spots, and the inscription 'The seal of the lepers'. It is possible that these may be intended to be depictions of Lazarus of Bethany and Lazarus the beggar, but they are just as likely to illustrate the dual nature of the twelfth-century order made up, as it was, of healthy and leper brothers.[19]

Gilchrist has pointed out how some medieval saints had 'a composite image' and there is clear evidence of such confusion in the case of Lazarus.[20] Indeed, Orme is in no doubt that Lazarus the bishop 'was identified with the beggar with sores in the gospel of St Luke'.[21] An important clue is provided in *The Cyrurgie of Guy de Chauliac*, which, speaking of Jesus, states 'He loved Lazer, the leprous man, more than other men', a clear reference, it would seem, to Christ's friend-

---

13 D.H. Farmer, *The Oxford Dictionary of Saints* (Oxford, 1992), pp. 292–3; J. Cumming (ed.), *A New Dictionary of Saints* (Tunbridge Wells, 1993), p. 190.

14 Farmer, *Saints*, pp. 292–3; Cumming, *Saints*, p. 190. There is also a possible confusion concerning the translation of the relics of St Nazarius from Milan to France.

15 P. Pradel, *Sculptures Romanes des Musées de France* (Paris, 1958), pp. 14, 32.

16 G.A. Lee, *Leper Hospitals in Medieval Ireland: with a short account of the military and hospitaller order of St Lazarus of Jerusalem* (Blackrock, Co. Dublin, 1996), pp. 25–6; L. Bellosi, *The Complete Works of Giotto* (Florence, 1981), pp. 45, 60.

17 Farmer, *Saints*, p. 292.

18 Jankrift, *Leprose*, p. 35.

19 Shahar, 'Lépreux', pp. 31–2. Unfortunately, Shahar does not illustrate this seal or give any indication of where it is to be found.

20 Gilchrist, *Contemplation and Action*, p. 41.

21 N. Orme and M. Webster, *The English Hospital, 1070–1570* (New Haven, London, 1995), p. 50.

ship with Lazarus of Bethany.[22] Though the Bible says that this Lazarus was sick, there is no suggestion that he was suffering from leprosy, so the idea must have come from the popular notion that this was the complaint of Lazarus the beggar. Thus the two individuals became conflated. The seals of the order in England focus more specifically on the priestly image, and here the most persistent representation is of a figure in full episcopal regalia.[23] All of this iconographical evidence, therefore, suggests that Lazarus of Bethany became the more dominant and enduring of the two, though possibly in his 'composite' form. A similar confusion took place in the case of Mary, the sister of Lazarus. Increasingly, St Mary of Bethany became identified with St Mary Magdalene, whose body, it was alleged, was buried at St Baume, near Marseilles, and whose relics were also claimed by Vézelay Abbey, next door to Autun. St Mary Magdalene, even more so than Lazarus, became a favourite dedicatee of medieval leper-houses.[24] Certainly a growing emphasis on this pair of prestigious saints was in line with the changing nature of the order in late-medieval Europe.

The order in the Holy Land, c.1130-1291

Though leprosy was a very ancient disease, and probably endemic in Europe since Roman times, it may well have been on the increase in the twelfth century if the number of hospital foundations is anything to go by. This horrific illness was probably more a fact of life in the Latin East than it was in the West, yet attitudes to it varied and were underpinned by a strange and contradictory theology that changed over time and space.[25] On the one hand (especially in the early Middle Ages) leprosy tended to be seen as a special reflection of Christ's suffering – in the words of St Ailred a veritable *imitatio Christi*; yet on the other (more specifically in the late Middle Ages) the sheer repulsiveness of the disease caused many commentators to regard it as a sign of sinfulness and evil life and a just punishment from God.[26] Shahar has argued that attitudes to leprosy were more tolerant in the East than the West, and there may be some truth in this point. Sources for the Latin kingdom suggest that leprosy did not generally imply moral judgement and was suffered simply 'by the will of God', an attitude that might owe something to the Moslem approach to the disease, which was 'more practical than moralistic'.[27] But, despite this, the inconsistency of approach was evident in Outremer as well as Europe.

The origins of the leper hospital of St Lazarus in Jerusalem are obscure and controversial. To compete with the Hospitallers, historians of the order have attempted to prove the ancient origins of the institution, thus enhancing its

[22] M.S. Ogden (ed.), *The Cyrurgie of Guy de Chauliac*, EETS, 265 (1971), p. 381.

[23] See Chapter 4, p. 114; Chapter 6, pp. 189, 192–3.

[24] Lee, *Leper Hospitals*, p. 19.

[25] P. Richards, *The Medieval Leper and his Northern Heirs* (Cambridge, 1977, reprinted 2000), p. 49; Shahar, 'Lépreux', pp. 21–2, 34, 38–9.

[26] Barber, 'St Lazarus', pp. 455–6; Shahar, 'Lépreux', p. 38; Jankrift, *Leprose*, pp. 5–29.

[27] Jankrift, *Leprose*, p. 40; Barber, 'St Lazarus', p. 455. See also S.N. Brody, *The Disease of the Soul. Leprosy in Medieval Literature* (New York, 1974), pp. 132–46; M.W. Dols, 'The Leper in Medieval Islamic Society', *Speculum*, 58 (1983), pp. 891–916.

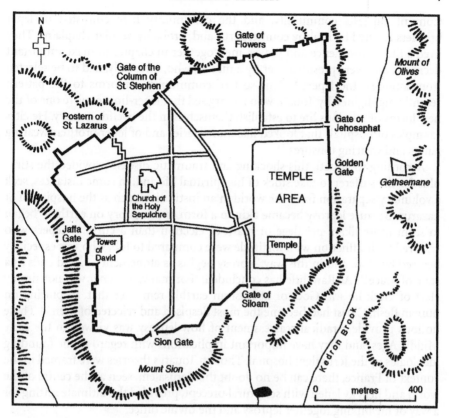

Map 1: Jerusalem in the twelfth century.

esteem, and the names of Judas Maccabeus and St Basil, among others, have been proposed as potential founders.[28] Although it is known that a leper hospital was established at Jerusalem by the Empress Eudoxia, wife of Arcadius (383–408), it cannot be linked, without doubt, to the crusading period and it is more reliable simply to follow medieval opinion and chart developments from the arrival of the 'first army of the Christians' in Jerusalem in 1099.[29] The best source we have for this early period is part of the order's Cartulary, containing about 40 charters and giving 'a precise picture of this hospitaller institution'.[30]

It would appear, from this source, that the order established itself in the 1130s on a site outside the St Lazarus postern, though the first unambiguous reference is a grant by King Fulk (1131–43) in 1142 giving land in Jerusalem to 'the church of St Lazarus and the convent of the sick who are called *miselli*' (Map 1).[31]

[28] Jankrift, *Leprose*, pp. 30–1. The Lazarites were interested in these foundation myths as early as the twelfth century.

[29] *Ibid*, p. 32.

[30] Hyacinthe, 'Saint-Lazare', p. 186. The Cartulary is printed in A. de Marsy (ed.), 'Fragment d'un Cartulaire de l'Ordre de Saint-Lazare en Terre Sainte', in *Archives de l'Orient Latin*, 2 (Paris, 1884, reprinted New York, 1978), pp. 121–57.

[31] Marsy, 'Fragment d'un Cartulaire', pp. 123–4. For the leper hospital in the 1130s, see J. Wilkinson, J. Hill and W. F. Ryan (eds), *Jerusalem Pilgrimage, 1099–1185*, Hakluyt Society, 167 (1988), p. 143.

Convent suggests community, and the community here consisted of leper brothers assisted by healthy counterparts, and, probably, secular chaplains. They lived a life of abstinence and prayer, met together in chapter to make important decisions and were presided over by a master, who, unusually, had to be selected from amongst the lepers.[32] This sort of community conforms to the pattern recently highlighted by Touati, who has argued that leper-houses were one of the new forms of religious life to establish themselves in the twelfth century. He cites examples of hospitals that looked like monasteries and of leper brothers wearing habits and wearing tonsures.[33]

According to Touati, this shocking and traumatic disease provided the stimulus for the sufferer to take stock of his spiritual life and, in some instances, seek a voluntary separation from the world in an institution such as the hospital of St Lazarus. Because leprosy became akin to a form of purgatory on earth, it 'began to seem more like a privilege or mark of election than a curse'.[34] Lepers who endured their affliction with fortitude were compared to Job, who was especially beloved by God; and in this way 'leprosy begins as atonement . . . and ends as a state of grace'.[35] As Rawcliffe has concluded: 'For many, the leper was not simply elect of God: he *was* God, or at least an earthly reminder that, in putting on human flesh, Christ had become the most despised and rejected of men.'[36] These notions provide a radical reassessment of how leprosy was viewed in the early Middle Ages, and they have important implications with regard to the founding ideologies of the Jerusalem hospital. Though Touati's theories were framed in the context of France, there can be no doubt that Jerusalem, seen as the centre of the world and heavily laden with scriptural precept, provided the ultimate setting for a way of life linking together leprosy and the divine office.

The leper hospital at Jerusalem must have been deeply inspired by notions such as these in the early years of its existence, and what little we know of its history suggests fairly wide-ranging interest and support. The first master for whom a name survives is Bartholomew, who appears in 1153. Barber has suggested that this Bartholomew may have been a Templar who left his order to reap the rewards of ministering to the sick.[37] 'That man, imitating Alberic, was accustomed to bring water from the ponds with great labour to the lepers of Jerusalem, whom he maintained with all necessities as far as he could.'[38] Alberic, Bartholomew's role model, had set an even more spirited example and illustrates the extent to which the hospital could stir up feelings of piety and a desire to serve. Clad in a goat-hair shirt and wearing his hair and beard in an outlandish

32 Hyacinthe, 'Saint-Lazare', p. 186; Barber, 'St Lazarus', pp. 444–6; Shahar, 'Lépreux', pp. 27–9; Jankrift, *Leprose*, pp. 58–9.

33 F.-O. Touati, *Maladie et société au moyen âge. La lépre, les lépreux et les léproseries dans la province ecclésiastique de Sens jusqu'au milieu de XIVᵉ siècle*, Bibliothèque du moyen âge, 11 (Paris, 1998), pp. 631–748.

34 C. Rawcliffe, 'Learning to love the Leper: aspects of institutional charity in Anglo-Norman England', *Anglo Norman Studies*, 23 (2001), pp. 241–2.

35 *Ibid*, p. 243.

36 *Ibid*, p. 245.

37 Barber, 'St Lazarus', p. 450.

38 B.Z. Kedar (ed.), Gerard of Nazareth, *De Conversatione Servatorum Dei*, in 'Gerard of Nazareth. A Neglected Twelfth-Century Writer in the Latin East', *Dumbarton Oaks Papers*, 37 (1983), p. 72.

style, Alberic was in the habit of whipping himself remorselessly and shouting at people who travelled past the *leprosarium*.[39] According to Gerard of Nazareth, he 'ate those things which the lepers had left, kissed each one daily after Mass, washed and wiped their feet, made their beds, and carried the weak on top of his shoulders'. After he had washed their feet, he made a remarkable show of self-abasement; 'the water mixed with the blood and discharge moved him to nausea, but he at once immersed his face and, horrible to say, took away not the least part'.[40]

Not everyone engaged in Alberic's dramatic and penitential behaviour, but the hospital, located just outside the north-west corner of the walls of Jerusalem, was ideally placed to attract interest from travellers. It lay on the route between the Mount of Olives and the Jordan, and sick pilgrims, especially those afflicted with leprosy who regarded bathing in the river as an essential part of the healing process, passed there regularly.[41] They are likely to have been inspired by the story of Naaman the Syrian who was cured of his leprosy after having bathed in the Jordan seven times, and alms giving, by those full of anticipation or grateful for a cure, was probably the first source of support that this embryonic community received.[42] If Christ was to be seen in the leper, the arguments for assisting the hospital by means of charitable giving were very great, and it is likely that a substantial income accrued from this source.

It is not known what rule was followed in the early years, though by 1255 the order was stated to be Augustinian. Jankrift, who has undertaken a detailed examination of the surviving statutes, believes that it only adopted this rule following the restrictions imposed by the Fourth Lateran Council in 1215 and that the Lazarite version of Augustinianism included some unexpected variants.[43] The statutes were certainly drawn up after 1154, and in the process the order took the advice of the Templars.[44] From the fragmentary survivals it is only possible to reconstruct a very sketchy picture of life in the convent. There were two sets of accommodation, one for the healthy brothers and one for the lepers, who ate and slept separately. The day was governed by a strict *horarium* based around services and meals, and punishments were imposed for transgressions of the rule. The hospital made little or no attempt to cure its sick inmates other than by providing a good diet, comfortable sleeping quarters and relieving their sufferings by bathing.

There appear to have been continual comings and goings. Jankrift suggests that the hospital was able to accommodate up to a thousand people under the supervision of a warden, providing them with clothing, shelter and care, though most of these must have been only temporary residents. Whether these 'guests' were pilgrims or migrant lepers visiting Jerusalem in hope of a cure, or both, is impossible to say.[45] Although only half the size of the great hospital of the order

---

[39] B. Hamilton, *The Leper King and his Heirs* (New York, 2000), p. 256.
[40] *Ibid.* Quoted in Barber, 'St Lazarus', p. 446.
[41] Barber, 'St Lazarus', pp. 440–1.
[42] II Kings, 5: 1–27.
[43] Jankrift, *Leprose*, pp. 72, 121–30. He rejects the view that the order ever followed the Rule of St Basil.
[44] *Ibid*, pp. 71–2.
[45] *Ibid*, pp. 60–8, 172–6.

of St John, the reputation of the institution was very high in the eyes of contemporaries, who believed that it fulfilled a useful function in terms of hospitality, potency of prayer and the containment of an extremely unpleasant disease.[46] Visiting crusaders, such as Roger de Mowbray, were impressed by what they saw, and the aristocracy of the Latin kingdom rallied round to support a foundation from which they stood to benefit more than most.

To the alms giving of the faithful was soon added a more permanent landed endowment, and the Cartulary underlines the fact that the hospital was supported by all classes in the Latin kingdom.[47] Fulk, Queen Melisende and Baldwin III (1143–62) all provided gifts, and Amalric I (1162–73), whose son Baldwin was leprous, was a special benefactor. In 1164 he promised the hospital one slave from every ten Moslem captives, and during the next decade gave 72 bezants *per annum* from the tolls of the Gate of David (1171) and a further 40 from the customs of Acre (1174).[48] Interestingly, the leper king, Baldwin IV (1173–85), does not appear to have specially favoured the order.[49] From the barons support was forthcoming from the count of Tripoli and the lords of Beirut and Caesarea, among others, and as early as 1150 the hospital was able to spend over 1000 bezants on the purchase of vineyards near Bethlehem, possibly the proceeds of alms giving.[50] By 1187 it had 'a modest economic base' comprising lands, tithes, rents and privileges and, even after the move to Acre in 1191, fresh gifts continued to come in until 1266.[51] It was certainly the most important institution caring for lepers in the crusader states.

Patrons gave, conventionally, out of concern for the health of their souls, but also because, given the prevalence of leprosy in the Holy Land, they knew that their turn might well come next. Indeed, many important people had personal connections with the order that went beyond mere gifts of land. Raymond of Tripoli was a *confrère*; Walter, lord of Beirut, considered entering the order; and Eustace, brother of Hugh, lord of Caesarea, abandoned secular life and became a Lazarite, though whether on account of leprosy or piety is not known.[52] Two of the early masters, who by definition had to be lepers, Walter de Novo Castro and Reynald de Fleury, were possibly members of the local aristocracy.[53] As Barber has put it, 'This close-knit, sometimes xenophobic community favoured St Lazarus because leprosy was endemic in the region and the Latins were therefore far more aware of their susceptibility to the disease than their contemporaries in the West.'[54]

Two documents are arguably particularly important in moulding the future of the order in this respect. First, the *Livre au Roi*, the legal code of the Latin

46 *Ibid*, p. 171; J. Riley-Smith, *Hospitallers. The History of the Order of St John* (London, 1999), p. 25.
47 Jankrift, *Leprose*, pp. 46–56.
48 *Ibid*, p. 442; J. Richard, *The Latin Kingdom of Jerusalem* (Amsterdam, 1979), p. 132; J.L. La Monte, *Feudal Monarchy in the Latin Kingdom of Jerusalem, 1100–1291* (Cambridge, Massachusetts, 1932), p. 145; C.R. Conder, *The Latin Kingdom of Jerusalem, 1099–1291* (London, 1897, reprinted 1973), p. 196.
49 H.E. Mayer, *The Crusades* (Oxford, 1972), p. 129.
50 Richard, *Latin Kingdom*, p. 139; Barber, 'St Lazarus', p. 442.
51 Barber, 'St Lazarus', pp. 446, 448; Shahar, 'Lépreux', p. 27. Shahar states that the last grant was in 1264.
52 Barber, 'St Lazarus', pp. 442–3.
53 *Ibid*, p. 443. For the case of Walter de Novo Castro, see Chapter 3, pp. 73–4.
54 Barber, 'St Lazarus', pp. 443–4.

kings drawn up *c.*1198–1205, which stated that a knight with leprosy should join the convent of St Lazarus 'where it is established that people with such an illness should be'.[55] Second, the *Règle du Temple* which provided Templar brothers afflicted with leprosy with the option of transferring to the hospital of St Lazarus.[56] The knights of St John never made such a rule – we must assume they felt capable of looking after their own sick knights – and the *Assises de la Cour de Bourgeois* is also silent on the matter.[57] This draws us to the conclusion that the convent of St Lazarus, perhaps because of its aristocratic connections, became regarded as a convenient receptacle for leprous knights, especially those from among the Templars.[58] This was to have profound consequences for the future development of the order in the Holy Land and in the West.

The links with the Templars, possibly stemming from the time of Bartholomew, become increasingly evident when the order withdrew from Jerusalem, following the fall of the city in 1187, and resettled at Acre. Here it adopted a mirror image of its earlier position, with a hospital and convent outside the city walls (Map 2).[59] However, when Louis IX (1226–70) extended the fortifications of Acre in the 1250s the hospital became incorporated into the northern suburb of Montmusart, behind the section of the wall protected by the Templars who supported the order by granting it free access to their water cistern.[60] In 1258, during the civil disturbances known as the War of St Sabas, the master of the Temple, Thomas Bérard, took refuge in the tower of St Lazarus when his own stronghold was subjected to crossfire between the Pisans, Genoese and Venetians, and in 1260 it was made compulsory for a leprous Templar to enter the order of St Lazarus.[61] As Shahar has argued, these were 'lepers like no others'. To ostracise them would have been unthinkable, so the obvious solution was to provide them with a role; 'a knight suffering from leprosy remained a knight and his scars and spots did not bring him any closer to other lepers of common birth'.[62] In this way the hospital confronted what Rawcliffe has termed the problem of 'high status or "noble" lepers whose rank merited more solicitous treatment', and it was factors such as these that encouraged the growing militari-

---

55 A.A. Beugnot (ed.), 'Le Livre au Roi', in *Assises de la Haute Cour, Recueil des Historiens des Croisades, Lois*, 1 (Paris, 1841), pp. 636–7; Shahar, 'Lépreux', pp. 20–1.

56 H. de Curzon (ed.), *La Règle du Temple*, Société de l'Histoire de France (Paris, 1886), pp. 239–40. There was no compulsion on a leprous knight to move, but if he did not do so he would have to live in isolation and his military role would therefore be curtailed. In the event of a transfer the Templars would supply his clothing and provide for his other needs for the rest of his life.

57 A. A. Beugnot (ed.), 'Assises de la Cour de Bourgeois', *Recueil des Historiens des Croisades, Lois*, 2 (Paris, 1843), p. 38. Though the hospital of St John did not accept lepers, the case of leper knights may have been different. Riley-Smith, *Hospitallers*, p. 22.

58 The problem of leprous members of religious orders was common enough and not confined to the Latin East. For cases involving the English Franciscans (1392) and Bridgettines (1487), see *CPapR, Letters 4, 1362–1404*, p. 454; *15, 1484–92*, p. 42.

59 Barber, 'St Lazarus', p. 447.

60 *Ibid*, p. 451; Jankrift, *Leprose*, pp. 73–4 See also, D. Jacoby, 'Montmusard, Suburb of Crusader Acre: the first stage of its development', in B.Z. Kedar, H.E. Mayer and R.C. Smale (eds), *Outremer. Studies in the History of the Crusading Kingdom of Jerusalem presented to Joshua Prawer* (Jerusalem, 1982), pp. 205–17.

61 Barber, 'St Lazarus', p. 451; Shahar, 'Lépreux', p. 26; Jankrift, *Leprose*, p. 79.

62 Shahar, 'Lépreux', p. 36.

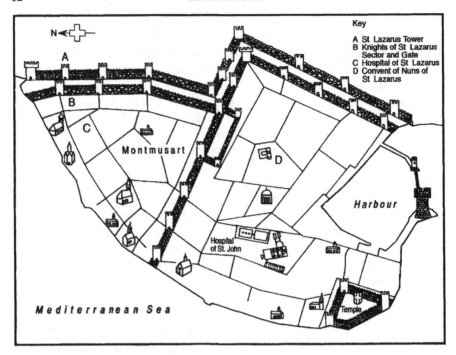

Map 2: Acre in the thirteenth century.

sation of the order along the lines experienced by the Hospitallers and the order of St Thomas of Acre.[63]

This new role, the origins of which are obscure but which Shahar believes date from the twelfth century, was certainly being clarified by the mid-thirteenth century. In 1234, for example, Gregory IX (1227–41) appealed for aid to help the order pay off its debts contracted in 'defence of the Holy Land', and in 1255 Alexander IV (1254–61) spoke of 'a convent of nobles, of active knights and others both healthy and leprous, for the purpose of driving out the enemies of the Christian name'.[64] In 1259 Matthew Paris included the Lazarites among 'defenders of the church fighting at Acre', and a map of the city, dating from the late thirteenth century, clearly shows the 'military convent of the brethren of St Lazarus' at Montmusart, complete with its own fortifications.[65] Indeed, there was also a tower of St Lazarus at Pain Perdu, near Caesarea, where the order had been granted the church in 1235, though Jankrift suggests that this did not have a

63 Rawcliffe, 'Learning to Love the Leper', p. 233. See A. Forey, 'The Militarisation of the Hospital of St John', in A. Forey, *Military Orders and Crusades* (Aldershot, 1994), no. ix; Forey, 'St Thomas of Acre', pp. 481–503; Jankrift, *Leprose*, p. 81.

64 L. Auvray (ed.), *Les Registres de Grégoire IX*, 1, BÉFAR, series 2 (Paris, 1896), p. 942; C. Bourel, J. de Loye, P. de Cenival and A. Coulon (eds), *Les Registres d'Alexandre IV*, 1, BÉFAR, series 2 (Paris, 1902), p. 122.

65 H.R. Luard (ed.), *Matthaei Parisiensis, Chronica Majora*, 5, Rolls Series, 57 (1880), p. 745; R. Vaughan, *Matthew Paris* (Cambridge, 1958), pl. 16; B. Dichter, *The Maps of Acre, an Historical Cartography* (Acre, 1973), pp. 17–18, 22–30.

military purpose and was, in fact, a hostel for itinerant lepers.[66] This develop-ment was probably not dissimilar to that of the order of St Thomas, which was transformed from a charitable organisation run by regular canons to a military order in the 1220s.[67]

The idea of leper knights might seem bizarre, but it was logical enough in the circumstances of the military and spiritual needs of the Latin kingdom. As we have seen, the hospital of St Lazarus had long been a refuge for men of the knightly class afflicted with leprosy, particularly Templars who were sworn to fight for the faith. The disease has a slow gestation period and can be diagnosed as much as seven years before serious debility begins to set in.[68] Baldwin IV, despite his leprosy, was an intelligent and courageous leader and an excellent horseman, instrumental in the defeat of Saladin at Mont Gisard in 1177.[69] Given the chronic shortage of manpower in the Holy Land, it made perfect sense to exploit the skills of trained fighting men, regardless of their physical condition, especially in the increasingly difficult circumstances of the thirteenth century. In a wider religious context these men brought the ideology of the cloister, charged with the belief that they were God's elect, onto the battlefield. Who knows what results might have been achieved by this daring strategy? The unusual nature of this extraordinary religious order should never be underestimated, and Shahar has summarised it as:

> Knights with leprosy who continued to perform their basic fighting function, an order in which brothers with leprosy lived alongside brothers enjoying good health under the authority of a master, himself suffering from leprosy – all this had never been heard of in the Europe of the twelfth and thirteenth centuries.[70]

Thus, the 'valiant knighthood' was born, a last line of defence for the Christians of the East, the 'living dead' mobilised in a desperate attempt to ward off the inroads of the Infidel. It was an image designed to inspire a medieval mindset moulded by notions of chivalry and the special relationship between God and his chosen sufferers. And this, as Nicholson has pointed out, was a society much preoccupied with public esteem and one in which the military orders, in general, received a good press from the laity.[71] The order of St Lazarus was to exploit this highly charged public perception of its role throughout its existence and long after it had ceased to be a reality.

It must be said, however, that in starkly practical terms the 'living dead' were not notably successful warriors. Every certain record we have of their activities speaks of military failure. Following the defeat of the crusaders at La Forbie in 1244, Robert de Nantes, Patriarch of Jerusalem, reported that 'all the leper

---

66 Barber, 'St Lazarus', p. 446; H.V. Michelant and G. Raynaud, *Itinéraires à Jerusalem*, Société de l'Histoire de France (Paris, 1882), p. 190; Jankrift, *Leprose*, p. 83.

67 Forey, 'St Thomas of Acre', pp. 481–9.

68 Barber, 'St Lazarus', p. 449.

69 S. Runciman, *A History of the Crusades*, 2 (Cambridge, 1952), pp. 417, 419–20, 432, 441; Shahar, 'Lépreux', pp. 37–8; Hamilton, *Leper King*, pp. 132–58.

70 Shahar, 'Lépreux', p. 32.

71 For a discussion of these issues, see Nicholson, *Templars*, though she fails to concede that the order of St Lazarus made any impact in this respect.

knights of the house of St Lazarus were killed', and during the crusade of Louis IX (1248–54) knights of the order were present at the disaster at Marsuna in 1250, when the king was captured by the Egyptians.[72] Joinville describes a particularly unfortunate incident, which occurred soon after in 1252:

> While the king was before Jaffa, the master of St Lazarus had spied out near Ramleh, a town some three good leagues away, a number of cattle and various other things from which he thought to collect some valuable booty. So being a man of no standing in the army, and who therefore did exactly as he pleased, he went off to that place without saying a word to the king. But after he had collected his spoils the Saracens attacked him, and so thoroughly defeated him that of all the men he had in his company no more than four escaped.[73]

To try to save the situation, a troop of Templars and Hospitallers was obliged to go to the rescue under the command of Joinville. The comment about the master 'being a man of no standing in the army', who was able to act as he pleased, is interesting and suggests that the order may have been functioning as a group of volunteers rather than regulars. Perhaps the leper knights traditionally undertook a foraging or scouting role, which would have distanced them from the main body of troops and helped to minimise the spread of infection. It would be over-harsh to apply Nicholson's judgement that the order was 'suicidally reckless' but, nevertheless, it is clear that the cumulative effect of these disasters was extremely serious.[74] As John, bishop of Jerusalem, put it in 1323, 'Brother knights and others of the aforesaid hospital have many times been horribly killed and their house in Jerusalem and in many other places in the Holy Land wholly devastated.'[75]

In 1253, immediately after the fiasco at Ramleh, Innocent IV (1243–54) altered the rules of the order at the request of the brothers to permit 'any healthy knight from amongst the brothers of the house' to be appointed master-general 'since all the leper knights of the said house have been miserably killed by the enemies of the faith'.[76] This was an important turning point, illustrating a clear movement away from the founding principles of the order. In 1255 Alexander IV spoke of 'active knights and others both healthy and leprous', and it seems that in the late thirteenth century, with leprosy less of a problem than it had been, fighting men were joining up on much the same terms as those attracted to the Templars, Hospitallers and Teutonic Knights.[77] And, of course, alongside these military activities the hospitaller vocation of the order went on much as before. Donations were still being made to the *mézeaux* of St Lazarus at Acre during the 1260s.[78] When the sultan of Cairo besieged the city in 1291 the order of St

---

72 G. Scalia (ed.), Salimbene de Adam, *Cronica*, 1 (Bari, 1966), p. 255; Luard, *Chronica Majora*, 5, p. 196.

73 M.R.B. Shaw (ed.), Joinville and Villehardouin, *Chronicles of the Crusades* (Harmondsworth, 1963), p. 300.

74 Nicholson, *Templars*, p. 70.

75 GRO, Berkeley Castle Muniments, J7/67/02/002/00/00 (MF 1297).

76 E. Berger (ed.), *Les Registres d'Innocent IV*, 1, BÉFAR, series 2 (Paris, 1884), pp. 476–7.

77 Bourel, *Registres d'Alexandre IV*, p. 122.

78 H.-F. Delaborde, *Chartes de Terre Sainte Provenant de l'Abbaye de Notre-Dame de Josaphat* (Paris, 1880), pp. 109–10; J.D. Le Roulx, *Cartulaire Général des Hospitaliers de Saint-Jean de Jérusalem, 1100–1310*, 3 (Paris, 1899), pp. 91–2.

Lazarus was able to muster a force of 25 knights.[79] On the night of 15/16 April a foray was made out of the St Lazarus Gate under William de Beaujeu, master of the Temple, to attempt to destroy the siege engines of the enemy, but the crusader force, which probably included troops of the order, came to grief when their horses tripped over the tent ropes of their opponents in the dark.[80] After a bitter siege the sultan ordered the final assault on 14 May, and Acre fell amidst scenes of unprecedented carnage. All of the knights of St Lazarus perished.[81] It was effectively the end of the crusader presence in the Holy Land and another watershed of immense significance for the order.

Papal support for the order

These military and hospitaller activities were supported, in part, by privileges granted by the papacy, which became particularly important as the landed endowment of the order in the Holy Land 'melted away' because of the successes of the Moslems after 1187.[82] It is not clear when the granting of these privileges began, but in his charter of confirmation, dated 1323, John, bishop of Jerusalem, said that 25 Popes had already contributed to them.[83] Counting back from the current Pope, John XXII (1316–34), we arrive at Urban III (1185–87) as the first supporter, which may not be too far wide of the mark since his pontificate preceded the crisis that gave rise to the Third Crusade. It can be deduced from the same document that the years between 1227 and 1285 represented a peak in the granting of papal privileges.[84] Gregory IX offered a 28-day indulgence to those giving alms (1234);[85] Innocent IV permitted the master to absolve brothers excommunicated for violent acts (1247);[86] Alexander IV provided a 100-day indulgence and income from the remission of crusading vows (1255);[87] and Urban IV (1261–64) released the order from episcopal control, putting it under the sole authority of the Patriarch of Jerusalem (1262).[88]

But it was Clement IV (1265–68), who in his younger days had been in the service of Louis IX, who was the most enthusiastic patron. In April 1265, following complaints that the secular clergy were not providing appropriate support for the activities of the order, the Pope issued a thoroughgoing confirmation of its privileges;[89] and in August of the same year he promulgated a

---

[79] This was not much fewer than the Templars and Hospitallers, who were estimated to have had about thirty knights each at Acre. However, the two larger orders had more knights spread around outlying garrisons since their commitments were greater than those of the Lazarites. Grassière, *Saint-Lazare*, p. 21; D. Seward, *The Monks of War: the military religious orders* (London, 1972), p. 81.

[80] Seward, *Monks of War*, p. 82.

[81] *Ibid*, p. 84.

[82] Jankrift, *Leprose*, pp. 99, 196–7.

[83] GRO, Berkeley Castle Muniments, J7/67/02/002/00/00 (MF 1297).

[84] It stated that the order's privileges were granted by Popes Gregory, Innocent, Alexander, Urban and Martin. This points to a sequence between Gregory IX (1227–41) and Martin IV (1281–85).

[85] Auvray, *Registres de Grégoire IX*, 1, p. 942.

[86] Berger, *Registres d'Innocent IV*, 1, pp. 476–7.

[87] Bourel, *Registres d'Alexandre IV*, 2, pp. 722–23. In addition Alexander IV granted confiscations from usurers when the original owners could not be found.

[88] J. Guiraud, *Les Registres d'Urbain IV*, 2, BÉFAR, series 2 (Paris, 1901), p. 61.

[89] S. Franco *et al.* (eds), *Bullarium Diplomatum et Privilegiorum Sanctorum Romanorum Pontificum*

further bull putting all of the leper-houses of the West under its protection and government.[90] This latter measure has been widely quoted by historians in England and France, who have taken the papal decree at face value and have assumed that it was implemented. The confusion has been made worse by the fact that some of them have mistakenly believed that all hospitals bearing the dedication of St Lazarus belonged to the order, and this is certainly not the case.[91]

Despite the fact that it was a genuine attempt to assist the order to improve its financial position, Clement IV's measure was fraught with problems because the Lazarites did not have the capacity to cope with sudden and dramatic expansion, and diocesan bishops and patrons were resentful about such ambitious schemes in any case.[92] There is no evidence that the Pope's grand design ever became a reality. Charles of Anjou (1266–85), for example, encountered serious difficulties when he attempted to enforce it in the kingdom of Sicily between 1268 and 1272. Not only did he propose that all lepers be confined in Lazarite houses but also that their property should pass to the order as well, a suggestion 'violently resisted' by their families.[93] Clement IV's initiative was the last attempt by the papacy to mobilise widespread support for the order, and its very limited success may well indicate that, by then, more negative attitudes were beginning to prevail about the Lazarites and what they stood for.[94]

European hospitals and preceptories

The Pope probably regarded the leper hospital at Acre as the template alongside which others should be measured, and he was no doubt aware that some patrons had already placed charitable institutions under the supervision of the Lazarites. Many of these were returning crusaders, such as the Emperor Frederick II (1220–50) in Italy and lesser noblemen in Germany and Switzerland.[95] The outstanding example was the hospital of St Mary Magdalene, Gotha, founded in 1227, which was given to the order by Queen Elizabeth of Hungary, the widow of the crusader Louis IV, landgrave of Thuringia.[96] Elizabeth, well known for her piety and austerities, was canonised as St Elizabeth of Marburg in 1235, and her virtues were extolled for subsequent generations in *The Golden Legend*: 'She cared for a woman with dreadful leprosy . . . bathing her, putting her in bed, cleansing and bandaging her sores, applying her salves, cutting her fingernails,

---

Taurinensis Editio, 3 (Turin, 1858), pp. 727–9. For Clement IV and Louis IX, see J.N.D. Kelly, *The Oxford Dictionary of Popes* (Oxford, 1988), pp. 196–7.

90　Franco, *Bullarium Diplomatum*, pp. 742–3.

91　See, for example, Grassière, *Saint-Lazare*, pp. 23–4. The railway station in Paris is a famous case in point. This site began life as a leper hospital dedicated to St Lazarus, but it was never connected with the order. It gained a fresh lease of life when it was granted to the *Lazarists*, the followers of St Vincent de Paul, in the seventeenth century. Farmer, *Saints*, pp. 481–2.

92　Jankrift, *Leprose*, p. 101.

93　R. Filangieri (ed.), *I Regestri della Cancellaria Angioina*, 2 (Naples, 1951), pp. 65–6; 7 (Naples, 1955), pp. 274–5; 8 (Naples, 1957), p. 110; Nicholson, *Templars*, p. 33.

94　Jankrift, *Leprose*, p. 101.

95　*Ibid*, pp. 91–3.

96　W.E. Tentzel, *Supplementum Historiae Gothanae* (Jena, 1702), pp. 66–7.

and kneeling at the sick woman's feet to loosen the laces of her shoes.'[97] Also in the imperial territories, a leper hospital at Sangerhausen was in the custody of the Lazarites from 1262.[98] In France an almshouse for the poor dedicated to St Thomas at Fontenay-le-Comte, Vendée, was staffed by brothers of 'Saint Ladre d'Outremer' in 1234;[99] and in 1235 the leper hospital of La Lande d'Airou, Manche, was given to the order by the local lord who had joined the crusader army at Acre.[100] The hospital of St Lazarus at Capua, in Naples, was not founded by the order but given to it in about 1226 on condition that lepers were supported there, and it is recorded that the brothers of Capua were tending to five lepers at Theanis in 1273.[101] Finally, the leper hospital of St Agatha, Messina, was described as being part of the order in 1266.[102]

Some of these hospitals, for example St Mary Magdalene and La Lande d'Airou, were associated with patrons who were crusaders, making their gifts easier to understand. No doubt they had an expectation that the order would take care of lepers in Europe just as it did in the Holy Land. The Pope, by endorsing this belief, evidently wished to support the Lazarites and to rationalise an untidy situation, but he was building his edifice on very slender foundations. Despite the belief of Charles of Anjou that the order was principally hospitaller, its involvement with the sick and suffering in western Europe was, in fact, relatively slight, both before and after Clement IV's decree. It seems that the order did not always share the enthusiasm of some of its patrons in this respect. Indeed, Hyacinthe has reassessed the hospitaller role of the Lazarites, outside Jerusalem and Acre, as 'modest' and has argued that 'we are above all talking about a land network providing a logistical support for the Crusade'.[103] Jankrift takes a similar view, and states that although there were more *leprosaria* in the West than in the Holy Land, the Lazarites had a much smaller share of them. They did not have the resources to replicate the work of the Jerusalem hospital outside of the Latin kingdom, and their European possessions were seen to fulfil a different purpose in any case.[104] Leprosy may have been the initial inspiration of the order in the Holy Land, but, as time went on, it became less and less the reality in Europe.

In France, where the order was always strongest, its 'land network' was based on the castle of Boigny, near Orléans, the principal house in France and eventually in Europe too (Plate 3). Louis VII (1137–80) viewed the Second Crusade in terms of a 'penitential pilgrimage' and had made a visit to a Paris leper hospital

97 Farmer, *Saints*, pp. 155–6; G. Ryan and H. Ripperger (eds), *The Golden Legend of Jacobus de Voragine* (New York, 1969), pp. 681, 685.
98 E. Sauer, *Der Lazariter-Orden und das Statutenbuch von Seedorf* (Freiburg, 1930), p. 38.
99 P. Marchegay, *Cartulaires du Bas-Poitou* (Les Roches-Barituad, 1877), p. 304.
100 AN, S 4841/B.
101 G. de Blasiis, *Della Vita e della opere di Pietro della Vigna* (Naples, 1860), pp. 230–2; Filangieri, *Registri Angioina*, 2, p. 65; 9 (Naples, 1957), p. 24.
102 S. Bottari, 'I Lebbrosari di Messina', in *Lazzaretti dell'Italia meridionale e della Sicilia*, Societa messinese di storia patria (Messina, 1989), pp. 19–29.
103 Hyacinthe, 'Saint-Lazare', p. 188.
104 Jankrift, *Leprose*, pp. 179–81.

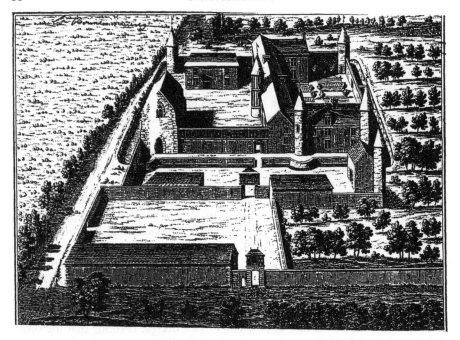

Plate 3: The castle of Boigny in 1699. Remnants of the medieval building can be seen among later adaptations.

before he set out.[105] Once in Outremer he provided the order with a pension of 10 livres, but 'at the request and prayer' of the brothers he agreed to exchange it for the gift of the royal castle of Boigny in 1154, where his marriage to Constance of Castile had been celebrated. Barber believes that this important gift 'suggests a conscious plan to plant houses in the West', and in this he is correct since substantial grants in England were made at about the same time.[106] Preceptories were established at Monlioust, Orne, before 1217;[107] at Grattemont, Normandy, in 1224;[108] at Posson, Cantal, before 1282;[109] and at Pastoral, Aveyron, probably also during the thirteenth century.[110] At Esztergom, in Hungary, there were *cruciferi* of St Lazarus in residence by 1181, and in 1233 land around the town was being administered by a master.[111] In the imperial territories three preceptories grew up around the hospital at Gotha in Thuringia: Braunsroda

---

[105] V.G. Berry (ed.), *Odo de Deuil, De Profectione Ludovici VII in orientem* (New York, 1948), pp. 16–17; Barber, 'St Lazarus', p. 447.

[106] Marsy, 'Fragment d'un Cartulaire', p. 132; Barber, 'St Lazarus', p. 447. For more or less contemporary English grants, see Chapter 2, pp. 34–5.

[107] AN, S 4891; 4894/B.

[108] Hyacinthe, 'Saint-Lazare', p. 189.

[109] AN, S 4866; 4884, doc. 9; Marsy, 'Fragment d'un Cartulaire', p. 132.

[110] I am grateful to Dr Hyacinthe for drawing my attention to this preceptory which he discovered through fieldwork.

[111] N. Knauz, *Magyar Sion*, 2 (Esztergom, 1866), p. 121; N. Knauz, *Monumenta Ecclesia Strigoniensis*, 1 (Esztergom, 1874), p. 297.

(1231), Breitenbach (1253) and Wackerhausen (1268).[112] At Meggersheim in Hesse another preceptory was functioning in 1253, the only one outside Thuringia.[113] These properties were supervised by a master of the order in Germany in 1266 who also appears to have had charge of a Swiss preceptory at Schlatt, Fribourg, which had under its authority smaller houses at Seedorf, Uri, and Gfenn, Zurich.[114]

The hospital of Capua, which had its own master by the fourteenth century, had churches at Barletta (1185) and Foggia (1233), the latter of which became a preceptory.[115] The main focus of land ownership in southern Italy was in Apulia, and particularly around Barletta, which had a 'St Lazarus' quarter of the town and was a major port of embarkation for expeditions to the East.[116] The foothold in Barletta, indeed, must have been an important resource, because it is likely to have been from here that men, money and supplies were shipped to the Holy Land. The scale of this land holding did not compare with that of the Templars and Hospitallers, but the function was similar.[117] Only in Spain, Scandinavia and the Low Countries were the activities of the order conspicuously absent.[118]

The purpose of these preceptories, each under its own master, was to return an annual contribution, a *responsium* or *apportum*, to the hospital in Jerusalem or Acre whence it could be employed at the discretion of the master-general and chapter.[119] The constitution of the order is extremely sketchy and the development of its hospitaller and landed interests appear to have been fairly random, but there were certainly provincial masters (as in England and Germany) who were accountable for a series of preceptories within their territories.[120] The best picture is provided by the statutes of Seedorf, Switzerland, drawn up between 1253 and 1291 and examined by Jankrift.[121] Though they provide a good deal of detail about day-to-day activities, the degree to which these practices were replicated in other parts of Europe remains uncertain. Two points of general interest do emerge, however. First, it appears that after 1250 leper brothers were in sharp decline and it was probably mainly, or even exclusively, healthy brothers who were admitted at Seedorf.[122] Second, as early as 1287 there was a move towards

112 C. Sagittarius, *Historia Gothana Plenior* (Jena, 1700), pp. 236–9; Tentzel, *Gothanae*, pp. 56–7, 66–7.
113 G.W.J. Wagner, *Die Vormaligen Geistlichen Stifte im Grossherzogth um Hessen*, 1 (Darmstadt, 1873), pp. 513–16.
114 *Fontes Rerum Bernensium*, 3 (Bern, 1880), p. 6; J. Escher and P. Schweizer (eds), *Urkundenbuch der Stadt und Landschaft Zurich* (Zurich, 1901), nos. 786, 1016, 1242, 1343, 1415, 1577, 1849; *Der Geschichtesfreund*, 12 (1856), pp. 2–17.
115 *Codice Diplomatico Pugliese*, 21 (Bari, 1976), p. 409.
116 *Codice Diplomatico Barese*, 8 (Bari, 1914), p. 187.
117 For the Templars, see M. Barber, *The New Knighthood. A History of the Order of the Temple* (Cambridge, 1994), especially pp. 229–79; for the Hospitallers, see Riley-Smith, *Hospitallers*, especially pp. 74–88.
118 Jankrift, *Leprose*, p. 91.
119 See Chapter 4, pp. 103, 105–7. The word 'preceptory' was another detail borrowed from the Templars, and it is noticeable that after their suppression the word 'commandary', favoured by the Hospitallers, tends to be used in France to describe these local outposts.
120 The relationship between the order and the English province is discussed in Chapter 3, pp. 66–7.
121 Jankrift, *Leprose*, pp. 102–11, 132–50.
122 *Ibid*, p. 106.

the recruitment of sisters, so that by 1327 the preceptory was spoken of as a 'convent of women'.[123]

These two factors demonstrate that, even before the fall of Acre, the Lazarite vocation was undergoing significant change, brought about by the beginnings of the decline of leprosy and the difficulty of attracting men to the cause. Just as the order started to detach itself from active involvement with leprosy, the image of the disease began to suffer serious setbacks from the position it had held at the time of the founding of the Jerusalem hospital. As the economic situation deteriorated across Europe in the early fourteenth century, lepers tended to be regarded as scapegoats for the sufferings of mankind rather than living embodiments of Christian suffering. The arrival of the Black Death in 1348 simply deepened this sense of ostracism and marginality, which rapidly became reflected in the writings of moralists and theologians.[124] The extent to which the collapse of the order in the Holy Land *contributed* to these new, more negative, attitudes is an interesting question but one on which it is impossible to reach a conclusion. Jankrift believes that the response of the order to these changes was to adopt a more spiritual agenda, employing the prayers of its healthy brothers to work for the benefit of society in subtly changing ways.[125] This appears to have been what happened at Seedorf, and the English experience was very similar. The fourteenth century was to be a period of profound change, and crisis, for the order of St Lazarus throughout Europe.

The order in Europe, 1291–2000

After the fall of Acre and the loss of all of its bases and properties in the Holy Land, the order was thrown back on its western European possessions. The master-general during this difficult period was a Frenchman, Thomas de Sainville, and it is possible that for a short time after 1291 he followed the example of the Templars by setting up a base on Cyprus.[126] In 1297 Boniface VIII (1294–1303) issued an indulgence to those who contributed to the rebuilding of the hospital of St Lazarus 'for the reception of paupers and the infirm'.[127] Unfortunately it is not stated where the proposed new hospital was to be, but it may have been on Cyprus since there is no evidence to suggest any such initiative in the West. It could well be that the plan was a failure and, with no estates on the island, it was only a matter of time before authority became more closely associated with the realities of landed power and royal support.

In this context the obvious headquarters was at Boigny and at some date after 1291 Sainville transferred the centre of operations to France.[128] This may have

---

123 *Ibid*, pp. 107–8.
124 Rawcliffe, 'Learning to Love the Leper', p. 235.
125 Jankrift, *Leprose*, pp. 110–11.
126 For Sainville, see AN, S 4866; 4891. The presence of a master-general on Cyprus is mentioned in PRO, SC 8/302/15081. This is the most likely period for him to have been there. Further evidence is provided by the statement in GRO, Berkeley Castle Muniments, J7/67/02/002/00/00 (MF 1297) that the order had bases in Jerusalem and 'many other places in the Holy Land'.
127 GRO, Berkeley Castle Muniments, J7/67/02/002/00/00 (MF 1297).
128 Jankrift, *Leprose*, p. 86.

happened soon after 1307, the date of Philip IV's (1285–1314) attack on the Templars, because in the following year the king took the order of St Lazarus under his personal protection.[129] By doing this he was continuing the patronage shown by Louis VII and Louis IX, but it was a significant move in terms of public relations coming, as it did, at the peak of Philip IV's campaign against the Templars, with whom the Lazarites were traditionally associated. From the king's point of view it demonstrated that he was not opposed to crusading orders *per se* and that, when the circumstances were right, he was prepared to work in the laudable tradition of St Louis by supporting them. In reality, the small wealth of the Lazarites and the widely dispersed nature of their holdings made them a much less appealing target.

Sainville died in 1312 after a long period in office that had seen the order undergo fundamental change, but, to his credit, it had at least survived during a dangerous and highly charged period. But Sainville and his successors were much less successful in carving out a new niche for themselves in the context of the continuation of the Crusade or in developing their hospitaller activities. They did not, for example, follow the lead of the order of St John in setting up a Mediterranean base or fitting out galleys to pursue a naval war against the Infidel; nor did they act purposefully to create a fresh start around the proposals of Clement IV's bull. Instead, they dug into their European preceptories and became what Moeller has termed 'veritable parasites', a role that the Templars might well have emulated had they been allowed to do so.[130] Demoralised because of their expulsion from the Holy Land and no doubt vilified by some because of the events of the lepers' plot of 1321, the Lazarites staggered on.[131]

It was undoubtedly a difficult time for them. In 1320, in response to repeated complaints about injuries, injustices and the unlawful seizure of their possessions, John XXII issued a bull threatening their detractors with excommunication.[132] But, in these circumstances, it was clear that this order without a purpose would soon begin to fragment, and schism became the abiding theme of the centuries that followed. With no uniting cause or focus to hold it together, apart from its monastic tradition, it was only a matter of time before the whole operation fell apart.[133] The French orientation became deeply resented by the English, and Capua was simply too far away, too culturally distinct, for effective management from Boigny. It seems that in the fourteenth century both Boigny and Capua claimed leadership and that the other provinces simply went their own way amid the general confusion.[134] In these circumstances it was undoubtedly the English province that proved the most tenacious in establishing a new independence and identity for itself in the fifteenth century.

---

129 Grassière, *Saint-Lazare*, pp. 25–6; Bagdonas, *Order of St Lazarus*, p. 15. For the circumstances of Philip IV's vendetta against the Templars see M. Barber, *The Trial of the Templars* (Cambridge, 1978). Pierre Dubois was critical of the military orders and wanted them brought together under the authority of the crown. Jankrift, *Leprose*, p. 111.
130 Herbermann, *Catholic Encyclopedia*, 9, p. 97.
131 Jankrift, *Leprose*, pp. 111, 116–19.
132 GRO, Berkeley Castle Muniments, J7/67/02/002/00/00 (MF 1297).
133 *CPapR, Letters 4, 1362–1404*, p. 84; Grassière, *Saint-Lazare*, p. 26.
134 Grassière, *Saint-Lazare*, pp. 26–7.

The late Middle Ages, of course, was a period that saw the birth and development of the cult of chivalry all over western Europe, and in many ways France provided the cultural dynamo that drove these developments on.[135] The earliest crusaders had not, at first, been characterised by a noble ideology. Rather they were men 'who massacred helpless Jews . . . and . . . could boast of riding up to their horses' knees in blood'.[136] However, with the passage of time and the achievement of the religious goals for which they had fought, these attitudes began to mellow, especially when their exploits passed into the pages of romantic literature. In the thirteenth century knighthood became more overtly religious and moral, 'when aspirants should be consecrated to knightly arms by fasting, vigil and solemn rites'.[137] Nowhere was this changing image more clearly displayed than among the military orders who, with their emphasis on charity and chastity, came to epitomise many of the burgeoning chivalric values. Even after the fall of Acre the aura of knightly virtues continued to glow, and in the fourteenth century they found a practical outlet in the Crusades of the Teutonic order in Lithuania: 'The Crusade to the Holy Land in the twelfth century had involved going and winning. In the fourteenth it was sufficient merely to go in order to guarantee oneself a name in the annals of knighthood.'[138]

With the defeat of the Teutonic order at Tannenburg in 1410, closing off this last possibility of 'holy war' outside Spain, and the continuing development of the myth by authors such as Froissart and Malory, the fifteenth-century knight was a far cry from his twelfth-century counterpart. Though uncompromising conflicts still raged across Europe, the brutal warfare of earlier times was now complemented by highly regulated tournaments with blunted weapons. Moncreiff characterises this 'nobler aspect of chivalry' with just a touch of cynicism: 'The wonder is that, what with tournaments, perilous quests, and chance encounters, any of these knights could ever reach a good old age, who, for all their martial vigour, seem to have been much given to swooning away, to shedding floods of tears, and to going mad under stress of sorrow.'[139] It cannot be imagined that the order of St Lazarus remained immune from such a culture shift. Detached from active crusading – and from leprosy – it was free to absorb the myth and, indeed, to become part of it. There can be little doubt that the order's continued survival in the late Middle Ages set it out on a path on which the code of romantic chivalry was gradually to envelope its identity and any sense of reality that remained from the past. Later members of the order may well have identified strongly with the charge given to Tristram's son at the tomb of Lancelot: 'Knight, be cruel to thine enemies, kind to thy friends, humble to the weak, and aim always to sustain the right and confound those who do wrong to widows, poor ladies, maidens, and orphans; and love the poor always and with all thy might, and withal love always the Holy Church.'[140] It pointed the way to the future.

---

135 For a full discussion of these developments, see M. Keen, *Chivalry* (Yale, 1984).
136 A.R.H. Moncreiff, *Romance and Legend of Chivalry* (London, nd), p. 33.
137 *Ibid*, p. 34.
138 S. Turnbull, *The Book of the Medieval Knight* (London, 1985), p. 87.
139 Moncreiff, *Romance and Legend*, p. 51.
140 *Ibid*, p. 10.

After the capture of Constantinople by the Turks in 1453, the papacy tried to initiate some schemes of reform in the hope of fanning the flames kindled by such romantic notions. In 1489 Innocent VIII (1484–92) ordered an amalgamation with the Hospitallers but, with the support of Charles VIII (1483–98), this was resisted by a powerful faction of French knights of St Lazarus, and the bulls were finally annulled by Pius IV (1559–65).[141] Despite this, the German branch was merged with the order of St John in 1490 and the Hungarian properties were swallowed up by the incursions of the Turks in 1540. At about the same time, the Reformation dealt a further body blow to the order and led to its activities in England and Switzerland being suspended.[142] Thus, of the old provinces, only France and Italy still survived in 1572 when Gregory XIII (1572–85) ordered a union with the order of St Maurice, but once again, in token of the old rivalry, the French proved obstinate. However, the Capuans agreed to accept the Pope's proposal and thereafter the mastership of the Italian branch became linked to the house of Savoy.

There was, indeed, a minor renaissance along the lines the revivalists hoped for. In the seventeenth century the order of St Maurice and St Lazarus maintained a house of knights at Turin, dedicated to land combat, and another at Nice, for naval warfare, but enthusiasm diminished in the eighteenth century and the order was suppressed at the time of the French Revolution. Revived as a secular order of knighthood by the king of Sardinia in 1816, it finally ceased to exist in 1946.[143] The order in France eventually found a new beginning thanks to Henry IV (1589–1610). Keen to make amends for his Huguenot background, Henry founded the military order of Our Lady of Mount Carmel, and in 1609 merged it with the French branch of St Lazarus under the mastership of the marquis de Nerestang.[144] Like its Italian counterpart the new French order enjoyed something of a revival in the seventeenth century. Louis XIV (1643–1715) was a special patron, and during the 1660s its ships were operating out of St Malo against the English. Indeed, between 1673 and 1691 the king's minister of war, the marquis de Louvois, was vicar-general with full authority over the affairs of the order in France.[145] But, again, the eighteenth century proved to be a period of relative stagnation. Louvois' successor, the marquis de Dangeau, directed his energies into the design of new and esoteric regalia and blunted his enthusiasms with protracted and pointless wrangles, such as whether or not the knights of St Lazarus shared with the Hospitallers the privilege of taking communion without removing their swords.[146] Suppressed by Clement XIV (1769–74) as a religious order in 1772, the whole lumbering edifice was swept away during the Revolution.

There followed a shadowy period in the order's history, when some have argued it ceased to exist altogether and others have alleged a thread of continuity,

141 Herbermann, *Catholic Encyclopedia*, 9, p. 97; Bagdonas, *Order of St Lazarus*, p. 16.
142 Hyacinthe, 'Saint-Lazare', p. 192.
143 Herbermann, *Catholic Encyclopedia*, 9, p. 97; Bagdonas, *Order of St Lazarus*, p. 19.
144 Grassière, *Saint-Lazare*, pp. 36–8; Herbermann, *Catholic Encyclopedia*, 9, p. 97; Bagdonas, *Order of St Lazarus*, p. 21.
145 Grassière, *Saint-Lazare*, pp. 41–2, Bagdonas, *Order of St Lazarus*, pp. 21–2.
146 LOSJ, Ms K 27/7.

but after 1910 it re-emerged, apparently redefined and reinvigorated.[147] Although during the twentieth century the 'new' order of St Lazarus spread across the world, being particularly active in the United States, Canada and Australia, it was not a period without difficulties. There has been tension between French and Spanish groups; misunderstandings between Catholics and Protestants; and disagreement over the influence of freemasons. The upshot of this was that in 1969 the order divided between the 'Malta Obedience' and the 'Paris Obedience', each with its own grand-master, and on a national level even further fragmentation appears to have taken place.[148] Scotland, for example, has three branches of the order, each of them claiming 'authenticity'.[149] Although there are moves afoot to resolve these difficulties, no solution has as yet been arrived at. Virtually all of the branches of the contemporary order are dedicated to charitable work of one sort or another, some of it involving leprosy, and it seems clear that a sense of history, tradition and pageantry looms large in persuading these present-day 'knights' to become involved and do what they do.[150] As the order's website explains, 'Its appeal lies in its long history, its strong religious affiliation and its heartfelt commitment to alleviating suffering. . . . Dedication to those high ideals binds these men and women together in the ancient tradition of chivalry'.[151] The order takes particular pride in the contribution it made during the 1990s to the restoration of Christianity in eastern Europe, and, in terms of the alleviation of suffering, its efforts have been manifest in the distribution of considerable quantities of food, clothing and medical supplies in the former Communist bloc.[152]

The order in England was revived in 1962 when the grand-master appointed Lord Mowbray, a direct descendent of Roger de Mowbray, the order's principal English patron, as grand-prior of England and Wales.[153] The present grand-prior is the duke of Westminster, and the honorary chaplains are the archbishop of Canterbury and the cardinal archbishop of Westminster, illustrating that the contemporary order is more firmly embedded in the 'establishment' than ever its medieval predecessor was. A marshal, from a military background, and two hospitallers, who are members of the medical profession, maintain links with the founding ideology in the Holy Land. Prospective members are invited to measure themselves against the following requirements:

> Membership of this order of chivalry is an honour, and one that can be shared by all who are deemed worthy. Membership is ecumenical, and open to all practising

147 http://www.kwtelecom.com/chivalry/lazarus. G.S. Sainty, 'The Order of St Lazarus. An Alternative Viewpoint'.

148 *Ibid.* 'The Order of St Lazarus. A Short History'; Bagdonas, *Order of St Lazarus*, pp. 27–8.

149 E. Casciani, 'Today's Knights', *The Scots Magazine* (July 1985), pp. 348–54. The three principal divisions in Scotland are the Grand Commandary of Lochore, the Grand Bailiwick of Scotland and the Great Priory of Scotland.

150 http://www.kwtelecom.com/chivalry/lazarus. 'The Order of St Lazarus. The Heraldry of the Order'; Bagdonas, *Order of St Lazarus*, pp. 36–41.

151 http://www.st-lazarus.net/world/history.htm. 'St Lazarus Net International'.

152 *Ibid*, 'History'.

153 Bagdonas, *Order of St Lazarus*, p. 27; http://www.users.globalnet.co.uk/~tyderwen/thegrand.htm. 'The Grand Priory of England and Wales'.

Christians, regardless of denomination and sex, and currently includes many married couples. Members are drawn from a wide range of professions and callings, but all who join make the provision to give service to the order. Membership requires a firm commitment to work for the good of the order by supporting its activities to the extent of one's abilities, whether this be by raising funds, devoting time to the order's charitable works, or by prayer.[154]

The order of St Lazarus, therefore, has proved to be exceptionally tenacious, not only in terms of its survival, but also by including in its present aims and objectives distinct echoes of the various phases of its past which have made it what it is today. From a national perspective it is curious that the English order should have been reborn as part of the continental tradition from which its medieval predecessor fought so hard to detach itself.

Archaeology and iconography

If the documentary history of the order is sketchy, its above-ground archaeological record seems to be equally poor – though this may be the result of an archive-based research bias on the part of recent historians. Virtually nothing survives to record its presence in the Holy Land. A mosque now covers the site of the leper hospital in Jerusalem, though a wall from the crusader period still survives.[155] At Acre almost everything was destroyed in 1291. Even archaeological remains of the important French preceptories appear to be slight. Boigny still stands and is inhabited, though it underwent very extensive alterations in the eighteenth century and its medieval character has been lost apart from the remnants of a moat and the impressive north-west and south-west towers.[156] There is a small, neglected chapel at Pastoral, its solid masonry suggestive of a thirteenth-century date. But undoubtedly the best survivals are at Grattemont, where the last remnants of the preceptory occupy a landscape even now reminiscent of medieval demesne farming.[157] The chapel of St Antony is a small and simple building with a steep pitched roof (Plate 4). Its east and west ends are of good stone with decorative vertical courses in ashlar, but the north and south walls are of poorer quality, being constructed in rubble and mortar and once probably covered with stucco. The door and windows, though impossible to date accurately, suggest a late twelfth or early thirteenth century date.

The interior of the chapel is a surprise. Against the south wall of the chancel there is a small wall-mounted memorial to Peter Potier, commander of Grattemont and vicar-general of the master-general William Desmares. Potier is depicted as a naked cadaver, with a book and chalice at his head and a lion at his feet. At the top of the monument is a shield of arms, supported by two flying angels, showing the cross of the order surrounded by three pots sprouting sprigs

---

154 http://www.users.globalnet.co.uk/~tyderwen/thegrand.htm. 'The Grand Priory of England and Wales'.
155 I am grateful to Dr Hyacinthe for this information.
156 AN, Engraving N. III. Loiret 77; E. Vignat, *Les Lépreux et les Chevaliers de Saint-Lazare de Jérusalem et de Notre Dame du Mont Carmel* (Orleans, 1884), p. 205.
157 A. Mutel, 'Recherches sur l'Ordre de Saint-Lazare de Jérusalem en Normandie', *Annales de Normandie*, 33, no. 2 (June 1983), pp. 121–42.

Plate 4: The chapel at Grattemont, Normandy. The simple style of architecture is
difficult to date, but is possibly from the thirteenth century.

of foliage, a pun on the name of the deceased. Neither Desmares nor Potier can
be dated accurately (the best estimate is late fifteenth century), but it appears to
have been Potier who initiated important changes at Grattemont, probably
connected with a healing cult of St Antony. The altar is flanked by two statues of
roughly contemporary date. To the south, St Damian, patron saint of physicians,
peers at a flask in his left hand and holds an empty purse in his right, suggestive
of the legend that he took no payment for his services.[158] He stands on a corbel
on which an angel, with wildly flowing robes and hair, prays over the arms of the
order. To the north, St Antony is even more remarkable, and he stands on an
elaborate plinth that not only identifies him as the principal cult image but also
closely associates him with the order of St Lazarus. Holding a staff in his right
hand and a book in his left, this stern guardian of the chapel emerges dramati-
cally from flames, among which are the pigs associated with his cult. Indeed,
both Antony and Damian claimed curative powers over animals as well as
people, and it could well be that it was partly a veterinary role that was perceived
for these two in this relatively remote, rural community.[159]

The most valuable iconographical evidence in the chapel, from an historian's
point of view, is the corbel on which Antony stands, because it provides virtually
our only contemporary depiction of the personnel of the order. In the centre of
the composition are the arms of St Lazarus, complete with helm, mantling and

158 Farmer, *Saints*, p. 113.
159 *Ibid*, pp. 25–6.

Plate 5: Fifteenth-century figures beneath the St Antony corbel at Grattemont, Normandy. Two knights (with swords and armour) and a robed brother (with a purse) are united in prayer to the left of the arms of the order.

crest in the form of a cross, and to each side three figures are represented (Plate 5). Four of these are knights, characterised by cloaks, swords and armour, and with helmets at their feet; the other two are to be identified as brothers, wearing long habits with purses hanging from their belts and books at their feet. Thus, the principal functions of the order – fighting, alms gathering (symbolic of their hospitaller vocation) and prayer – are depicted. To place these activities very firmly in a Christian context, both knights and brothers wear huge crosses suspended from collars. The sculptures at Grattemont are remarkable and unique survivals and, despite the alterations made to the chapel in the seventeenth and eighteenth centuries, it remains a highly evocative place, a glimpse of the order of St Lazarus before its medieval foundations were entirely shot away by Reformation and Revolution.

With the exception of the representations at Grattemont, very little survives to create an impression of what brothers of St Lazarus looked like, and some of the Grattemont evidence is contradictory, especially with regard to heraldry. The medieval arms of the order are generally taken to be a green *couped* cross on a white field, but at Grattemont, where some early colouring has survived, the field is green and the cross (which is a passion cross, not a *couped* cross) appears to be a light green or dirty white.[160] Nevertheless, documentary evidence for the green

---

[160] For the *couped* cross, see A.C. Fox-Davies, *A Complete Guide to Heraldry* (1929, reprinted London, 1993), p. 129. For the heraldry of St Lazarus, see http://www.kwtelecom.com/chivalry/lazarus. 'The Order of St Lazarus. The Heraldry of the Order'.

cross in medieval Europe is reasonably strong. In 1314 Sigfried de Flatte, commander of Seedorf, ordered that it should be worn by brothers on their habits; in 1419 a similar order was repeated by Robert le Conte, commander of Grattemont, and extended to servants and retainers of the house.[161] England, where we know that brothers similarly wore a habit bearing the 'mark' of the order, may have broken step with continental practice, certainly after the schism of the fourteenth century.[162] The common seal of the English province shows a plain cross (not *couped*) and the lion rampant of the order's principal patrons, the Mowbrays. Yet by the sixteenth century the only arms recorded by John Leland were those of the Mowbrays.[163]

There is no evidence of the use of the green cross in England prior to the revival of interest in the order in recent years. On the contrary, the only surviving clues point to a red cross on white, the same as the arms used by the Templars. In the early seventeenth century the antiquary William Burton and the herald William Wyrley, Rouge Croix, visited the churches of Leicestershire prior to the heralds' visitation of 1619. In the abandoned collegiate church at Burton Lazars, built by the order in the fifteenth century, they both recorded, amongst other coats, a shield bearing a cross on a plain background. In the notebook in the College of Arms, ascribed to Wyrley, no colours are provided;[164] but Burton, in his subsequent *Description of Leicestershire* published in 1622, gives the blazon as *Argent, a cross gules*.[165] We must assume he was providing an accurate record of what he saw. His description was followed by the eighteenth-century antiquarians Nichols and Throsby and by the compilers of the new and improved edition of Sir William Dugdale's *Monasticon* in 1830.[166] Having said that, the arms of Burton Lazars hospital do not appear in any of the classic sixteenth-century books of arms, and it may be assumed that the brethren adopted the red cross, in abeyance since the suppression of the Templars, during the late Middle Ages to differentiate the order in England from the continental branch from which it had recently seceded.[167] The red cross also had the advantage of linking the brethren with the patriotic cult of St George, which helped assert both their chivalric and nationalistic credentials during this time of change.[168] For this, it seems, Burton is our earliest and sole authority.

Only two medieval representations of masters-general survive, once more creating contrasting and contradictory images. The earliest is that of Thomas de Sainville, who is depicted on an engraving of his memorial slab once in the

161 http://www.kwtelcom.com/chivalry/lazarus. 'The Order of St Lazarus. The Heraldry of the Order'.
162 PRO E 40/11147; *DCAD*, 5, p. 100. See Chapter 3, p. 0.
163 See Chapter 4, pp. 111–12; J. Leland, *De Rebus Britannicis Collectanea*, 1 (London, 1774), p. 72.
164 CA, Vincent Mss, 197, f. 39v.
165 W. Burton, *The Description of Leicestershire* (London, 1622), p. 64.
166 Nichols, *Leicestershire*, 2 pt 1, p. 269, pl. 51, fig. 2; J. Throsby, *The Supplementary Volume to the Leicestershire Views: containing a series of excursions in the year 1790, to the villages and places of note in the county* (London, 1790), p. 177; W. Dugdale (revised by J. Caley, H. Ellis and B. Bandinel), *Monasticon Anglicanum*, 6 pt 2 (London, 1830), pp. 632, 983; J. Woodward, *A Treatise on Ecclesiastical Heraldry* (Edinburgh and London, 1894), p. 360.
167 For example, CA, L Series, Ms 10.
168 See Chapter 3, p. 92.

Plate 6: Thomas de Sainville, master-general of the order
of St Lazarus, who died in 1312. From his memorial, once
in the chapel at Boigny.

chapel at Boigny and dated 1312 (Plate 6).[169] He wears a long round-necked
cloak or mantle, which is laced at the collar and charged with the *couped* cross of
the order on the left shoulder; beneath this there is a long undergarment, with
buttoned sleeves, fastened with a heavy belt. He has no armour, sword or surcoat,
and his monument stands apart from more obviously 'military' memorials such
as that of Kuno von Liebensteyn, knight of the Teutonic order, at Nowemaisto,
Poland.[170] Although Sainville does not look particularly knightly, neither is he
quite the monk described by Jankrift.[171] He may simply have been a
non-knightly brother, though, paradoxically, the pronouncement of Innocent IV
in 1253 states clearly that the master-general should be a knight.

169 Bagdonas, *Order of St Lazarus*, p. 12.
170 Seward, *Monks of War*, opposite p. 114.
171 Jankrift, *Leprose*, pp. 110–11.

Plate 7: James de Besnes, master-general of the
order of St Lazarus. From his seal, originally
attached to a document dated 1382.

James de Besnes is depicted on his seal as master-general, which is attached to
a document dated 1382 surviving in the Smitmer-Löschner collection in the
Österreichischen Staatsarchivs (Plate 7).[172] This image, showing Besnes in
armour on a galloping horse and brandishing a sword, is borrowed from the
seals of royal chanceries and important noblemen across Europe, and is a far cry
from the less obviously secular *persona* represented on Sainville's monument.
Not only does his shield proudly bear the *couped* cross of the order, his horse
wears trappings ostentatiously festooned with the same device. The seal points to
the shift in attitude that was connected with the changing nature of the order in
the fourteenth century. As the Lazarites became further removed from the reality
of warfare and the Crusade, so the myth of chivalry and knighthood took root.
Indeed, one cannot help feeling there is something slightly Ruritanian about the
knights of Grattemont, their beaky close-helms unsuitable for any type of
conflict other than the joust. By the late fifteenth century the iconography of the
order was already looking forward to its later mythology, rather than back to the
harsh realities of the crusading era when the leper knights perished *en masse* at
the hands of the Infidel. It was the beginning of the set of quasi-knightly values
still espoused by the order today.

In terms of its military contribution to the crusader states, the order of St
Lazarus paled into insignificance alongside the Templars and the knights of St
John. It simply did not have the resources in terms of lands or manpower to
compete with them. The ideology of Christian knighthood was something
common to them all, but the Lazarites brought a fresh ingredient in the form of

---

[172] OS, Smitmer-Löschner Collection Catalogue, p. 92.

their physical suffering – they were the only order of *leper* knights. In terms of the way in which leprosy was perceived in the twelfth and thirteenth centuries, this made them something very special, knights touched with a veritable messianic presence; even their humblest followers were potentially 'the heirs of Christ'.[173] They became, by virtue of this unique identity, the divine warriors of the Crusades. In this context the military failures are more easily understood, because the Lazarites were not to be judged against the Templars and Hospitallers in a starkly practical and utilitarian sense. Having the leper knights on the battlefield was more like parading a holy relic, a talismanic presence that brought benefits by the very fact of their being there. All of this gave birth to a potent myth that long survived the fall of Acre. Indeed, the Lazarites were the most determined of all that it should live on. If the crusading days of the order came to an end in 1291, the memories of leprosy and chivalry endured, constantly reinterpreted to meet the demands of time and place, constantly exploited to guarantee the survival and prosperity of the order. The following chapters analyse how this underlying theme of continuity and change developed in England from the foundation of the order in the twelfth century until its suppression by Henry VIII in 1544.

---

[173] GRO, Berkeley Castle Muniments, J7/67/02/002/00/00 (MF 1297).

2

Lands and Patrons

heartily beseeching you as a good lord unto me and my poor house
(Letter of Sir Thomas Norton, c.1520)

Patrons and their motives

The prosperity and well being of virtually all medieval religious orders depended on their ability to accumulate and maintain an estate consisting of both temporal and spiritual property. This chapter deals with the landed estate of the order of St Lazarus and its spiritual property is discussed in Chapter 6. For orders established at the time, the twelfth century was a golden age of opportunity, growth and expansion. Orme estimates that at least 259 out of a total of 585 hospital foundations (44 per cent) dated from the period 1080–1200; and if that period is extended to 1300 the number of foundations becomes 475, 81 per cent of the eventual total.[1] Yet, as Satchell has pointed out, the landed endowment of leper hospitals, in particular, was far from generous and they were forced to rely on other money-raising expedients, such as alms gathering, to make ends meet.[2] These years, stretching roughly from the capture of Jerusalem in 1099 to the fall of Acre in 1291, coincided with a widespread enthusiasm for the Crusade, and gifts of land to the military orders, if anything, outstripped those to hospital foundations of a more general nature. An order that was both leprous and military was to find itself in a unique and interesting position.

For the order of St Lazarus there are comparatively few original documents of twelfth- or thirteenth-century date to plot these acquisitions in detail. Most of the surviving charters are transcriptions appearing in a Cartulary drawn up by the master Walter de Lynton and bearing the date 12 December 1404 (Plate 8).[3] In it Lynton states that he had 'ordained that a book be made for the greater security of all charters etc of the hospital of Burton St Lazarus of Jerusalem in England', but the reality does not quite match up to this optimistic expectation.[4] Most of the documents enrolled relate to Leicestershire, and though there is a substantial section dealing with Carlton-le-Moorland, Lincolnshire, nothing is

[1] Orme and Webster, *English Hospital*, p. 11.
[2] M. Satchell, 'The Emergence of Leper-Houses in Medieval England, 1100–1250', University of Oxford, D.Phil. thesis (1998), pp. viii, 150–2, 158–9.
[3] BL, Cart, ff. 1a–250 (plus end paper).
[4] *Ibid*, f. 1a.

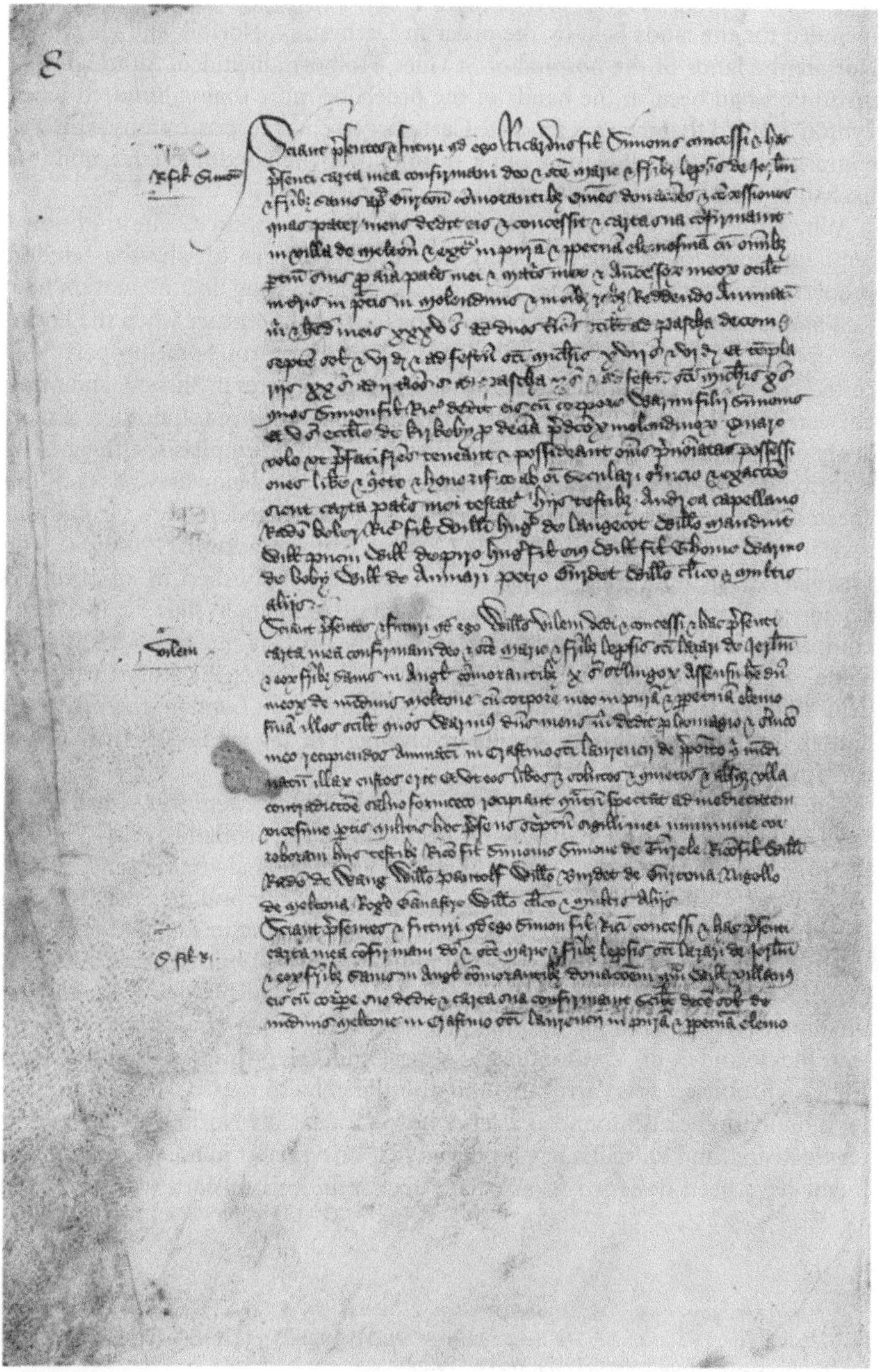

Plate 8: The Burton Lazars Cartulary drawn up in 1404. This page records gifts of property in Melton Mowbray.

included for the lands held by the order in Derbyshire, Norfolk and elsewhere. Nor are the lands of the hospital of St Giles, Holborn, included. Although that institution had been in the hands of the order for more than a hundred years, Lynton decided to draw up a separate Cartulary to cover its possessions. This was completed in 1402, following a bitter dispute over the London estates, and it is likely that the Burton Lazars Cartulary was prompted by it.[5]

Why is the Burton Lazars Cartulary such a patchy source? The traditional semi-autonomy of St Giles's provides an explanation as to why the London property does not appear, and further gaps in the surviving documentation may well have been caused by the disputes of the fourteenth century when the Locko preceptory had attempted to free itself from central control. Some property was certainly disposed of prior to 1404 (for example, the estates in Sussex), and other charters may simply have been lost or accidentally destroyed. Indeed, a certain laxity of administration is hinted at by Lynton when he emphasises 'the greater security' needed for the extant documents. One of the major drawbacks of the charters that do survive is that very few of them are dated, though virtually all appear to be in the range c.1160–1337, with a concentration c.1190–1250. The Cartulary is an important source, and it has been published in an abridged version and subjected to fairly detailed examination by Walker in his thesis comparing the patronage of the Templars and the order of St Lazarus.[6] Although some of these issues are discussed here, the chapter takes the story further by exploring the reasons for the late growth of an estate in London, the privileges and exemptions of the order and its involvement in the feudal structure of the early medieval period.

The initial grants of property to the order in Britain were somewhat piece-meal, as might be expected. Before his death David I of Scotland (1124–53) gave the order the church of St Giles, Edinburgh, and also lands in the same place.[7] These were prestigious gifts by the king in his capital city, and they may indicate that the order was established in Scotland before it came to England. The first English grant was a gift of land at Wymondham, Norfolk, by William d'Aubigny, earl of Arundel.[8] This is to be dated before 1146, and as such is one of the earliest unambiguous grants to the hospital in Jerusalem anywhere in Europe. Aubigny was the founder of Wymondham Abbey and, according to the Waltham Abbey chronicler, was 'arrogant and inordinately conceited'. In addition to Wymondham, he also founded a leper hospital near his Norfolk stronghold at Castle Rising, and Rawcliffe has suggested that this interest in the plight of lepers might have been designed to associate this 'ambitious upstart' with the good

---

5   BL, Harl Mss, 4015.
6   T. Bourne and D. Marcombe, *The Burton Lazars Cartulary: a medieval Leicestershire estate*, UNCLH, Record Series, 6 (Nottingham, 1987); Walker, 'Patronage'.
7   G.W.S. Barrow (ed.), *Regista Regum Scottorum*, 2 (Edinburgh, 1971), pp. 116–17.
8   A.S. Napier and W.H. Stephenson, *The Crawford Collection of Early Charters and Documents now in the Bodleian Library* (Anecdota Oxoniensa), pt 7 (Oxford, 1895), p. 31; F. Blomefield, *History of Norfolk*, 2 (1732, 2nd edition London, 1805), pp. 504–5; R. Taylor, *Index Monasticus: abbeys and other monasteries . . . formerly established in the Diocese of Norwich and the ancient Kingdom of East Anglia* (London, 1821), p. 36.

deeds of his wife, Adeliza of Louvain (widow of Henry I), and provide the 'moral authority' that such foundations could bestow.[9] It seems he wanted to advertise his humility and concern for the poor in a very practical and highly visible fashion. The statement in Dugdale's *Monasticon* that the gift was 'for the endowment of a cell for leprous brothers' is purely speculative, and, if he had this sort of end in view, the plan misfired.[10] It is unlikely that the size of the grant justified such a deployment of resources from the Holy Land, and the order appears to have waited until Aubigny's cousin, Roger de Mowbray, provided a more generous endowment elsewhere before it began seriously to consider colonisation in England.

Mowbray's grant is recorded as the first charter enrolled on the Burton Lazars Cartulary, and it granted to 'God and Holy Mary and the lepers of St Lazarus of Jerusalem' two carucates of land, a house and the site of a mill at Burton, near Melton Mowbray in Leicestershire.[11] Among the witnesses were Roger's sons, Nigel and Robert, and since Roger de Mowbray did not marry until 1142/3 it is unlikely that his sons were able to act as witnesses until at least the 1150s. The *Victoria County History* suggests a date no earlier than 1138 and before 1162, with the latter end of the range (c.1155–62) looking the most likely.[12] Additional credence is given to this possibility by a charter of Henry II in favour of the 'lepers of St Lazarus of Jerusalem' dated at Stamford, Lincolnshire, probably in December 1157.[13] The content of this document is unknown, but it is likely to have been a grant of privileges rather than land. The king may well have been aware that Mowbray was about to give, or had recently given, an English estate to the order and he probably felt it appropriate to weigh in with his own support at the same time. A date of 1157 may therefore be as close as we are likely to get to Mowbray's initial grant.

There may possibly have been a small community of lepers already resident at Burton before Mowbray sealed his first charter.[14] This informal group, indeed, might have provided his inspiration, because Burton, given the unusual qualities of its situation and water, was no ordinary site and was land particularly suitable for the foundation of a leper hospital. Since Mowbray's gift overshadowed that of Aubigny, and probably had the support of Henry II, it must have persuaded the authorities in Jerusalem of the advantages of establishing a presence in England, to consolidate what was already held and to solicit further gifts. Roger de Mowbray's critical importance in these developments caused him to be regarded by the English Lazarites as their founder, and they soon came to use the lion rampant of the Mowbrays as part of their arms.[15] Burton, known generally as

---

9 Rawcliffe, 'Learning to Love the Leper', p. 250. As successor of the pious Queen Matilda, Adeliza had much to live up to. She was a major benefactor of leper hospitals at Wilton, Wiltshire, and Arundel, Sussex.

10 Dugdale, *Monasticon*, 6 pt 2, pp. 769–70.

11 BL, Cart, f. 1a.

12 *VCH, Leicestershire*, 2 (London, 1954), p. 36.

13 R.W. Eyton, *Court, Household and Itinerary of King Henry II* (London, 1878), p. 31. The charter was witnessed by Earl Reginald, Richard de Lucy and Richard de Canvill.

14 See Chapter 5, p. 146.

15 PRO, SC 8/302/15081.

Plate 9: The seal of Roger de Mowbray, founder of the order of England, who granted lands at Burton Lazars, Leicestershire.

Burton St Lazarus or Burton Lazars, very quickly became the site of a house that was to form the hub of the order's administrative activities for the next four hundred years.

Roger de Mowbray, born in about 1120, was one of the most notable land-owners of the twelfth century, having inherited an extensive estate from his father, Nigel d'Aubigny, a loyal supporter of Henry I (Plate 9). By virtue of his birth, ancestry and marriage he was related to many of the wealthiest and most powerful families in the land, including the earls of Surrey, Norfolk, Northumberland and Lincoln (Table 1). The centre of his estate was on the Isle of Axholme in Lincolnshire, but the Mowbrays also owned important lands in Yorkshire and Leicestershire, especially around Melton Mowbray, that formed

part of their demesne.[16] Although Roger de Mowbray became involved in political manoeuvres which weakened his feudal authority, his support for religious
institutions provided a more constructive outlet for his undoubted energy and
enthusiasm. He founded a Cistercian house at Byland; established the Augustinian canons at Newburgh; the Templars at Temple Balsall; and in addition to
this was a patron of the Benedictines, Gilbertines and Premonstratensians.

But Mowbray was no armchair evangelist, and his generosity was matched by
practical action. On three occasions he travelled to the Holy Land. On the first of
these he fought in the Second Crusade, and on the last he was captured at the
battle of Hattin in 1187, by then a veteran warrior well advanced into his sixties.
In this misfortune his earlier generosity served him well, since he was ransomed
by the Templars and Hospitallers, who both stood in his debt for lands. He died
in the Holy Land in 1188, and, though it has been suggested that he was 'a gentleman who was tainted with the disease [i.e. leprosy]', there is no evidence to back
such a statement.[17] Apart from his passion for the Crusade, there is no known
factor that might explain Mowbray's support for the Lazarites other than his
relationship with William d'Aubigny, the first English benefactor.[18] It is likely
that the reasons for his patronage of a leper order were no less cynical that those
of his cousin. If Touati and Rawcliffe are correct, and lepers *did* represent a
branch of the 'new spirituality' of the twelfth century, Mowbray was identifying
himself with an ideal charged with real authority and power.[19]

Roger de Mowbray's patronage was continued by his son, Nigel, who died
overseas with the crusader army in 1191, and, in all, the Cartulary records four-
teen Mowbray charters executed by five different members of the family.[20] The
Belers, descendants of Roger de Mowbray's brothers, Hamo and Ralph, were
equally enthusiastic benefactors and provided the order with many early gifts
around Kirby Bellars.[21] Although Nigel de Mowbray's grandson, Roger, was
elevated to the peerage as the first Baron Mowbray in 1295, the loyal support of
the family was not always untarnished by political failure. John, second Baron
Mowbray, became a notable supporter of Thomas, second earl of Lancaster, in
his quarrel with Edward II. Captured at the battle of Boroughbridge, Mowbray
was executed and hung in chains at York in 1322, his lands being forfeit to the
crown and his widow and son being imprisoned in the Tower.[22] But the eclipse of
the Mowbrays did not last long and was reversed with the accession of Edward
III in 1327. John Mowbray, fifth baron, was created earl of Nottingham in 1377,
and his son, Thomas Mowbray, sixth baron, not only succeeded to the earldom

---

16 D.E. Greenway, *Charters of the Honour of Mowbray, 1107–1191* (London, 1972); T. North, 'The
Mowbrays, Lords of Melton', *Transactions of the Leicestershire Architectural and Archaeological Society,* 1
pt 3 (1864). For Roger de Mowbray, see *DNB*, 13, pp. 1124–7. At the time of the Leicestershire Survey
(1124–29) Roger de Mowbray held eleven carucates and seven bovates in Burton; the Honour of Blyth
held three carucates there; and seven bovates belonged to Henry de Ferrers. J. Curtis, *History of
Leicestershire* (London, 1831), p. 252.

17 G. Newman, *Prize Essays in Leprosy,* New Sydenham Society (London, 1895), p. 18.

18 Greenway, *Mowbray Charters*, pp. xxvi–ix.

19 See Chapter 1, p. 8.

20 Walker, 'Patronage', p. 116.

21 BL, Cart, ff. 104–5, 111.

22 *DNB*, 13, pp. 1114–16.

Table 1: The family of Roger de Mowbray

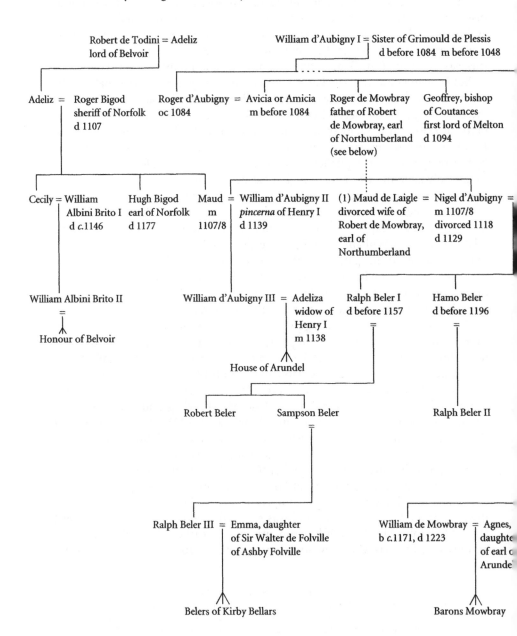

Sources: J.G. Nichols, *History and Antiquities of Leicestershire*, 2 pt 1 (London, 1795), p. 263 (Mowbray), p. 278 (Bele⸱
T. North, 'The Mowbrays, Lords of Melton', *TLAS*, 1 pt 3 (1864), p. 226; J.-P. Yeatman, *The Feudal History of the Co⸱*
of Derby, 4 sect 8 (London, 1905), pp. 392–3; G.F. Farnham, *Leicester Medieval Pedigrees* (Leicester, 1925), p. 42.

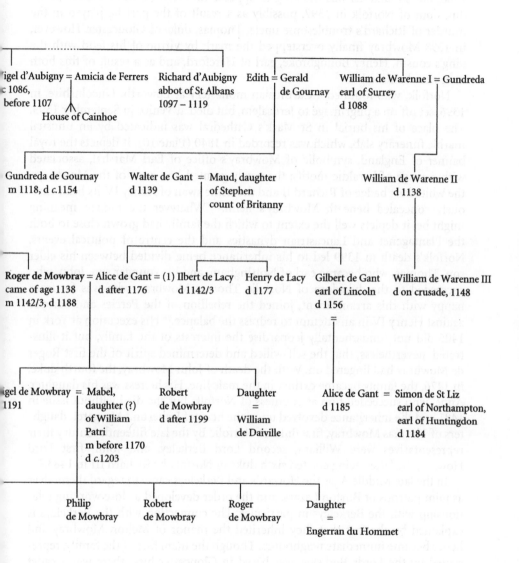

Nigel d'Aubigny = Amicia de Ferrers
c 1086,
before 1107

House of Cainhoe

Richard d'Aubigny
abbot of St Albans
1097 – 1119

Edith = Gerald
de Gournay

William de Warenne I = Gundreda
earl of Surrey
d 1088

Gundreda de Gournay
m 1118, d c.1154

Walter de Gant = Maud, daughter
d 1139   of Stephen
              count of Britanny

William de Warenne II
d 1138

Roger de Mowbray = Alice de Gant = (1) Ilbert de Lacy
came of age 1138   d after 1176   d 1142/3
m 1142/3, d 1188

Henry de Lacy
d 1177

Gilbert de Gant
earl of Lincoln
d 1156

William de Warenne III
d on crusade, 1148

Nigel de Mowbray = Mabel,
1191   daughter (?)
                 of William
                 Patri
                 m before 1170
                 d c.1203

Robert
de Mowbray
d after 1199

Daughter
=
William
de Daiville

Alice de Gant = Simon de St Liz
d 1185   earl of Northampton,
                earl of Huntingdon
                d 1184

Philip
de Mowbray

Robert
de Mowbray

Roger
de Mowbray

Daughter
=
Engerran du Hommet

but also became influential during the reign of Richard II.[23] Not always in harmony with the king's policies, Mowbray was among the Lords Appellant in 1386, but so anxious was the king to appease him that he was elevated to the dukedom of Norfolk in 1397, possibly as a result of the part he played in the murder of Richard's troublesome uncle, Thomas, duke of Gloucester. However, in 1398 Mowbray finally overstepped the mark by virtue of his feud with the king's cousin, Henry Bolingbroke, earl of Hereford, and as a result of this both men were banished.[24]

Norfolk, who founded a Carthusian monastery at Epworth, Lincolnshire, in 1396, set off on a pilgrimage to Jerusalem, but died at Venice in September 1399. The place of his burial in St Mark's Cathedral was indicated by an unusual marble funerary slab, which was recorded in 1840 (Plate 10). It depicts the royal banner of England, symbolic of Mowbray's office of Earl Marshal, associated with a range of heraldic motifs: the newly granted lion crest of the Mowbrays, the white hart badge of Richard II and the white swan of Henry IV, its head curiously concealed beneath Mowbray's helm.[25] Whatever the hidden meaning might be, it depicts well the extent to which the family had grown close to both the Plantagenet and Lancastrian dynasties and the centre of political events. Norfolk's death in 1399 led to his inheritance being divided between his elder son, Thomas, who became earl of Nottingham, and his younger son, John, who succeeded to the dukedom of Norfolk. Thomas Mowbray, who was far from happy with this arrangement, joined the rebellion of the Percies and Scropes against Henry IV in an attempt to redress the balance.[26] His execution at York in 1405 did not fundamentally jeopardise the interests of the family, but it illustrated, nevertheless, that the self-willed and determined spirit of the first Roger de Mowbray had lingered on. With the death of John Mowbray, the fourth duke, in 1476, the family became extinct in the male line. His heiress was his daughter, Anne, who succeeded him as countess of Norfolk, but she died without issue in 1481 and the inheritance devolved upon the heirs of Isabel and Margaret, daughters of Thomas Mowbray, first duke of Norfolk. By the late fifteenth century their representatives were William, second Lord Berkeley, and John, first Lord Howard, the latter being created sixth duke of Norfolk by Richard III in 1483.[27]

In the late Middle Ages the Howards and Berkeleys came to regard themselves as joint patrons of Burton Lazars, and the order developed a close working relationship with the Berkeleys in particular. The connection with the Berkeleys is explained by the fact that they inherited the manor of Melton Mowbray and hence became immediate neighbours. Though the main line of the family, represented by the Lords Berkeley, was based in Gloucestershire, there was a cadet

23 *Ibid*, p. 1117.
24 *Ibid*, pp. 1127–33; H.A. Doubleday and H. de Walden (eds), *The Complete Peerage*, 9 (London, 1936), pp. 376–7.
25 R. Brown, 'Achievement of Thomas Mowbray, Duke of Norfolk', *Archaeologia*, 29 (1842), pp. 387–9. The view that this monument may relate to a visit by Henry IV as earl of Derby is expressed in J. Foster, *The Dictionary of Heraldry. Feudal Coats of Arms and Pedigrees* (London, 1992), p. 144.
26 *DNB*, 13, pp. 1133–4.
27 *Complete Peerage*, 9, p. 385; *DNB*, 10, pp. 42–4. John Howard, duke of Norfolk, was killed at Bosworth in 1485. For the Berkeleys, see V. Gibbs (ed.), *The Complete Peerage*, 2 (London, 1912), pp. 133–8.

Plate 10: An enigmatic memorial, generally considered to be that of
Thomas Mowbray, first duke of Norfolk, who died at Venice in 1399.

branch in Leicestershire, the Berkeleys of Wymondham.[28] Both families had links with the order; and both, confusingly, often christened their sons Maurice. It seems that these links were mutually profitable, and there is no suggestion of the hostility that soured the relationship between the Lords Berkeley and another Leicestershire religious house in which they had an interest, Croxton Kerrial.[29] In 1492 and 1494 Maurice, third Lord Berkeley, and Sir George Sutton were joined, with others, in some complex transactions over land, latterly involving the manors of Scalford and Saxby, Leicestershire.[30] This Lord Berkeley died in 1506, and when in 1514 his widow, Isabel, gave the Austin friars of London £72 13s 4d to repair their house and set up special prayers for the family to be known as 'Berkeley's Mass', Sir Thomas Norton was appointed to supervise the agreement and receive a forfeit of £1 0s 0d on behalf of the Lazarites if the intercessions were not performed. [31] Isabel's son, Maurice, fourth Lord Berkeley, was evidently short of ready money and in the same year as this agreement he borrowed £100 from Sir Thomas Norton (who had been privy to the financial dealings of the family since 1492, at least), pledging the manor of Melton Mowbray as security.[32] Although in his will of 1520 Lord Berkeley acknowledged his debt as still outstanding, it appears that the master had received permission to collect the rents of certain of his lands to pay it off.[33]

Yet, that this was a relationship of some deference is indicated in a letter from Norton to Thomas, fifth Lord Berkeley, concerning a windmill at Melton Mowbray, which the master considered damaging to the interests of the order:

> My right reverend lord and founder, my duty in every part considered, I recommend me unto you with my sincere and daily prayer, heartily beseeching you as a good lord unto me and my poor house, as my lord your brother, whose soul God pardon, ever hath been in time past . . . And thus Almighty Jesu have you in his most blessed keeping. Amen.[34]

At about the same time a black gelding was found wandering in Melton Mowbray and was impounded by John Oldham, the master's collector of tithes for the town. After eight weeks in the pound, so as not to infringe Berkeley's manorial rights, Oldham, by order of the master, 'did turn the said gelding out of the parsonage yard into the street, whereupon the officers of the said Lord Berkeley did seize the same gelding to the use of the said Lord Berkeley'.[35] After the Reformation one of the principal areas of the Burton Lazars demesne was known as 'Berkeleys', simply because it had become a traditional fief of the Wymondham family.

28 R.P. Taylor, *The Berkeleys of Wymondham* (Wymondham, 1980).
29 S. Jack, 'Monastic Lands in Leicestershire and their Administration on the Eve of the Dissolution', *TLAHS*, 41 (1965–66), p. 13.
30 LRO, Gretton (Sherard) Mss, DG40/189; 40/283.
31 I.H. Jeayes (ed.), *Descriptive Catalogue of the Charters and Muniments in the possession of the Rt Hon Lord Fitz-Hardinge at Berkeley Castle* (Bristol, 1892), p. 203.
32 MH, Lothian Mss, Box 23, no. 108.
33 PRO, PROB 11/21, f. 109 (Sir Richard Sutton, 1524); MH, Lothian Mss, Box 23, no. 108. The lands were at Melton Mowbray, Cold Overton, Sileby and Seagrave.
34 MH, Lothian Mss, Box 25.
35 PRO, E 134/27 and 28 Eliz 1/Mich 26.

This relationship of 'good lordship', be it with the Mowbrays, Berkeleys or Howards, usually worked to the advantage of the order and only occasional disputes over property rights upset the general sense of harmony, for example in 1364 when John Mowbray, fourth baron, accused Nicholas de Dover of cutting down trees on an ancient motte in Melton Mowbray, the ownership of which was in dispute between them.[36] However, the fact that this same Mowbray was killed by the Turks four years later on his way to the Holy Land indicates that the old crusading impulses of the family were far from dead, and probably served to strengthen the emotional link between the order and its principal English patrons. By virtue of their strong positions at court and enduring traditions of piety, the Mowbrays and Howards, in particular, were capable of exercising positive influence in support of their 'poor house'.

There were, of course, other benefactors from among the Anglo-Norman baronage, such as William de Ferrers, third earl of Derby, the probable grantor of the order's Derbyshire property around Spondon.[37] Interestingly, his family had long established connections with Burton Lazars, where they gave a portion of their demesne tithes to Tutbury Priory before 1100.[38] The Mowbrays and Ferrers were related, and Roger de Mowbray also had a relationship, through marriage, with the Gants, Lacys and St Lizs who were grantors of spiritualities to the order in Yorkshire and the East Midlands.[39] These contacts were based on the marriage of Alice de Gant (daughter of Walter de Gant and sister of Gilbert de Gant, earl of Lincoln), first with Ilbert de Lacy and second with Roger de Mowbray himself. Earl Gilbert's daughter, Alice, married Simon de St Liz, earl of Huntingdon (see Table 1).[40] This was a very close-knit and introspective world, strengthened by links of family and feudal loyalty, and though relationships were not always harmonious (for example, the feud of Gilbert de Gant and Henry de Lacy over the Pontefract lands) indissoluble bonds still remained. Even in far-off Northumberland, where the Lazarites came to own the property of Harehope hospital, Roger de Mowbray had family ties with the local aristocracy.[41]

Among the knightly families, the Burdets were important patrons in Leicestershire, with gifts at Cold Newton, and the Amundevilles in Lincolnshire, with grants at Carlton-le-Moorland.[42] However, it was among the lesser gentry that the impulse to give was most sustained, with the Rampanes providing generous endowments at Kirby Bellars, the Newtons at Cold Newton and the Thorps at Thorpe Satchville and Twyford.[43] Although gifts such as these gave the order a substantial foothold in a number of townships before 1200, an analysis of land grants recorded in the Cartulary clearly indicates that the larger grants, such as those made by Mowbray and Aubigny, were very much the exception rather

36 BL, Cart, f. 13; PRO, KB 27/416, m.42 (Farnham, 1, pp. 259–60).
37 D. Marcombe, 'The Preceptory of the Knights of St Lazarus at Locko', DAJ, 111 (1991), pp. 51–2.
38 A. Saltman (ed.), The Cartulary of Tutbury Priory, HMC (1965), pp. 24, 43, 63, 65.
39 Greenway, Mowbray Charters, pp. 260–1; North, 'The Mowbrays', p. 226.
40 VCH, Leicestershire, 1 (1907, reprinted London, 1969), p. 312; VCH, Yorkshire, 2 (London, 1912), p. 161.
41 J.C. Hodgson, 'The Hospital of St Lazarus and the Manor of Harehope', AA, 3rd series, 19 (1922), p. 77.
42 BL, Cart, ff. 81, 203, 207, 245–9.
43 Ibid, ff. 93–7, 173–7, 187–93.

than the rule. A proper assessment of this source is difficult because many of the charters are imprecise when it comes to the amount of land being granted, but in over 200 charters in which areas *are* specified, two-thirds comprise gifts of less than a bovate, in other words tofts and crofts, collections of selions or measured acreage in the open field.[44]

The givers of these gifts, many of which must date from the twelfth or early thirteenth centuries, came from a level of society beneath the resident gentry of the townships, effectively peasant farmers. Henry Aboneton of Billesdon, for example, made 10 separate grants comprising an acre, a selion, two roods or a portion of meadow. His widow, Agnes, and his son, Simon, added to this with two further grants, making a total of 12 charters over two generations.[45] Similarly, Philip the Miller of Kirby Bellars made two grants comprising two acres and half a selion; his widow, Matilda, added a bovate and a messuage, and his son, Walter, made a further six grants comprising two and a half acres, three and three quarter roods and a toft. In all there were nine charters enrolled over two generations.[46] Many of these small gifts have left virtually no record because of the Leicestershire bias of the Cartulary. In Yorkshire, for example, the *Valor Ecclesiasticus* of 1535 records lands at Pontefract valued at £7 0s 0d. However, the *Quo Warranto* inquests of 1293–4 make it clear that this estate was, in fact, made up of fragments of land in no fewer than 13 different townships, spanning the three Ridings.[47] Thus, the impulse to give cut across class boundaries, and, though the estates of the order tended to be centred on the more substantial gifts of the nobility and gentry, the donations of poorer people formed an important supplement. This was something quite unlike the pattern of patronage noted by Satchell for most leper hospitals where the gifts of the larger patrons were conspicuous by their absence. It was, however, very similar to the expansion of the Templars and the order of St John which, similarly, shared benefactors from a wide cross-section of society. Indeed, Gervers has concluded that 'the order [of St John] unquestionably drew most of its patrons from among the middle and lesser landlords, not to mention the peasants'.[48]

Why did such a wide range of people give to the order of St Lazarus? Like grantees to all religious orders, their principal motive was spiritual benefit, and phrases such as 'for the salvation of his soul and of his ancestors and successors' are commonplace among all classes.[49] Some gifts carried more specific conditions. Richard Burdet, for example, stated that his grant was 'for the salvation of

---

44 Charters often note imprecise amounts of land, such as 'all his meadow' or 'a piece of wood'. *Ibid*, ff. 189, 200.

45 *Ibid*, ff. 157–63.

46 *Ibid*, f. 192.

47 *Valor*, 4, p. 153; B. English (ed.), *Yorkshire Hundred and Quo Warranto Rolls*, YAS, Record Series, 151 (1993 and 1994), p. 266. The townships were Pontefract, Foulsnape, Darrington, Ferrybridge, Birkin, Norton-next-Campsall, Went Bridge, Azerley, Mickley, Abbeford, Silton, Hunmanby and Thirsk. I am grateful to Dr Ted Connell for this reference.

48 M. Gervers (ed.), *The Cartulary of the Knights of St John of Jerusalem in England, secunda camera, Essex*, Records of Social and Economic History, new series, 6 (1982), p. xxxviii; Gilchrist, *Contemplation and Action*, pp. 66–7. Even the small order of St Thomas of Acre enjoyed a wide range of support. Forey, 'St Thomas of Acre', p. 489.

49 BL, Cart, f. 33.

the Lord Henry, son of Matilda, his father, William Burdet, his ancestors, successors and himself'.[50] As Thompson has stated, the monastic expansion of the twelfth century was fuelled by 'the exchange of temporal support for the spiritual benefits which would secure or ease the path of the lords in the after life'.[51] In the case of the order of St Lazarus these 'spiritual benefits', effectively prayers for the souls of founders and benefactors in purgatory, might have been considered all the more potent since they were being undertaken, partly, by leper brothers who stood in a special relationship with God.[52] A significant minority of benefactors, however, abandoned a concern for purgatory altogether and made their gifts merely 'in respect of charity' or 'in respect of divine piety', William de Aumari requesting 'the lighting of a burning lamp in the chapel of the hospital at all canonical hours and at masses'.[53]

Alongside these clear-cut religious concerns there were others, a tiny minority by comparison, which overlapped with more secular considerations. Nigel de Amundeville, giving half a bovate in Carlton-le-Moorland 'at the start of his journey from England to the Holy Land', expected it back when he returned, but was so impressed by 'the great honours made to him by the brethren of St Lazarus in parts across the sea' he changed his mind and commanded his son to allow them to keep it.[54] Another member of the same family, Elias de Amundeville, gave a carucate in Carlton-le-Moorland in about 1195 'because a certain daughter of his was a leper'.[55] William Beler's gift in 1286 was 'for the promotion of his nephew, Roger Beler' and William Wisman noted a claim for sustenance in return for a virgate of land.[56] Two individuals pledged further virgates in return for money loaned 'in his [or her] greatest necessity'.[57] Among this wide mix of motives it must be remembered that a large number of charters record no form of motivation at all, either 'religious' or 'secular'. This does not mean that there was none, but it perhaps suggests that these transactions were more likely to have been sales or exchanges than gifts inspired by an expectation of reward or recompense. It is, of course, notoriously difficult to separate out motives in acts of benevolence, but the examples we have at the very least provide important clues as to the dual function of the order. On the one hand, it provided conventional spiritual services, such as could be expected of any monastic community or parish church; and on the other, more practical assistance, occasionally in the context of its main declared objectives, crusading and leprosy.

Yet when we try to take further these key notions of crusading and leprosy by looking more closely at the content of the Cartulary and the people mentioned in it, we are provided with only a little additional support. Some of the early

50 Ibid, f. 81.
51 B. Thompson, 'Monasteries and their Patrons at Foundation and Dissolution', TRHS, 6th series, 4 (1994), p. 107.
52 Rawcliffe, 'Learning to Love the Leper', p. 243.
53 BL, Cart, ff. 22, 98, 100.
54 Ibid, f. 249.
55 Rot Hund, 1, p. 284 .
56 BL, Cart, ff. 111, 119.
57 Ibid, ff. 73, 163.

patrons – Roger de Mowbray, Henry de Lacy, William de Ferrers and William Burdet amongst others – were indeed crusaders.[58] Nevertheless, Walker has calculated that only 10 identifiable supporters of Burton Lazars, out of a possible 14, definitely went on crusade, a figure that constitutes between five per cent and seven per cent of the 200 or so patrons named in the Cartulary – about the same proportion of crusaders as can be found in society at large, in fact.[59] Leprosy gets an even poorer showing. Only one patron, Robert FitzPernel, earl of Leicester, can be demonstrated from other sources to have been a leper; and one more, Elias de Amundeville, to have had a leper in his immediate family.[60] Satchell believes that personal exposure to leprosy by patrons was an important motive for their support of leper-houses, and in this he may well be correct.[61] The problem is that it can only be proved in a very few cases. So the conclusion that the economic well being of the order in England was driven on, even in the first instance, by *active* crusading or *active* involvement with leprosy cannot be sustained beyond dispute. It was there in the background, perhaps, but it was not demonstrably of primary importance.

Instead, Walker's analysis of the motives of Burton Lazars patrons places emphasis on three principal areas. Family loyalty, which can be seen in noble families such as the Mowbrays, gentry such as the Burdets and peasants such as the Abonetons; the impact of lordship, which encouraged lesser people to follow the example of their feudal superiors; and 'social and geographical association', which dictated a very localised form of patronage.[62] The last point is particularly significant. Allowing for the fact that the most substantial patrons and the biggest grants came from furthest away, it is notable, by contrast, that 92 per cent of grants and 79 per cent of patrons came from within a 10 mile radius of Burton Lazars.[63] This parish-pump patronage requires further explanation. First, Burton Lazars was fortunate in that it had few local competitors. Only the small Hospitaller commandary of Old Dalby and the Premonstratensian abbey of Owston were close, and Kirby Bellars Priory, an immediate neighbour, was not founded until 1359, when the popular enthusiasm to give had long since subsided.[64] Second, it is possible that many of these smaller grants do not so much represent gifts as attempts by the Lazarites to buy up minor parcels of land to consolidate their demesne holding around Burton.[65] The imprecise nature of the enrolled charters prevents a firm conclusion being reached on this point, but the nature of the activities of the order in the thirteenth century and the charters without a stated motive provide ample grounds for suspicion. Third, and a point

58 Walker, 'Patronage', pp. 52–4.
59 Walker, 'Patronage', p. 55.
60 *Ibid*, p. 66. William the Leper, son of Robert, earl of Leicester, founded St Leonard's hospital, Leicester, in the late twelfth century. Orme and Webster, *English Hospital*, p. 112.
61 Satchell, 'Leper-Houses', pp. ix, 221–2.
62 *Ibid*, pp. 152, 217, 288.
63 *Ibid*, pp. 231–5.
64 Vaudey Abbey, near Bourne, Lincolnshire, had substantial holdings at Burton Lazars but cannot be accounted a 'local' house in terms of its immediate influence on potential patrons.
65 Satchell, 'Leper-Houses', pp. 238–40.

not developed by Walker, we may be encountering here a manifestation of popular crusading.

Walker, by concentrating on noble and knightly crusaders, took only a very limited view of the movement. Since Walker's thesis in 1990 the work of Evans has placed a spotlight on the role of peasants and artisans who, though they do not often crop up in conventional sources, can nevertheless be proven to have been active in the Crusade in all sorts of ways. Harper-Bill, looking back from the fourteenth century, has backed up this view, pointing out how 'the crusading ideal had been at the centre of Christian life even for those who never ventured beyond their own locality'.[66] On the estates of the Hospitallers, Gervers detects an upsurge in land grants from poorer people during the 1230s and speculates that these might have been inspired by the fact that Jerusalem was temporarily back in Christian hands between 1229 and 1244.[67] Unfortunately, no direct comparison is possible with the order of St Lazarus because of the deficiencies of dating in the Cartulary charters, but it is at least possible that the highly localised patronage of Burton Lazars was an attempt by men of humbler status to associate themselves with the great crusading ideal, without actually making the dangerous and expensive journey overseas. This was a trend that Popes such as Innocent III (1198–1216) and Honorius III (1216–27) were anxious to encourage, since they were being forced to become increasingly inventive to finance expeditions to the Holy Land. The granting of privileges to crusading orders, in the hope of attracting new patrons to augment their estates, was an obvious expedient.[68]

Perhaps these lesser patrons of Burton Lazars were *cruci signati*, who, unable to fulfil their vows because of poverty or other circumstances, compensated with small grants of land. This form of surrogate crusading was probably encouraged by the papal privileges the order enjoyed, and in this the Lazarites and other military orders were able to attract a type of benefactor rather different from the monasteries and run-of-the-mill leper-houses, which did not have quite the same glamorous appeal in the world of the underprivileged.[69] No doubt this was another issue that widened the rift between the order of St Lazarus and other groups in the church that did not enjoy the benefit of such privileges or such a positive popular image.[70] Yet it was these circumstances, fuelled by the hazy vision of the leper knight fighting for the faith, which probably helped the estates of the order expand in the way they did during the thirteenth century. Thus, although *active* crusading may not have been a prime motive, *passive* crusading may well have figured much more prominently than Walker allows for. These, indeed, were the 'armchair crusaders' highlighted by Gilchrist.[71]

[66] M. Evans, 'The Crusades and Society in the English Midlands, c.1160–1307', University of Nottingham, Ph.D. thesis (1997); C. Harper-Bill, 'The English Church and English Religion after the Black Death', in M. Ormrod and P. Lindley (eds), *The Black Death in England* (Stamford, 1996), p. 81.

[67] Gervers, *Hospitaller Cartulary*, p. xlvi.

[68] J.A. Brundage, *Medieval Canon Law and the Crusader* (Madison, Wisconsin, Milwaukee and London, 1969), pp. 114–15; J.M. Powell, *Anatomy of a Crusade, 1213–1221* (Philadelphia, 1986), pp. 89–106.

[69] For the spiritual privileges of the order, which may have been linked to land grants, see Chapter 6, pp. 180–2.

[70] See Chapter 1, pp. 15–16; Chapter 6, p. 178.

[71] Gilchrist, *Contemplation and Action*, p. 67.

The extent of the estate in 1291

The few instances of dating in the Cartulary indicate that donations began to lapse in the second half of the thirteenth century and were all but terminated by the statute of mortmain in 1279, a situation once more paralleled on the estates of the order of St John. This dramatic change in the climate of benefaction is also evident in the case of the leper-houses, where Satchell notes the issue of only eighteen mortmain licences between 1308 and 1349, most of them involving the appointment of chaplains. This contrasts sharply with 934 licences obtained for the support of chantries over the same period.[72] Even if spiritual priorities were changing, there is some evidence of limited growth of the Lazarite estate after 1279, notably a licence to acquire in excess of 160 acres from various donors in Spondon in 1312, but such instances are rare.[73] By the time of the 1291 *Taxatio* the land holding profile of the order had been established, and, apart from two notable additions that evaded the restrictions of mortmain, this pattern was to survive up to the Dissolution.

As can be seen from Table 2, the greatest concentration of estates was in Leicestershire, particularly around Burton Lazars, but there were also substantial outlying properties in Lincolnshire and Norfolk and, to a lesser extent, in Derbyshire. The lands in Yorkshire and Northumberland (part of the Northern Province) are not included in the printed version of the *Taxatio*, but their relatively small scale is unlikely to make a major difference to the total.[74] Robinson states that 'It is probable that the assessment was calculated on the rent that possessions could be expected to yield, and that a minimum would surely have been given.'[75] Moreover, it is notoriously difficult to convert a rent valuation into an acreage, but for the Essex estates of the Hospitallers Gervers has suggested an annual rent for arable in the thirteenth century of somewhere between 3.5d and 5.3d per acre.[76] East Midland land values were probably lower, and on this basis it would be unlikely if Burton Lazars rents exceeded 4d per acre: indeed, they may well have been much lower in places. Nevertheless, this sort of calculation leaves us with an estimated acreage of 3,769, not including the Yorkshire and Northumberland properties.

Bearing in mind the possibility of a minimum figure returned for the *Taxatio* and the fairly generous multiple of 4d derived from Gervers, it seems likely that the Lazarite landed estate may have exceeded 5,000 acres, nationwide, in 1291. This estimate, of course, does not include spiritualities, with which the order was particularly well endowed.[77] Nor does it include payments of alms made on a regular basis by certain individuals as a substitute for gifts of property. The leprous earl of Leicester, for example, had granted 10s *per annum* for ever out of

---

72 Satchell, 'Leper-Houses', p. 205.
73 The grantors were, once again, minor individuals: John de Sutherne (19 acres), Thomas le Fevre (17 acres and 3 roods), Thomas Poer (90½ acres), Alice de Lokage (a toft), Robert de Sallowe (37 acres and 4s rent). *CPR, 1307–13*, p. 513; PRO, C 143/89/5.
74 Walker, 'Patronage', pp. 269–77.
75 D.M. Robinson, *The Geography of Augustinian Settlement in Medieval England and Wales*, BAR, British series, 80 (1980), p. 113.
76 Gervers, *Hospitaller Cartulary*, p. lxxviii.
77 For a discussion of spiritualities, see Chapter 6, pp. 197–201.

Table 2: Temporalities according to the *Taxatio* (Southern Province)

County	£	s	d
Derbyshire	5	6	10
Leicestershire	31	16	0
Lincolnshire	13	1	9¾
Norfolk	12	18	2
Northamptonshire		7	8
Rutland		3	7
Suffolk		18	0
Total	64	12	9¾

Source: *Taxatio*, pp. 54, 55, 71, 111, 132, 264.

the manor of Leicester, and Earl Warenne had similarly earmarked 13s 4d from the annual profits of Stamford fair.[78] Inquisitions prove that both payments stood the test of time and were still being rendered by Henry, first duke of Lancaster, and the town of Stamford in the fourteenth century.[79]

Henry II's grant of alms and the gift of St Giles's, Holborn

The most generous, and most troublesome, grant of alms was made by Henry II and was to have profound long-term consequences for the order. On 25 January 1176 the king ordained that 40 marks *per annum* [£26 13s 4d] was to be paid by the Treasurer on the feast of St Michael until such time as suitable endowments could be found to replace it.[80] The gift, confirmed by Richard I, John and Henry III, became an eagerly anticipated source of revenue.[81] It is difficult to determine the consistency with which the pension was paid in the early years, but by the reign of Henry III evidence from the Liberate Rolls suggests that payment was becoming increasingly erratic. Between 1229 (the date of Henry III's confirmation) and 1259 19 payments are recorded totalling 750 marks [£500], a sum that was actually less than a third of the order's entitlement. A double payment in 1257 suggests an attempt to clear some arrears, and a reduction to 30 marks [£20] in 1259 may reflect the beginnings of a period of difficulty for the Treasury caused by the civil wars.[82] Certainly after 1260 payments appear to collapse entirely, and at about this time three petitions were directed to the king, by the English Lazarites and those 'over the sea', requesting him to confirm Henry II's charter or discharge it with the long-awaited grant of property.[83] Though the

---

[78] BL, Cart, f. 231; *CLR, 1240–45*, pp. 39, 254; *Cal Inq 9*, p. 44; J. Harley, F.M. Stenton and F. Bickley (eds), *Hastings Mss*, 1, HMC (1928), p. 341.

[79] *Cal Inq 11*, p. 93.

[80] T.D. Hardy (ed.), *Syllabus in English of the documents relating to England and other kingdoms contained in the collection known as 'Rymer's Foedera'*, 1 (London, 1869), p. 6; PRO, SC 8/219/10908.

[81] Hardy, *'Rymer's Foedera'*, 1, p. 7; *Rot Chart*, 1 pt 1, p. 67; *CR, 1226–57*, p. 94.

[82] *CLR, 1226–40*, pp. 104, 144, 235, 238, 500; *1240–45*, pp. 182, 285; *1245–51*, pp. 44, 115, 178, 232, 283, 384; *1251–60*, pp. 124, 172, 213, 284, 370 (80 marks), 485 (30 marks).

[83] PRO, SC 8/54/2654; 8/219/10908; 8/163/8103. None of these petitions is dated.

pension was paid again in 1281, concern became increasingly serious thereafter since arrears of 700 marks [£466 13s 4d] had built up.[84]

A solution, of sorts, emerged as a result of discussions between the order and John de Kirkeby, Treasurer (1284–90) and bishop of Ely (1286–90). A man with a formidable reputation as a financial manager, Kirkeby was the son of Sir William Kirkeby of Melton Mowbray and therefore might be regarded as being sympathetic to the order. Moreover, after the mid-1280s he was locked in a bitter conflict with the city of London, as a result of which the mayoralty was suspended and not restored until 1298.[85] Probably in the late 1280s, it was suggested that the outstanding debt be written off and remitted to a single payment of 80 marks [£53 6s 8d] and that the order should receive a grant of the leper hospital of St Giles, Holborn, as a future recompense for the royal pension.[86] But, whatever Kirkeby's attitude to the order, St Giles's was a poisoned chalice. Situated on the south side of the Roman road from London to Oxford, it commanded a prominent position on the outskirts of the city. Its founder was Queen Matilda, who had placed it under the supervision of the city of London whence most of its inmates were drawn.[87] However, in 1246 the crown had begun to show an interest in the patronage of the hospital and a series of disagreements culminated in an acrimonious clash with the city authorities in 1286. There were further quarrels with the bishops of London over rights of visitation, all of which became mixed up with Edward I's more general breakdown of relations with the Londoners during this period.[88]

Kirkeby's scheme to offload St Giles's on the Lazarites could therefore be seen as an astute move on the part of the crown, divorcing it from a troublesome sibling and discharging its pension obligation at a stroke. It may even have been inspired by some glimmerings of piety, since in the mid-thirteenth century it had been reported that the lepers were trying to live as a religious community, and a connection with the order of St Lazarus, in line with Clement IV's decree, might have been seen as a way of encouraging this positive development.[89] The plan was formally noted on the Parliament Roll in 1290 along with a request by Edward I that the Chancellor should visit the house and 'certify if the king would be able to confer the said hospital without the prejudice of any'.[90] Just to demonstrate the king's good will and that no course of action had been finally decided upon, the Treasury paid the traditional pension of 40 marks [£26 13s 4d] in 1291.[91] But events were outpacing the king's cautious approach because of Kirkeby's growing hostility to the Londoners. John de Kirkeby died in 1290 and, in a dramatic escalation of the conflict, either he, or his successor as Treasurer,

84   CCR, 1279–88, p. 100; PRO, SC 8/57/2818.
85   DNB, 11, pp. 204–6; Nichols, Leicestershire, 2 pt 1, p. 224.
86   PRO, SC 8/57/2818; 8/97/4812.
87   M.B. Honeybourne, 'The Leper Hospitals of the London Area', Transactions of the London and Middlesex Archaeological Society, 21 pt 1 (1967), pp. 20–1; Satchell, 'Leper-Houses', pp. 312–13.
88   Honeybourne, 'Leper Hospitals', pp. 20–1.
89   Ibid, p. 21.
90   Rot Parl, 1, p. 53; PRO, SC 9/2/No.85.
91   F. Devon (ed.), Issues of the Exchequer, Henry III–Henry VI (London, 1837), p. 101.

William de Marche, encouraged the Lazarites to take possession of St Giles's 'without the hand of the king'.[92]

Initially they were barred by Henry de Durham, the warden, and when he was ordered to hand over the hospital a stream of bitter complaints was directed to the king by the citizens of London.[93] It was alleged that St Giles's had been 'sold' to the Lazarites against its charters, bulls and even the provisions of Magna Carta. To this was added deep suspicion about the motives of the order and the way in which the grant had been procured. The transaction, it was said, had been brought about 'by council of some people who by certain reasons are friends of the brethren of the order of St Lazarus', presumably a sideswipe at Kirkeby's Leicestershire origins, and the new occupiers, who had no respect for tradition, merely wished 'to appropriate all to their religion'.[94] In view of this, the king was requested to remove the Lazarites 'and to allow the said sick to have and enjoy the state which their predecessors had . . . for they are all to be disinherited if the king and his council do not put things right'.[95] In 1293 a commission reported that the hospital was indeed a free chapel, in the gift of the crown, and that its master enjoyed spiritual jurisdiction in the parish and precinct of St Giles without interference from the bishop of London or the archbishop of Canterbury in the event of a vacancy.[96] Eventually, on 4 April 1299 St Giles's was finally, and formally, granted to the order of St Lazarus by Letters Patent (Plate 11).[97] This was hardly a sudden impulse, as Honeybourne has claimed, but the measured conclusion of ten years of difficult and acrimonious negotiation.[98]

The London estate and its problems

In taking over St Giles's the order assumed responsibility for a ready-made estate, which had grown up since the foundation of the hospital during the reign of Henry I. Most of these land grants were already in place by 1250, and for this reason the development of the London estate has not been carefully examined for the purposes of this study, though all surviving charters were enrolled on the St Giles's Cartulary drawn up by Walter de Lynton in 1402.[99] The estate was extensive, but it differed markedly in character from that of Burton Lazars since it was made up, largely, of burgage property in the city of London and the suburb of Holborn. The Cartulary notes no fewer than 58 urban, suburban and rural parishes in which the hospital held land.[100] Surviving rentals are invariably fragmentary, but a survey drawn up by the city authorities in 1392 notes 20 properties belonging to St Giles's spread over 15 or 16 parishes and totalling

92 PRO, SC 8/324/E617A.
93 PRO, SC 8/57/2818. Henry de Durham was appointed warden of St Giles by the king in 1286. *CPR, 1281–92*, pp. 252, 423.
94 PRO, SC 8/49/2448.
95 PRO, SC 8/324/E617A.
96 Honeybourne, 'Leper Hospitals', pp. 21–2.
97 *CPR, 1292–1301*, p. 404.
98 Honeybourne, 'Leper Hospitals', p. 22.
99 BL, Harl Mss, 4015.
100 BL, Harl Mss, 4015, ff. 4–119; Satchell, 'Leper-Houses', pp. 155–6.

Plate 11: Seal of St Giles's Hospital, Holborn, showing
St Giles as an abbot. The hospital was founded by
Queen Matilda for lepers and given to Burton Lazars
by Edward I in 1299.

£10 2s 1d.[101] The limitation of this document is that it does not include Holborn,
the area in which the parish of 'St Giles of the Lepers' and most of its holdings
were situated, but fortunately a more comprehensive survey, compiled in 1544,
lists the lands in Holborn along with properties in a further 36 city parishes.[102]
The fact that the hospital's stake in city parishes had more than doubled between
1392 and 1544 suggests substantial expansion and an active policy of property
purchase in the fifteenth century. Its tenants included confraternities, city
companies and the landlords of numerous inns, not to mention some influential
individuals such as the bishops of Salisbury and Ely and the sheriffs of London,

---

101 A.K. McHardy (ed.), *The Church in London, 1375–1392*, LonRS, 13 (1977), pp. 43, 46, 47, 48, 49, 52,
      54, 55, 61, 62, 65, 66, 67, 70. The most substantial rent of £2 was paid by Stephen Spelman for a tene-
      ment in Queenhithe (p. 52).
102 *Ibid*, p. 89; PRO, C 78/1/1.

Surrey and Sussex.[103] The annual value of this estate was noted as £80 in a peti-tion that probably dates from the 1390s, yet by the time of the *Valor Ecclesiasticus* in 1535 its rents had been increased by more than half.[104] St Giles's was therefore fully integrated into the social and commercial life of the capital, and because of this it posed different administrative problems from those of a rural estate in midland England.

The order was already well acquainted with one problem inherited with St Giles's, and that was the difficulty of collecting royal gifts of alms. Henry II had granted £3 *per annum* to the lepers of St Giles's at about the same time as the grant to the order of St Lazarus, but after 1299 the payment was more often than not ignored. There was a suggestion that administrative problems played a part in this, particularly the transfer of the Exchequer from London to York as a result of Edward I's Scottish wars, but in reality the king may have felt that he was absolved from this payment by virtue of his grant of the hospital to the order. In 1315 the master petitioned Parliament on the matter, and in 1318, after an exam-ination of evidences by the Exchequer, it was agreed that the payment should be made, but that the arrears should be met 'in the debts due from them [i.e. the order] for tenths and other things at the Exchequer'.[105] Since the order denied that any tenths were due to the crown, and the whole issue was the subject of another acrimonious dispute, the judgment could only be accounted a mixed blessing, but the payment to St Giles's appears to have survived since it was still being made by Henry VII as 'yearly alms' between 1486 and 1489.[106]

Holy Innocents', Lincoln

The final package of property that came to the order was the estate of Holy Inno-cents' Hospital, Lincoln, first granted in reversion by Henry VI in 1457 for a yearly rent of £1 to the Exchequer 'and for prayers to be made for the good estate of the king and Queen Margaret and for their souls after death and the souls of the king's progenitors'.[107] This grant was probably obtained through the growing influence of the master, Sir William Sutton, and when Henry VI was deposed in 1461 it was noted in the Act of Resumption of Edward IV that the gift was not to be prejudiced, and a new patent was issued later in the same year with no mention of a yearly rent to the Exchequer, or, indeed, of prayers for the Lancastrian royal house.[108] Though Holy Innocents' had a long and distin-guished history, with the exception of a payment from the manor of Nettleham, its lands were of small value and did not compare with the properties of either Burton Lazars or St Giles's. It is likely that this grant, especially bearing in mind the intercessionary obligations that were a condition of it, was a measure of support offered by the crown to the building of the new collegiate church at

103 PRO, C 78/1/1.
104 PRO, SC 8/324/E617B. For the *Valor* valuation, see below.
105 *CCR, 1313–18*, p. 541; *Rot Parl*, 1, p. 344.
106 W. Campbell (ed.), *Materials for a History of the Reign of Henry VII*, 2, Rolls Series, 60 (London, 1877), pp. 80, 222, 390, 558.
107 *CPR, 1452–61*, p. 359. For the foundation of Holy Innocents', see Satchell, 'Leper-Houses', pp. 329–30.
108 *CPR, 1461–67*, p. 123; *Rot Parl*, 5, pp. 472, 521, 602.

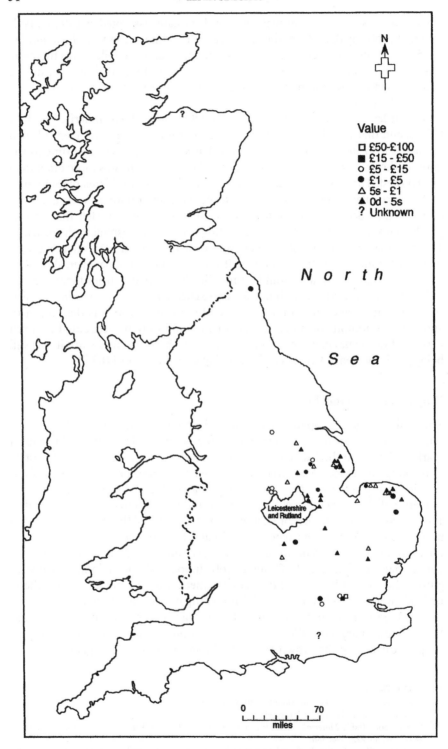

Map 3: Distribution of temporalities (excluding Leicestershire and Rutland).

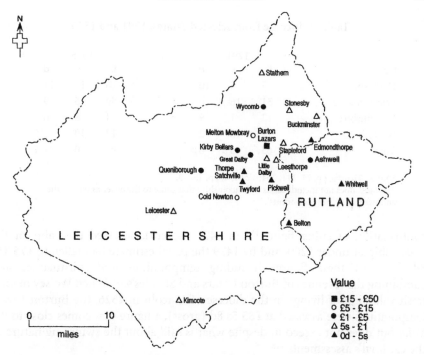

Map 4: Distribution of temporalities, Leicestershire and Rutland.

Burton Lazars.[109] Like Eton College and King's College, Cambridge, it can be seen as the sort of project of which the pious Henry VI would have approved.

The value of the estate

When the *Valor Ecclesiasticus* was drawn up in 1535 the order possessed landed estates that rested on three quite separate accumulations of property – Burton Lazars, St Giles's and Holy Innocents' – though all were returned under 'Burton Lazars' for the purposes of the survey (Map 3).[110] The total gross valuation of the temporal property was put at £271 10s 8¾d (£259 0s 2¾d after deductions), and it is possible, with one or two minor uncertainties, to separate out the values of the three integral parts.[111] The burgeoning St Giles's estate was the most lucrative (£133 1s 3d gross); closely followed by Burton Lazars (£111 16s 1¾d gross), with Holy Innocents' showing a poor third (£26 13s 4d gross).[112] Leicestershire and Rutland were always the heartlands of the important midland properties (Map 4). The *Valor*, of course, is subject to the same reservation about under–valuation as the *Taxatio*, and very little survives by way of independent

---

109 See Chapter 3, pp. 92–9.
110 *Valor*, 4, pp. 152–3.
111 For a valuation of the entire estate (i.e. spiritualities and temporalities), see Chapter 7, pp. 218–19.
112 Holy Innocents', in fact, appears twice in the *Valor*, once under Burton Lazars and once under the city of Lincoln. The latter was clearly regarded as a mistake, however. *Valor*, 4, p. 29.

Table 3: Income from selected estates, 1291 and 1535

County	1291			1535		
	£	s	d	£	s	d
Derbyshire	5	6	10	26	14	11
Leicestershire	31	16	0	50	6	9
Lincolnshire	13	1	9¾	4	8	0
Norfolk	12	18	2	12	10	5¼
Total	63	3	6¾	94	0	1¼

Source: *Taxatio*, pp. 71, 111, 264; *Valor*, 4, pp. 152–3.
The table does not include lands in Lincolnshire that came to the order as part of the endowment of Holy Innocents'.

confirmation of either figure.[113] In 1421 the curia assessed the value of the mastership at under £200, and by 1479 the papal estimate had fallen to £75 16s 8d, both of these figures including temporalities *and* spiritualities and combining the revenues of Burton Lazars and St Giles's.[114] When Wolsey made a fresh valuation of livings in the diocese of Lincoln in 1526, the Burton Lazars temporalities were assessed at £85 5s 8d (gross), a figure that comes close to the *Valor* but does not exceed it, despite what is said about the swingeing nature of the cardinal's assessments.[115]

Comparing the *Taxatio* and the *Valor* in areas where the information seems more or less complete, a very variable picture begins to emerge. From Table 3 it appears that income from land rose in Leicestershire and Derbyshire (most markedly so in the latter); remained constant in Norfolk and fell off in Lincolnshire. The Derbyshire increase is explained, at least in part, by augmentations to the estate after 1291, and the relative isolation of the Norfolk properties probably resulted in fossilised rents lingering on longer there than in other areas. However, the collapse of income from Lincolnshire is puzzling and may be explained by the sale of lands for which no record has survived.[116] Certainly the order had no aversion to selling off estates if the need arose, either to settle debts or invest in something more attractive. It seems that a good deal of the Kings Lynn property was sold after 1270, for example, perhaps reflecting the declining importance of the relationship with the Holy Land, and in the early sixteenth century Sir Thomas Norton was selling a plot in London to one Geoffrey Knight.[117] But despite these fluctuations, it is clear that the overall economic

---

113   For a recent reappraisal of the *Valor*, see C. Harrison, 'The *Valor Ecclesiasticus*: a re-appraisal based on the Staffordshire returns', *StS*, 11 (1999), pp. 28–50.

114   *CPapR, Letters 7, 1417–31*, pp. 181–2; *13 pt1, 1471–84*, p. 3. The 1479 figure is based on Lunt's estimate of a gold curial florin at 4s 4d.

115   H. Salter (ed.), *A Subsidy Collected in the Diocese of Lincoln in 1526*, Oxford Historical Society, 58 (1909), p. 120.

116   The Lincolnshire figure excludes the properties of Holy Innocents'. When these are taken into account Lincolnshire temporalities came to £31 1s 1¾d in 1535.

117   D.M. Owen, *The Making of Kings Lynn*, Records of Social and Economic History, new series, 9 (1984), pp. 186–7; E. and P. Rutledge, 'Kings Lynn and Great Yarmouth. Two Thirteenth-Century Surveys', *Norfolk Archaeology*, 37 pt 1 (1978), pp. 94, 108; Nichols, *Leicestershire*, 2 pt 1, p. 276.

Graph 1: Temporalities according to the *Taxatio* (Southern Province)
and the *Valor Ecclesiasticus*

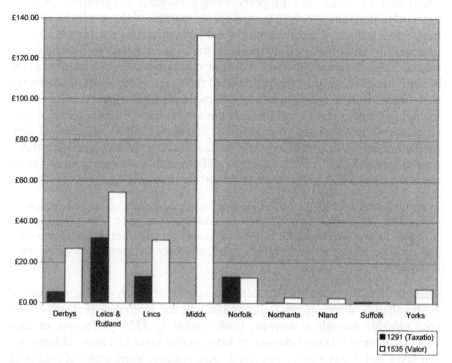

Source: *Taxatio*, pp, 54, 55, 71, 111, 132, 264: *Valor*, 4, pp. 152–3.

position was much stronger in 1535 than it was in 1291. Income had gone up by
more than a third, and this had transpired in spite of the fact that the military
orders, in general, lost favour with the public because of the fall of Acre in 1291
and the revelations in the trial of the Templars between 1307 and 1312.[118] The
order circumvented the restrictions of the statute of mortmain by two significant
royal grants in 1299 and 1457, which ensured that its estates continued to grow
at a time when those of many other religious orders remained unaltered, or even
shrank. It is these additions that are reflected in Graph 1, showing (by 1535) a
recovery of the position in Lincolnshire (thanks to the grant of Holy Innocents')
and the outstanding importance of St Giles's Middlesex estates. The Hospitallers,
of course, enjoyed a similar windfall when many of the expropriated estates of
the Templars were confirmed to them by statute in 1324, but these often raised
problems of title and management similar to those encountered by the Lazarites
at St Giles's.[119]

---

[118] Gilchrist, *Contemplation and Action*, p. 68.
[119] *Ibid.*

Privileges and feudal obligations

The extent to which this property-owning religious corporation could be expected to participate in the practical preoccupations of the secular world must have been a subject of debate from the earliest years of its foundation, and the Lazarites, for their part, actively pursued the cause of privilege based on their special status. In charters that are no longer extant (apart from a synopsis of one of them in the Cartulary), Henry II placed the order under his personal protection, freed it from tolls and customary payments to the Exchequer and granted it the right to hold its lands free from customary services.[120] Though one of these charters may have been the one issued at Stamford in 1157, we know of them chiefly because John confirmed them in 1200, adding his own personal protection to that of his father.[121] It was these privileges that were summarised in the master's response to the Yorkshire *Quo Warranto* inquest of 1293–4:

> all their lands and men . . . are free from toll, passage and all custom of shire, hundred, wapentake; from gelds, scots, scutages, Danegeld, except justice of murdrum and larceny. And if it should happen that murdrum or larceny money should be given, they are completely free, and only the justice remains to the king.[122]

Henry II similarly granted to the demesne tenants of St Giles's freedom from 'all gelds and aids, amercements, customs and tolls etc', a privilege that was considered valuable enough to warrant confirmation in 1393.[123] Because of these charters the order claimed exemption from secular taxes, just as it did from clerical taxes, but it was a battle not finally won without some bruising confrontations. Later kings did not necessarily offer the same sympathetic support as their predecessors.

Before 1290 the order petitioned Edward I to be freed from the fifteenth, for themselves and their tenants, 'as they have nothing to sustain the poor brethren overseas'.[124] For the twelfth of 1296 and the twentieth of 1327 the temporalities obtained by the order in Leicestershire and Derbyshire since 1291 were assessed, though the sums raised in each case were pardoned. During the 1330s, as Edward III's problems in Scotland and France deepened, there were fresh levies of fifteenths and tenths, once more taking into account the post-1291 endowments of the order.[125] Evidently attempts were made to collect this money, since in 1337 the taxers and collectors of Middlesex were ordered to give temporary respite to St Giles's, and in 1344 the order formally complained that 'they are now

---

120 BL, Cart, f. 204.
121 *Rot Chart*, pp. 67–8; Nichols, *Leicestershire*, 2 pt 1, Appendix xvi, Charters 8, 11; Eyton, *Court, Household and Itinerary of King Henry II*, p. 31.
122 English, *Yorkshire Hundred and Quo Warranto Rolls*, p. 266. The order was free to seek the king's grace on any matter contained in its charters. A similar claim is registered under Northumberland. See W. Illingworth and J. Caley (eds), *Placita de Quo Waranto* (London, 1818), p. 586.
123 E. Williams, *Early Holborn and the Legal Quarter of London*, 2 (London, 1927), no. 1632.
124 PRO, SC 8/54/2654.
125 The sums pardoned were: 1s 2d (Leics), 1296; 2s 0d (Leics), 10s 0d (Derbys), 1327; 5s 0d (Leics), £1 6s 8d (Derbys), 1332; 13s 4d (Derbys), 1336; 13s 4d (Derbys), 5s 0d (Leics), 1337. PRO, E 359/14; 372/151.

grievously distrained by the treasurer and barons of the Exchequer of the ninth, wools, tenths and fifteenths granted to the king by the commonalty of the realm from the twelfth year of his reign'.[126] The king stepped back from confrontation with a body of men 'founded on behalf of lepers and to fight against the enemies of the cross' and issued an exemption on the Patent Rolls, which was confirmed in 1378.[127] Only in the city of London does the indemnity not seem to have been upheld. When the aldermen were required to value property in their wards with a view to raising a fifteenth for the use of the city, it was specifically stated that the properties of St Giles's were to be included.[128] Nevertheless, despite these minor hiccups, the Lazarites were able to exploit their perceived association with crusading and leprosy to win benefits in the secular sphere, just as they did in the ecclesiastical.

The question of feudal obligations and revenue could be equally fraught, once more because of the somewhat ambivalent position and image of the order. Many of the Leicestershire estates fell within the Honour of Mowbray, and the active patronage of the lord, along with many of his leading tenants, ensured that most early grants were made 'in pure and perpetual alms without any service'.[129] Indeed, in his initial grant Roger de Mowbray not only made his own gift in this fashion but also decreed that 'Whatever my vassals have given or shall give to them . . . to be holden of them in perpetual alms, freely and quietly from all secular services.'[130] As we have seen, Henry II upheld the view that the lands of the order should be free from customary payments, but experience proved that these exemptions were not to be universal, either because lands were not granted in alms in the first place (hence laying an obligation of feudal service upon them) or because lords, beset by hard times, later attempted to exploit land grants to religious houses in just the same way as they did the rest of their 'secular' estate.

In the context of the first point, some land grants made a specific exemption of feudal service, or part of it. William de Mowbray, for example, released the order from foreign service on five bovates in Leesthorpe, and Robert de Chevercourt granted a similar privilege on all holdings in his fee at Burton.[131] On other occasions service was commuted to nominal payments or the gift of symbolic items such as roses, pairs of gloves or needles.[132] For the gift of a bovate in Melton Mowbray from Matilda Karles, for example, the brethren were freed from all exactions and demands 'except for the payment of 3s *per annum* to the chief lord of the fee'.[133] These payments, in lieu of service, comprised *socage*, and indicate clearly that the brethren were not entirely free from feudal entanglements. The estate was therefore a strange hybrid, with most lands discharged from service but others bearing the normal burdens of a secular landlord. No

126 *CPR, 1343–45*, p. 224.
127 *CPR, 1377–81*, p. 290.
128 R.R. Sharpe (ed.), *CLBCL, H*, p. 155.
129 BL, Cart, f. 210.
130 *Ibid*, f. 1a.
131 *Ibid*, ff. 2, 50, 91.
132 *Ibid*, f. 235.
133 *Ibid*, f. 11.

grants made in *frankalmoign* have been encountered, in other words gifts made in return for the spiritual service of the grantor receiving a place in the prayers of the grantee. Although grants such as this are common enough to monastic houses within the Honour of Mowbray, the fact that they are not made in the context of the order of St Lazarus suggests that, at this early stage of its history, its primary purpose was not considered to be intercessionary. This was a role that became more pronounced in the later Middle Ages as the rigours of feudalism began to collapse.[134]

In many townships, where only small portions of land were involved, *socage* payments were the appropriate remuneration for the chief lord, but in some villages the holdings of the Lazarites were substantial enough to comprise a knight's fee, or a fraction of it. At Spondon, for example, the order held two-thirds of a fee and in neighbouring Locko one-twentieth of a fee.[135] The case of Locko, where the order was merely one of many local landowners, was a common situation, and even at Burton Lazars, which took its name from the commanding presence of their preceptory, the holding of the Lazarites was significantly smaller than that of the Cistercian monks of Vaudey Abbey, Lincolnshire, who owned half a fee there.[136] Carlton-le-Moorland comprised:

> One knight's fee, where twelve carucates make a fee, held by Nigel de Amundeville: whereof he held in demesne thirty-four bovates . . . the abbot of Thornton holds sixteen bovates whereof four are in alms, the master of the knights of the Temple holds 38½ bovates in alms, the master of the hospital of St Lazarus holds 7½ bovates in alms.[137]

If in Carlton the status of the holding of the order negated the obligation to provide a fraction of a knight for service in the king's wars, on other manors *scutage* might be paid by holders of portions of fees in lieu of supplying an armed man. Only on two manors, Cold Newton and Kirby Bellars, were the territories of the order substantial enough to command a full fee, though in 1361 their holdings in Burton, Melton Mowbray and Queniborough were also considered sufficient to justify that description.[138] In this context the master was liable from time to time to make payments to the crown. In 1271 a quittance is recorded by which he is stated to have satisfied the king and the Lord Edward of a twentieth incident on behalf of himself and his villeins, and in 1320 and 1346 aids of £1 6s 8d were levied on the portions of knights' fees at Spondon and Locko.[139] Payments such as these were only logged by constant use of Inquisi-

---

134 Although Greenway makes a clear distinction between grants 'in alms' and grants 'in frankalmoign', there is some evidence to suggest that they were regarded as interchangeable. The confirmation of property in Kirby Bellars to the chapel of St Peter by the order in 1324 was made 'in pure and perpetual alms', yet the version of the grant that appears on the Patent Rolls states that the gift had been made 'in frankalmoign'. BL, Cart, f. 106; *CPR, 1317–21*, p. 394. For a discussion of this grant, see below, pp. 62–3.

135 *Cal Inq* 3, pp. 312–13.

136 *Ibid*, p. 360. According to the Hundred Rolls (1276), Vaudey Abbey had eight carucates in Burton Lazars and the Lazarites had four. Curtis, *Leicestershire*, p. 251.

137 *Cal Inq* 4, p. 305.

138 *Cal Inq* 3, p. 360; *11*, p. 141; *12*, p. 191; *15*, p. 132.

139 *CPR, 1266–72*, pp. 575, 580; *Feudal Aids, 1284–1431*, 1 (London, 1899), pp. 151, 158.

tions to determine royal rights, because even the limited experience of Burton Lazars indicates that the extent and ownership of knights' fees was frequently in dispute.

At Cold Newton, where the order received what appears to be a release of seigniorial rights from William Burdet, conflict centred on the Marmion family who held lands in the township by knight service and were in the homage of the master.[140] In her work on the Honour of Mowbray Greenway states that 'On the incidents of wardship and marriage the charters are silent . . . we have no means of knowing how the custody of minors and their estates normally operated. Similarly there are no direct statements on the marriages of wards and of widows.'[141] If the case of Cold Newton is anything to go by, contemporaries were not much better informed. In the 1270s the Marmions suffered two deaths as a result of which under-age heirs stood next in line for property. In the first of these the heir was forcibly removed by a relative, Mauncer Marmion, and in the second Mauncer's own son was seized by the master, John de Horbling, 'in the name of wardship', by which he claimed custody of the lands until the heir came of age.[142] The Marmions responded by stating that they held of Richard de Tours and that the master did not have a valid claim, and in 1288 Tours confirmed this position by initiating his own litigation against the order.[143] This seems to have prompted the new master, Robert de Dalby, to take direct and drastic action. On Thursday, 16 August 1288, backed by three of his brethren and a dozen laymen, some of whom appear to have been shipped in from Derbyshire, he entered the property of the Marmions and was alleged to have removed £40 worth of goods, placing an essoiner in residence to administer the estate.[144] Agnes, the widow of Mauncer Marmion, removed the heir to a safe place, and in 1290 Richard de Tours hit back and ejected the essoiner 'with force and arms', causing damage estimated at £100 in the process.[145]

William Marmion, the heir in question, survived the crisis and grew up to enjoy his lands, but his own death in about 1323 triggered another, remarkably similar, series of difficulties. His widow, Lucy, proceeded against the master, William de Tye, in a plea of dower, and Robert Burdet stepped in and abducted the Marmion heir at either Little or Great Dalby 'whose marriage belongs to Robert Burdet'.[146] The result of the disagreement is unknown, but as late as 1336 bad blood still existed between the order and the Marmions when the master

---

[140] BL, Cart, f. 207; Nichols, *Leicestershire*, 3 pt 1 (London, 1800), p. 338.

[141] Greenway, *Mowbray Charters*, pp. xxxviii–ix.

[142] PRO, CP 40/5, m.66d (Farnham, 1, p. 254); CP 40/82, m.62 (Farnham, 1, pp. 256–7); CP 40/17, m.100 (Farnham, 2, p. 50).

[143] PRO, CP 40/17, m.100 (Farnham, 2, p. 50).

[144] PRO, JUST 1/1279, m.31; KB 27/118, m.15 (Farnham, 2, pp. 50–1). Dalby had close contacts with Derbyshire where he was involved in a violent dispute with the abbot of Dale and had dealings with Edmund, earl of Lancaster.

[145] PRO, CP 40/82, m.62 (Farnham, 2, p. 51). Mauncer Marmion's widow had remarried with Geoffrey de Skeftington.

[146] PRO, CP 40/271, m.9d (Farnham, 1, p. 258). The claim is puzzling, since in the Inquisition Post Mortem of Roger de Mowbray (1299) the fee of Newton Burdet was stated to be held under him by the master. CP 40/247, m.181d (Farnham, 2, p. 51). For evidence of other contemporary problems between the Burdets and the order, see Chapter 5, pp. 160–1; Chapter 6, pp. 200, 202–3.

Plate 12: The tomb effigy of Roger Beler, chief baron of the Exchequer and a
notable patron of the order, who was murdered in 1326. Kirby Bellars church,
Leicestershire.

accused William Marmion of detaining some of his cattle.[147] The exercise of
feudal rights of lordship could therefore be an extremely untidy business, the
order anxious to enforce them because of their financial benefits (particularly
useful in the wake of the statute of mortmain), but the legal right to exercise
them apparently split three ways in this case, between the Lazarites, the Tours
and the Burdets.

At Kirby Bellars the complexities of feudal law once more encroached, but
here violent confrontation was averted, and the order may well have benefited by
its ownership of the fee. In 1277, on the death of Alice Beler, John de Horbling
'broke' the family house at Kirby and seized and sold goods to the damage of the
executors.[148] However, an arbitration was agreed upon and the matter seems to
have been settled amicably, so much so that a grandson of Alice, Roger Beler,
became a major supporter of the order during the troubled years of the early
fourteenth century (Plate 12).[149] As a young man he was probably placed in the
household of Edmund, first earl of Lancaster, and he subsequently rose in the
royal service to become chief baron of the Exchequer and a notable supporter of
Edmund's son, Thomas, second earl of Lancaster, during the domestic upheavals

---

[147] PRO, CP 40/308, m.345 (Farnham, 1, p. 258).
[148] BL, Cart, f. 109.
[149] Walker, 'Patronage', p. 292; G.F. Farnham, *Leicestershire Medieval Pedigrees* (Leicester, 1925), p. 42;
Nichols, *Leicestershire*, 2 pt 1, p. 278.

of Edward II's reign. Cleverly, he survived Lancaster's fall, came to terms with Edward II and re-emerged as a leading follower of the Despensers.[150] Thus he was able to provide for the order some of the support it lacked because of John Mowbray's fall from grace in 1322.

Like many successful men of his generation Roger Beler wished to found a chantry, and in 1316 he received permission from the master, John Crispin, as lord of the fee of Kirby, to appropriate three virgates to the embryonic chapel of St Peter.[151] By 1319 the new foundation had grown to incorporate a warden and twelve chaplains, and an arrangement was worked out between Beler and the new master, Richard de Leighton, to provide for its better maintenance. Part of the agreement was that the master should be allowed to present one of the chaplains to the college, which indeed he did, for a while, before the privilege lapsed. As part of a prospective endowment, Roger Beler granted to the master a messuage and carucate in Kirby, only to have this immediately transferred to his chantry 'in *frankalmoign*' in return for an annual rent of £1 6s 8d. The transaction was recorded on the Patent Rolls and confirmed by the order in 1324.[152]

Interestingly, this arrangement was accompanied by a loan of £250 from Beler to the master (which was repaid to Beler's widow in 1331), and another of 100 marks [£66 13s 4d] from William de Melton, chaplain.[153] Why the master needed such a large sum of money is not apparent, though it may not be unconnected with the economic difficulties that characterised the years 1315–22.[154] Beler was using his knowledge of the law to put his endowment beyond dispute by working in conjunction with the lord of the fee; and his wealth clearly made it worthwhile for the lord to co-operate in the scheme. Roger Beler was murdered near Rearsby in 1326, a victim of the notorious Folville gang, and in 1359 his widow, Alice, and son, Roger, expressed their desire to convert his chantry foundation into a priory for Augustinian canons. The Lazarites duly confirmed their charters and welcomed the new prior and convent as neighbours, a foundation located a mere five miles from the preceptory at Burton.[155]

One of the expectations placed on even a minor feudal potentate, such as the master of St Lazarus, was that he should provide hospitality for the king and his entourage when it passed through the area. Two examples of such visits have been discovered at Burton from published itineraries, though there may well have been more. In September 1216 King John paused at 'Berton' which, since it punctuated his journey between Lincoln and Bedford, could well have been Burton Lazars.[156] A more clear-cut case occurred on the weekend of 1–2 September 1291 when Edward I visited Burton and Tilton *en route* from Grantham to Daventry.[157] As ever on these occasions the king was accompanied

---

150 *DNB*, 2, pp. 144–5.
151 BL, Cart, f. 107.
152 *CPR, 1317–21*, p. 394; BL, Cart, ff. 104, 108.
153 *CCR, 1318–23*, p. 498; *1330–33*, p. 327.
154 See Chapter 4, p. 129.
155 *CChartR, 1341–1417*, pp. 164–5.
156 T.D. Hardy, 'Itinarium Johannis Regis Anglicie', *Archaeologia*, 22 pt 1 (1828), p. 159.
157 H. Gough (ed.), *Itinerary of King Edward I throughout his reign, AD 1272–1307*, 2 (Paisley, 1900), p. 85; *Itinerary of Edward I, pt 2, 1291–1307*, List and Index Society, 132 (1976), p. 12.

by a small army of administrators who issued at Burton documents permitting the abbot of Pipewell to travel overseas to attend the General Chapter of the Cistercians and ordering the royal justices to take action in the case of Roger de Scaldewell's lands, among others.[158] The visit, which no doubt enabled the king to hear mass in the chapel of the brethren on Sunday, was possibly prompted by the fall of Acre earlier in the same year, and it may be that important verbal agreements were struck concerning the future of Tilton hospital and the hotly debated question of St Giles's.[159] Bishops of Lincoln visited too, generally to break their itineraries around their huge diocese, which stretched from the Humber to the Thames. John Dalderby, for example, is recorded as being at Burton Lazars three times during his 21-year pontificate, and on one of these occasions he stayed for three days (29 September–1 October, 1301).[160]

Instances such as these provided visual symbols of solidarity within the feudal hierarchy and helped heal the wounds caused by the inevitable collisions between the prerogatives of the crown and the bishops and those of lesser lords. In 1235 a servant of the master, Robert de Erdington, hanged himself, possibly at Foulsnape hospital, and the master seized his goods valued at £2 2s. However, the king directed a writ to the sheriff of Yorkshire ordering him to recover the money, 'which said chattels belong to the king by occasion of the said hanging and not to the said master'. But the case had a twist that was typical of the attitude of central government to the order:

> and after he [i.e. the sheriff] shall have received that money to the king's use, so that having acknowledged that he received the money as belonging to the king for the deed aforesaid, on the second or third day afterwards he caused the said master to have the money by way of charity, of the gift of the king, so that by occasion of this grace of the king, the master cannot possibly lay claim of his own in process of time to any chattels of his men to whom a misfortune of this kind may happen.[161]

But the crown was not always so magnanimous in defence of its rights. Roger Mortimer, earl of March, who virtually ruled the country during the early years of Edward III's reign, seized corn and other goods of the order at Nottingham in 1330 under colour of purveyance. With a grim irony he was hanged, drawn and quartered at Tyburn, outside the walls of St Giles's, later in the same year, no doubt receiving his 'last sustenance' from a brother of the order according to custom.[162] Nine years later, in 1339, the master, Hugh Michel, was also on the receiving end of the judicial system, being imprisoned at Oakham Castle 'for trespass of vert and venison' in the royal forest of Rutland, but the king granted him bail to appear at the next eyre.[163] This may well be another example of a policy of harassment directed against a master whose behaviour was suspect in

---

158 CPR, 1281–92, p. 443; CCR, 1288–96, p. 202.
159 The alleged failure of the brethren to honour traditional obligations at Tilton lapsed at about the same time as Edward I's visit to Burton Lazars. See Chapter 5, pp. 160–1.
160 LAO, Dalderby Memoranda, ff. 37, 169, 395. The other visits were in 1309 and 1318.
161 Close Rolls, 1234–37, p. 59 (Farnham, 1, p. 253).
162 Rot Parl, 2, p. 51; PRO, SC 8/266/13294; DNB, 13, pp. 1033–41.
163 CCR, 1339–41, p. 148.

the eyes of the crown.[164] Land at Choseley, occupied by a tenant who was an outlaw, was seized by Edward III for a year and a day in 1356, and in 1404 there was a similar case involving 'cups, pieces and jewels of silver, and other goods' belonging to Sir Hugh Mortimer.[165] Mortimer, who was an outlaw and dead by 1404, possibly sought refuge with the order in the context of its rights of sanctuary, since these items were said to be in the hands of Walter de Lynton and Sir John Berkeley of Wymondham after his death. However, they were removed by Sir John Eynesford and Henry Stainton, and 'unlawfully taken and withheld' in defiance of the king's rights. The crown, therefore, proved itself capable of protecting its legal and judicial prerogatives, but in the firm belief that justice should be tempered with mercy where the affairs of the order were concerned.

The order of St Lazarus built up a moderate landed estate scattered over a very considerable geographic area because of the benevolence of an extremely wide set of patrons. It received all of the benefits that Satchell believes to be characteristic of leper hospitals (grants of land, gifts of alms and remission of economic burdens), but on a much larger scale than most. Only the largest hospitals, such as Sherburn and Harbledown, were comparable in this respect. In terms of the pattern of patronage, the order of St Lazarus actually had closer parallels with the monastic and military orders, and it successfully outmanoeuvred the restrictions of the statute of mortmain by receiving two substantial gifts from the crown after 1279. Benefactors included kings, noblemen and gentry, but it was the peasant farmers who made up the majority in terms of numbers of grants, if not in terms of the volume of property granted. The scattered nature of the estate meant that it was not always easy to administer, and the gift of St Giles's by Edward I, though perceived to be a solution to an ongoing problem, in fact only created a new set of difficulties. After 1299 the order had to cope with a group of surly and rebellious tenants in London who had a clear expectation that the support of lepers was part of the Lazarite way of life. They found it hard to understand that masters such as Robert de Dalby felt more at home making armed assaults on their feudal tenants, or entertaining the king at Burton, than ministering to the sick of the capital. Yet the inescapable irony was that it was on those lepers that the prosperity of the 'poor house' ultimately depended, because patrons gave with that image very much to the forefront of their minds, and kings granted immunities and privileges for precisely the same reasons. By becoming part of the property-owning world, with its taxes and feudal entanglements, the order inevitably distanced itself from the wellspring that provided its inspiration, yet those properties were needed to sustain its work both in the Holy Land and in England. It was a dilemma debated at length by other religious orders that professed poverty as part of their ideology, and it would be difficult to believe that it did not result in some prolonged heart-searching among the Lazarites too.

[164] See Chapter 3, pp. 76–7.
[165] *CCR, 1354–60*, p. 287; *1402–5*, p. 309.

3

Crusading, Crisis and Revival

preceptor and custodian of all the alms of St Lazarus on this side of the sea

(Charter of Matthew de Crembre, late twelfth/early thirteenth century)

The English province

The order of St Lazarus in England underwent far reaching organisational change during the 400 years of its existence. Central to this development was the relationship between the English province and the master-general, and this fundamental issue was to have repercussions in many different areas. One of these concerned the question of authority and control; another touched on the important matter of funds, and, in particular, where and how they were to be directed. The order also had to respond to changing economic circumstances and different notions of piety among the laity, especially after 1350. But these potential difficulties could not have been predicted in the euphoria of the twelfth and thirteenth centuries, when patrons, inspired by the potent image of the leper knight, gave generously to the hospitals in Jerusalem and Acre to speed forth the Crusade. By 1291 the English estate had reached considerable proportions, and the chief preceptory at Burton Lazars was administering dependencies in several different parts of the country. Although this provided much-needed revenue for the work of the order in the Latin kingdom, little is known about the precise relationship between the master-general in the Holy Land and his subordinates in western Europe.

What is clear, even in the early years, is that the master of Burton was an important figure, and increasingly so as the extent of the English estate grew in the late twelfth and early thirteenth centuries (Appendix 1). Modes of description varied considerably. After 1150 there are references to a 'prior', or one member of the order being deemed to act 'for the other brethren in England'.[1] By the thirteenth century more obviously legalistic forms were in use, such as 'preceptor of all the alms of St Lazarus in England and warden of the brethren in England'; 'preceptor and custodian of all the alms of St Lazarus on this side of

---

[1] BL, Cart, ff. 5, 32, 203; LRO, DE2242/5; PRO, CP 25/1/121/6, no. 130 (Farnham, 1, p. 252); *Feet of Fines, Lincolnshire, 1199–1215*, PRS, new series, 29 (1953) p. 92. 'Prior' may have had a precise meaning, for which see Chapter 5, pp. 152–3.

the sea'; 'master of the house of St Lazarus in England and its convent'; or 'master of the house of St Lazarus, Burton, and proctor in England of the lepers of St Lazarus of Jerusalem'.[2] These cumbersome formulae disguise what came to be at least two quite distinct offices, which are highlighted by individuals mentioned in a charter of 1289: 'Robert, master of the hospital of Burton St Lazarus' and 'Brother Geoffrey, preceptor of the hospital of Burton St Lazarus'.[3] The master (in this instance Robert de Dalby) had authority over the entire English province, which included Scotland; the preceptor, we must assume, was responsible for the management of his own house. In the early years the prior may have been responsible for the leper brothers, and the fact that he disappears as an officer after the early thirteenth century possibly reflects the declining importance of this short-lived branch of the order. It is probable that the distinction between master, prior and preceptor took time to evolve, but by the late thirteenth century the master of Burton was clearly regarded as having a provincial jurisdiction under the master-general. He was, indeed, 'perpetual and provincial general of the said order in England'.[4]

How were the early masters of Burton Lazars appointed? In about 1390, the master, Nicholas de Dover, recorded both the means of election traditionally employed and the succession of masters, as he recalled it, from the time of King John to the present.[5] According to Dover, when a new master was required representatives were summoned from the various English preceptories to a General Chapter held at Burton. At that gathering a candidate would be elected and notified to the master-general, who was expected to provide merely verbal confirmation of the appointment. Dover does not highlight any of the potential difficulties implicit in this seemingly straightforward procedure. What if the representatives of the preceptories were not agreed on a candidate? What happened in the event of a deadlock? And was the master-general obliged to confirm a candidate of whom he disapproved? The fact that Dover said that the master-general's confirmation did not take the form of a written document is unusual, and suggests either that he was being economical with the truth or that there was, in reality, a very *ad hoc* approach to the appointment of this senior provincial official.

Having described the process of election, Dover went on to list nine masters, including himself, who served between the early thirteenth century and the late fourteenth century, a period of almost 200 years.[6] All of these, with the exception of Henry de Cadeby, are readily identifiable from other sources, and in each instance Dover emphasised an uncontested succession, in other words a new master taking over without controversy on the death of his predecessor. Unfortu-

2   BL, Cotton Mss, Claudius A xiii, f. 21; Cart, f. 91; Cotton Mss, Vespasian E xxiii, f. 77; *CCR, 1279–88*, p. 100. See also, Harl Mss, 3868, f. 16; W.P.W. Phillimore (ed.), *Rotuli Hugonis de Welles*, 2, LRS, 6 (1913), pp. 278, 279; *CPR, 1216–25*, pp. 443, 536; W.H. Blaauw, 'Dureford Abbey. Its fortunes and misfortunes', *Sussex Archaeological Collection*, 8 (1856), pp. 58–9.

3   PRO, KB 27/118, m.15.

4   PRO, SC 8/302/15081.

5   *Ibid.*

6   These are: Henry de Cadeby; Richard Bustard; Robert de Dalby; Richard de Sulegrave; William de Thame; Hugh Michel; Thomas de Kirkeby; Robert Haliday; Nicholas de Dover.

nately, other than linking them in roughly with the reigns of monarchs, there is no attempt to provide dates for the accession and death of the masters listed. Significantly, Nicholas de Dover drew up this important document in the context of a dispute in which he was resisting a royal nominee to the mastership of Burton, and the historical situation was certainly more complicated than he knew or chose to admit. While there is no precedent for a royal nominee before 1398, there is considerable evidence to shed doubt on Dover's account.

Although there are no alternative sources against which to test Nicholas de Dover's allegations about the means of election in the early years, there are some which question his order of succession. His list appears to be over-simplified and leaves out certain individuals who are consistently described as masters in other documents, for example Roger de Reresby and John de Horbling in the thirteenth century and William de Aumenyl in the fourteenth.[7] Another master, Sir Richard de Sulegrave, is chronologically misplaced. The only documentary reference places him in 1271/72, before Robert de Dalby's mastership, not after it as stated by Dover.[8] Moreover, the office does not appear necessarily to have been for life. John de Horbling, master in 1281, was once more an ordinary brother in 1284 serving under the new master, Robert de Dalby.[9] Most important of all, Dover fails to mention the major dispute over the mastership in the fourteenth century involving Geoffrey de Chaddesden.[10] Certainly this titanic conflict generated documentation from Boigny since 'letters of appointment' are spoken of in the context of the election of Robert Haliday, though by this stage the earlier process may well have been modified. Chaddesden, who was probably doing very unconventional things to back up a weak claim to the mastership, also obtained confirmations of his appointment from the Pope and the Patriarch of Jerusalem.

There are at least three possible explanations for these inaccuracies on the part of Dover. First, that he was simply ill informed, which is possible since (with the exception of his failure to mention the Chaddesden dispute) he is noticeably more confident about matters within living memory than those in the distant past. Second, that the jumble of nomenclature in the thirteenth century (master, preceptor, custodian, prior etc) is creating a smoke screen and that some of the individuals who appear to be 'masters' (for example, Reresby, Horbling and Aumenyl) are in reality 'preceptors' or 'priors'. In other words, that Dover's order of succession is essentially correct. Third, that there were, in fact, varying customs of appointment and removal (especially during the upheavals of the fourteenth century) and that Dover merely picked out those examples that suited his case best. Given the fragmentary survival of sources, it is impossible to be clear on this point, but the most likely explanations are that some masters had been forgotten about or that their case histories did not fit in satisfactorily with what Nicholas de Dover was trying to prove. The late fourteenth century was a period when Burton Lazars was distancing itself not only from the influence of

---

[7]   See Appendix 1.
[8]   C. Parkin, *History of Norfolk*, 8 (London, 1808), pp. 493–4.
[9]   PRO, JUST 1/462, m.21; CP 40/39, m.15 (Farnham, 1, p. 255).
[10] See below, pp. 78–83.

the crown but also from that of Boigny, so Dover's agenda would have been to stress the traditional 'independence' of his house. Hence inconvenient details, such as Haliday's letters of appointment from the master-general, are likely to have been glossed over in the interests of building a bright new future for the order in England.

Once appointed, the principal duty of the master in the thirteenth century was to dispatch an annual contribution, or *apportum*, from the English province to the Holy Land. The scale of this is not known, but the Derbyshire preceptory of Locko was obliged to contribute £20 *per annum*, a substantial sum, probably equivalent to about a third of its net income.[11] Fighting men might well have been involved too, and the Lazarites enjoyed special privileges at Dover, under the authority of the king, to enable them to send men and money out of the realm without hindrance. In 1256, following the disaster at Ramleh, the master-general, Miles, was in England drumming up support for the cause, and along with one William de Hereford he was given free passage 'with their brethren, men, horses and equipment'.[12] In spite of references such as this, it should not be imagined that the operation of the order of St Lazarus in England came anywhere close to that of the Templars or Hospitallers in terms of its scale.[13] The hierarchy of the larger military orders, with their knights, sergeants and chaplains, was simply not replicated by the Lazarites. Even the master of Burton Lazars was only rarely a knight before the fifteenth century, and he and his staff were engaged, basically, in a service capacity to ensure a regular flow of money and supplies to the Holy Land.

We know very little about the masters of the lesser houses or 'cells'. For five of them (Carlton-le-Moorland, Foulsnape, Tilton, Westwade and Harting) no names survive at all. For three (Choseley, Locko and Threckingham) there is one. Only Harehope (six names) and St Giles's, Holborn, (nine names) provide more detailed information.[14] However, it is clear from what does survive that masters could be transferred fairly frequently from house to house, and a surviving document for Harehope dated 1308 lays down a system of five-year contracts for their management.[15] Certainly, at about this period, John Crispin moved from St Giles's to Burton and William de Thame from Burton to Harehope, suggesting that the practice may have been widespread.[16] Under normal circumstances the master of Burton had wide authority to effect these changes and to conduct routine business such as law-suits and the presenting of clerks to benefices, but he was constrained by the need to work in harmony with his brethren meeting in chapter. Each year the preceptors of the daughter houses were expected to attend a General Chapter at Burton Lazars where they received 'advice and help' with regard to their charges, and it is likely that this annual gathering considered

---

11 *CCR, 1346–49*, p. 338. For a discussion of this, see Chapter 4, pp. 105–6.
12 *Close Rolls, 1256–59*, p. 130
13 Gilchrist, *Contemplation and Action*, p. 64. In 1338 the Hospitallers had 31 knights, 47 sergeants and 78 chaplains spread around 37 commanderies in England.
14 See Appendix 1.
15 GRO, Berkeley Castle Muniments, J7/67/02/001/00/00 (MF 1354).
16 See Appendix 1.

Plate 13: This small, bearded figure, clad in hood and
cowl, may represent a thirteenth-century brother of St
Lazarus. From Burton Lazars parish church.

other important provincial matters too.[17] If this represented the normality of life
for the order, under special circumstances the master could be overruled by
commissaries sent by the master-general to carry out specific visitations or
enquiries.[18] In the early fourteenth century, for example, Richard de Leighton
and Thomas de Sutton figure prominently as 'general attorneys' of the
master-general in England, an attempt, perhaps, to exercise closer direct control
after the centre of operations had shifted from Acre to Boigny.[19]

Brothers of St Lazarus came under the jurisdiction of the master of Burton,
who had sole rights of admission to the English branch of the order, and they

17 GRO, Berkeley Castle Muniments, J7/67/02/001/00/00 (MF 1354).
18 BL, Cotton Mss, Claudius A xiii, f. 21. A grant made 'with the common counsel of all the Chapter'.
19 *CPR, 1307–13*, p. 344; *1313–17*, pp. 1, 214; *1317–21*, p. 131.

lived according to the rule developed by St Augustine, bishop of Hippo, in the fifth century (Plate 13). This encouraged a more flexible way of life than the stricter rule of St Benedict, and because of this it was often adopted by groups, such as the Lazarites, who were developing a role which was not exclusively monastic.[20] Nevertheless, at the heart of the Augustinian code stood the round of eight daily services, the *opus Dei*, which represented the core of the community's spiritual life. These devotions continued with only minor variations throughout the year, and any aspiring brother would be obliged to accept this liturgical discipline as his most enduring and demanding task. Despite various shifts in emphasis that were to take place between the twelfth and sixteenth centuries, the critical importance of prayer remained constant throughout.

In terms of their social origins, brothers are likely to have been men of middling rank comparable to lay brothers in the monasteries, 'more menial and less spiritual than monks'.[21] They wore a habit, which was possibly grey, and certainly bore a distinctive 'mark', probably the *couped* cross of St Lazarus.[22] There is some evidence to suggest that they may have been bearded, a nuance possibly borrowed from the Templars or designed, in the early years, to mask the scars of leprosy.[23] The vows they took are unrecorded, but, as in the Holy Land, the vocation probably catered for brothers (both healthy and leprous) and chaplains to provide the spiritual support for their activities.[24] The term 'brother' is one of the most ambiguous and controversial with which the historian of medieval hospitals has to contend. On the one hand, it suggests a healthy assistant to the master; on the other, a sick member of the foundation. This is a problem of terminology particularly common in leper-houses, and when we are confronted with 'brothers' of Burton Lazars it is not immediately clear whether the healthy or sick are intended, or, indeed, brothers of the confraternity.[25] Chapter 5 argues that it is doubtful if leper brothers were ever a major feature of the order in England.

The extent to which healthy brothers sought ordination to the priesthood, a trend that was becoming more common in other religious orders as the medieval period progressed, is not known.[26] Certainly from the fourteenth century it seems that an increasing number of brothers were in priest's orders and, in the fifteenth century, when the English province fell under the direct supervision of the papacy, some received dispensations to hold secular benefices, a function that was considered incompatible with their traditional hospitaller vocation.[27] Another difficult area is marriage. The general assumption must be that brothers were celibate, as part of their vows, but there are two clear-cut examples of

---

20 Orme and Webster, *English Hospital*, p. 70.

21 *Ibid*, p. 81.

22 The evidence for the grey habit is provided by Bowyer's, coloured, sixteenth-century illustration. HL, HM 160, f. 160. For the 'mark', see *DCAD*, 5, p. 100.

23 The brother depicted in HL, HM 160, f. 160 is bearded; as is the possible sculpture of a brother in Burton Lazars church. See Plates 13, 29.

24 See Chapter 1, pp. 7–8, 9–10.

25 Orme and Webster, *English Hospital*, pp. 80, 112. Orme states that Burton Lazars supported eight brothers and a number of lepers, a statement presumably derived from Dugdale. *Ibid*, p. 72.

26 For leper brothers, see Chapter 1, pp. 7–8; Chapter 5, pp. 152–3.

27 *CPapR, Letters 11, 1455–64*, p. 126; *13 pt 2, 1471–84*, p. 836.

individuals having been married and fathering children – Brother John de Rotomago in the thirteenth century and the master Sir William Sutton in the fifteenth – though both of these may have been men who entered the religious life after the deaths of their wives.[28]

By the fifteenth century papal documents occasionally classify the order as one of crutched friars or *fratres cruciferi*, along with the brethren of St Thomas of Acre and St Bartholomew's, Gloucester. The *cruciferi*, one of the lesser orders of friars, were Augustinian hospitallers who were strongest in Italy yet who made some limited inroads into England in the thirteenth century. Although in the twelfth century the Hungarian Lazarites were described as *cruciferi*, the revival of this description in the late Middle Ages may be no more than a misunderstanding, on the part of papal bureaucrats, of the true status of the order of St Lazarus and, indeed, of other English hospitals too.[29] In common with the other military orders, the Lazarites did not have a scholarly tradition, and, with the exception of Dr Thomas Legh, no member of the order has been traced as having a degree or studied at university. The books recorded at St Giles's in 1371 and 1391 were sufficient to conduct the liturgy and provide elementary instruction in the lives of the fathers and martyrs, but little else.[30]

Since the Lazarites enjoyed exemption from episcopal control and no record of internal visitation has survived, we know virtually nothing of the quality of their spiritual life. The constant comings and goings of the early brothers in terms of the administration of their estates and the collection of alms must have created some difficulties with regard to their ability to adhere to the Rule, because one of the papal privileges recited by the bishop of Jerusalem in 1323 permitted an indulgence to those 'diligently administering matters who will have carelessly omitted the divine office'.[31] Two random cases involving brothers were heard by the royal courts and the papal curia in the fifteenth century. The first concerned Thomas Poutrell, alias Robert Norton, who was 'wandering about in secular habit, despising the habit of religion, to the peril of his soul and the scandal of that order'.[32] The king ordered his arrest in 1428 so that he could be delivered up to the master for punishment 'according to the rule', and in the following year Walter de Lynton was pursuing a suit against Sir Gilbert Keighley of Hille, Yorkshire, and William Keighley of London alleging their abduction of Poutrell.[33]

The second, a more complex case, developed from a dispensation granted to Hugh Spalding to hold a secular benefice in 1450.[34] Spalding eventually obtained

[28] BL, Cotton Mss, Claudius A xiii, f. 21; J.P. Rylands (ed.), *The Visitation of Cheshire in the year 1580*, HS, 18 (1882), p. 220.

[29] *CPapR, Letters 11, 1455–64*, p. 126; D. Knowles and R.N. Hadcock, *Medieval Religious Houses in England and Wales* (1953, 2nd edition London, 1971), pp. 208–9; Knauz, *Magyar Sion*, 2, p. 121.

[30] PRO, E 326/12434; E 315/38. A book called *Martyrology* and another entitled *Lives of the Fathers* were present on both occasions. For the lack of a scholarly tradition amongst the Hospitallers, see Gilchrist, *Contemplation and Action*, pp. 63–4.

[31] GRO, Berkeley Castle Muniments, J7/67/02/002/00/00 (MF 1297).

[32] *CCR, 1422–29*, pp. 418–19.

[33] PRO, CP 40/675, m.505d (Farnham, 1, p. 262).

[34] *CPapR, Letters, 10, 1447–55*, p. 72. Spalding also required dispensation on the grounds of his illegitimacy.

the living of Doddinghurst, Middlesex, and evidently preferred the life of a secular since 'he was acting as, wore the habit of, and was reputed to be a secular priest and was under sentence of apostasy by the said order'. By 1479 the attempts of Sir William Sutton to bring him back into the fold had failed, and Spalding petitioned the papacy to be absolved. The Pope was in a difficult dilemma since the curia had permitted the breach of regulations in the first place yet wished to see the authority of the master upheld. Accordingly, it was decided that Spalding was to continue to wear the habit of St Lazarus 'beneath a becoming mantle or priestly vestment of a becoming colour without incurring apostasy'.[35] It was an untidy compromise, which provided evidence of the changing priorities of brothers in the late Middle Ages. However, the comparative infrequency of recourse to outside agencies indicates that the disciplinary sanctions of the order were for the most part monitored effectively by its own officers.

Despite its international connections, the English province sustained a fair degree of autonomy, even in the thirteenth century. Little evidence has survived concerning the names of brothers, but, when it has, prosopographical analysis suggests a recruitment firmly based in the East Midlands, reflecting the landed interests of the order. The locative surnames of Martin de Hale, Nicholas de Flore and William Croxton are fairly typical, pointing to origins in Lincolnshire, Northamptonshire and Leicestershire respectively.[36] The names of masters present a similar pattern. John de Horbling probably came from Lincolnshire, Robert de Dalby from Leicestershire and Geoffrey de Chaddesden from Derbyshire.[37] On the other hand, there was no reason why brothers from other parts of Europe should not have come to work in England, or why Englishmen should not have gone overseas to serve the interests of the order in France or the Holy Land. The surname of the English brother, John de Rotomago, is the Latinised form of Rouen;[38] Terry de Alemanius, master in 1235, was possibly German; and William de Aumenyl, master in 1321, sounds more likely to have been French than English.[39] John Paris, a brother of Locko in 1333, is possibly to be identified with John de Paris who appears as master-general before 1357, but whether he was a Frenchman serving in England or an Englishman who went on to become head of the order in France is by no means clear on surname evidence alone.[40]

Apart from Paris, there are three further examples of English brothers who may have progressed to hold senior positions in the order. First, Walter de Novo Castro, who appears as master of Harehope in 1189 and later became master of Burton Lazars. Is he the same Walter de Novo Castro who occurs as

---

35 *CPapR, Letters, 13, pt 1, 1471–84*, pp. 7–8.

36 PRO, CP 40/5, m.66d (Farnham, 1, p. 254); JUST 1/1279, m.31 (Farnham, 2, p. 50); *CPR, 1381–85*, p. 463.

37 PRO, KB 27/114, m.4d (Farnham, 2, p. 50); KB 27/33, m.8d (Farnham, 3, p. 109); *CPR 1354–58*, p. 43. Orme points out that very little research has been undertaken on this aspect of hospital history. Orme and Webster, *English Hospital*, p. 80.

38 BL, Cotton Mss, Claudius A xiii, f. 21.

39 See Appendix 1.

40 W.H. Stevenson (ed.), *Middleton Mss*, HMC (London, 1911), p. 18; AN, S 4884, doc. 9.

master-general between 1228 and 1234?[41] Second, Sir Richard de Sulegrave, who is mentioned in a deed concerning Kings Lynn dated to 1271/72.[42] The description of Sulegrave is unusual. Not only is he described as 'knight', the only member of the order in England to have this distinction in the thirteenth century, but also 'master of the whole order of St Lazarus of Jerusalem'. These two points may be significant, especially bearing in mind the fact that between 1240 and 1277 there is a gap in the list of identifiable masters-general.[43] Third, Sir Adam Veau, master of Burton Lazars in 1308 and master-general of the order in 1327.[44] As in the case of John Paris, surname evidence alone does not provide indisputable evidence of nationality, but all of these cases, taken together, argue for an active interchange of personnel across the Channel. Despite the growing French dominance of the order, the English influence appears to have remained strong, reflecting the importance of the estates located there.

The number of brothers in England was never very great compared with even medium-sized monasteries. In 1277/78 the preceptory at Burton Lazars was staffed by the master, John de Horbling, and eight brothers; and 11 years later a new master had taken over, Robert de Dalby, who had seven brothers under his command.[45] Continuity of personnel was small, with only three of the community from 1277/78 possibly still being active in 1289.[46] During this period, with population and agricultural profits at a high level, the order was probably at its peak, mobilising all of the efforts it could to retain its base at Acre in the face of growing encroachments by the Moslems. In addition to Burton Lazars, there were perhaps up to eight subsidiary houses functioning at this time, and if each was staffed by two brothers it would suggest that the total strength of the order in England was a little over 20, most of its manpower being fairly widely dispersed. The gift of St Giles's in 1299 immediately put the order under pressure to increase its numbers, and the closure of some of the older hospitals, for example Tilton, may not be unconnected with this essential redistribution of the workforce.[47] It was probably not so easy to recruit new brothers in the changed circumstances following the fall of Acre, and certainly it has been pointed out that a crisis of recruitment hit the Templars at about this time.[48]

In 1355, after a series of complaints about staffing, St Giles's hospital was

---

41 See Appendix 1. AN, S 4841/B, doc. 16; Marsy, 'Fragment d'un Cartulaire', chart xxxiv, xxxv. His surname and connection with Harehope suggest that he may have come from Newcastle-upon-Tyne. However, Barber believes him to have been a member of the aristocracy of the Latin kingdom. Are we dealing with two people here?

42 Parkin, *Norfolk*, 8, pp. 493–4. Parkin describes the charter as 'remarkable'.

43 An unnamed master-general occurs in 1240. Marsy, 'Fragment d'un Cartulaire', chart xxxix, pp. 156–7.

44 GRO, Berkeley Castle Muniments, J7/67/02/001/00/00 (MF 1354); AN, S 4884, doc. 9. Sir Adam Veau may have been a member of the prolific medieval English family of Vaux.

45 PRO, KB 27/33 m.7 lists John de Horbling, master, and the brothers Osbert, Reyner, Geoffrey, John, William, Roger, Ralph and John (1277/78). KB 27/118 m.15 lists Robert, master, and the brothers Henry de Gateby, Nicholas de Flore, John de London, Simon de Thorpe, Geoffrey, preceptor of Burton, Ralph de Esseby and Ralph de Hermothorp (1289).

46 Only John de London, Geoffrey, preceptor of Burton, and Ralph de Esseby or Ralph de Hermothorp could have carried over from the earlier date.

47 See Chapter 5, pp. 160–1.

48 R. Studd, 'From Preceptor to Prisoner of the Church: Ralph Tanet of Keele and the last of the Templars', *StS*, 8 (1996), pp. 43–9.

directed to maintain a complement of eight: a warden, three brothers, two sisters and two chaplains.[49] These sisters of St Lazarus, who were at work in the fourteenth century, appear to be a new phenomenon, and may be comparable to the community of women who took over at Seedorf following the fall of Acre.[50] Despite its well-intentioned desire to reform abuses at St Giles's, the 1355 directive may well have been over-optimistic in view of the impact of the Black Death. According to Harper-Bill, the effects of the plague on virtually all religious houses were 'devastating and demoralising, totally destructive both to the liturgical round ... and of the economic structure which sustained their existence in this world'.[51] Certainly the evidence of the clerical poll-tax indicates that the earlier numbers had fallen considerably. In 1377 only three members of the order were resident at Burton Lazars (Nicholas de Dover, master, Brother William Borough and John 'chaplain there'); and in 1381 St Giles's was down to four (William Croxton, warden, Brother Nicholas and William and Henry 'celebrants').[52]

With many of the cells already closed, or on the verge of closure, the number of brothers spread around the outlying dependencies must also have been reduced. By 1380 there may well have been 10, or fewer, brothers of St Lazarus nationwide, representing a decline of at least 50 per cent over the preceding hundred years. These small numbers of clerical staff were not unusual for the military orders, since in 1377 the Hospitaller commandary at Eagle, Lincolnshire, returned a complement of only two, similar to Burton Lazars.[53] The broader community of the Lazarites, comprising lepers, corrodians and *famuli*, was more numerous than these small numbers of professed brothers might suggest, and there was a growing confraternity of lay folk who, confusingly, were often termed 'brethren'.[54] Nevertheless, it appears that by the end of the fourteenth century the combined effects of demographic collapse, schism and the loss of a sense of purpose had taken their toll. The English order had reached its lowest point.

The years of crisis, c.1330–1420

As the decline in numbers suggests, the fourteenth century was a period of crisis for the Lazarites as it was for many other religious orders. The Templars disappeared entirely, and in the 1320s rival branches of the order of St Thomas of Acre, based in England and Cyprus, fell into bitter conflict.[55] According to Touati, the positive image that leprosy enjoyed in the twelfth century was gradu-

49 *CPapR, Petitions 1, 1342–1419*, p. 270.
50 See Chapter 1, pp. 19–20. The Hospitallers had a house for women at Buckland, Somerset. Gilchrist, *Contemplation and Action*, p. 64.
51 Harper-Bill, 'English Church', p. 97.
52 A.K. McHardy (ed.), *Clerical Poll-Taxes for the Diocese of Lincoln, 1377–1381*, LRS, 81 (1992), pp. 16, 36; McHardy, *Church in London*, p. 38.
53 McHardy, *Lincoln Poll-Taxes*, p. 36.
54 For the *famuli*, see Chapter 4, p. 115; for lepers, see Chapter 5, pp. 156, 161, 166; for the confraternity, see Chapter 6, pp. 186–94.
55 Forey, 'St Thomas of Acre', pp. 496–500.

ally eroded into something much less favourable, reaching its nadir, perhaps, in the events of the lepers' plot of 1321.[56] If during the good years of the thirteenth century England had shared as a more or less equal partner in an international order with a unified sense of purpose, all that was to change after 1291.

First, the tendency towards schism among the continental Lazarites, with growing conflict between Boigny and Capua, opened the door to those who might have had personal ambitions or aspirations towards national autonomy. Second, the grant by Edward I of the 'royal' hospital of St Giles's, Holborn, not only had the effect of drawing the Lazarites closer to the crown, but also of involving them in ongoing conflicts with the citizens of London, one of the less fortunate legacies of the king's gift.[57] Third, as the royal and papal bureaucracies became more complex, there was an increasing desire to discover new sources of revenue with which to reward officers. Hospitals and colleges, which did not have cure of souls, came to be regarded as classic targets in this respect and fair game for speculators. Finally, the growing French orientation of the order sat ill at ease with the political tension between England and France, which eventually erupted when Edward III crossed the Channel with an army in 1338, commencing a conflict which was destined to drag on for more than a century. After 1340 all religious orders that had links with France were regarded with suspicion, and the Lazarites, whose principal purpose was military, might even have been seen in this light as potentially treasonable. When the deteriorating economic situation is added to these political uncertainties, it is not difficult to see why the fourteenth century was a more challenging time for the Lazarites than for other religious orders with a purely English orientation. Though they escaped the vortex that sent the Templars to their ruin in 1312, the period was nevertheless a testing one.

It seems that the difficulties began while Hugh Michel, whose name suggests he may have been a French brother, was master of Burton Lazars during the 1330s and 1340s. It is possible that after the fall of Acre, as the whole order became more introspective, the French began to take a closer interest in the lucrative English estates and that this became a point of friction. The conflict probably took the form of disagreement within the chapter about the loyalty due to Boigny in the context of Edward III's war with France, and the upshot was that Michel, no doubt finding himself outnumbered by an 'English' faction at Burton, withdrew to the preceptory at Locko in Derbyshire and persuaded the master-general to grant him the house for life in return for the traditional annual *apportum* of £20, payable directly to Boigny and not to Burton Lazars (Plan 1).[58] In June 1347 Michel was summoned before the council 'to answer those things that be set forth to him', apparently the controversial question of funds being transferred from Locko to the 'superior house' of the order in France.[59] By the end of July the revenues in question were in the hands of the crown and were

56 Satchell, 'Leper-Houses', p. 20.
57 *CPR, 1292–1301*, p. 404. For a full discussion, see Chapter 4, pp. 123–4.
58 PRO, SC 8/210/10456.
59 *CCR, 1346–49*, p. 295.

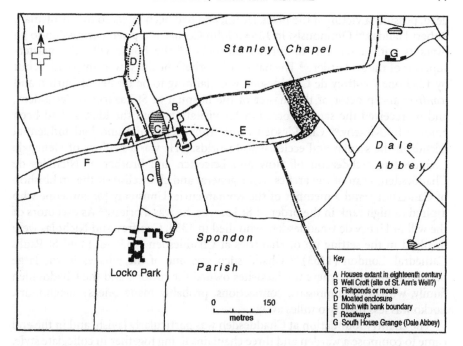

Plan 1: Locko Preceptory.

granted to the warden and scholars of King's Hall, Cambridge, 'to be received by them at the hands of the preceptor as a gift from the king'.[60]

Michel was still in office in August, when Edward III was attempting to extract a further 'loan' from him, but by October he had been deposed as master of Burton and replaced by Thomas de Kirkeby. In that month the king granted to Kirkeby, master of Burton 'and of the whole order of the same in England', protection for a year to visit houses and manors and to correct offences, effectively giving his endorsement to the changes that had taken place.[61] These events seem to indicate that authority, once unambiguously vested in the master-general, was now coming from the crown. This was clearly an important watershed, because when later in the century the master-general, James de Besnes, looked back on the disintegration of the order, he pinpointed the years around 1350 as being critical.[62] Hugh Michel died in 1352, holding out at Locko to the bitter end, and on his death the order petitioned the king to discharge the payment to King's Hall 'that their troubles will be ended'.[63] Though the king appears to have agreed to this request, the troubles of the Lazarites were, in fact, only just beginning.

Thomas de Kirkeby did not last long as master of Burton. By 1350 he was

---

[60] The warden and scholars were said to be in the process of erecting new buildings. *CCR, 1346–49*, p. 338; *CPR, 1345–48*, pp. 408, 429; *Rot Parl*, 2, p. 454.

[61] *CPR, 1345–48*, p. 414; *CCR, 1346–49*, p. 382.

[62] *CPapR, Letters, 4, 1362–1404*, p. 84.

[63] PRO, SC 8/210/10456; 8/210/10457.

dead, possibly a victim of the Black Death, and had been replaced by a Scotsman, Robert Haliday.[64] Ominously, in 1353 a John Corbet was given permission to go overseas with a servant 'to further business of the house with the master-superior of the said order'.[65] The nature of Corbet's business was unspecified, but by 1354 one Geoffrey de Chaddesden was claiming to be master of Burton and 'confrère and proctor of the master of the hospital of St Lazarus of Jerusalem', and he received the same protection for visitation from the king as had been enjoyed by Kirkeby.[66] Chaddesden came from Derbyshire and had influential friends in the secular and ecclesiastical worlds.[67] He was a nephew of Henry de Chaddesden, archdeacon of Stow and Leicester, and brother of Nicholas de Chaddesden, dean of the arches, vicar-general and chancellor of the archbishop of Canterbury, and a member of the Roman curia. Unusually for someone who aspired to high rank in the order of St Lazarus, he was a priest.[68] As executors of the will of Henry de Chaddesden, who died in 1354, Geoffrey and Nicholas were involved in the setting up of chantries at Chaddesden (1356–81) and St Paul's Cathedral, London (1363).[69] Chaddesden was one of the villages in the large parish of Spondon, where the Lazarites owned the rectory, and the Chaddesden family, with their impressive connections, probably made uneasy neighbours. Locko was less than two miles away.

The chantry foundation at Chaddesden was particularly lavish, and in the end came to comprise a warden and three chaplains living together in collegiate style. In the mid-fourteenth century the chapel was enlarged by the addition of north and south aisles, to accommodate the new chantry, and impressive architectural embellishments – a painted reredos, sedilia and piscina for each of the two new chapels – still record their presence (Plate 14). In 1546 the chantry was valued at £36 13s 4d, its widely dispersed properties including an inn known as the *Mermaid* on London Bridge.[70] According to Cholerton, this was a foundation 'well on the way to becoming one of the wealthiest of such establishments in Derbyshire', and it is likely that happenings at Chaddesden were causing envy

64 *Ordre Militaire de Notre-Dame*, p. 69. In a charter of 1349 Haliday is described as witnessing 'for the house of St Lazarus of Burton' rather than the more conventional form of 'master'. It suggests that he may have replaced Kirkeby, though, as yet, without formal election. BL, Cotton Mss, Claudius A xiii, f. 69.

65 *CPR, 1350–54*, p. 502.

66 *CPR, 1354–58*, pp. 43, 284, 352.

67 The Chaddesdens flourished in the thirteenth and fourteenth centuries. An early member of the family was Ralph de Chaddesden, archdeacon of Coventry and chancellor of Coventry and Lichfield. He died in about 1276 and was buried in a remarkable tomb at Sawley, Derbyshire. See J.C. Cox, *Notes on the Churches of Derbyshire*, 4 (Chesterfield, 1879), p. 384; V. Sekules, 'A Lost Tomb from Sawley', in A. Borg and A. Martindale (eds), *The Vanishing Past: studies of mediaeval art, liturgy and metrology*, BAR, International Series, 111 (1981), pp. 173–7.

68 H.P.F. King (ed.), John Le Neve, *Fasti Ecclesiae Anglicanae, 1300–1541,1, Lincoln Diocese*, (London, 1962), pp. 12, 18; J.M. Horn (ed.), *Fasti, 5, St Paul's London* (London, 1963), p. 70; B. Jones (ed.), *Fasti, 10, Coventry and Lichfield Diocese* (London, 1964), p. 53; J.C. Cox, *Notes on the Churches of Derbyshire*, 3 (Chesterfield, 1875), p. 304. For Nicholas de Chaddesden, see A.B. Emden, *A Biographical Register of the University of Oxford to AD 1500*, 1 (Oxford, 1957), pp. 380–1.

69 PRO, C 143/318/13; 143/343/7; 143/346/14; 143/356/18; 143/385/8; 143/398/8; 143/399/10.

70 P. Cholerton, *The Church of St Mary the Virgin, Chaddesden: a guide and history* (Chaddesden, 1997), pp. 7–9, 11–12, 45–50.

Plate 14: Fourteenth-century piscina and sedilia, in the Decorated style, from the former Chaddesden chantry in Chaddesden church, Derbyshire.

and concern with the authorities at Burton Lazars.[71] The chapel of ease at Chaddesden appears to have been new in the fourteenth century, and the first documentary reference to it is in 1347 when Roger Northburgh, bishop of Coventry and Lichfield (1322–59), licensed burials there so long as the fees continued to be collected by the vicar of Spondon.[72] It may have been felt that the very considerable sums of money being ploughed into Chaddesden might have been better spent in the refurbishment of the mother church following the disastrous fire at Spondon in 1340.[73] It was a significant rebuff to the master of Burton, as rector of the parish, that the Chaddesden family determined that after the deaths of Henry de Chaddesden's executors the patronage of the four chantry priests should be in the hands of the abbots of Dale and Darley.[74] This stood in sharp contrast to the situation at Kirby Bellars where the local family, in founding their chantry, had co-operated fully with the Lazarites.[75]

Chaddesden's secular supporters included prominent Derbyshire gentlemen such as Sir Robert de Twyford, Godfrey Foljambe the Younger and John Curzon of Kedleston.[76] From its regional power base, it is clear that this was another faction clustered around the preceptory of Locko, probably attempting to perpetuate the tradition of independence already established by Hugh Michel.[77] It has been suggested that the Chaddesdens and Twyfords were one and the same family, and certainly the Twyfords, who originated from Twyford-on-Thames, were related to the Lords Pipard and through them to the Ferrers and Aubignys.[78] It is possible, therefore, that the Derbyshire episode was an instance of the descendants of founders and benefactors attempting to win back their endowments in view of perceived shifts of emphasis on the part of the order.[79] If that was the case, they received support at the highest levels, because the Foljambes and Curzons had close contacts with the household of John of Gaunt by way of the Duchy of Lancaster.[80] Sir Godfrey Foljambe, 'one of the duke's closest associates', was Steward of the Honour of Tutbury and also chief steward of Gaunt's lands.[81]

But despite his impressive Derbyshire patrons, Chaddesden was unable to command the support of the majority of English brethren, and in July 1354 he was challenged by Robert Haliday whose letters of appointment, unusually, were

---

71 *Ibid*, p. 49.
72 *Ibid*, p. 44.
73 See Chapter 6, p. 212.
74 Cox, *Derbyshire Churches*, 3, p. 306
75 See Chapter 2, pp. 62–3.
76 *CCR, 1369–74*, pp. 432–3, 437–8.
77 Marcombe, 'Locko', pp. 54–5.
78 For information on the possible Twyford/Chaddesden connection I am grateful to Syd Lusted of the Spondon Local History Society. M.J. Sayer, 'Twyford of Kirk Langley and Spondon: problems in the history of a medieval Derbyshire family', *DAJ*, 94 (1974), pp. 26–31; M.J. Sayer, 'Twyford of Kirk Langley and Spondon: some problems resolved', *DAJ*, 97 (1977), pp. 23–26; S.P.H. Statham, 'Ralph Fitz-Nicholas', *JDANHS*, 58, new series, 11 (1937), pp. 57–66; J.P. Yeatman, 'Pedigree of the Albinis', *The Feudal History of the County of Derby*, 4 sect 8 (London, 1905), pp. 392–3.
79 For other examples of difficulties with the heirs of founders and benefactors, see Chapter 6, pp. 200, 202–3.
80 R. Somerville, *History of the Duchy of Lancaster, 1, 1265–1603* (London, 1953), pp. 54, 112, 123, 126, 366, 373, 375, 377, 381, 523, 539.
81 *Ibid*, pp. 112, 366, 381

from the master-general of the order at Boigny.[82] This, of course, raises questions about the nature of Chaddesden's appointment – was he a nominee of the Capuan house, perhaps, or the recipient of a papal grant of the mastership? Though he appears not to have had the backing of the authorities at Boigny, Edward III showed him limited support, probably because of the influence of Gaunt. As the conflicting forces pulled in their separate directions, there was a fear that St Giles's, always a loose link in the chain, was abandoning its traditional alignment with Burton Lazars and that the order was falling apart.[83]

Robert Haliday died soon after 1358 and was replaced as master of Burton by Nicholas de Dover, who was confirmed in person by the master-general of the order in Rome.[84] However, in 1363 Chaddesden approached the Patriarch of Jerusalem for collation as master of Burton 'in all rights that used to equal Robert Haliday'. Since 1262 the order had, in theory, been under the sole authority of the Patriarch, but Chaddesden also took the precaution of having his collation confirmed by the Pope.[85] To counteract this Dover was granted permission by the king to go overseas in 1364 to present an alternative case to the curia.[86] His return to England introduced a period of utter confusion. In 1365 officers of the crown were ordered to arrest Chaddesden, now described merely as 'chaplain', 'brother of Burton Lazars' and 'a vagabond . . . to the scandal of his order'. Upon capture the reprobate was to be delivered up to Nicholas de Dover 'to be chastised according to the rule of his order'.[87] Dover evidently caught up with his rival, because in 1369 a commission of *oyer et terminer*, probably issued by the influence of John of Gaunt, was directed to Sir Godfrey Foljambe, Sir Ralph Basset and others 'touching the evildoers who imprisoned Geoffrey de Chaddesden, master of the hospital of Burton Lazars, who is in the king's protection, at Burton Lazars . . . , detained him in such strait keeping as to endanger his life and took him thence to places unknown whereby he could not be found to be replevied.'[88] Yet, confusingly, only six weeks later a further commission was issued in favour of Dover ordering the arrest of Chaddesden.[89]

Can any pattern be discerned in these apparently contradictory statements? First, it is clear that Nicholas de Dover was regarded as the legitimate successor of Robert Haliday and that both men enjoyed practical support amongst the brethren of Burton and probably from Boigny too – how else was Dover able to imprison Chaddesden at Burton and regard the community as 'his fellows'?[90] Since this was a traditional, English and essentially nationalistic faction, it is likely to have received support and encouragement from the king, and it is no doubt significant that the second order for Chaddesden's arrest comes soon after

82 *Ordre Militaire de Notre-Dame*, p. 69; BL, Cotton Mss, Claudius A xiii, ff. 25, 69; *CCR, 1354–60*, p. 498.
83 *CPR, 1361–64*, p. 253.
84 PRO, SC 8/302/15081.
85 W.B. Lunt and E.B. Graves, *Accounts Rendered by Papal Collectors in England, 1317–78* (Philadelphia, 1968), p. 199.
86 *CPR, 1361–64*, p. 508.
87 *CPR, 1364–67*, p. 206.
88 *CPR, 1367–70*, p. 259.
89 *Ibid*, p. 266.
90 *CCR, 1369–74*, pp. 432–3, 437–8.

Gaunt's probable commission directed to the investigation of his grievances. It is possible that it exposed facts that displeased the king. Second, Chaddesden's 1363 appointment is noted in the accounts of the papal collectors, and in 1371 Arnold Garnerii commented 'it is not having an effect', with the marginal note 'useless'.[91] In the same year (1371) the master-general, John de Comti, was petitioning the Pope in an attempt to bring back the English province to its proper obedience, an indication that he believed that his authority had been seriously challenged.[92] Whether he felt threatened by Dover, Chaddesden, or both, is not clear, but the most likely explanation is that Chaddesden, given his legal and curial connections, was a papal provisor, opposed by a group of traditionalist brethren who, ultimately, had the support of the crown and the authorities at Boigny. The king's position was ambivalent because of Chaddesden's impressive clerical and lay backers, to whom he felt the need to defer, particularly when the duke of Lancaster was active in their support. And the master-general was in a difficult position too, because he feared that the issues raised might well get out of hand and act to his detriment over the long term, which, of course, they did. All of this helped to prolong the conflict. But underlying everything was the issue of how the master was to be appointed, a controversy that had contemporary parallels in other English religious houses subject to mother houses overseas, and helps explain Nicholas de Dover's ambiguous statements on the matter.

As a result of Dover's appeal to Rome, Urban V (1362–70) issued a commission on 29 March 1370 to William Clown, abbot of Leicester, ordering him to hear and determine the matter.[93] Clown was an excellent choice as an adjudicator. A man of rare qualities, he had the confidence of both Edward III and John of Gaunt. 'A lover of peace himself, he acted as a peacemaker . . . not merely by example but by practical handling of disputes and discords'.[94] It is clear from the instructions to Clown where the Pope's loyalties lay. Dover, he said, had been 'canonically received' as master and had governed 'laudably, quietly and in peace' until disturbed by the false claims of Chaddesden, which had caused the order to be 'unduly oppressed'. Clown was to decide the matter without appeal, and if, 'through favour, hatred or fear', witnesses failed to turn up they were to be compelled to do so. There is no record of the abbot's decision, but in 1372 there was a further hearing before the chancellor, Sir Robert de Thorpe, which probably confirmed the judgment of the ecclesiastical court. Each side produced its bulls and documents from Rome, and, 'to have peace henceforward', Chaddesden agreed to give up and cancel all his evidences and renounce his claim to the mastership in return for a pension of 40 marks [£26 13s 4d] *per annum* to be paid at the college of Newarke, Leicester. Each side agreed not to pursue any further suits against the other, and Dover, now undisputed master of

---

91 Lunt and Graves, *Accounts*, pp. 235, 274, 330, 369.

92 AN, S 4884, doc. 9; M. Secousse, *Ordonnances des Roys de France*, 3 (Paris, 1782), p. 263; *CPapR, Letters*, 4, *1362–1404*, p. 84.

93 ASV, Register Avinioni 171, f. 356, doc. no. lxi. The commission is summarised in M. Hayez and A-M. Hayez (eds), *Lettres Communes des Papes du XIV siècle: Urbain V (1362–1370)*, 9, BÉFAR, series 3 (Rome, 1983), p. 357.

94 A.H. Thompson, *The Abbey of St Mary of the Meadows, Leicester* (Leicester, 1949), p. 28.

Burton Lazars, promised not to harass Chaddesden in respect of 'any profession or obedience on his part'.[95]

Chaddesden, in the end, had not done badly out of it all. Since 1344 he had been rector of Long Whatton, Leicestershire, and his income from this preferment, as well as his pension, must have set him up comfortably for the rest of his life.[96] It is tempting to believe that Dover raised the money to pay off Chaddesden by leasing out the lands of the troublesome preceptory at Locko and closing it down to forestall any future difficulties. Certainly it disappears from the records at about this time, but whether or not its closure can be specifically linked with the end of the Chaddesden episode cannot be proven.[97] When Dover obtained a confirmation of the appointment, by him, of William Croxton as warden of St Giles's in 1374 he took the precaution of reciting his full titles as he saw them: 'Brother Nicholas de Dover, governor, warden and master of the conventual house of Burton Lazars, and of the convent of that place, and lieutenant and vicar-general in spiritualities and temporalities of the general master of the order of the knighthood of St Lazarus of Jerusalem in England and Scotland.'[98] It was a statement of unprecedented complexity, but it spelt out carefully the legal position which, significantly, did not involve a breach with the central administration of the order in France. Indeed, in later documents Dover reverted to the traditional thirteenth century usage, 'he being master and proctor-general of that order in England'.[99] Yet there is evidence that after 1370 the master-general began to regard England increasingly as a lost cause. Orme has argued that the fourteenth century saw the end of 'internationalism' in the hospital sector and that 'even what remained . . . became heavily anglicised'.[100] This was certainly the case at Burton Lazars. In practical terms the connections with Boigny were being shed, though a legalistic deference to the past ensured that this was not as yet stated in unambiguous terms.[101]

The ambivalence of the position of Burton Lazars after the conflicts of the mid-fourteenth century led directly to another problem that touched on the status of the order in England and was connected with the governmental attack on alien religious houses that characterised this period. Several hospitals with mother houses overseas, such as St Mary Rouncivall and St Anthony of Vienne, had royal-appointed wardens imposed upon them during the reign of Richard II, and the Lazarites were forced to fight hard to resist a similar fate.[102] At the height of the dispute between Dover and Chaddesden, Edward III had taken possession of St Giles's, Holborn, and given it to Geoffrey de Birston, an act

---

95   CCR, 1369–74, pp. 432–3, 437–8. For Thorpe, see DNB, 19, p. 801.
96   PRO, C 143/343/7; 143/385/8; 143/399/10. The patron of Long Whatton was Leicester Abbey and Chaddesden was still rector there in 1382. However, Thompson does not include him in the list of incumbents. Thompson, Leicester Abbey, pp. 176–7. Cholerton notes that Chaddesden exchanged Long Whatton for Eggington, Derbyshire, in 1344; and that between 1349 and 1351 he was also vicar of Longford, Derbyshire. Cholerton, Chaddesden, p. 46.
97   For a later case involving Locko, see PRO, E 134/42 Eliz 1/Hil 17.
98   CPR, 1370–74, p. 418.
99   Ibid, 1377–81, p. 290.
100 Orme and Webster, English Hospital, p. 75.
101 CPR, 1388–92, p.120; 1399–1401, p. 434; 1422–29, pp. 268–9.
102 Orme and Webster, English Hospital, p. 74.

reversed in 1371 when Nicholas de Dover nominated William Croxton and had his action recorded on the Patent Rolls.[103] However, the precedent for a revival of royal interest in the London hospital was set, and in 1385 Richard II asserted his right to appoint visitors.[104] Four years later another royal visitation revealed continued evidence of maladministration, and the king responded by appointing two royal clerks as the chief executive officers of the order in England, Richard Clifford as master of Burton Lazars and John Macclesfield as warden of St Giles's.[105] Macclesfield was a relatively obscure character whose highest preferments were prebends at York and Wells, but Clifford was a favourite of Richard II, who became keeper of the privy seal in 1388 and was at the beginning of a long and successful career that culminated in his appointment as bishop of London in 1407.[106] It is interesting to speculate whether John of Gaunt was active in these matters, still smarting, perhaps, after his defeat in the Chaddesden case. Nevertheless, Nicholas de Dover petitioned the Chancellor concerning Clifford's appointment to Burton Lazars, and this appears to have had the desired effect since there is no evidence that the nomination ever became effective.[107] This was Dover's last recorded act. Soon after this the veteran campaigner, in office for 'well nigh forty years', died and was replaced as master at Burton by Walter de Lynton.[108]

The more serious dispute, with which Lynton had to contend, involved St Giles's, where the king compounded his grant of the mastership to Macclesfield by handing over the property of the hospital to the Carthusian abbey of St Mary Graces on Tower Hill in return for an annuity of 110 marks [£73 6s 8d] out of the church of Scarborough.[109] In 1391 the abbots of St Mary Graces and Dore, accompanied by Giles Francis and Roger Chanuder of Southwark, entered St Giles's with 'swords, staffs, daggers, bows and arrows' intent on mayhem. In the process of this violent assault they were alleged to have taken away animals, furnishings and other materials (including books, vestments and ecclesiastical ornaments) worth over £1,000.[110] Lynton promptly petitioned the king for redress, reminding him that his grant to the abbot had been made in the wake of an *inspeximus* obtained by Dover in 1387, the king 'recollecting not his confirmation'.[111] An acrimonious dispute followed, during which Lynton alleged he was 'daily vexed and disturbed and prevented from taking the rents . . . and profits as he ought to do and was unlawfully wearied with costs, travail and expenses for defence of his right.'[112] With the tide running strongly against Richard II in 1399, Lynton at last took the law into his own hands and, supported by a group of armed men, regained possession of St Giles's by force, turning out

---

103 *CPR, 1370–74*, p. 418.
104 *CPR, 1381–85*, p. 596.
105 *CPR, 1388–92*, pp. 117, 120.
106 For Clifford, see *DNB*, 4, pp. 525–6. For Macclesfield, see B. Jones (ed.), *Fasti, 8, Bath and Wells Diocese* (London, 1964), pp. 34–5; B. Jones (ed.), *Fasti, 6, Northern Province* (London, 1963), p. 28.
107 Despite the fact that a writ of *de intendendo* was directed to the tenants. PRO, SC 8/302/15081.
108 *Ibid.*
109 *CPR, 1396–99*, pp. 47–8.
110 PRO, E 315/38, no. 171.
111 *CCR, 1399–1402*, pp. 450–1.
112 *Ibid.*

the servants of the abbot. He may well have been encouraged in this by an unexpected recantation on the part of Richard II soon after his deposition, who apparently:

> humbly and with great contrition prayed the king [Henry IV] to succour the master of the hospital of Burton St Lazarus that the latter might be restored to his hospital of St Giles without London, to ease the conscience and soul of the said late king, declaring that by sinister information he had done the master an injury in expelling him from the hospital and making a grant of it to others and that the king granted the supplication, ordering the master to remind him of it another time.[113]

In 1401 Lynton secured writs in Parliament that compelled the abbot to appear in Chancery, and by 1402 judgment had been given in his favour, by the king in person, and he was once more in undisputed possession of St Giles's.[114] The only explanation of this strange turn of events is that Richard II, at the end of his reign and quite possibly anticipating his own demise, faced a genuine crisis of conscience, accepting that he had behaved badly to a poor religious order having the approbation of God.

Macclesfield was bought off with a pension of 10 marks [£6 13s 4d] *per annum*, and guaranteed possession of a house and garden in the hospital.[115] He lived on until 1422, and, despite a fear that he was planning to travel overseas to pursue a case before the curia in 1419, does not appear to have presented any further difficulties.[116] Lynton consolidated his position by drawing up cartularies for Burton Lazars and St Giles's and obtaining new confirmations of charters from the king in 1401 and 1414.[117] These were wise precautions, because the events of the 1390s had posed a considerable threat. Richard II had attacked the order when it was at its weakest in an attempt to command its patronage and make it a mere adjunct of the crown, an action he lived to regret if his personal testimony is to be believed. Henry IV may well have been more sympathetic and appears to have abandoned the hostility to the order shown by his father, John of Gaunt, in the Chaddesden case. The role of Walter de Lynton is also noteworthy because he proved to be an able successor of Nicholas de Dover. But neither of these doughty fighters did much to engender fundamental constitutional change. Like Dover, Lynton continued to regard himself as 'proctor of the order in England', despite the fact that the title was by now little more than a legal fiction.[118]

---

113 *CPR, 1401–05*, p. 120.

114 *CCR, 1399–1402*, pp. 450–1; *1402–05*, pp. 16–17; PRO, E 315/35, no. 8.

115 In 1393/4 Macclesfield had procured a lease, probably of the master's house, from the abbot of St Mary Graces for one rose a year. The lease was regranted by Walter de Lynton in 1402 and renewed in 1420. Williams, *Early Holborn*, no. 1633; *CPR, 1416–22*, pp. 310–11.

116 *CCR, 1419–22*, pp. 38–9, 44, 48. When his will was proved in 1422 Macclesfield was described as of St Benet, Fynke, London, and Burton Lazars, Leicestershire. He mentioned his lodging at St Giles's and entitlement to a quantity of hay and straw from the master of Burton Lazars. PRO, PROB 11/2B (John Macclesfield, 1422).

117 BL, Cart; Harl Mss, 4015; *CPR, 1399–1401*, p. 434; *1413–16*, p. 248.

118 *CPR, 1399–1401*, p. 434; *1413–16*, p. 248; *1422–29*, pp. 268–9.

The order redefined, c.1420–1500

The particular problems of the order of St Lazarus underline the fact that the early fifteenth century was a difficult period for the hospitals in general. The Hospitallers had been specifically targeted during the Peasants' Revolt when their property at Highbury was attacked and their prior, Sir Robert Hales, beheaded.[119] The complaints of the Lollards about the corruption and inertia of many hospitals helped fuel a petition to Parliament in 1410, and in 1414 the House of Commons demanded widespread reforms.[120] Though Henry V successfully prevaricated, many churchmen were becoming apprehensive about what the future held, and the impetus of the age was for change. The order of St Thomas, which shared similar origins to those of St Lazarus and also endured a bitter conflict in the fourteenth century, was forced to adapt to these changing circumstances. It adopted the Augustinian rule in favour of that of the Teutonic order (which it had followed since its foundation), demonstrated a growing interest in chantries and *obits* and established a grammar school at London.[121] This sort of survival mechanism was replicated by the Lazarites, their innovations drawing them ever closer to the spiritual, social and intellectual preoccupations of the fifteenth century.

With a history of difficulties in their dealings with the mother house at Boigny and the crown, the English Lazarites turned to the papacy as the ultimate authority that might guarantee their continued survival and independence in these difficult times. Accordingly, when he determined to resign the mastership in 1421, Lynton did so before the bishop of Ostia, vice-chancellor of the Roman church, who was also given authority by the Pope to collate his successor, Sir Geoffrey Shriggley.[122] Henry VI clearly had no objection to these developments, because in 1439 he granted permission to Shriggley to obtain new bulls regulating the election of masters.[123] When these were eventually granted, the crucial point was that henceforward elections were to be in the hands of the English brethren 'and that such elect shall, without any confirmation, be true and undoubted masters of the said house'.[124] At the same time it was also stated that the master had to be a professed brother, that he had power to admit new brethren and could not be less than 30 years of age without special dispensation from the Pope.[125] Despite this important clarification, which should have made a repeat of the Clifford episode impossible, some legal anomalies still remained, chiefly with regard to the order's relationship with Boigny and the Patriarch of Jerusalem.

To resolve these difficulties, when Shriggley died or resigned in about 1450, the new master, Sir William Sutton, approached Nicholas V (1447–55) not only for a ratification of his own election, the first under the new regulations, but also

---

119 N. Saul, *Richard II* (1997, reprinted New Haven and London, 1999), p. 69.
120 Orme and Webster, *English Hospital*, pp. 32, 132, 135–6.
121 Forey, 'St Thomas of Acre', pp. 500–3.
122 *CPapR, Letters, 7, 1417–31*, pp. 181–2.
123 *CPR, 1436–41*, p. 362.
124 *CPapR, Letters, 10, 1447–55*, p. 81.
125 *CPapR, Letters, 13 pt 1, 1471–84*, pp. 369–70.

for a clear statement that the authority of the Patriarch had lapsed and that the order in England was 'under the protection and subjection of St Peter and the apostolic see' and no other ecclesiastical person.[126] Finally, when Sutton was riding high in the favour of Edward IV in 1479, he obtained a further grant from Sixtus IV (1471–84) confirming all previous privileges but also formally releasing Burton Lazars from any subjection to the French mother house:

> although the said house or hospital is said to be dependent on the house of Boigny . . . the master and brethren of Burton have for about eighty years behaved as though free from any obedience to Boigny: that the two houses are so much apart that if the master and brethren of Burton had to have recourse to Boigny for all their affairs, its revenues would hardly suffice therefore, and that such recourse would moreover be unsafe, in as much as there have long been wars and dissentions between the English and French: alleging, furthermore, that Nicholas V made a similar grant to the master and brethren of the house of St Anthony, London.[127]

For this important confirmation of independence the order in England paid the Pope 12 florins *per annum*, at Christmas, as compensation for first fruits and other dues 'and in token of the said immediate subjection'. John de Gigles, the papal collector responsible for this payment, rated the florin as equivalent to 4s 4d and therefore expected to draw £2 12s each year from Burton Lazars.[128]

The events of 1421–79 tidied up an unsatisfactory situation and led to the abandonment by the order in England of any notion that it was subservient to the master-general at Boigny. The extent to which these constitutional changes were imposed on the order by the crown, driven on by its own sense of national-istic identity or perceived as a means of solving the financial difficulties of the period, must remain an open question.[129] It is likely that they all played a part. After the mid-fifteenth century the generally accepted description of the order became 'Burton St Lazarus of Jerusalem in England', an international corpora-tion effectively nationalised.[130] This gave kings greater confidence in their deal-ings with it, and in the fifteenth century the Lazarites enjoyed a renewed vigour and status, enhanced because notions of crusade and chivalry were once more becoming fashionable. Constantinople fell to the Turks in 1453, creating a new Moslem threat to the West, and the writings of Sir Thomas Malory and others were enthusiastically embraced at the Yorkist court.[131] These things almost certainly impacted on the way in which the order was perceived, and it probably deliberately adapted its activities to match that perception.

The master who dominated this period was Sir William Sutton, who not only obtained the important papal grants of 1450 and 1479, but also took full advan-

---

126 *CPapR, Letters, 10, 1447–55*, p. 81.
127 *CPapR, Letters, 13 pt 1, 1471–84*, p. 3.
128 W.E. Lunt, *Financial Relations of the Papacy with England, 2, 1327–1534* (Cambridge, Massachusetts, 1962), p. 63.
129 See Chapter 4, pp. 130–31.
130 *LP, 1 pt 1, 1509–13*, p. 221.
131 J. Cowen (ed.), *Sir Thomas Malory, Le Morte D'Arthur*, 2 vols (1969, reprinted Harmondsworth, 1986).

tage of them. Sutton was the first identifiable master to come from a family of leading gentry, which suggests that the new rules may have made it possible to nominate men of more substance to the post. He was of the Suttons of Sutton, a Cheshire family 'of great worth and worship', who were hereditary foresters of Macclesfield Forest and who had won a military reputation in the French wars. Anthony Sutton, who was probably a relative, had been Henry V's page and 'bore his armour' during the Agincourt campaign. By way of this same Anthony Sutton, the master appears to have been related to the influential Leicestershire families of Howby, Villiers and Beler, descendants of the ancient lords of Melton Mowbray. During the Wars of the Roses the Suttons turned their skills to the support of the Yorkist cause and provided men to fight under Sir Thomas Fitton at Bloreheath in 1459.[132] Very soon after his appointment in 1450 Sutton received from the Pope the privilege of selecting his own confessor and maintaining a portable altar, but in the same year he demonstrated that he was also prepared to conform to some of the more disordered habits of the gentry by pursuing a violent feud against Robert Shriggley, probably a relative of his predecessor, attacking his property at Gaulby and Prestwold and threatening his servants.[133] This same sense of determination showed through in 1457 when he obtained from the crown a grant in reversion of the hospital of Holy Innocents', Lincoln.[134] But after 1461 Sutton settled down to become a loyal supporter of the Yorkist cause in Leicestershire and an associate of Edward IV's favourite William, Lord Hastings, who was attempting to build up a regional power base in the midlands. He was a JP and commissioner of array, and also participated in various governmental commissions such as those involving the complaints of the abbot of Leicester (1464/5) and the loss of revenues to the Exchequer within the county (1473).[135]

Sutton's knightly status, which was shared with his predecessor and which before the fifteenth century had been a rarity, merits some comment, because after 1450 all of the heads of the order in England used the title 'Sir' before their names. The designation is particularly interesting coming at a time when clergy of all complexions were making increasing use of courtesy titles such as 'Sir' and 'Dom'. But that the master of Burton was not using the word in this context is indicated by the use of the description 'knight' after his name and the fact that there is no evidence that any of the late-medieval masters were in priest's orders.[136] By contrast, many brothers by this time *were* ordained and, in terms of their abilities and status, had more in common with chantry priests and vicars choral than with the head of their order. It seems that the adoption of this title by

132 G. Ormerod, *The History of the County Palatine and City and Chester*, 3 (London, 1819), pp. 544, 758–9; Rylands, *Visitation of Cheshire, 1580*, p. 220; G.J. Armytage and J.P. Rylands, *The Visitation of Cheshire, 1613*, HS, 59 (1909), p. 230; J. Fetherston (ed.), *The Visitation of the County of Leicester in the year 1619*, HS, 2 (1870), pp. 29–30.

133 PRO, CP 40/759, m.244 (Farnham, 1, p. 262); *CPapR, Letters, 10, 1447–55*, pp. 93, 220. John Hemington, priest of the order, also received permission to select his confessor in 1450. *Ibid*, p. 220.

134 *CPR, 1452–61*, p. 359.

135 *Ibid*, p. 669; *1461–67*, pp. 346, 462; *1467–77*, p. 405; *1476–85*, p. 563; Thompson, *Leicester Abbey*, p. 71; E. Acheson, *A Gentry Community. Leicestershire in the Fifteenth Century, c.1422–c.1485* (Cambridge, 1992), p. 130. He obtained an *inspeximus* and confirmation of charters in 1462. *CPR, 1461–67*, pp. 136–7.

136 The only 'master' who was ordained was Geoffrey de Chaddesden.

the master was designed to set him apart, and, with the exception of Sir Richard de Sulegrave and Sir Adam Veau, its use in the late Middle Ages is the only instance of the order in England being, in any sense, a 'knighthood'.

In the scale of 'aristocratic precedence' knights were placed below barons and above esquires, though how precisely they got there was an ongoing matter of debate.[137] Rigby has pointed out that the English nobility was 'by no means a unified or closed legal caste' and that one of the few generally accepted definitions of knighthood was economic, the recipient of the honour being expected to have a landed income of more than £40 per annum. Though the master of Burton Lazars might be said to be well within this financial bracket, it was a benchmark that applied only to tax payers and for most assessments the order was exempt.[138] More convincing is Keen's explanation that crusading bestowed a 'distinct place of priority in the knightly scale of values' and that 'To take part in a crusade and to be armed against the Infidel carries a special, sovereign honour.'[139] Though the fifteenth-century masters are unlikely to have been active crusaders, they were, in theory, 'armed against the Infidel', and therefore capable of reaping the social rewards of their state of military readiness. Nevertheless, the origins of the chivalric honours of the period are difficult to determine. Whether these masters were created knights by the crown by virtue of their office, or whether they enjoyed the privilege because of family connections or increasingly tenuous links with the Crusade, is not apparent. What is clear is that the generally accepted perception of the master's status took a quantum leap in the fifteenth century, reconnecting him with the leper knights of Jerusalem who were so integral to the order's founding ideology.

If, by the eve of the Reformation, a sharp gulf divided the knightly master of Burton from most of his brethren, it raises the question of whether or not the new electoral practices of 1439 permitted a master to emerge from the more broad-based confraternity, containing, as it certainly did, members of the gentry and aristocracy who were often termed 'brothers'.[140] But the bull of 1439 said that the master had to be a professed brother, and the more likely explanation is that social polarisation was taking place within the order. This interpretation is borne out by the case of Sir Thomas Ratcliffe, who became master in 1526 and enjoyed the customary knightly designation. The fact that he was a brother in 1518 indicates clearly that he did not arise directly from the ranks of the confraternity and that his election followed the guidelines of the 1439 bull.[141] Yet one does not see a man of Ratcliffe's stature as a mere chantry priest made good. During the difficulties of the 1530s he had no qualms about approaching Henry VIII in person, indicating that he was an individual possessing the confidence and charisma that came with gentility.[142] The less socially elevated brothers who

---

137 Keen, Chivalry, p. 168.
138 S.H. Rigby, English Society in the Later Middle Ages: class, status and gender (Basingstoke, 1995), p. 202.
139 Keen, Chivalry, pp. 170–1.
140 See Chapter 6, p. 193.
141 LJRO, B/C/10 (Thomas Byrde, 1518). Thomas Ratcliffe, brother of the 'holy' hospital of Burton Lazars, was one of the supervisors of Byrde's will.
142 See Chapter 7, p. 220.

appointed him must have thought that he was the obvious man for the job. It is as if, in its last years, the order of St Lazarus was attempting to recreate itself according to its own mythology – knights, brothers and the sick once more conjoined in a unique spiritual and temporal union. That this new set of relationships was never truly egalitarian is firmly suggested by the position of the master who now lorded it over his brethren in a way that had not been apparent in the past. No longer *primus inter pares*, the master had become a country squire with a strange, quasi-ecclesiastical role to play.

This recrafting of the order in a new knightly context was taking place alongside the production of one of England's most influential works of chivalry, Sir Thomas Malory's *Le Morte D'Arthur*, completed in about 1469 and published in 1485.[143] It tells of the gallant deeds of King Arthur and the Knights of the Round Table, who were unified by bonds of indissoluble Christian brotherhood – the archetypal military order, in fact. 'The story of the Knights of the Round Table, is, quintessentially, the story of the greatest company of Christian knights that the world has ever known.'[144] The lives of Arthur and his knights were motivated by an all-pervading sense of mission and quest, which Cowen has linked to the Christian obsession of winning back Jerusalem from the Infidel.[145] Indeed, one of Caxton's first books, *Godfrey of Boloyne*, published in 1481, told the tale of the only successful siege of Jerusalem, from a Christian point of view, and there are obvious parallels between the two works of literature.[146] The great preoccupation of King Arthur's knights was the quest for the Holy Grail, which carried with it similar crusading undertones. In Wolfram von Eschenbach's *Parzival* the Grail Castle is guarded by Templars, and virtually all of the stories are characterised by an absence of conventional churchmen. Instead, religion is represented by hermits, people 'divorced . . . from the world of the organised ecclesiastical hierarchy', many of whom had begun life as knights and had taken to a life of 'holy contemplation' when their strength failed them.[147] These liminal characters have a strong resonance with the leper knights of St Lazarus, and the friendship between Christ and Lazarus of Bethany drew the order still closer to the mystical traditions of the Grail quest.

All of this stirred up powerful wellsprings of spirituality in the medieval mind. As Keen has put it:

> The Grail story not only made it possible for chivalrous romance to become a vehicle for eucharistic mysticism: it was also . . . the medium through which the chivalrous story of Arthur and his knights was linked into the sacred history of Christianity, as recounted in the Bible.[148]

From the point of view of the order this provided opportunities for exploitation comparable to the myths that had served them so well during the golden age of

---

143 S. Hart (ed.), *One in Specyal: immortalizers of King Arthur* (Presteigne, 1985), p. 4.
144 Keen, *Chivalry*, p. 118.
145 Cowen, *Le Morte D'Arthur*, 1, p. xviii.
146 Hart, *One in Specyal*, p. 12.
147 Keen, *Chivalry*, pp. 59, 61–2.
148 *Ibid*, p. 118.

the Crusade. Malory himself carried through the ideal of Christian knighthood into his life, and the last words of *Le Morte D'Arthur* speak of his unfailing belief in prayers for the dead. 'I pray you all, gentlemen and gentlewomen that read this book of Arthur and his knights ... pray for me while I am alive. ... And when I am dead, I pray you all pray for my soul.'[149]

Malory's Arthurian ideologies found their ultimate embodiment in the person of Anthony Woodville, second Earl Rivers, the brother-in-law of Edward IV, who was himself a crusader and instrumental in the publication of another significant work, the *Order of Chivalry*, in 1484.[150] A man who represented all the classic Arthurian virtues, Ross has also seen in him 'a strange streak of melancholy and asceticism', characterised by the hair shirt he wore beneath his rich secular dress.[151] Rivers was an important figure at the court of Edward IV, and he no doubt influenced the king in some of his more knightly pursuits, for example his patronage of the order of the Garter and the rebuilding of St George's chapel, Windsor. Richard III, to whom the *Order of Chivalry* was dedicated, shared many of these attitudes, though, for political reasons, he was generally at odds with Rivers. As king, Richard is remembered as the founder of the College of Arms and the man who harboured dreams of reviving the Crusade against the Turks.[152]

The climax of this Yorkist passion for chivalry came in June 1467 at the great Smithfield tournament, a star-spangled set of jousts during which Rivers took on the most celebrated European knight of the day, Antony, bastard of Burgundy, and fought out a memorable draw.[153] Lord Hastings was closely involved in the planning for this occasion and John, Lord Howard, took charge of the protocol on behalf of John Mowbray, fourth duke of Norfolk, the Earl Marshal. It is not difficult to see how the order of St Lazarus might have become caught up in the jollifications.[154] Norfolk and Howard were successive patrons of the order; Hastings was a known associate of Sir William Sutton; and Richard III was to visit Melton Mowbray, and possibly even Burton Lazars, in September 1484.[155] The Leicestershire connection is further strengthened by the fact that Queen Elizabeth Woodville's first husband, Sir John Grey of Groby, came from the county. More important, the Lazarites identified strongly with much of the ideology held dear by Malory, Woodville and the Arthurians – they were Christians, knights and crusaders, and, to gild the lily, they could affect more than a suggestion of hermit-like romantic melancholy. Indeed, Bowyer's sixteenth century lampoon of the Lazarites – mixing up the notions of courtliness and asceticism – has clear parallels with Woodville.[156] The leper knight was, by then,

---

[149] M. Clive, *This Sun of York: a biography of Edward IV* (1973, reprinted London, 1975), p. 143.

[150] Hart, *One in Specyal*, p. 13.

[151] C. Ross, *Edward IV* (1974, reprinted London, 1975), p. 98.

[152] P.M. Kendall, *Richard the Third* (1955, reprinted London, 1961), pp. 320, 322; J. Hughes, *The Religious Life of Richard III. Piety and Prayer in the North of England* (Stroud, 1997), pp. 28–56.

[153] Kendall, *Richard the Third*, pp. 65–7; Hart, *One in Specyal*, pp. 12–13; Clive, *Sun of York*, pp. 120–3.

[154] Kendall, *Richard the Third*, pp. 65–7.

[155] *CPR, 1476–83*, p. 474.

[156] See Chapter 6, pp. 184–5.

such a bizarre curiosity that it can easily be imagined that no pageant was complete without him.

There is sufficient evidence from the sculptures at Grattemont to suggest that the order in France was beginning to embrace a chivalric myth at about this time, and Malory, during his somewhat chequered career, certainly enjoyed the support of the order's patron, John Mowbray, third duke of Norfolk.[157] It therefore seems likely that the genre of knighthood embraced by the English order in the fifteenth century had more to do with this growing mythology of Christian chivalry than with a reality rooted in the past. In a world of 'historical likelihood' and 'romantic impossibility' the Lazarites could draw from their history all that was needed to make their mark in a changing world, not unlike Edward III's order of the Garter, 'a parody, albeit profoundly serious, of a religious community'.[158] Above all, perhaps, their new-found Englishness was wonderfully Arthurian and was a means of placing their former internationalism firmly in a patriotic context. This important point is best illustrated by the order's adoption of the red cross as its arms, probably at about this time. This simple device captured some potent and highly charged symbolism – of the Templars, who had been prime movers in the Crusade, and the cult of St George which flourished in England soon after their suppression. George, the classic 'heavenly warrior', had been a saint of special importance to the early crusaders and had appeared to protect their armies at Jerusalem and Antioch. After the thirteenth century he became absorbed into the myth-making of the English monarchy, transferring his allegiance to the struggle against the French. The fact that St George was also traditionally invoked in the cure of leprosy, probably because of the scaly skin of the dragon that he overcame, made this new connection all the more appealing.[159] The order of St Lazarus, claiming ever more ancient origins, could now move to the chivalric and spiritual high ground. The foundation of a myth was laid.

In terms of the religious life of the order, which was inseparably bound up with these knightly aspirations, it was almost certainly Sir William Sutton who launched it on its most ambitious spiritual and architectural scheme to date, the construction of the collegiate church at Burton Lazars. This was inspired by the preoccupation with masses for the dead that dominated the thinking of the late Middle Ages and the fact that the liturgy, based on the Sarum Rite, was becoming increasingly complex and was demanding ever larger spaces for effective worship.[160] As Harper-Bill has put it, 'never . . . has God been bombarded with such a barrage of masses as rose from late-medieval England'.[161] Many hospitals, such as St Leonard's, York, and St John's, Bridgwater, were falling into line with the requirements of the age, and numerous lay people would have echoed Malory's belief in the efficacy of their prayers. In a starkly practical sense,

---

157 See Chapter 1, pp. 26–7, 30. For Malory's career, see P.J.C. Field, *The Life and Times of Sir Thomas Malory* (Cambridge, 1993); and for his connection with Norfolk, see C. Carpenter, 'Sir Thomas Malory and Fifteenth-Century Local Politics', *Bulletin of the Institute of Historical Research*, 53 (1980), pp. 37–40.

158 Cowen, *Le Morte D'Arthur*, 1, p. xviii; Harper-Bill, 'English Church', p. 108.

159 S. Riches, *St George: hero, martyr and myth* (Stroud, 2000), p. 123; see also pp. 1–35, 101–39.

160 Duffy, *Stripping of the Altars*, pp. 338–76, especially pp. 368–76.

161 Harper-Bill, 'English Church', p. 111.

Rawcliffe reminds us that 'music and ritual attracted more worshippers', and the resources derived from chantry endowments could be very profitable indeed.[162] 'The transformation of many hospitals into collegiate churches or glorified chantry chapels was by no means unusual, and reflects a common response to the pressures of economic and social change.'[163] If the Lazarites were to keep pace with these developing trends and find a way ahead after the difficulties of the fourteenth century, a major investment in church building might just have provided the right answer.

There are many examples of new foundations in the late Middle Ages that combined a hospital and collegiate function, but many fewer which, like the order of St Lazarus, started out as a hospital and later added a college.[164] The outstanding example, which might have provided an inspiration since it was local and shared contacts with the duchy of Lancaster, was the Hospital and the New College of the Annunciation of St Mary in the Newarke at Leicester. Initially founded by Henry, third earl of Lancaster, as a hospital in 1330, it was transformed into a collegiate foundation by his son, Henry, first duke of Lancaster, in 1355.[165] This was exactly the type of transformation the Lazarites hoped to achieve at Burton, the difference being that the changes were being imposed on a preceptory rather than a hospital in the accepted sense of the word. Such a transformation was for the first time possible because resources that had previously gone overseas as *apporta* could now be invested in England at the discretion of the master. The building of the new church, like the new concepts of chivalry, can therefore be seen as an expression of burgeoning confidence, a celebration of national independence and the privileges that were being obtained from the papacy.

The initial inspiration for the plan is not clear, but it may have owed something to the patron of the house, John Mowbray, third duke of Norfolk, who was an inveterate pilgrim and influential in the government of Henry VI prior to his death in 1461.[166] Surprisingly, this major development was brought about with the generation of virtually no documentary record, though some significant pointers exist to prove the case. When John Leland visited Burton Lazars in the early sixteenth century he considered it to be 'a very fair hospital and collegiate church'.[167] A little later the monastic pension lists for the Lincoln diocese describe its redundant inmates as *consocii*, or fellows, a mode of description also employed for the personnel of the collegiate foundations of Newarke, Leicester,

---

162 C. Rawcliffe, *Medicine for the Soul: the life, death and resurrection of an English medieval hospital, St Giles, Norwich, c.1249–1550* (Stroud, 1999), pp. 55, 106.

163 *Ibid*, p. 107.

164 New foundations include Pontefract (1385); Higham Ferrars (1423); and Tattershall (1439). Orme and Webster, *English Hospital*, p.143. For the late medieval preoccupation with church building and improvement, see Harper-Bill, 'English Church', pp. 120–1.

165 A.H. Thompson, *The History of the Hospital and the New College of the Annunciation of St Mary in the Newarke, Leicester* (Leicester, 1937), pp. 11–40.

166 *DNB*, 13, p. 1121. Between 1446 and 1457 Norfolk received permission to visit Jerusalem, Rome and many other sites. In November 1456 he made a pilgrimage on foot from Framlingham to the shrine of Our Lady of Walsingham.

167 L.T. Smith (ed.), *Leland's Itinerary in England*, 4 (London, 1909), p. 19.

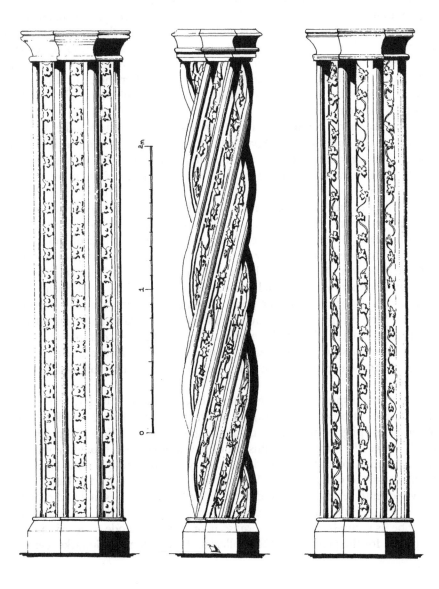

Plate 15: Reconstruction of Perpendicular columns, probably from the collegiate church at Burton Lazars. The decorative schemes are: fleurons (left); white bryony (centre); maple (right).

and Noseley, near Market Harborough.[168] The sixteenth-century master Sir Thomas Norton thought of himself as a 'daily bedeman', in other words one who prays, and in 1544 there were six brothers at Burton who were still assisting his successor in that task.[169] It therefore seems clear that at Burton Lazars, even more so than at St Giles's, the intercessionary activities of the order had come to supersede all others, and that by the sixteenth century the old preceptory, because of its new function, was once more restored to the numbers it had enjoyed before the Black Death. Moreover, it now had attached to it many of the ancillary services that might be expected of a collegiate institution, including a school to train choristers to sing in the choir.[170] The extent to which it also acted as a mausoleum for patrons, benefactors and members of the confraternity cannot be determined because of the lack of documentary and archaeological evidence. However, it would be highly unlikely if this impressive new church, with its constant round of liturgy, was not regarded as a very desirable place in which to be laid to rest.

It is impossible to trace the footprint of Sutton's church with any confidence among the dispersed and fragmentary earthworks extant at Burton today. However, Leland's phrase 'very fair' is a significant clue, because it is also applied to the substantial and newly built churches of Rotherham, Yorkshire, and Bunbury, Cheshire, and is suggestive of a building of some size and status. Both churches, which still survive, are basically Perpendicular in style, and Rotherham 'is one of the largest and stateliest of parish churches in Yorkshire'.[171] Could Burton Lazars have been similar? The discovery of the Burton House stones in 2000 enables a picture to be obtained of what it might have looked like.[172] Probably erected in the years after 1450 in an up-to-date Perpendicular style, its architecture placed a strong emphasis on leaf and flower decoration deep-cut into limestone. It is possible that the church was entered through a doorway flanked with spandrels bearing the red cross of the order and the arms of Sir William Sutton.[173] The body of the church was lined with octagonal columns, some of them decorated with fleurons, some with trailing maple leaves and the most spectacular with spiralling stems of white bryony, not dissimilar in style to the 'apprentice pillar' at Rosslyn chapel, near Edinburgh (Plate 15).[174] The building was further enhanced by heraldic stained glass and specially commissioned floor tiles adorned with religious imagery and more coats of arms (Plate 16).[175] The

---

168 G.A.J. Hodgett (ed.), *The State of the Ex-Religious and former Chantry Priests in the Diocese of Lincoln, 1547–1574*, LRS, 53 (1959), pp. 82, 84, 86.

169 MH, Lothian Mss, Box 25; LAO, PD 1545/42.

170 *CPapR, Letters, 13 pt 1, 1471–84*, p. 3. For the educational role of collegiate foundations, see Orme and Webster, *English Hospital*, pp. 63–6.

171 N. Pevsner, *The Buildings of England. Yorkshire. The West Riding* (Harmondsworth, 1959), pp. 418–20; N. Pevsner and E. Hubbard, *The Buildings of England. Cheshire* (Harmondsworth, 1971), p. 119.

172 See Chapter 7, pp. 241–5.

173 CA, Vincent Mss, 197, f. 39v. Wyrley joins together these two coats of arms, a suggestion, perhaps, that they may have been linked in some architectural scheme.

174 For the details of this reconstruction and a discussion of the imagery, see Chapter 7, pp. 244–5.

175 CA, Vincent Mss, 197, ff. 30, 39v.

Plate 16: Part of the 'pavement' of fifteenth-century glazed tiles discovered at Burton Lazars in 1913 and now in the British Museum. Heraldic and religious imagery predominates.

preponderance of heraldry is significant and links the rebuilding firmly with the chivalric preoccupations of the day. It is not always easy to identify medieval coats of arms, especially when the colouring is absent (as in floor tiles), but at least three distinct categories can be differentiated. First, old patrons of the order such as the Mowbrays and Ferrers. Second, families such as the Bohuns, Greys, Zouches, Willoughbys and Chaworths, who do not crop up in the Cartulary and who may be later supporters or even contributors to the rebuilding.[176] Third, the family closely associated with the mastership in the late Middle Ages, the Suttons.[177]

Nor was the new church devoid of devotional *foci* for visitors and pilgrims. There was an image of St Lazarus where the faithful were encouraged to make offerings, and William Wyrley, who visited the building in the early seventeenth century, noted the presence of the arms of Simon de Montfort (Plate 17).[178] Why these should have been represented, and commented upon, is an interesting question. The earls of Leicester, and indeed Simon de Montfort himself, were patrons of the house, and following his bodily dismemberment after the battle of Evesham in 1265 Earl Simon became the centre of a cult with relics dispersed as far afield as Alnwick Abbey in Northumberland.[179] Finucane comments that 'in many a house of friars and nuns he was a popular saint' and in Westminster Abbey there was a monument to him, intriguingly, bearing his arms.[180] He was invoked by the Franciscans as the 'guardian of the English people', and his bravery, piety and crusading activities caused him to be regarded as 'the flower of all chivalry'.[181] It could well be that Simon de Montfort's unique set of moral credentials fitted unusually well with the programme of image-building that the Lazarites were engaged in during the fifteenth century, and it is not beyond the bounds of possibility that he had some sort of memorial at Burton Lazars. In 1503, to enhance the majesty of the liturgy, William Sutton, rector of St Stephen, Walbrook, bequeathed 'an altar cloth of white damask richly embroidered' and 'a corporas case richly embroidered with verdure and a corporas in the same and also my best carpet containing in length three yards and in breadth a yard and a half'.[182] Verdure is a form of Flemish tapestry characterised by leaf decoration and the gift of a corporas case in this style was probably designed to compliment

---

[176] N.R. Whitcomb, *The Medieval Floor-Tiles of Leicestershire* (Leicester, 1956), p. 125; CA, Vincent Mss, 197, ff. 30, 39v; Nichols, *Leicestershire*, 2 pt 1, p. 278; J. Foster, *Some Feudal Coats of Arms* (1901, reprinted Bristol, 1984), pp. 51, 117, 177, 263, 268; the Greys and Zouches had contacts with the manor of Burton Lazars. Nichols, *Leicestershire*, 2 pt 1, p. 265.

[177] CA, Vincent Mss, 197, f. 30. One of the unidentified coats of arms from Eye Kettleby is *Argent, three locks sable*. Could this be a punning reference to the preceptory at Locko?

[178] *Ibid*, f. 39v.

[179] BL, Cart, f. 111. Simon de Montfort confirmed the pension of Robert, earl of Leicester, in 1233. For Alnwick Abbey's involvement with the cult, see *LP, 10, 1536*, p. 142. Alnwick was close to the Lazarite outpost at Harehope.

[180] R.C. Finucane, *Miracles and Pilgrims. Popular Beliefs in Medieval England* (London, Melbourne and Toronto, 1977), p. 133.

[181] *DNB, 13*, pp. 741–2.

[182] The 'carpet' is likely to have been a covering for the altar. CCA, Dcc, Reg F, f. 198 (William Sutton, 1503).

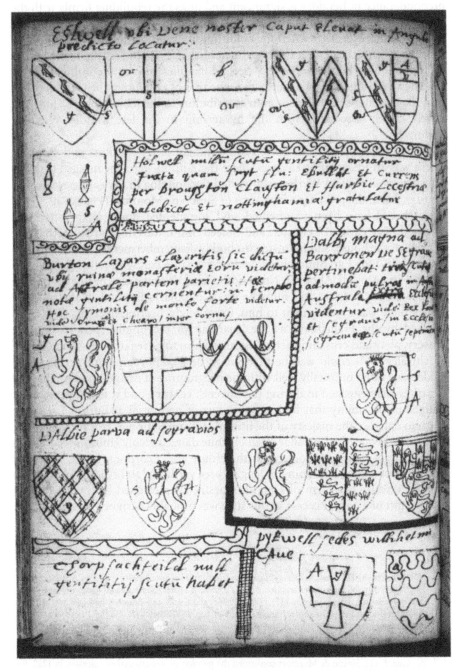

Plate 17: Three coats of arms (centre) associated with the collegiate church at Burton Lazars. Simon de Montfort, earl of Leicester (left); order of St Lazarus (centre), joined to Sutton (right). From the notebook of William Wyrley, Rouge Croix, c.1600.

the repeating leaf motifs in the architecture and enhance a sense of colour co-ordination.

By the late fifteenth century, therefore, Burton Lazars was firmly established as a college of chantry priests, under the leadership of an Arthurian-style 'redcrosse knight', maintaining a regular round of services for the souls of founders and benefactors in a setting of much-enhanced architectural magnificence.[183] In the context of Yorkist England's preoccupation with chivalry and liturgy, this was state-of-the-art. Sir William Sutton resigned in 1483, the same year as Lord Hastings' execution by Richard III, and he was replaced as master by a probable relative, George Sutton. Like Dover and Lynton before him, Sir William Sutton played an important part in moulding the development of the order in England, and his mastership in many ways represented a culmination of their efforts. Politically he had managed to translate a close alignment with the house of Lancaster into an equally firm bonding with the new house of York. Spiritually he had redefined the priorities of the order and brought it to the attention of a wider public by an ostentatious display of building and the development of new, evocative perceptions of the past.

This path to national autonomy had been long and hard and was punctuated by two bitter confrontations, the first prompted by a possible papal provisor and the second by an attempt on the part of the crown to nominate the masters of Burton Lazars and St Giles's. Both represented moves by outside agencies to command the wealth and patronage of the order in England when it was perceived to be weak because of internal feuds and the loss of a sense of direction. Yet both attempts were successfully resisted, and the English order managed to sustain an uneasy harmony with the authorities at Boigny until the early fifteenth century. But, for the master-general, the confidence won by the English brethren in these disputes, under the successful leadership of Dover and Lynton, was to have dire consequences, because it ultimately persuaded the province to break free and go its own, separate way. Ironically, the allies in this were the old adversaries of the fourteenth century, the papacy and the crown, who came to settle for financial contributions and administrative service rather than the direct control they had aspired to in the first instance.

It is surprising, perhaps, that such a small order as St Lazarus should have shown such spirit in the face of apparently overwhelming odds, but here the crusading traditions of the leper knights arguably stood it in good stead. Psychologically its militaristic instincts had become channelled into a taste for litigation. By 1420 the worst of its problems were over, and the order in England looked forward to a phase of its development which was very different from the pioneer years of the thirteenth century. Under Shriggley and Sir William Sutton the English Lazarites finally obtained privileges from the Pope guaranteeing their independence, and Sutton, by his construction of the collegiate church, set the final seal on these developments by creating a new focal point and religious ideology for them. What had remained constant in all of this was the Augus-

183 Riches, St George, pp. 175, 183–5, 186.

tinian dedication to the *opus Dei*, which continued to be at the core of the Lazarite vocation when much else had fallen away. When Innocent VIII ordered the amalgamation of the orders of St Lazarus and St John in Europe in 1489 the English branch had already been independent for ten years, *de iure* as well as *de facto*.

4

Land and Livelihood

The manor of Burton is in circuit six miles exceeding good ground,
both arable land, meadow and pasture
(Survey of Burton Lazars, 1563)

The outlying estates

Whatever debates were engaged in with regard to the paradox of a begging order administering an estate, there can be no doubt that these lands, once granted, were the property of the hospital in the Holy Land and that, in the first instance, the English brethren merely managed them as agents of the mother house. Their fundamental duty, in the early years, was to return an agreed measure of income from the province to their superiors, a relationship that was constantly subject to tension since the master-general was unable to rely on his estates in Palestine because of the ebb and flow of the Crusade. Similarly, for the order of St John this 'collection and transfer of funds . . . was from the start the *raison d'être* of the Hospitallers establishment in Europe'.[1] The vast majority of the provincial lands were in England, and though there were also holdings in Scotland, it appears that the Lazarites never established footholds in Wales or Ireland.[2]

In its capacity of land management the order of St Lazarus faced some major economic and political challenges. First, how to administer an estate that had grown up sporadically over a very wide area, often with small, isolated pockets of land. Second, how to exploit that estate given the changing economic climate of medieval England. Third, how to justify and utilise its income in view of the declining emphasis placed on crusading in the fourteenth and fifteenth centuries and the controversial loyalty of Boigny to the French royal house. The Hospitallers, with 'neutral' bases on Cyprus and Rhodes, did not face the last of these problems to quite the same extent, but the economic and managerial difficulties were certainly shared. Writing about monastic estates in Leicestershire at the time of the Dissolution, Jack has warned pessimistically that 'Very little can

---

[1] Gervers, *Hospitaller Cartulary*, p. lxviii.
[2] A. Gwynn and R.N. Hadcock, *Medieval Religious Houses. Ireland* (London, 1970). 'Dr Logan has found no evidence that any of the leper hospitals in Ireland belonged to the order of St Lazarus', p. 344. See also Lee, *Leper Hospitals*, p. 9. Lee quotes a letter from R.N. Hadcock expressing the curious conclusion that 'while he came across no evidence of the order having been there, he thought it most probable that some of the leper-houses were of this order'.

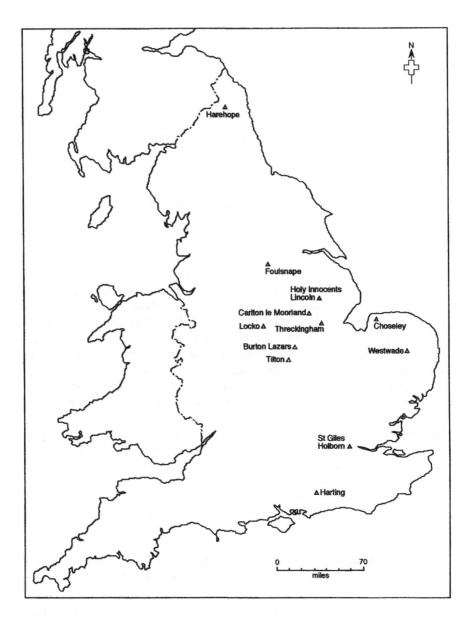

Map 5: Hospitals and preceptories.

be said of Burton Lazars. The long list of villages . . . in which it held small rents suggests that its property was not very concentrated.'[3] The statement is partly true. The order did, indeed, hold a good deal of dispersed land. But it also consolidated a valuable demesne at Burton Lazars, which stood it in good stead until the time of the suppression.

The response to the administrative challenge, at least before 1350, rested on a series of preceptories, or hospitals, of which Burton Lazars was the chief (Map 5). These preceptories might be specially established with an economic and managerial aim in view (for example, Choseley), or they might take advantage of an institution for the care of the sick that already existed and had been granted to the order (for example, Harehope). In all there were 11 of these stretching the length of the country, from Harehope in Northumberland to Harting in Sussex, though with a notable concentration in the East Midlands and East Anglia. Not all were functioning at the same time. In the thirteenth century, for example, Harting was disposed of and St Giles's, Holborn, was gained, making the picture a very variable one over the four hundred years of the order's existence. Gilchrist has demonstrated that these smaller houses of the military orders are an ambiguous and under-researched set of institutions.[4] Terminology wavers between 'preceptory', 'camera' and 'grange', and for the Lazarites the picture is further complicated by the fact that some doubled up as 'hospitals' in the true sense of the word. Basically they functioned as central points for the production and distribution of agricultural produce, the larger ones displaying some of the characteristics of manorial complexes but the smaller ones having more in common with farms.[5]

The order probably developed six of these outposts to manage specific packages of property under the authority of Burton Lazars – Harehope for the northern estates; Locko for Derbyshire; Choseley for Norfolk; Carlton or Threckingham for Lincolnshire; Foulsnape for Yorkshire and, after 1299, St Giles's for London. It is likely that some houses (for example, Tilton and Westwade) never had a managerial function in terms of the estates of the order. The pattern has all the hallmarks of random development rather than the planned expansion which characterised larger orders such as the Cistercians and Templars. St Giles's, since it was a substantial independent foundation, always enjoyed a special status and had its own seal (see Plate 11), but the other preceptories were more ephemeral and could be expanded and contracted at the whim of the master of Burton as economic forces dictated. This created a particular problem when a unit of land management overlapped with an institution for the care of the sick (as at Carlton-le-Moorland), and the economic ambitions of the Lazarites ran into conflict with the more altruistic objectives of founders.

With the exception of Burton Lazars, only two houses have left clear evidence on the landscape – Harehope and Tilton. In 1955 it was believed that the buildings at Harehope were 'too fragmentary and spoiled to be surveyable', though a large stone cistern is still a highly visible feature. Some thirteenth- and

3   Jack, 'Monastic Lands', p. 11.
4   Gilchrist, *Contemplation and Action*, pp. 87–93.
5   *Ibid*, pp. 70, 74, 101, 105.

Plate 18: Choseley Manor, Norfolk, possibly the site of a preceptory of the order
of St Lazarus. A nineteenth-century house (in the foreground) has been built up
against an older structure, possibly with medieval origins.

fourteenth-century worked stone windows and a doorway at nearby Eglingham
Hall, which Hodgson viewed in 1893, are reputed to have come from the site.[6] At
Tilton there is no hint of structural remains, just earthworks, suggesting that it
may have been even more short-lived than Harehope. This is probably true,
because it was too close to Burton Lazars to give it much independent viability
after its initial purpose as a base for the leper brothers had been fulfilled. Since
the surviving features are in the parish of Cold Newton, not Tilton-on-the-Hill,
it is not generally conceded that they constitute 'Tilton Hospital', though it is
difficult to see what else they could be if that attribution is not upheld. Topographical references to 'the Spital Field at Tilton Newton' and 'the North Field of
the Spital' would appear to be suggestive of its true function.[7] At Choseley there
is a house that probably dates from soon after the Dissolution, though there is a
possibility that this is associated with a portion of the estate, Willy's Manor, not
owned by Burton Lazars (Plate 18). Nevertheless, archaeological finds of pottery
and human skeletal remains confirm pre-Domesday settlement, and the presence of a chapel suggests a degree of interaction between the owner of the house
and the small secular community that lived near it.[8] Faint landscape imprints

6   Hodgson, 'Hospital of St Lazarus'; Northumberland County Council, SMR ID 3618.
7   Nichols, *Leicestershire*, 3 pt 1, p. 349.
8   Norfolk Landscape Archaeology, SMR 21554 (Choseley Farm, Choseley); Burton Lazars Research
    Group, *The Preceptory of the Order of St Lazarus at Choseley* (2000). Willy's Manor, comprising 600
    acres, was the portion of Choseley not given to Burton Lazars by Walter Gifford, earl of Buckingham.

can be discerned at Locko and Carlton-le-Moorland; but at Foulsnape, Harting, Westwade, Threckingham, Holy Innocents', Lincoln and St Giles's, Holborn, no physical trace appears to have survived.[9]

What several of these smaller houses share with Burton is an isolated hilltop position, location near a parish boundary or within an extra-parochial enclave and proximity to major road junctions and water supplies. They were, essentially, liminal spots. All of the evidence derived from the landscape, particularly at Locko, suggests that in form they were similar to the small Templar preceptory at South Witham, Lincolnshire, the excavation of which by Mayes between 1965 and 1967 enables us to gain an impression of the location of key buildings such as a hall, chapel, gatehouse and barns.[10] These arrangements were more typical of a manor than a monastery, and they are replicated at the Lazarite preceptory of Grattemont in Normandy, indicative that the order did not differ significantly from the Templars in this respect.[11] It is clear that there were free-standing chapels at St Giles's, Holy Innocents', Locko and Choseley, which must have provided them with some status in the pecking order of daughter houses, but others may have been closer to Temple Manor at Stroud, Kent, where chapel and hall were merged into one.[12] These smaller houses were governed by a resident 'preceptor' or 'master' who was accountable for their management and income under the master of Burton.

A clear administrative picture is obtained at Locko, where in 1291 the preceptor was responsible for enclosed manors at Spondon and Locko, rented lands, stock, a windmill, the collection of assize rents and the management of a court. All of this brought in £5 6s 10d *per annum*, but he was also probably charged with the collection of the rectorial tithes of Spondon parish valued at a handsome £33 6s 8d.[13] This compact estate was administered from the Locko preceptory, which was located, typically, near a crossroads and parish boundary and comprised a moated feature, outbuildings and fishponds (see Plan 1). There was a chapel dedicated to St Mary Magdalene and a spring known locally as St Ann's Well, so the spiritual welfare of the resident brethren, and indeed of passing travellers, was not ignored.[14] According to the *Taxatio*, the preceptory accounted for £38 13s 6d, but it is likely that the rectory alone could have been worth as much as double that figure, which, if extended to the lands also, would provide a 'real' income of £77 7s. Out of this the preceptor would be expected to deduct the running costs of the estate, leaving a net income of, say, £60 *per annum*. On the estates of the Hospitallers it was customary for local commanderies to return a third of their net income to the mother house as a *responsium*, and Templar preceptories followed the same practice with their

9 For Locko, see Marcombe, 'Locko', pp. 51–63.

10 'South Witham', *Current Archaeology*, 9 (July 1968), pp. 232–7; Gilchrist, *Contemplation and Action*, pp. 69, 81–6.

11 For an excellent case study, from the Templar estates, see E. Gooder, *Temple Balsall: the Warwickshire preceptory of the Templars and their fate* (Chichester, 1995).

12 Gilchrist, *Contemplation and Action*, pp. 87–90.

13 *Taxatio*, pp. 246, 264.

14 Marcombe, 'Locko', pp. 51–63; G. Turbutt, *A History of Derbyshire*, 2 (Cardiff, 1999), pp. 800–3.

confrariae.[15] It appears that a similar custom prevailed on the estates of St Lazarus, since in 1347 Locko was stated to owe an annual *apportum* of £20 to Boigny.[16] The circumstances of this payment are somewhat unusual because of the rift between Hugh Michel and the Burton Lazars community, but, nevertheless, it probably reflects what was generally expected from Locko in the thirteenth century, effectively a third of its net income.

Harehope too was situated at a crossroads near a parish boundary.[17] Hannah's Well, which appears in later sources, may well be a post-Reformation corruption of an earlier name, perhaps St Ann's Well, providing another echo of Locko. A *Quo Warranto* inquest of 1292 indicates that the master of Harehope claimed rights in 15 Northumberland townships, though it would appear that the holdings of the order in all of these places were small.[18] One of his tasks was the management of the estates in Scotland. These may once have been quite extensive, but their administration was complicated by the circumstances of the war of independence and its aftermath. Before 1153 David I had granted lands at Spitalton and St Giles's Grange, Edinburgh, and in addition to this the order owned land at Linlithgow and Elgin.[19] Spottiswoode has claimed that the hospital of St Mary Magdalene, Linlithgow, was 'formerly governed by the Lazarites' and that 'Lanark belonged likewise to this sect'.[20] Easson, however, has found no evidence to back either of these claims. In fact, he points out that the Edinburgh land was granted by Robert II (1371–90) to his son John, earl of Carrick, in 1376, and it is likely that the other Scottish estates suffered a similar fate at about the same time, or before.[21]

For Harehope, a unique contract has survived from 1308 between Sir Adam Veau, master of Burton Lazars, and Roger de Robeby, chaplain, granting him supervision of 'our houses in the borders of Northumberland and the kingdom of Scotland up to the end of his life'.[22] The preceptory, which was evidently in debt because of the circumstances of the Anglo-Scottish war, was obliged to contribute 10 marks [£6 13s 4d] *per annum* to Burton Lazars, but only in times of peace. During the term of his office, Robeby was to strive to pay off all existing debts within five years and he was not to behave in a way that challenged the prerogatives of the master of Burton. He was not empowered to admit brethren or sisters to the order; he could not sell any of the lands or goods of the preceptory without consent; and he was specifically prohibited from taking

15 Gervers, *Hospitaller Cartulary*, p. lxviii; Gilchrist, *Contemplation and Action*, p. 65.
16 *CCR, 1346–49*, p. 338.
17 UNCLH, J.M. Allsop, 'Site notes and interpretation of the earthworks of Harehope Hospital in the parish of Eglingham, Northumberland', MFR, 01/02 (2001).
18 Hodgson, 'Hospital of St Lazarus', p. 78. The townships were Ditchburn, Mitford, Newbiggin-by-the-Sea, Bewick, Eglingham, Charlton, Shipley, Warenford, Lanton, Branton, Brandon, Hedgley, Wooperton, Titlington and Crawley.
19 Barrow, *Regista Regum Scottorum*, 2, pp. 116–17; D.E. Easson, *Medieval Religious Houses. Scotland* (1957, 2nd edition, I.B. Cowan and D.E. Easson, London, 1976), pp. 161, 163.
20 J. Spottiswoode, *An Account of all the Religious Houses that were in Scotland at the time of the Reformation*, included in R. Keith, *An Historical Catalogue of the Scottish Bishops* (Edinburgh, 1824), pp. 467, 477.
21 J.M. Thomson (ed.), *Registrum Magni Sigilli Regum Scottorum, 1306–1424* (Edinburgh, 1912), p. 213; Easson, *Medieval Religious Houses. Scotland*, pp. 150, 162–3.
22 GRO, Berkeley Castle Muniments, J7/67/02/001/00/00 (MF 1354).

timber from Harehope Wood other than for repairs to the buildings or as fuel for the kitchen. If the same rule is applied to Harehope as Locko, a contribution of £6 13s 4d would translate into an annual net income of about £20. When the *Valor Ecclesiasticus* was drawn up, however, this exclusively Northumbrian estate was valued at only £2 13s 4d and a little later, in 1538/9, Sir Thomas Hilton, farmer of the dissolved priory of Tynemouth, accounted for £1 of yearly rent payable by the master, Dr Thomas Legh, for the lordship and lands there.[23] These figures would suggest that a very considerable portion of the income of the preceptory had been lost after 1308, and most of these losses would appear to have been in Scotland. Harehope was therefore significantly less successful than Locko in economic terms. Not only was much of its estate simply wiped out by changing political circumstances, it also had to contend with low land values in Northumberland, which was constantly subject to the impact of wars with Scotland and the unwelcome attention of border reivers. It was also more dispersed and without the benefit of lucrative spiritualities, and conscientious masters must have expended a good deal of energy in the supervision of this fragmented little estate, high in the Cheviots.

Despite the problems of Harehope, consolidated estates were comparatively easy to manage, but a difficulty arose where extraneous fragments lay between the boundaries of two accounting centres. A classic problem area was Northamptonshire, where the small estates of the order were inconveniently placed for easy rent collection from either Burton or Choseley. In order to avoid the problem of wasted journeys, it was specified in the lease of a toft to the hospital of St Leonard, Northampton, in 1301/2 that if the annual rent of 1s failed to be paid 'the brother or messenger sent to collect the rent shall be ministered to at the expense of the said master and brethren of the said hospital [i.e. St Leonard's] until the farm be fully paid'.[24] Not far away at Clopton the order enjoyed an annual rent charge of 2s by grant of one Walter Moyne in 1225. However, in about 1317 his descendants ceased to pay, so that by 1329 arrears of £1 4s had built up. Although the matter came to court, the master failed to prosecute his case when a jury was summoned – less a comment on his rights, perhaps, as on the inconvenience of some of these small and isolated benefits enjoyed by the order.[25]

One pocket of land that was probably more useful than most was the tenement in Kings Lynn known as Lazar Hill, held by the order as early as 1271. Nearby was a row of houses on Dampgate, adjacent to the Milneflet, giving access to the Ouse and the sea.[26] Kings Lynn was the only seaport in which the Lazarites had a foothold before 1299, and because of this it may have served a similar function to Barletta, conveniently placed for the distribution of resources from the East Midland and East Anglian estates. Indeed, rationalisation was to be

23 *Valor*, 4, p. 153; Hodgson, 'Hospital of St Lazarus', p. 79.

24 J.C. Cox, *The Records of the Borough of Northampton*, 2 (Northampton, 1898), p. 330.

25 PRO, JUST 1/633, m.85d; copied in Bod Lib, Ms Top Northants C 18, f. 168; D.W. Sutherland (ed.), *Eyre of Northamptonshire, 3–4 Edward III*, SS, 98 (1983), pp. 567–8.

26 Parkin, *Norfolk*, 8, pp. 493–4; Rutledge, 'Kings Lynn and Great Yarmouth', pp. 94, 108; Owen, *Making of Kings Lynn*, pp. 186–7.

Plate 19: The preceptory at Burton Lazars surrounded by vestiges of ridge and furrow, the features accentuated by a light dusting of snow.

a major theme of Lazarite land management, and it was to be demonstrated in a willingness to rent land, in order to consolidate particular holdings, as well as abandoning it if it was considered utterly impractical. As early as the twelfth century the order was renting land at South Croxton, Leicestershire, from Malton Priory, and by 1535 it was a tenant of three further religious institutions and also of the king for land in Spondon.[27] Odd leases of other lands have survived in the archives of the British Library.[28]

The Burton Lazars demesne

This policy of consolidation was most evident at the great preceptory of Burton formed around the two carucates granted by Roger de Mowbray in the mid-twelfth century (Plate 19). Brown has argued that the village layout at Burton Lazars and its units of tenure are basically Saxon, perhaps dating from the period c.950–975.[29] Certainly at the time of the Conquest not all of the parish was under the plough. However, the expansion of population in the twelfth century created a need for more land, and in response to this the open fields expanded into less fertile areas, making possible the land grants that religious houses such as Burton and Vaudey Abbey received there. At this period Burton Lazars comprised two open fields encompassing about 2,800 acres. The preceptory was located on a 50-acre site deliberately carved out from the area under cultivation. Although the order received extensive land grants in Leicestershire, and particularly in Burton Lazars and Melton Mowbray, these were not always ideally placed for the sort of consolidated estate that ecclesiastical landlords hoped for. Accordingly, a policy of sale and exchange was embarked upon. Some of the properties obtained in this way were specifically stated to be 'towards the courtyard of the said brethren' or 'laying outside the gate of the brethren', giving them a clear context in relation to the preceptory.[30]

In about 1248 the master Terry de Alemanius, with the agreement of the chapter, took the decision to sell the outlying estate and hospital at Harting, Sussex, to Dureford Abbey for £80, the money to be applied to the purchase of other lands.[31] Abbot Valentine of Dureford had ambitions to extend the possessions of his house, and as an adjunct to the purchase of Harting he also took steps to buy out the interest of the St Lazarus tenants, the most important of which was Shulbred Priory. Although he encountered difficulties with the feudal lord, Walter de Upton, who disapproved of his ambitious schemes, the abbot's

---

[27] BL, Cotton Mss, Claudius D xi, f. 217. The other institutions were Westminster Abbey, Kirby Bellars Priory and St John's Hospital, Northampton. In all £3 6s 10d was paid out in rent in 1535. *Valor*, 4, p. 153.

[28] BL, Add Chart, 33635; Cart, f. 119.

[29] A.E. Brown, 'Burton Lazars, Leicestershire: a planned medieval landscape?', *Landscape History*, 18 (1996), pp. 31–45.

[30] BL, Cart, ff. 56, 70; see also ff. 21, 30, 32, 44, 46, 48, 49, 51, 54, 65, 101, 250.

[31] BL, Cotton Mss, Vespasian E xxiii, f. 57v; *VCH, Sussex*, 2 (1907, reprinted London, 1973), p. 103; Blaauw, 'Dureford Abbey', pp. 58–9. Similarly, in the early thirteenth century the order sold a toft in Newark to William de Tolney, burgess. C.W. Foster (ed.), *Registrum Antiquissimum*, 3, LRS, 29 (1935), p. 258.

plea was upheld by the justices at Lewes and the bargain held good.[32] There is no clue as to how the proceeds of the sale were spent, but it is significant that they came at the peak of an acrimonious competition between the Lazarites and the Cistercian monks of Vaudey Abbey for economic supremacy in Burton Lazars. The monks possessed a grange and a considerable estate at Burton, and as early as 1216 exchanges of land had been negotiated between the two orders.[33] However, by 1235 some tension had entered the relationship since it was stated that no new enclosures were to be set up in the open fields without the consent of both parties.[34] Fresh arrangements concerning houses and lands were made in 1254 and 1260, but both sides were prepared to admit that 'many disagreements have arisen between them'.[35]

So intense had these become by 1264 that Bishop Richard de Gravesend of Lincoln (1258–79) was called in to arbitrate. It was decided that in the event of a conflict the injured party should approach the other and make known his complaint 'in a friendly manner and either by themselves or with judgement of good men, transgression should be corrected within a month'. If these sober counsels did not prevail, the earl of Leicester could be called upon to levy a fine of £5 on the offender, who, if a religious person, was to be corrected by his superiors, or, if a layman, removed from the service of his house.[36] This was at least an improvement on the arbitrary and violent behaviour of some members of the aristocracy, and it seems to have defused the worst of the tension, possibly because the age of expansion was drawing to a close in any case. By 1276 the order had doubled its stake in Burton to four carucates, but it still only commanded half of the territory of Vaudey.[37] However, when surrounding parishes such as Melton Mowbray, Kirby Bellars and Great Dalby are taken into account – and none of these was very far from the preceptory for the purposes of management – the Lazarite estate was by far the greater of the two. Nevertheless, it was only at Burton that the order appears to have followed an active and sometimes aggressive policy of building up a consolidated holding immediately adjacent to its preceptory.

This, of course, raises the important question of how the Burton estate was managed and what it was actually used for. There is no evidence from either Burton Lazars or St Giles's to support the existence of a managerial structure of obedientiaries that reflected that of the larger monasteries. Lazarite administration was more *ad hoc*, with extensive use of 'proctors' or 'messengers' to undertake specific tasks under the authority of the master.[38] Brother John Paris, robbed of £3 by Eustace and Laurence de Folville when they were 'riding with an armed force against the king's peace' in 1332/33, was fulfilling just such a role, possibly collecting rents at Spondon or transferring money to Burton

32 BL, Cotton Mss, Vespasian E xxiii, ff. 58, 61, 73v; Blaauw, 'Dureford Abbey', pp. 58–9.
33 BL, Cart, ff. 60, 62.
34 *Ibid*, f. 59.
35 *Ibid*, f. 64; Nichols, *Leicestershire*, 2 pt 1, p. 274.
36 BL, Cart, f. 61.
37 *Rot Hund*, 1, p. 240.
38 *CLR, 1240–45*, p. 285.

Plate 20: Twelfth-century lease of land at Wymondham, Norfolk, from Robert, son of Hugh, prior of the hospital of St Lazarus, to Alice, wife of Ralph de Chare.

Lazars.[39] In quieter moments, regular business was carried out in the chapter house at Burton and validated by the use of beeswax and resin seals. The order of St Lazarus used an unusually wide array of these, and the fact that many of them have survived, as matrices, modern casts or contemporary impressions, enables us to piece together a picture of administrative priorities. The seals have the additional benefit of introducing us to the iconography deemed important by the order – in other words, the messages it wished to convey to the world – and also the quality of engraving it was prepared to commission. The earliest example, quite distinctive in form, is dated to c.1150 and is attached to a grant of land at Wymondham, Norfolk (Plate 20).[40] The seal, which may relate to the hospital in Jerusalem rather than the English province, is a vesica showing a plain cross with crescents in the top two quarters and stars in the bottom ones. If this was indeed a seal used by the lepers of Jerusalem, it was not long before the English brethren gained a device of their own.

By the early thirteenth century there was a provincial common seal, circular in shape and showing a cleric in vestments holding a leper's clapper in his right hand.[41] Unfortunately, the only impression of this is imperfect and the matrix

39 W.H. Stevenson (ed.), *Middleton Mss*, HMC (London, 1911), p. 278.
40 LRO, DE2242/5.
41 PRO, E 327/50; R.H. Ellis, *Catalogue of Seals in the Public Record Office, Monastic Seals*, 1 (London, 1986), p. 15.

Plate 21: The common seal of the order of St Lazarus of Jerusalem
in England. The central figure (probably a brother of the order)
holds a book and a clapper and is flanked by the arms of the
order (right) and those of the Mowbrays (left).

must have been lost, stolen or destroyed because by 1351 another version had
been generated (Plate 21). It is not difficult to imagine the common seal being a
target for the ambitions of both sides during the troubled years of the mid-fourteenth century. The new circular seal, which is very similar to its predecessor,
displays a sexfoil within which stands the tubby demi-figure of a tonsured cleric
with two small crosses above his shoulders.[42] Another cross is suspended around
his neck, similar to the collars worn by the figures at Grattemont. In his right
hand he holds a clapper and in his left a closed book. Also within the sexfoil are
two shields, one showing the lion rampant of the Mowbrays, the other the plain
cross of St Lazarus, and the initials BZ, presumably signifying Burton Lazars. The
inscription reads S'COMMUNE: ORDINIS: MILICIE: HOSPITALIS: SCI: LAZARI: DE:
BORTONE. The fact that the same seal crops up again in 1515 proves that it had a
long life, probably serving the order right up to the Dissolution.[43]

The purpose of the common seal was to validate the most important transac-

---

42 PRO, E 329/334; BL, Seal lxvi 47; W. de G. Birch, *Catalogue of Seals in the Department of Manuscripts in
the British Museum*, 1 (London, 1887), no. 2789.
43 PRO, E 329/334; Ellis, *Catalogue of Seals*, 1, p. 15.

Plate 22: The seal of the preceptory of Burton Lazars. St Lazarus
of Bethany delivers a blessing, while a brother of the order prays
in a niche below.

tions, and as a piece of iconography it made some firm statements about the
aims and aspirations of the order. It is likely that the clerical figure on the seal
represents a brother rather than St Lazarus himself, because on this occasion the
omission of the episcopal regalia, commonplace on the confraternity seals, is
surely significant.[44] He holds objects symbolic of his monastic and
intercessionary vocation – a clapper and a book. The clapper is especially interesting and its relevance has been discussed by Touati and Satchell. Touati is
convinced that in the early period, at least, it was symbolic of the religious vocation; but Satchell, in more practical vein, has asked 'were these signals to solicit
alms or warn off the healthy?'[45] If the clapper was indeed a religious symbol and

---

[44] See Chapter 6, pp. 189, 192–3.
[45] Touati, *Maladie et Société*, pp. 417–20; Satchell, 'Leper-Houses', p. 166.

a call to alms giving, its presence on the common seal must have been a carefully selected detail designed to inspire the generosity of the faithful. Similarly, the arms of the Mowbrays were a reminder of aristocratic patronage and the crusaders' cross recalled noble deeds of arms. Neither the seals of the Templars nor the Hospitallers speak so eloquently of their perceived role in society, and this mix of imagery must have been designed to make an unambiguous statement to the patrons on whom the order depended for land grants and financial support.[46]

In the sixteenth century another seal appears bearing the inscription SIGILLU: DOM: BORTO: SCANTI: LAZARI, suggesting that it applied to the preceptory of Burton Lazars alone (Plate 22).[47] This example, which survives only in the form of a modern impression from a matrix, is oval and has the central device of a bishop, probably St Lazarus, seated on a canopied throne, his right hand raised in benediction and his left holding a pastoral staff. Under the bishop's feet there is a small figure beneath a plain canopy, his arms raised in prayer, a characterisation, perhaps, of the intercessionary role of Burton Lazars during the last phase of its existence. Also from the later fifteenth or early sixteenth centuries privy seals have survived for two masters, Sir George Sutton and Sir Thomas Norton. Sutton's seal shows St Giles as an abbot with a wounded hind leaping up to him;[48] Norton's shows a St Julian's cross.[49] These seals did not carry the same weight as the institutional seals and were designed to execute business over which the master was deemed to have personal jurisdiction. But, as with the common seal, both were deeply symbolic. St Giles was a popular hospital dedication, especially for those concerned with leprosy, and the tale of the holy hermit and the wounded hind was well known.[50] St Julian the Hospitaller is less frequently met with in England, but *The Golden Legend* recounted the apocryphal story of a young nobleman who was charitable to the poor and to lepers.[51] What better symbolism for a knightly master steeped in a late-medieval world of myth, chivalry and romance?

If the formal business of the chapter house was the preserve of the professed brethren, a whole range of lesser functionaries was required to ensure that more mundane matters ran smoothly. To this end, secular servants, such as Thomas de Bybir, gatekeeper at Burton in 1284, or Richard Cook, cook at St Giles's in 1321, were supported on semi-permanent contracts. Both men received leases as part of their emoluments, and Bybir also qualified for a livery of a loaf of bread and a cooked meal each day.[52] But the most revealing information about the establishment at Burton Lazars comes from the lay subsidy, or poll-tax, return of 1381, which included secular servants of the house, though not professed brethren. In

46   P.D.A. Harvey and A. McGuiness, *A Guide to British Medieval Seals* (London, 1996), p. 102.
47   BL, Seal D.CH. 37; Birch, *Catalogue of Seals*, 1, no. 2795.
48   *Ibid*, nos. 3512–15.
49   LRO, 10D34/123. Norton also used the leaping hind motif, which was probably specifically connected with the mastership of St Giles's. Birch, *Catalogue of Seals*, 1, nos. 3516–18.
50   Farmer, *Saints*, pp. 205–6.
51   *Ibid*, pp. 273–4.
52   PRO, JUST 1/462 m.15; BL, Harl Mss, 4015, f. 177b. Bybir complained that he had been unlawfully deprived of his livery by the master. Cook received what must have been a very favourable lease of two shops in Holborn, for his life and that of his wife, for 6s *per annum*, the first two years being rent free.

this document four men are specifically stated as being in the service of the master: a shepherd, servant, clerk and *cognatus*. However, this might not represent the full complement of the preceptory by any means. In other parts of the return it is clear that the enumerator recorded household members in succession to one another. At Burton Lazars, for example, Joan Auntel, farmer, is followed by Henry 'her servant' and Sarah 'her maid'. If we take the first name clearly connected with the preceptory (John, the master's shepherd) and the last (John, the master's *cognatus*), thirteen names separate them: four ploughmen, three labourers, one shepherd, one husbandman, one tailor, one servant, one clerk and one unidentified individual. Indeed, the name immediately before that of the master's shepherd is that of William Laughton, cook, and there might be a strong argument for associating such an occupation with the preceptory too. In other words, we could well be looking at a secular staff of at least sixteen, six employed in an administrative and service capacity and a further ten working on the land.[53]

In the lay subsidy of 1524 there were twelve men assessed on wages alone at Burton Lazars (i.e. labourers and servants), but it is impossible to associate these specifically with the hospital. However, in a return of men liable for military service in 1539 'the place of Burton Lazars' (i.e. the preceptory) returned eight, 'servants to Dr Legh'.[54] These estate servants comprised the *famuli*, a common feature on the lands of the Templars and Hospitallers. There is little indication of their ethos and material culture, but Gilchrist has commented that where archaeological evidence has survived for other military orders it is illustrative of activities such as hunting, hawking and feasting. In other words, these were secular and homosocial communities and the small finds associated with them seem to be more typical of castles than monasteries.[55] The degree of manpower suggested by the Burton Lazars *famuli* would argue for a substantial demesne estate directly managed from Burton, a point which fits well with the moves towards consolidation in the thirteenth century, but conflicts with the practice of the Hospitallers who were placing growing emphasis on the collection of rents rather than on direct farming.[56]

---

53 PRO, E 179/133/34, m.3, c.1 (Farnham, 1, pp. 260–1); C.E. Fenwick (ed.), *The Poll Taxes of 1377, 1379 and 1381, pt 1, Bedfordshire-Lincolnshire*, Records of Social and Economic History, new series, 27 (Oxford, 1998), pp. 591–2. Another peculiarity of the 1381 return is the presence at Burton Lazars of Thomas o'the Castell and Peter del Castel. Was the preceptory known locally as 'the castle'? Some substance for this theory is provided by the survival, in the nineteenth century, of an oral tradition that suggested that the site of the preceptory was 'the remains of a fortified camp and that they had been used, if not thrown up, in war time. They also tell us that there must have been a skirmish (we will not say battle) here.' W.B. Twowell, *Leicestershire Village History, Past and Present, 1, Burton Lazars* (Melton Mowbray, 1882), pp. 160–1.

54 Farnham, 1, p. 264; *LP, 14*, p. 275. Allowing for the fact that some servants of the preceptory might have been deemed unfit for military service, the number of people employed there may have fallen, slightly since 1381. The men returned in 1539 were Henry Hertwell, Henry Foxe, William Chambers, John Peynton, Richard Smyth, Nicholas Lowes, Robert Webster and Robert Diccon. With the exception of Diccon, all were classed as archers. PRO, SP 1/145, f. 26d.

55 Gilchrist, *Contemplation and Action*, p. 105.

56 Gervers, *Hospitaller Cartulary*, p. lxix. On the other hand, Wolsey's valuation of 1526 states that only £2 of temporalities were held as demesne. This compares with £6 at Kirby Bellars, a house with a much smaller income. Salter, *Lincoln Subsidy*, p. 120.

The question of land use is difficult to determine, but certainly there is consistent evidence for an interest in livestock, particularly sheep, the presence of which is indicated at Burton by the two shepherds noted in 1381. All of the religious houses of Leicestershire invested heavily in wool, and Melton Mowbray was a well-known centre of the trade, with local merchants, such as Walter Prest, who occupied lands in Burton Lazars, making fortunes in the thirteenth century by way of exports from Boston and Hull.[57] Although the pasture lands of Burton provided grazing close at hand, it is likely that the order also made use of sheep runs on outlying estates, such as Billesdon and Cold Newton. Newton had grazing for one hundred sheep, and a lease of a bovate at Billesdon in 1257 specifically reserved the pasture for the sheep of the order.[58] From these estates sheep could easily be moved to Burton for shearing and sorting. The earthworks on site would seem to confirm this, because several of the enclosures appear to relate to the management and watering of livestock. Moreover, a wide trackway, or 'drove road', leaves the preceptory to connect with Sandy Lane and thence to Melton Mowbray.

Brown suggests that by the early fourteenth century the area of arable land at Burton was contracting, the first parts to be returned to grass being those newly colonised in the twelfth century.[59] This would suggest an increase in the volume of livestock rearing, a view confirmed by a growing number of references to enclosures – and their associated social problems – in the sixteenth century. In 1553 the duke of Northumberland's lease of the former Lazarite demesnes to Henry Alicock mentions the 'new close', 'a close . . . lately enclosed by Thomas Legh, knight' and 'the ditches lately made by command of the said duke'. Moreover, Alicock might be required to provide 500 fat sheep and 30 fat oxen for the duke's household in lieu of rent.[60] In the late sixteenth century a series of depositions, taken in the context of a dispute among members of the Hartopp family, confirms the extent to which the former hospital lands were a notable breeding ground for 'great cattle' and sheep. These animals were periodically driven to London to be sold, and, though the size of the flocks is not specified, between 1,200 and 1,300 sheep were stated to have died on one occasion because of 'the rot'.[61] It is likely that the Elizabethan Hartopps were continuing in a tradition long established by the order of St Lazarus and that this trend had intensified during the period of Sir Thomas Legh's mastership.

In 1563 figures for the former Lazarite estate in Leicestershire suggest that only a third of it was arable, and for the former Burton Lazars demesne, more specifically, a little over a half was under the plough.[62] A terrier of 1700, copied

57 Nichols, *Leicestershire*, 2 pt 1, p. 266. Burton Lazars, however, does not figure in the trading records of Prest, neither is it recorded among the religious houses that sold their wool directly to Italian merchants.

58 BL, Cart, ff.155, 176, 198, 248. At Carlton-le-Moorland there was pasture for 60 sheep, 9 animals, 2 horses and 10 pigs. Sheep must also have been important to the economy of the Harehope preceptory where the land was suitable for little else. Cart, f. 248.

59 Brown, 'Burton Lazars', p. 44.

60 *CPR, 1554–55*, pp. 318–19.

61 PRO, E 134/37 Eliz 1/Trin 10.

62 PRO, E 326/12927. For the situation in Leicestershire in 1563, see n. 72.

Table 4: Land use on the Burton Lazars demesne, c.1552–3

Land use	Area in acres
Arable	588.375
Pasture	469.75
Unidentified	57.5
Total	1115.625

Source: A. E. Brown, 'Burton Lazars, Leicestershire: a planned
medieval landscape?', *Landscape History*, 18 (1996), p. 36.

from an 'old rental or survey' probably dating from 1552–3, provides the break-down of the former hospital lands at Burton indicated in Table 4. At the time of the Tithe Award, in 1845, 62 per cent of the parish of Burton Lazars was still under pasture, indicating that, proportionally, land usage had remained constant since the sixteenth century, even if specific fields and closes might have changed their function along the way.[63] Although the survey of 1552–3 provides a fair reflection of land use at the time of the Dissolution, it takes no account of the topographical changes initiated by four hundred years of Lazarite land management. By the early sixteenth century consolidation of holdings and enclosure, most strongly represented on Burton's ecclesiastical estates, had all but put an end to the common field system. Working from the Burton Lazars and Woodford cartularies, and linking these up with evidence from the Tithe Award, Brown has reconstructed a remarkably full picture of field boundaries in the parish of Burton Lazars on the eve of the Dissolution (Map 6).[64] Since these correspond almost exactly with the lands owned by the Hartopps and the diocese of Ely in the nineteenth century, it is likely that they formed the core of the Lazarite demesne. As Brown has concluded, 'The effect of this was in the end, and probably finally around the time of the Dissolution, to produce a zone of early enclosed fields.'[65]

One of the difficulties implicit in Table 4 is that the acreages represent the position at Burton Lazars *after* the exchange of the Vaudey Abbey lands had been finalised in 1536, bringing to an end many years of competition between the two religious houses.[66] In other words, the order only enjoyed this extensive estate, based on Vaudey Grange, for the last eight years of its existence. Prior to 1536 the Lazarite stake in Burton was much smaller, probably about half of what it eventually came to own. It is difficult now to separate the 'core' estate of pre-1536 from the 'extended' estate of post-1536 since the documentation is much stronger for the latter than for the former. But there are indications from both that suggest that some portions were retained in demesne and others rented out on lease. Because of their ephemeral nature, leases, across the whole estate, have survived much less commonly than land grants, but for the early thirteenth

---

63 LRO, DE746/5.
64 BL, Cart; Cotton Mss, Claudius A xiii (Woodford Cartulary); LRO, DE746/5.
65 Brown, 'Burton Lazars', p. 34.
66 *SR*, 3 pt 2, 28 Hen VIII, c.42, pp. 701–3. See Chapter 7, p. 220.

Map 6: Burton Lazars, c. 1520.

century there are two, though they both relate to lands some distance away from Burton Lazars. For the master Osbert de Stanford there is a lease of a virgate in Upton, Sussex, to Thomas Gorie;[67] and for Terry de Alemanius a lease of half a virgate in Offord D'Arcy, Huntingdonshire, to John de Sok.[68] Conditions varied significantly. Though no term of years is mentioned in either case, Gorie paid 7s *per annum* for his virgate, while Sok paid only a little less, 6s 6d, for half as much land. The difference between the leases was that Gorie paid an entry fine of 3½ marks [£2 6s 8d], which presumably justified his lower rent. Both tenants were expected to pay in two annual instalments due at Easter and Michaelmas. It is likely that this flexible approach, balancing rents against entry fines, was

67 BL, Cotton Mss, Vespasian E xxiii, f. 58v.
68 BL, Add Chart, 33635.

repeated across the St Lazarus estates. Early sixteenth-century leasing policy is suggested by Sir Thomas Norton's lease of a tenement at Burton to Thomas Cumberland in 1525. Cumberland held for 10 years and his annual rent of £1 6s 8d was payable in three instalments at Easter, Lammas and Martinmas.[69] It is not clear at what point the order introduced leases for specific terms or the notion of three rent days as opposed to two.

After the Dissolution evidence for management is provided by a detailed rental made in 1563 for Robert Dudley, earl of Leicester, and preserved at Longleat House.[70] There are two obvious caveats when considering this important document. First, it deals with the 'extended' estate and therefore mixes Burton Lazars and former Vaudey lands with no obvious distinction between them. Second, it was drawn up twenty years after the Dissolution, a period during which the duke of Northumberland had started to initiate wide-ranging changes on the local landscape. However, if we assume that little had altered in terms of how the lands were actually divided up, we may be looking at a compelling snapshot of the hospital during the last years of its existence. The Longleat survey covers what it calls 'Burton Lazarus, alias Burton Lisle' made up of three components – the old demesne of the hospital at Burton (with an associated pasture in Leesthorpe); non-demesne lands at Burton; and other Leicestershire properties formerly belonging to the order in places such as Melton Mowbray, Great Dalby and Stapleford. Except for the grant of the Vaudey lands in 1536, this probably represents something like the area administered from the Burton preceptory when separate accounting centres were in use prior to the fifteenth century. The three tenants of the demesne – Henry Owtered, Henry Alicock and Thomas Hartopp – paid between them £166 3s 8d, including 17s 'for the issues of the manor'. The other properties at Burton comprised 25 tenements, six cottages, one house and two mills. These properties were leased to a variety of tenants at rents ranging from £3 13s 8d to 2s and accounted for only £30 5s 0½d, bringing the total income for Burton Lazars (demesne and non-demesne) to £196 8s 8½d. When the other Leicestershire lands were added the grand total came to £221 2s 0½d, with a deduction of £10 allowed for the bailiff's fee. Decays were comparatively small, and the conclusion of Dudley's surveyor was extremely positive:

> The manor of Burton is in circuit six miles exceeding good ground both arable land, meadow and pasture whereof the manor with the demesne is parcel which containeth the fourth part of the circuit thereof ... the said manor of Burton to be enclosed and ditched will be made very profitable and great enhancement of rent may be increased with the contentation of the tenants.[71]

Evidence from documents and from the landscape therefore points in the same direction. The order appears to have built up a consolidated estate of

---

[69] PRO, E 118/1/62.

[70] LH, marquis of Bath Mss, Dudley Papers, III/33, ff. 130–2. See also G.D. Owen (ed.), *Marquess of Bath Mss*, 5 (Talbot, Dudley and Devereux Papers, 1533–1659), HMC (1980), pp. 164, 167; *CPR, 1560–63*, pp. 189–91.

[71] LH, marquis of Bath Mss, Dudley Papers, III/33, f. 132.

moderate size based on its preceptory at Burton, greatly enhanced by the Vaudey exchange in 1536. Much of this was made up of early enclosures. In 1563 the Leicestershire estate of Burton Lazars comprised more than 9,000 acres and 200 houses, though this figure includes the whole of the county and not just the immediate demesne of the old preceptory.[72] Even in the late Middle Ages, when demesne cultivation was less fashionable among religious orders, the Lazarites seem to have maintained an active interest in farming, perhaps encouraged by the suitability of their lands for the raising of good-quality sheep and cattle. In this they had more in common with monastic houses and the preceptories of the military orders than with the leper hospitals, which tended to have a very limited stake in demesne farming.[73] Although the inflation of the 1540s and 1550s might cast doubt on the figures returned in the 1563 survey as an accurate measure of the wealth of the order on the eve of the Dissolution, there can be no doubt that its principal property, granted by Roger de Mowbray in the twelfth century, was a very desirable one and remained the jewel in the Lazarite crown.

The St Giles's demesne

The same tradition of active demesne farming survived at St Giles's at least until 1400 and possibly longer. As early as the reign of Henry II a small home farm was being worked outside the gate of the hospital, and in 1321 a lease was granted to William de North Mimms, farrier, on condition that he maintained the two ploughs belonging to the house, shod seven farm horses and the master's horse, and bound one set of cartwheels each year, the iron to be provided by the brethren.[74] Two inventories survive for the house from the late fourteenth century. One, dated June 1371, was completed when William Croxton handed over the wardenship to Geoffrey de Birston; and the other, dated September 1391, when the accomplices of the abbot of St Mary Graces absconded with what was alleged to be the entire property of the house.[75] Thus they are useful in providing a picture of demesne farming at different times of the year; at the height of summer while the crops were still on the ground, and in early September after the harvest had been gathered and before animals had been culled in readiness for the winter. There are some obvious comparisons and contrasts between the information derived from these documents, and these are to be seen in Table 5 (1371) and Table 6 (1391). The hospital had 105 acres under cultivation in 1371 and the staple crops, in both cases, were barley, wheat, peas and beans and oats. The fact that the 1391 inventory was taken while threshing was still in progress (some cereals had already been processed and others were standing in ricks) makes it difficult to estimate a total acreage or volume of crops

---

[72] PRO, E 326/12927. In Leicestershire the former properties of the order comprised 3,000 acres of arable; 3,000 of meadow; 2,000 of pasture; 1,000 of wood; and 40 of heath. In addition, there were 200 houses or cottages (with gardens and orchards); five watermills; and four dovecotes.

[73] Satchell, 'Leper-Houses', p. 162.

[74] Williams, *Early Holborn*, 2, nos. 1611, 1239; Honeybourne, 'Leper Hospitals', pp. 22–3.

[75] PRO, E 326/12434 (1371); E 315/38 (1391).

Table 5 Animals, crops and equipment at St Giles's, June 1371

Animals	Crops	Equipment
2 horses	wheat (29 acres)	1 cart
6 oxen	rye (8 acres)	harness for 6 cart horses
25 'great pigs'	barley (44 acres)	3 ploughs plus equipment
20 piglets	peas and beans (16 acres)	1 winnowing fan
	oats (8 acres)	2 winnowing cloths
		3 sacks

Source: PRO, E 326/12434.

Table 6: Animals, crops and equipment taken away from St Giles's, September 1391

Animals	Crops	Equipment
8 horses	wheat (8 quarters)	2 carts
12 oxen	malt (20 quarters)	2 dung carts
2 cows	barley (8 quarters)	harness for carts
4 boars	peas and beans (5 quarters)	2 ploughs plus equipment
12 sows	wheat, barley, oats, peas and beans in ricks	4 sets of harness
140 pigs	hay in ricks	2 winnowing fans
60 geese		2 winnowing sheets
40 capons		23 forks, spades, shovels, mattocks and picks
6 cocks		
40 chickens		
100 pullets		
20 yearlings		

Source: PRO, E 315/38.

for the later year, but, significantly, the hospital seems to have abandoned the cultivation of rye and a large quantity of malt was in store, suggesting an expansion of its brewing activities. Numbers of horses, oxen and cows rose between the two dates, and pigs increased, substantially, from 45 to 156. There is no mention of poultry in 1371, but in 1391 the number of birds stood at 266. In terms of equipment, although the three ploughs of 1371 were reduced to two by 1391, carts had increased from one to four.

How are these discrepancies to be explained? The second inventory, of course, was made by Walter de Lynton in the context of a legal dispute, and he will have wished to maximise his losses to try to impress potential adjudicators. Litigants notoriously exaggerated their damages in circumstances such as these. But, nevertheless, the increases in pigs, poultry and malt may well be significant, and all of these clues appear to be pointing in the same direction. These were all commodities that could be aimed at the ever-expanding London market for food and drink that lay just beyond the gates of St Giles's.[76] Indeed, it is logical to suppose that the increased number of carts might have been required to take some of this produce to market. How the citizens of London responded to purchasing meat and ale produced in a leper hospital is another matter altogether, and raises questions about the prevalence of the disease and the way in which it was perceived by the community at large. Laws passed in London and other cities consistently discouraged trade with lepers, and the rite of *separatio*, suspect though it may be in a fourteenth-century English context, made it clear that they were 'to avoid markets, mills, bakeries and inns' where food might be contaminated.[77] The rule of the leper-house of St Julian, St Albans, stated 'he [the leper] must not approach the bread or beer . . . because it is not right for men of such a disease to handle what is destined for the common use of men'.[78]

However, all of these regulations were difficult to enforce, and in reality there was more contact between lepers and healthy individuals than the legislators would have wished for. Moreover, Satchell has argued that leper-houses were not situated with a view to protecting healthy people from the disease, as has traditionally been supposed. Far from being located in out-of-the-way places, they tended to be prominently situated and close to centres of population, and instances of interaction between lepers and healthy people are commonplace.[79] In 1372, for example, John Mayn, a London baker suffering from the disease, was threatened with the pillory because he had disobeyed several orders to leave the city.[80] It could have been, of course, that customers had no idea where or how the St Giles's foodstuffs were produced, and their provenance may have been further disguised by the intervention of middle men. On the other hand, it may be that buyers, like John Mayn's customers, were not unduly concerned where their food came from and that St Giles's could compete openly and freely alongside other providers, a scenario that might be preferred by Satchell, who suggests that 'fear of infection was not very important'.[81]

Whatever the perception of leprosy, it seems that what was still a fairly conventional demesne farm in 1371 probably geared itself up to the demands of the London market and changed in character, somewhat, over the next twenty years. This was not an experience or an opportunity shared by all religious houses. Many of them withdrew from demesne farming almost entirely after 1350, but it is clear that the Lazarites continued to sustain a limited stake in the market because of the close proximity of their major houses to towns that were able to receive their surpluses. Though the case of Burton Lazars is not so clear cut as that of St Giles's, Melton Mowbray was on its doorstep, and in 1330 corn was being sold as far afield as Nottingham.[82] It must have reached there either from Locko or from Burton itself.

---

[76] F. Sheppard, *London. A History* (Oxford, 1998), pp. 103–5.
[77] Orme and Webster, *English Hospital*, p. 31.
[78] Satchell, 'Leper-Houses', p. 226.
[79] *Ibid*, pp. 227–31.
[80] Orme and Webster, *English Hospital*, pp. 28–9.
[81] Satchell, 'Leper-Houses', p. 227.
[82] PRO, SC 8/266/13294; *Rot Parl*, 2, p. 51.

Relations with tenants

If demesne farming was constantly subject to the laws of supply and demand, tenanted land, which accounted for the majority in terms of overall acreage, posed different problems of administration. In general very little evidence has survived in this area, but the hostile reaction of some of the tenants of St Giles's following its absorption by the Lazarites in 1299 indicates that rents were not always paid without prevarication.[83] Here a deep resentment lingered on because of Edward I's gift of the hospital to the order and long-standing grievances over the appointment of wardens and brethren.[84] When in 1302 the master went to collect two years' rent arrears from John Orpedman, a fishmonger of Bridge Street, accompanied by the mayor's sergeant, he was assaulted when he attempted to distrain a fish lying on Orpedman's stall.

> On a later occasion the defendant admitted the plaintiff and his men, and then closed the doors behind them, so that the master with difficulty escaped into the shop in front. The defendant sent the master's men after him, kicking and ill-treating them, and when the plaintiff raised the hue and cry the defendant took him by the neck and pushed him out of the shop-door and ill-treated him.[85]

The master prosecuted Orpedman before the mayor's court alleging assault, damages and wrongful imprisonment, but the fishmonger demanded a jury, which returned a verdict not at all favourable to the landlord. The master's alleged damages of £40 were reduced to 2s and the assault and wrongful imprisonment rejected. Indeed, the jurors returned that Orpedman had acted not out of malice but only to prevent his fish being thrown down into the mud.[86] In 1305, just as the protracted Orpedman case ground to a halt, another very similar dispute emerged when the master seized 20lb of wax for rent arrears at the house of Peter Adrian in Soper's Lane. Adrian promptly retrieved his wax, and when the case came to court he alleged that the disputed rent was not payable since his house did not belong to St Giles's.[87]

The problem of rent collection in London had become so acute by 1314/15 that the master petitioned Parliament requesting that the mayor and sheriffs be compelled to provide more visible support for his efforts.[88] But, although it was ordered that incidents of resistance should be reported to the king, the battles continued. Simon de Creppin had ceased to pay his rent on three shops before the petition to Parliament and continued to do so after it. When the master seized a ewer and a basin from two of his associates another brawl ensued during which the distrained items were recovered. The matter was heard before the eyre of London in 1320/21 and although Creppin followed Adrian's defence of

---

83 C.W. Foster (ed.), *Final Concords of the County of Lincoln*, 2, LRS, 17 (1920), p. 122; PRO, CP 40/342, m.290 (Farnham, 1, pp. 258–9); BL, Cart, f. 176.

84 See Chapter 2, pp. 49–51.

85 A.H. Thomas (ed.), *Calendar of Early Mayors' Court Rolls of the City of London, 1298–1307* (Cambridge, 1924), p. 219.

86 *Ibid*, pp. 125, 131, 219.

87 *Ibid*, p. 230.

88 *Rot Parl*, 1, pp. 323–4.

suggesting that the master was not entitled to the rent, the court found against him and ordered him to pay the arrears as well as £2 0s 0d damages.[89] This was a more satisfactory outcome than the disastrous Orpedman case, and it suggests that the petition to Parliament might have had some effect of concentrating the minds of London's legal officers on the problems of the order. By then the tenants of St Giles's had had twenty years to adjust to a new style of management, a style perhaps more rigorous than that which had gone before.

But the respite was short-lived. The difficulties endured by the order later in . the fourteenth century, and especially the expropriation of its London properties under Richard II, encouraged fresh encroachments and disobedience on the part of tenants. When Walter de Lynton and Sir Geoffrey Shriggley attempted to sort things out in the early fifteenth century the London properties were high on the agenda because in some of them rents had been unpaid for as long as 25 years. Between 1411 and 1436 Lynton and Shriggley prosecuted at least 13 cases against tenants and one against two individuals, Henry Whitby and Richard Lye, for failing to obey a judgment of the court in favour of the master.[90] A feature of these cases is that two-thirds involved other ecclesiastical landlords, London clergy or religious houses such as Notley and Woburn Abbeys, who appear to have been taking advantage of the Lazarite misfortunes to claim title to St Giles's lands. In the cases in which judgments are recorded the recovery campaign seems to have been broadly successful, and on one occasion, in a prosecution involving a block of tenements in the parish of St Mildred, Bread Street, in 1429, Shriggley succeeded in winning damages of £3, costs of £2 and £17 12s in arrears of rent.[91]

This is not to say that the order was always so fortunate. In 1382 positions were reversed when on two occasions the abbot of Westminster prosecuted the master and his tenants for encroachments in the parishes of St Benet, Sherehog, and St Michael, Queenhithe. In both cases damages were awarded in favour of the abbot, and in one of them the jury specifically exonerated the tenant, John Walcote, draper, and blamed the master for the offence.[92] It was not unusual for ecclesiastical landlords to squabble among themselves where landed property was concerned – that had been proven in the thirteenth-century disputes at Burton Lazars – but it is possible that these quarrels were sharpened by the sense of resentment that some of the more conventional religious orders felt about the privileges of the Lazarites.[93] The conflicts were encouraged by the ambivalent legal position of St Giles's in the fourteenth century, fuelled by the order's unpopular lack of provision for lepers and triggered by the jealously guarded privileges of the city of London and major religious houses. Such doughty opponents were not to be found on the tenanted lands of midland England.

[89] H.M. Cam (ed.), *Eyre of London, 14 Edward II*, SS, 86 (1969), pp. 144–7. The prosecution was against Simon de Creppin, Richard de Breyehesle and Agnes, his wife.

[90] H.M. Chew (ed.), *London Possessory Assizes: a Calendar*, LonRS, 1 (1965), pp. 32, 60–2, 73–4, 76, 104–5; A.H. Thomas (ed.), *Calendar of Plea and Memoranda Rolls of the City of London, AD 1413–1437* (Cambridge, 1953), pp. 35–6, 168, 180–1, 188, 205, 220, 250, 258, 272, 293.

[91] Chew, *London Possessory Assizes*, pp. 104–5.

[92] *Ibid*, p. 62.

[93] See Chapter 6, p. 178.

Industrial activity and milling

Evidence of direct involvement with industrial activity in the preceptories and hospitals of the order is slight. In 1371 St Giles's had seven vats and in 1391 a mashing-vat and an ale-vat, as well as a wide range of containers, tubs and sieves. It is difficult to know if these brewing operations catered only for the hospital's quite extensive community of clergy, *famuli*, lepers and corrodians or for a wider market. In the latter year there were eight barrels standing empty and another eight 'full of ale', which may point to brewing on a semi-commercial scale.[94] It is also significant, perhaps, that the St Giles's estate included a number of inns and alehouses, and it is possible that the hospital was manufacturing alcohol for some of its own outlets in Holborn and the city.[95] Metalworking was also carried out, because in 1391 the brethren of St Giles's had 1000 lb of 'old iron' and 15 fothers of lead and tin stockpiled at the hospital.[96] 15 fothers [about 14½ tons] is such a weight as to suggest trading or major building works; but the 'old iron' may well have been for the use of the successor of the farrier who was based there in 1321. Nevertheless, 1000 lb of iron is a large amount of metal [about half a ton] and along with the lead and tin it raises questions about what exactly it was being used for.

In the far north, at Harehope, a large stone cistern with a capacity of about 500 gallons, carved from outcropping sandstone, has caused debate amongst local historians for many years (Plate 23). Though the tank is well positioned to collect rainwater and, by means of pipes, provide a supply to the hospital, there is a view that it may well be a post-medieval feature. Holmes comments: 'Altogether the excavation has a modern appearance, but there are on each side of it what appears to be work of prehistoric date.'[97] The most persistent theory, based on an oral tradition, was put forward by Holmes in 1901 and suggests that it was used for the production of juniper wine.[98] Also at Harehope there is evidence of quarrying on the high ground above the hospital, and in particular the production of millstones, but whether this represents medieval or post-medieval activity similarly cannot be verified for certain.

Milling with water- or wind-powered mills at Burton Lazars, Melton Mowbray, Whissendine, Choseley and Spondon provides better-documented evidence of commercial enterprise, though this was an activity carried out mainly by tenants rather than the brethren themselves. In the twelfth and thirteenth centuries pensions were also received out of mills at Thirsk, Masham and Carlton-le-Moorland, though these were quite quickly exchanged for land.[99] Man Mill, situated in a kink in the river Eye to the north of Burton Lazars, was probably part of Roger de Mowbray's original endowment, and its footings, leats

94 PRO, E 326/12434 (1371); E 315/38 (1391).

95 See Chapter 2, p. 52; Chapter 7, p. 220.

96 PRO, E 315/38.

97 S. Holmes, 'Trough on Harehope Moor, Northumberland', *Proceedings of the Society of Antiquaries of Newcastle-upon-Tyne*, 2nd series, 9 (1901), p. 142.

98 *Ibid*, pp. 142–3. In 1901 juniper berries were still plentiful in the area, though the trees were 'of great age'.

99 BL, Cart, ff. 1a, 4, 245, 247.

Plate 23: Stone cistern on Harehope Moor, Northumberland. A water supply for
the hospital, or a vat for the manufacture of juniper wine?

and dam have been located by archaeological survey work (Plan 2).[100] Although
it was an important feature in the landscape in the thirteenth century, giving its
name to one of the open fields of Burton, by 1563 it was in decay and was leased
out on favourable terms in hope of re-edification.[101] In a similar condition in the
same year was a malt mill at Burton, though the nature of its power and the
extent to which it had previously been worked to the profit of the order are not
clear.[102]

The most important mills were the two watermills on the Eye at Melton
Mowbray, granted by Simon, son of Richard, the original grant having been
made to his uncle, Warin, by Roger de Mowbray.[103] The gift to the order is therefore unlikely to have been made before 1200, and it was specified that the
brethren were to render £3 *per annum* for all services and 5s to the priory of
Monks Kirby, Warwickshire, for mill tithes. However, the grant caused considerable dissatisfaction. The monks of Kirby were unhappy with the composition,
and the Pope ordered an arbitration by the abbot of Stoneleigh and the priors of
Kenilworth and Coventry by which the annual sum was raised from 5s to

---

100 UNCLH, J.M. Allsop and M. Hatton, 'Earthwork Survey of Man Mill (Mannemilne), possession of
     the medieval order of St Lazarus on the River Eye at Burton Lazars', MFR, 00/01 (2000). For a case
     involving Man Mill, see PRO, E 134/31 Eliz 1/East 6.
101 Brown, 'Burton Lazars', pp. 36–7; LH, marquis of Bath Mss, Dudley Papers, III/33, f. 132.
102 LH, marquis of Bath Mss, Dudley Papers, III/33, f. 132.
103 BL, Cart, ff. 7–8.

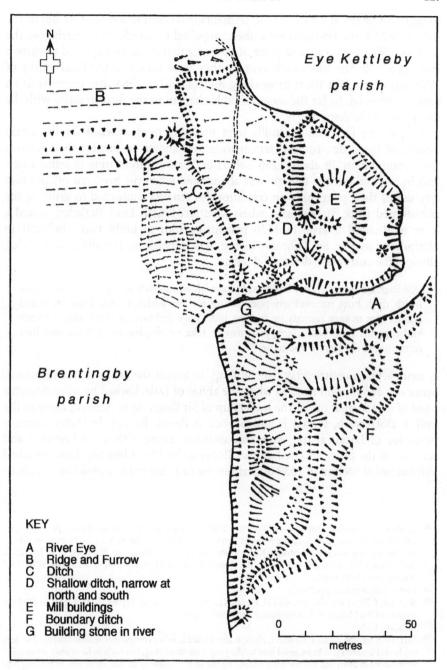

KEY

A River Eye
B Ridge and Furrow
C Ditch
D Shallow ditch, narrow at
   north and south
E Mill buildings
F Boundary ditch
G Building stone in river

Eye Kettleby
parish

Brentingby
parish

0   50

metres

Plan 2: Man Mill, Burton Lazars.

6s 8d.[104] More serious, in 1210 the Templars laid claim to a rent of £1 out of the mills to which the brethren were also compelled to accede.[105] Nevertheless, the Melton mills were a valuable piece of property that could be expected to show a good profit. In the fourteenth century they were leased to the local family of Waltham who sublet them to working millers, and in 1563 they commanded a rent of £10 6s 8d, by far the most valuable element in the Burton estate with the exception of the demesne.[106]

Despite the fact that the mills were probably never worked for the direct benefit of the order, some determination was shown to protect their tenants from competition. In about 1250 Robert de Ver was threatening to build a new mill in Melton, but the scheme was abandoned when the brethren offered him free use of their own mills on condition his tenants continued to grind at the accustomed price.[107] Similarly, when Maurice, fourth Lord Berkeley, issued a lease to Richard Sharpe in 1520 permitting him to build two windmills in Melton, the master, Sir Thomas Norton, was impelled to complain to Berkeley, albeit in the customary deferential terms:

> One Richard Sharpe, lately bailiff of Melton Mowbray, hath set up a windmill there which doth hurt me and my poor house for the which I have been purposed against him to seek remedy by the law, but I have forborn for displeasing of your lordship this time beseeching you now to take no displeasure if I account him according to the law for the same.[108]

A more serious controversy over milling, in which the law was not respected, broke out at Spondon in 1283 when the abbot of Dale, backed by a considerable band of armed men under the leadership of Sir Roger de St Andrew, came to the mill at Borrowash, looted it and burned it down. Robert de Dalby, possibly preceptor of Locko at the time, was assaulted along with other brethren and servants of the order.[109] The fact that Roger de Waltham had his sluice smashed and burned at Melton in 1339 underlines the fact that milling could be a particu-

---

104 T. Madox, *Formulare Anglicanum* (London, 1702), p. 28; Nichols, *Leicestershire*, 2 pt 1, pp. 125, 239–40. In the fourteenth century Lewes Priory, which owned the rectory of Melton Mowbray, bought out the interest of Monks Kirby Priory in the mill tithes. See BL, Cart, f. 9; *DCAD*, 4, pp. 232–3; *CPR, 1350–54*, pp. 530–1; P.E. Hunt, *Notes on Medieval Melton Mowbray, 1077–1507* (Grantham, 1965), p. 61.

105 Curtis, *Leicestershire*, pp. 252–3.

106 BL, Cart, f. 73; Hunt, *Notes*, p. 46; LH, marquis of Bath Mss, Dudley Papers III/33, f. 131. In 1381 the tenants of the Melton mills were Henry and Robert Bote.

107 BL, Cart, f. 15.

108 MH, Lothian Mss, Box 25, Bundle 1. Norton also hinted at other complaints against Sharpe: 'Further, my lord, I beseech you to be good lord to the poor man this bringer in such as he convey to you. For verily he hath been full hastily dealt withall by the same person as he can show you in putting him from his office, and if the lordship of your lordship of Dalby be not otherwise looked unto than it has been now of late it will be to your great loss, I say.' For Berkeley's lease to Sharpe, see Box 24, Bundle 1, no. 90.

109 *CPR, 1281–92*, p. 93; *Cal Inq, Misc 1, 1219–1307*, p. 378. For St Andrew, see C. Moor (ed.), *Knights of Edward I*, 4, HS, 83 (1931), p. 169. A writ was directed to Thomas de Bray and the sheriff of Derby to investigate. Bray was the steward of Edmund, earl of Lancaster, and could be accounted a supporter of the order since he was one of the arbitrators it named in the dispute with the executors of Alice Beler in 1277. BL, Cart, f. 109.

larly provocative activity when questions of monopoly, costing and environ-
mental damage through flooding are taken into account.[110]

Difficulties and responses

Most of the conflicts occasioned by day-to-day problems of estate management
were not so violent as those sometimes generated by the mills. A territorial
dispute broke out at Burton in 1364 involving alleged trespass, and another at
Spondon in 1515.[111] At St Giles's there was concern that the activities of the
order were encroaching on traditional rights of way. In 1372 the warden was
stated to have failed to maintain one of his ditches for five years, and by 1383 the
situation was so serious that the highway was flooded. Moreover, Nicholas de
Exton, a corrodian and fishmonger of London, had deliberately blocked up path-
ways and removed footbridges, a reflection, perhaps, of the fact that he regarded
his residence at the hospital principally as a means of escape from an unpleasant
civic feud in which he was involved.[112] One or two cases concerning small sums
of money look as if they might have been prosecutions of tenants who had failed
to pay their rents.[113]

But, with the exception of occasional incidents such as these, the sources
record very little about routine difficulties of management outside London. Nor
is it possible to obtain much of a picture of how priorities changed over a period
of time. The thirteenth century was, in general, an age of prosperity for the religious orders, and this seems to have been true for the Lazarites who expanded
and consolidated their estates and attempted to tighten their feudal control. The
fourteenth century was different. Climatic change and serious economic depression characterised the years 1315–22, and following this there was a period of
prolonged warfare and high taxation with which to contend. Most serious of all,
the Black Death devastated the population in 1349 and thereafter became
endemic, creating labour shortages on demesne farms and a difficulty in finding
occupiers for tenanted land.[114] As the feudal authority of lords weakened,
income from this source dried up too: it was 'the culmination of a chain of disasters and the beginning of a long period of economic conditions disadvantageous
to landlords'.[115]

The impact of all of this was potentially very damaging for the hospitals.
During the 'great famine' of 1315–22 the receiver-general's accounts of St Giles's,
Norwich, show annual income fluctuating between £75 and £105, and St
Bartholomew's, Bristol, never recovered from these difficult years, being said to
be 'greatly decayed' in 1344.[116] The plague simply made a bad situation worse,

110 BL, Cart, f. 73; Hunt, Notes, p. 46.
111 PRO, KB 27/416, m.36 (Farnham, 1, p. 259); CP 40/1011, m.274 (Farnham, 1, p. 264).
112 C.T. Flower (ed.), Public Works in Mediaeval Law, 2, SS, 40 (1923), pp. 65–6. For Exton, see Chapter 5,
     p. 164.
113 CPR, 1467–77, p. 501; PRO, CP 40/489, m.7d (Farnham, 1, p. 261); CP 40/839, m.7; CP 40/882, m.7d
     (Farnham, 1, p. 263); W.D. Macray et al. (eds), Various Collections, 2, HMC (1903), p. 20.
114 Rawcliffe, Medicine for the Soul, pp. 65–6.
115 Harper-Bill, 'English Church', p. 100.
116 Ibid, pp. 65, 84.

and by the 1370s the cumulative impact of many years of crisis was beginning to have a general effect. At St Leonard's, York, income fell from £1263 *per annum* in 1287 to £310 in 1535; and St Paul's, Norwich, suffered a decline of two-thirds in its revenues between 1363 and 1533.[117] Little wonder that Rawcliffe speaks of the 'blighted blooms and withered leaves' of late-medieval hospitals, and Orme has suggested that in the fourteenth century, as a result of the economic crisis, about a hundred foundations – 20 per cent of the original total – disappeared entirely.[118] Those that survived were forced to look at their activities very critically to ensure they did not go the same way. Among the military orders, the Hospitallers suffered particularly in the early part of the century, though here it has been suggested that the massive financial demands placed on them by the capture of Rhodes in 1309 played no small part in this.

It is unlikely that the order of St Lazarus was involved in this campaign, but certainly the years after 1309 were difficult ones, characterised by a number of petitions to Parliament to guarantee their financial privileges or to enforce payment of rent by tenants. It is possible that Roger Beler, chief baron of the Exchequer, was a loyal supporter during these years, since it seems clear that the order had at least one friend at court who was prepared to use legal knowledge and political influence on its behalf. Indeed, in 1319, at the height of the crisis, Beler loaned the master the very considerable sum of £250, which may have been a way of confronting some of the difficulties emerging during these years.[119] However, by 1355 the situation was once more parlous, and the order petitioned the Pope that 'The said hospital [St Giles's] has suffered loss by fire and is burdened by debts, and that the lands which they used to cultivate and those let to farm to seculars, are, by reason of the horrible mortality, now uncultivated.'[120] By 1367, if the representations of the order are to be believed, St Giles's was 'so miserably dilapidated and depressed . . . that its goods do not suffice to maintain the pious works with which it is charged.'[121]

It is difficult to know how much credence to give to these complaints. The fire referred to in 1355 may be that at Spondon (with no direct connection with St Giles's); the hospital owned very little land under cultivation (most of its property being urban); and the inventory of 1371 does not immediately evoke a picture of miserable dilapidation. On the other hand, the London estate suffered particular problems in the fourteenth century because of the transfer of ownership and the bitter dispute over the appointment of the warden (both of which factors made it difficult to collect rents). What cannot be denied is that there was a climate of economic decay and, rightly or wrongly, religious houses latched on to this as a means of consolidating their positions by grants of favours.

The hospitals came up with a range of solutions to these economic difficulties, some of them more successful than others. At St Giles's, Norwich, these included the acquisition of new property, the sale of corrodies and a greater

117 *Ibid*, p. 65.
118 *Ibid*; Orme and Webster, *English Hospital*, p. 129.
119 See Chapter 2, pp. 62–3.
120 *CPapR, Petitions 1, 1342–1419*, p. 270.
121 *CPR, 1364–67*, p. 388.

emphasis on the spiritual services offered by the institution.[122] There is evidence that the Lazarites replicated all of these expedients with some success.[123] Faced with comparable problems, the Hospitallers began to centralise management on their principal house at Clerkenwell, and a very similar policy appears to have been followed by the order of St Lazarus.[124] During the fourteenth century almost all of the lesser preceptories and hospitals disappeared as working units and their affairs were subjected directly to Burton Lazars. Choseley, always a tiny settlement, seems to have been in steady decline after the Black Death, and the mention of a 'master of Choseley' in 1428 is the last reference to a resident member of the order handling affairs there.[125]

In the fifteenth century the policy appears to have been to rent off these outlying estates to local gentry and possibly to alienate the most inconvenient packages altogether if and when the need arose. The 'missing' Lincolnshire property might be accounted for in this way, and by 1535 Westwade chapel, Norfolk, was being administered by Wymondham Abbey.[126] Nearby, at Choseley, the Inquisition on Enclosures and Evictions, taken in 1517 and relating to decays occasioned since 1488, revealed a depressing picture of what had once been a flourishing estate based around the preceptory. 'Also dwellings of Burton Lazar in the aforesaid vill are laid waste and the inhabitants therein have departed and three hundred acres belonging to the said dwellings of which sixty are ploughed, however the rest are in pasture and by the aforesaid decay the church at the same place has fallen down.'[127] By the 1520s the 'meadows and pastures' of Choseley had been in the hands of Sir Thomas Lovell's family for at least 40 years, 'pastured with my master's sheep', and leased from the order for £2 10s per annum.[128]

The lack of brethren of St Lazarus in these places was made up for by the appointment of a receiver and a number of lay bailiffs to oversee the most important estates.[129] These people, it seems, did very well out of the lands they were supposed to look after. William Faunt, a prominent lawyer and the order's bailiff at Melton Mowbray, enjoyed a choice lease of the manor of Cold Newton and the rectory and advowson of Lowesby.[130] His success story was an indication of the extent to which the gentry had come to dominate the order's affairs by the

122 Rawcliffe, *Medicine for the Soul*, pp. 84–6.
123 See Chapter 2, p. 52; Chapter 5, pp. 163–6; Chapter 6, pp. 181–94.
124 Gervers, *Hospitaller Cartulary*, p. lvi.
125 Parkin, *Norfolk*, 10 (London, 1809), p. 348; Norfolk Landscape Archaeology, SMR 21554 (Choseley Farm, Choseley). Pottery finds at Carlton-le-Moorland confirm an abandonment c.1350, but here the situation is complicated by two adjacent sites (both of which fulfil the documentary criteria): the site referred to, therefore, might not be the leper hospital, but the rival site is even more ephemeral and was probably deserted at an earlier date.
126 Blomefield, *Norfolk*, 2, pp. 504–5; Taylor, *Index Monasticus*, p. 36; *Valor*, 3, p. 322.
127 I.S. Leadam, 'The Inquisition of 1517, Inclosures and Evictions', 2, *TRHS*, new series, 7 (1893), p. 168.
128 J.H. Round (ed.), *Rutland Mss*, 4, HMC (1905), p. 262; *LP, 4 pt 1, 1524–26*, p. 154.
129 Nicholas Walwin, master's receiver, appears in 1527. *LP, 4 pt 2, 1526–28*, p. 1367. In 1535 there were bailiffs of Melton Mowbray, Cold Newton, Spondon, Derby and St Giles's, Choseley and Wymondham, Nettleham and Ashby Puerorum, Northampton, Pontefract and Kedington. *Valor*, 4, p. 153.
130 *CPR, 1553–4*, pp. 169–70; Fetherston, *Visitation of Leicestershire, 1619*, p. 28; Jack, 'Monastic Lands', pp. 16–17.

eve of the Reformation, and the potential implications of this were ominous. According to Harper-Bill, 'The long-term result of this shift was to place monastic lands, in all but name, in the hands of prosperous peasants, yeomen and knights whose successors would ultimately be eager, when the chance was offered by the crown, to acquire outright ownership.'[131] Faunt, indeed, did just that. He established his home at Cold Newton and in 1554 obtained a grant of the former Lazarite property from Queen Mary, proving that Protestantism was not a necessary prerequisite for those profiting from church lands during the period of the Reformation.[132]

Thus, although direct farming continued at Burton, the order detached itself more and more from active land management at the periphery as time went on. A thirteenth-century brother would have spent much of his career travelling around preceptories and properties raising money for the Crusade; his fifteenth-century counterpart led a much more static life devoted primarily to prayer and intercession.[133] With knightly and religious gentlemen running the affairs of the order from a position of some magnificence at Burton Lazars, secular gentlemen reaped the rewards of the estates in the localities. In this fundamental transition there is little evidence that the order suffered the financial hardship it sometimes claimed. The estate had continued to expand throughout the period of economic difficulties, and the Lazarites as often lent money as borrowed it. Even in the late 1380s, when St Giles's was 'miserably depressed and in debt', Nicholas de Dover was capable of extending a loan of £80 to the abbot of Croyland;[134] and in 1514 Maurice, fourth Lord Berkeley, mortgaged some important properties to Sir Thomas Norton in return for an advance of £100.[135]

This apparent contradiction is partly explained by the ambiguity surrounding the affairs of an individual house and the affairs of the order. Burton Lazars might well have been in a much stronger position than St Giles's in the second half of the fourteenth century, for example. Without the detailed estate accounts that survive for some institutions, it is impossible to be more specific, and even when these do exist, as at St Giles's, Norwich, the monetary contributions made by patrons of all social classes – which may have been quite considerable – are impossible to quantify.[136] But, in general terms, it would be difficult to resist the

---

131 Harper-Bill, 'English Church', p. 101.

132 PRO, LR 2/87, f. 292; *CPR, 1553–4*, pp. 169–70; S.T. Bindoff, *The House of Commons, 1509–1558*, 2 (London, 1982), pp. 121–2. See also PRO, E 134/3 Chas 1/Mich 11.

133 The distinction is underlined by an analysis of the number of disputes over property in which the order was involved. These were most numerous in the thirteenth century, when the estate was being formed and actively managed, and least numerous in the fifteenth century with its more static reliance on rents.

134 *CPR, 1388–92*, p. 143; PRO, CP 40/574, m.448 (Farnham, 1, p. 262). It is clear that the transaction was a loan because the abbot failed to pay and Walter de Lynton prosecuted him in 1404. For other financial transactions involving Lynton, see *CCR, 1399–1402*, pp. 501, 504; PRO, CP 40/629, m.250 (Farnham, 1, p. 262).

135 MH, Lothian Mss, Box 23, no. 108. In June 1520 Norton was one of the officials administering the manor of Melton Mowbray, presumably under the terms of this mortgage. *Ibid*, Box 35. Berkeley permitted Norton to receive the revenues of the manors of Melton Mowbray, Cold Overton, Sileby and Seagrave until the debt was paid off.

136 Rawcliffe, *Medicine for the Soul*, p. 102.

conclusion that the order survived with some comfort, even though modes of management changed and statements for public consumption might sometimes have indicated otherwise. It weathered the economic storms of the fourteenth century, and in the course of these confronted the damage done by a disastrous fire at Spondon.[137]

Why had the order of St Lazarus prospered when many other hospital foundations had gone to the wall or seriously curtailed their activities? Jack has stated that 'Economic policy and financial stability varied widely from house to house,' the principal determining factors in Leicestershire being the nature of the estate and the approach of the monks to its management.[138] For the Lazarites the constitutional changes that were taking place during the period of the worst economic upheavals in the fourteenth century were to be critical. The most significant administrative contrast between the twelfth and sixteenth centuries was the fact that on the eve of the Reformation no contribution at all was being made to the order overseas. When exactly payments to Boigny were finally suspended is not clear, but it was probably the product of gradual erosion and changing attitudes rather than a sudden break. As early as 1347 the king seized the revenues of Locko on account of the war with France, and in about 1400 the order as a whole was acting 'as though free from any obedience to Boigny'.[139] Certainly by the fifteenth century it was commonplace to speak of 'the order of St Lazarus of Jerusalem in England', and in 1450 and 1479 official confirmations of independence were received from the curia. This was a transition brought about with the full support of the crown, and was a move similar to the 'naturalisation' being imposed on other alien houses at about the same time.

This new, national identity had important and far-reaching financial consequences. First, it was viewed by some, particularly the heirs of founders and benefactors, as a fundamental betrayal, since it was quite evident that endowments given in good faith for the support of the Crusade were now being used in a very different way. Indeed, they were not even held by the same order, championing the same goals, to which they had been granted. Second, in real terms, the order in England was becoming much more prosperous since it was no longer required to return a substantial portion of its profits to a mother house overseas. Its revenues were thus increased by a third 'at a stroke', even before the profits of any new lands are taken into account. This meant that the headship of the English order became viewed as an attractive proposition for gentry speculators, such as the Suttons, who now had it in their power to spend what they gathered in. Ironically, the second development tended to cancel out the first, and the feelings of bitterness experienced by disillusioned families of patrons were lessened when they discovered in the reinvented order avenues of advancement, which had not hitherto existed.

We know little of how the fifteenth-century masters handled these burgeoning revenues. There were certainly improvements undertaken in the churches of Threckingham and Lowesby, and an impressive and up-to-date

---

137 See Chapter 6, p. 212.
138 Jack, 'Monastic Lands', p. 26.
139 *CCR, 1346–49*, p. 338; *CPR, 1345–48*, pp. 408, 429; *CPapR, Letters 13 pt 1, 1471–84*, p. 3.

collegiate church was constructed at Burton. But it is also notable that no support was offered to the Crusade or to the sick over and above that which was appointed by custom. The management of property had always been an overriding concern, but by the late Middle Ages the distribution of its profits had shifted decisively. This helped to change the face of the order, and it also created the precedent for the closer involvement of the laity in its affairs which was to culminate with the appointment of Dr Thomas Legh as master in 1538.

5

Care and Community

There is something uncommonly salubrious in the air here, as well as in the water
(Nichols, *Leicestershire*)

Medieval lepers and leprosy

The order of St Lazarus was 'founded on lepers' and throughout its 400-year history in England it relentlessly projected the image of the suffering leper to solicit gifts of land and win privileges from the crown and papacy. Leprosy indisputably lay at the root of the order's founding ideology, but the extent to which this sustained exploitation was justified is a question very much open to debate. Not only is leprosy a very unpleasant disease, it is also an extraordinarily complex one, and modern medical research has identified it in at least five different forms.[1] The most serious is low-resistant lepromatous leprosy (Hansen's disease), which was prevalent in Europe and the Holy Land in the early Middle Ages and is spread by droplet infection. However, it is not easy to contract this strain of leprosy. Hamilton notes, 'Contrary to popular belief, it is difficult to transmit from person to person and usually close contact is required for months or years before the disease is passed from one person to another.'[2] In the Middle Ages it was therefore very much a malady associated with specific families and households, and it has been estimated that this sort of regular and prolonged exposure to the bacterium increases the risk of infection by up to 20 per cent.[3]

After infection symptoms may not appear for between five and ten years, though the sufferer is capable of spreading the disease during this long incubation period. The bacterium prefers the cooler extremities of the body, and it is in

---

[1] V. Möller-Christensen, 'Evidence of Leprosy in Earlier Peoples', in D. Brothwell and A.T. Sandison (eds), *Diseases in Antiquity* (Springfield, Illinois, 1967), pp. 295–306; J.G. Andersen, *Studies in the Medieval Diagnosis of Leprosy in Denmark* (Copenhagen, 1969); K. Manchester, 'Tuberculosis and Leprosy in Antiquity: an interpretation', *MH*, 28 (1984), pp. 162–73; J. Cule, 'The Diagnosis, Care and Treatment of Leprosy in Wales and the Border in the Middle Ages', *Transactions of the British Society for the History of Pharmacy*, 1, no. 1 (1970), pp. 29–58. See also Richards, *Medieval Leper*. For the most recent discussion of the nature of medieval leprosy, see Hamilton, *Leper King*. Appendix by P. Mitchell on Baldwin IV's leprosy; L. Demaitre, 'The Description and Diagnosis of Leprosy by Fourteenth-Century Physicians', *Bulletin of the History of Medicine*, 59 (1985); Touati, *Maladie et société*.
[2] Hamilton, *Leper King*, p. 247.
[3] Rawcliffe, 'Learning to Love the Leper', p. 234.

these areas where its early effects are most apparent, attacking the nervous system, invading bone and impeding blood circulation. The damage done in this way leads to localised anaesthesia, and because of this the leper becomes prone to injury at points of pressure on the hands and feet. The absence of any sensation of pain often leads to ulceration of untreated injuries and, ultimately, serious damage to these vulnerable parts of the body. In its later stages lepromatous leprosy is grotesquely disfiguring, with distortion of the facial features and the degeneration of hands and feet. However, in terms of the archaeological evidence, Manchester estimates that no more than 50 per cent of victims exhibit these extreme characteristics. Alongside this there co-existed a tuberculoid form of the disease, which displayed many similar characteristics, but which was less serious, the major difference being that tuberculoid leprosy heals spontaneously in most cases but lepromatous leprosy does not.[4] Satchell acknowledges that today it is extremely difficult to diagnose which variety of the disease medieval lepers were actually suffering from, given the vagaries of description and diagnosis. The whole study is bedevilled by 'confused and shifting terminology'.[5] To get around this, Mitchell uses the phrase 'leprosy complex disease' to describe the condition when a precise diagnosis cannot be arrived at, which, historically, is generally the case.[6]

The best hard evidence is from excavated cemeteries, and recent work at the hospitals of St James and St Mary Magdalene, Chichester; South Acre, Norfolk; and St Margaret, High Wycombe, Buckinghamshire, has revealed inmates with both of the major types of the disease and, indeed, with no trace of it at all.[7] Satchell concludes, however, that a 'significant proportion' of these burials, though well under half in most cases, were suffering from Hansen's disease.[8] As a general rule, lepromatous leprosy is most strongly represented among male burials of the earlier period, chiefly the twelfth century, and tuberculoid leprosy is most evident in mixed burials of the later Middle Ages. When leprosy is first introduced into a population it is epidemic and affects perhaps 10 to 30 per cent of all age groups. When, after a number of years, it becomes endemic, it tends to develop in childhood or adolescence and affects only one to five per cent of people.[9] Even at its most virulent, therefore, leprosy is only likely to affect a small proportion of the population, and Satchell argues, convincingly, that the expansion of hospital provision for the disease in twelfth-century England was not based on an 'epidemiological crisis'.[10] The best explanation that can be arrived at is that because of its unpleasant visual manifestations and the growing urbanisation of the period – not to mention the spiritual benefits these foundations brought to their patrons – the disease assumed a higher profile than in reality it deserved.[11]

The earliest evidence of leprosy in England is provided by the Poundbury feet,

4 Hamilton, *Leper King*, pp. 247–9.
5 Rawcliffe, 'Learning to Love the Leper', p. 232.
6 Hamilton, *Leper King*, p. 254.
7 Gilchrist, *Contemplation and Action*, pp. 42–3.
8 Satchell, 'Leper-Houses', pp. 58, 67.
9 Hamilton, *Leper King*, pp. 247–9.
10 Satchell, 'Leper-Houses', p. vi.
11 Rawcliffe, 'Learning to Love the Leper', p. 233.

a partial leprous skeleton discovered in Dorset and dating from the last years of the Roman occupation, and, though the disease was probably endemic by the eleventh century, it appears that a new epidemic arrived from China at about this time.[12] By the Norman period hospitals were being founded for the containment and care of lepers, and their rapid expansion up to 1250 has recently been charted by Satchell, who has counted no fewer than 299 leper-houses, most of them small and many of them transitory.[13] These foundations reached a peak in the twelfth century, coinciding with the popularity of monasticism and the crusading ideal, but they declined thereafter. Certainly lepromatous leprosy was already in sharp retreat by 1300, by the fifteenth century it was rare and by the sixteenth it was virtually eliminated. Manchester has suggested that this decline was caused by the upsurge of tuberculosis, which was a notable feature of the late Middle Ages, but it is just as likely that climatic change, diet and improved hygiene also played a part. As the most virulent strain of leprosy became virtually extinct, the old hospitals were left with little or nothing to do and were forced to radically reconsider their role in society. As Orme has stated, 'by the fourteenth century many leper-houses were changing into hospitals for the general poor and infirm'.[14]

Though medieval leper hospitals were principally concerned with the care of the spirit rather than the body, there were measures that it was believed could alleviate the worst physical suffering. Mitchell describes dietary treatments, the use of drugs and ointments, blood-letting and sexual abstinence, but possibly the most widely recommended of the medieval treatments was bathing in water that might have had a mineral or sulphurous content. Such immersions were believed to be beneficial to the sick in general and to lepers in particular.[15] This approach frequently became confused with the idea of a holy river or well, and hence a 'miraculous' cure, but washing may well have provided some temporary relief, either physical or psychological. Indeed, the earliest Lazarites probably encouraged bathing in the Jordan as an antidote to the disease.[16] Certainly Harbledown Hospital, near Canterbury, was situated next to a famous spring,

12 R. Reader, 'New Evidence for the Antiquity of Leprosy in early Britain', *Journal of Archaeological Science*, 1 (1974), pp. 205–7. See also K. Manchester, 'A Leprous Skeleton of the 7th century from Eccles, Kent, and the present evidence for Leprosy in early Britain', *Journal of Archaeological Science*, 8 (1981), pp. 205–9; Orme and Webster, *English Hospital*, p. 23.

13 Satchell, 'Leper-Houses', pp. 81, 113. They are listed in a Gazetteer. R.M. Clay, *The Medieval Hospitals of England* (1909, reprinted London, 1966), mentioned about 260, and this was added to by Knowles and Hadcock, *Medieval Religious Houses*, taking the total to about 300. For the debate on the extent of the disease, see R.I. Moore, *The Foundation of a Persecuting Society* (Oxford, 1987), pp. 45–57, 73–9. For medieval hospitals, and leper hospitals in particular, there is a growing literature following on from the pioneer study of Clay in 1909. See, for example, Orme and Webster, *English Hospital*, pp. 23–31, 139–41; M. Rubin, 'Development and Change in English Hospitals, 1100–1500', in L. Granshaw and R. Porter (eds), *The Hospital in History* (London, 1989), pp. 41–59; C. Rawcliffe, 'The Hospitals of Later Medieval London', *MH*, 28 (1984), pp. 1–21; P.H. Cullum, 'Hospitals and Charitable Provision in Medieval Yorkshire, 936–1547', University of York, D.Phil. thesis (1989); R. Gilchrist, 'Christian Bodies and Souls: the archaeology of life and death in later medieval hospitals', in S. Bassett (ed.), *Death in Towns: urban responses to the dying and dead, 1000–1600* (London, 1992), pp. 101–18; Rawcliffe, *Medicine for the Soul*.

14 Orme and Webster, *English Hospital*, p. 29.

15 Hamilton, *Leper King*, pp. 254–5; Satchell, 'Leper-Houses', p. 147.

16 See Chapter 1, p. 9.

and 'cures' were also noted at the shrine of St Thomas Becket and other centres of pilgrimage.

Legend and science are united in their emphasis on the importance of water. A leper called Ramp, the alleged founder of a hospital at Beccles, Suffolk, was cured by bathing in a sacred spring; at the hospital of St John the Baptist, Oxford, archaeological evidence suggestive of healing rituals involving immersion has recently come to light; and the water of the Lepers' Well at Breewood Hospital, Staffordshire, was found to have a sulphurous content when it was analysed in 1979.[17] Sherburn Hospital, near Durham, one of the largest medieval foundations for lepers, provides a good picture of these commonsense measures, based on the *regimen sanitatis*, combined with preparation for death by close attention to the divine office. Inmates were expected to attend chapel regularly and were provided with proper shoes and clothing and a considerable degree of domestic comfort. Moreover, careful attention was paid to their diet, and the regular washing of clothes and bodies was strictly enjoined. Whereas in the earliest hospitals patients had been cared for communally in a long hall or ward, by the early fourteenth century individual 'leper houses' had been adopted at Sherburn to permit a greater degree of privacy.[18]

How this institutional care was funded is a rather more difficult point on which practice varied considerably. Some hospitals were deliberately endowed to cater for the poor, rather like the *cremetts* who provided a substantial section of the population of St Leonard's, York, though none of these was leprous.[19] Certainly the popular image which has survived, particularly in medieval illustrations, is of the poor, often itinerant, leper.[20] Because of this many authors have tended to exaggerate the importance of charitable provision and have ignored the fact that places in leper hospitals were just as often purchased for cash or landed endowments. The Lazarite hospitals at Jerusalem and Acre were targeted principally at the knightly class, and even at Sherburn it was assumed that the inmates would have servants and friends who would be prepared to travel to visit them.[21] The research of Satchell confirms that 'Many leper-houses required payment for admission' and the emoluments that these prosperous patients brought with them were important in keeping these institutions on an even keel financially.[22]

Significantly, the only possible portrait we have of a leper connected with the order of St Lazarus in England is of a member of the aristocracy (Plate 24). In the Angel Choir of Lincoln Cathedral, constructed between 1255 and 1280 in honour of St Hugh, there are a number of carved stone corbels that may relate to incidents from the life of the saint. One of these, on the north side of the choir,

17 Rawcliffe, *Medicine for the Soul*, p. 37; Satchell, 'Leper Houses', p. 146.

18 J.R. Boyle, *The County of Durham* (London, 1892), pp. 469–72. Sherburn was dedicated to the Blessed Virgin, St Lazarus and his sisters Mary and Martha, but had no connection with the order.

19 P.H. Cullum, *Cremetts and Corrodies: care of the poor and sick in St Leonard's Hospital, York, in the Middle Ages*, Borthwick Paper, 79 (1991), pp. 9–13.

20 Richards, *Medieval Leper*, cover illustration. 'Sum good my gentyll mayster for god sake', says the unfortunate, begging leper.

21 See Chapter 1, pp. 11–12.

22 Satchell, 'Leper-Houses', p. ix.

Plate 24: Thirteenth-century head of a leper from the north aisle of the Angel Choir, Lincoln Cathedral. Possibly Robert FitzPernel, earl of Leicester.

shows a man in an advanced state of lepromatous leprosy, his eyes fixed, his nose collapsed and his mouth locked in a grotesque, gaping smile. Could this be Robert FitzPernel, earl of Leicester, who died in 1204 and was a patron of the order of St Lazarus? According to the *Magna Vita*, Earl Robert unjustly obtained one of Lincoln's episcopal estates and was smitten with leprosy for his sins. Not only this, his sin was visited on his son, who, under the name of William the Leper, was a benefactor of the hospital of St Leonard, Leicester.[23] Frozen in stone,

---

[23] D.L. Douie and D.H. Farmer (eds), *Magna Vita Sancti Hugonis. The Life of St Hugh of Lincoln*, 2 (Edinburgh, 1962), p. 84. I am grateful to Kate Holland for pointing this out to me. This, and other leper imagery in Lincoln Cathedral, is to be the subject of a forthcoming paper.

it would have seemed appropriate that Earl Robert should stand as an exemplar for future generations, his doleful countenance solemnly pointed out to pilgrims wending their way to the shrines behind the high altar.

The cause and spread of the disease was little understood in the Middle Ages and its unpleasant manifestations laid it open to 'negative and positive interpretations'.[24] In particular, the impact it made on the behaviour of its victims was a subject of widespread speculation. The popular belief that lepers were fired by an inordinate sexual appetite, for example, was perpetuated in a range of late-medieval chivalric romances, and the story of Troilus and Cressida recounted the tale of how a high-spirited young woman named Yseut, the wife of King Mark and 'little more than a harlot', received the reward for her immoral life by being sent to live amongst the 'leper-folk' where she, in turn, contracted the disease.[25] Ivain, the leader of the lepers, says to the king:

> 'Give Yseut to us and we will possess her in common. No women ever had a worse end. Sire, there is such lust in us that no woman on earth could tolerate intercourse with us for a single day. The very clothes stick to our bodies. . . . If you give her to us lepers, when she sees our low hovels and looks at our dishes and has to sleep with us . . . when she sees our court and all its discomforts, she would rather be dead than alive . . . She would rather have been burnt.'[26]

Not surprisingly, with sex-crazed lepers in their midst, the attitudes of healthy people were often suspicious. The notion that leprosy was a punishment for sin, as in the case of Earl Robert, was widely held, and the disease was frequently compared with other cankers, such as heresy, which undermined the wellbeing of mankind. In obedience to the Book of Leviticus, in which the Israelites were punished with leprosy for worshipping the golden calf, lepers were to be isolated from centres of population, and the typical medieval leper hospital came to occupy a marginal site on the edge of a town.[27] These notions of seclusion were underlined by the Councils of Westminster (1175 and 1200) and the Third Lateran Council (1179), and in the thirteenth century Henry de Bracton spelt out legal limitations on what a leper could and could not do.[28] In a society rife with rumours about the unpredictable behaviour of lepers, it is not surprising that paranoid fantasies often became focused on this ostracised minority. The lepers' plot of 1321, for example, linked them with Jews and Moslems as part of a sinister conspiracy to overthrow Christianity.[29]

On the other hand, leprosy was sometimes seen as a special mark of divine favour, and uninfected individuals, such as St Hugh, bishop of Lincoln (1186–1200), and Queen Matilda, could mingle freely with sufferers on terms of some physical intimacy. Hugh, for example, not only visited the leper hospitals of his diocese (which probably included at least two institutions managed by the

---

24 Satchell, 'Leper-Houses', p. 21.
25 C. Rawcliffe, *Medicine and Society in Later Medieval England* (Stroud, 1995), pp. 15–16.
26 Orme and Webster, *English Hospital*, p. 26.
27 Leviticus 13: 45–6; Gilchrist, *Contemplation and Action*, p. 40.
28 Orme and Webster, *English Hospital*, pp. 26–7.
29 Rawcliffe, *Medicine and Society*, pp. 14–17; M. Barber, 'Lepers, Jews and Moslems: the plot to overthrow Christendom in 1321', *History*, 66 (1981), pp. 1–17 .

Lazarites), but also took some delight in embracing their inmates, kissing those 'swollen and livid faces, deformed and sanious, with the eyelids everted, the eyeballs dug out, and the lips wasted away, faces which were impossible to touch close or even to behold afar off'.[30] Actions such as these brought their perpetrators closer to Christ's suffering. Touati, in his research on the ecclesiastical province of Sens, has recently amplified this 'positive' image of leprosy by suggesting that lepers, by virtue of their sickness, 'were seen as a category of the religious' and that this was an attitude that was particularly prevalent in the twelfth and thirteenth centuries, just when the hospitals were expanding.[31] Though Satchell believes that Touati's conclusions are 'irrefutable' with regard to France, they nevertheless leave a difficult question when they are applied to England. If lepers were looked on as the religious, why did institutions dedicated to their support fail to pick up the sort of endowments usually associated with monasteries?[32] Among the ordinary leper-houses Satchell found little evidence of generous benefaction, but the order of St Lazarus, of course, was an exception, having a leprous ideology *and* the endowments of a monastery. For this reason it must seriously be considered as the most convincing example of Touati's theory and also its principal manifestation in England. 'The healthy preferred to reserve their major benefaction to religious houses which offered more substantial and enduring spiritual services,' and this must surely have been regarded as true for Burton Lazars.[33]

The fact that the order of St Lazarus prospered as long as it did by association with this unpleasant disease would seem to question two well-established 'negative' benchmarks. First, the notion that leprosy was most commonly associated with sinfulness. If that was the case, why should people so readily have given money and lands to those marked by the judgment of God? Perhaps, on the contrary, the more pragmatic approach suggested by Shahar and Touati for the Latin kingdom and France was characteristic of England too, once the much-quoted literary and theological sources are set aside.[34] Second, the idea that lepers were cut off from Christian society as marginal, mistrusted pariahs. In fact, there was always more contact between leper hospitals and the outside world than is popularly believed. In the fourteenth century healthy people clamoured for placements in them, and in 1334 only one inmate at Holy Innocents', Lincoln, out of a complement of nine, was a leper.[35] Because of the paucity of our sources it is unlikely that these contradictions in the medieval attitude to leprosy will ever be fully reconciled, but enough has survived to illustrate clearly the limitations of a monochrome approach to the problem. The order of St Lazarus was working in a difficult area that raised high and sometimes conflicting emotions.

30 J.F. Dimock (ed.), *Magna Vita S. Hugonis Episcopi Lincolniensis*, Rolls Series, 37 (London, 1864), pp. 163–4; D.H. Farmer, *Saint Hugh of Lincoln* (London, 1985), pp. 45–6.
31 Touati, *Maladie et Société*, pp. 631–748; Satchell, 'Leper-Houses', pp. ix, 19–21.
32 Satchell, 'Leper-Houses', pp. 237, 246.
33 *Ibid*, p. 244.
34 See Chapter 1, pp. 6, 8.
35 See below, p. 162; Orme and Webster, *English Hospital*, pp. 28–9.

Burton Lazars: *Leprosarium* or preceptory?

The belief that Burton Lazars was a leper hospital, similar to Sherburn or Harbledown, was first suggested by William Burton in his *Description of Leicestershire* published in 1622. Burton, it seems, relied heavily on the work of Leland and Stow, though he certainly visited the place and it is possible that he was the recipient of some oral tradition that had survived the sixty years or so since the Dissolution.[36] Nichols, writing in the late eighteenth century, followed the lead of Burton, and by the time of the additions to Dugdale's *Monasticon* in 1830 an orthodoxy, of sorts, had been established. Burton Lazars was 'a well endowed hospital consisting of a master and eight sound, as well as several poor leprous brethren, which was the chief of the spittles or lazar-houses in England, but dependant upon the great house at Jerusalem'.[37]

Despite the lack of clear authority for such statements, which cannot be referenced to extant documents, many subsequent writers have followed them and have added their own embellishments about the site and the part played by the Lazarites in the treatment of leprosy. Rothery, for example, states that:

> The earthworks at the site of the hospital today suggest an elaborate system of moats possibly for isolation purposes. . . . There would also be bathing areas for the afflicted. . . . Harbouring inmates . . . with such a dread disease in any case, would not encourage casual callers. Only the truly sick and destitute would feel moved to make their way down the footpath and knock at the door of the almonry.[38]

The authors of the *Victoria County History* were more measured in their judgement, and Satchell, wisely, distanced himself almost entirely from a consideration of the order. Nevertheless, the commonly held view, most recently expressed by Gilchrist, is that Burton Lazars was a *leprosarium* of very considerable importance.[39] It is necessary to examine carefully what evidence there is to support this notion from topography, archaeology and contemporary documents, since it is critical to our understanding of the activities of the order in England.

The location of Burton Lazars has always been seen as one of its most remarkable features, and its situation on a hilltop caused Nichols to make some interesting comments on the curative effects of the environment:

> There is something uncommonly salubrious in the air here, as well as in the water, which perhaps may increase its effects, situated as it is upon a gentle ascent, surrounded by high hills. To give an instance of this: during the disorders of the murrain among the larger cattle . . . most alarmingly within a century past, the lands in Burton, heretofore the hospital lands, where the pure spring rises, were a happy asylum against the ravages of the murrain: the occupants at such time taking in distempered cattle, where they found a certain cure, to their great emolument.[40]

---

36 Burton, *Leicestershire*, p. 64.
37 Dugdale, *Monasticon*, 6 pt 2, p. 632.
38 C.D. Rothery, *Burton Lazars: story of a village* (1980, 2nd edition Burton Lazars, 1984), pp. 28–9.
39 *VCH, Leicestershire*, 2, pp. 36–9; Gilchrist, *Contemplation and Action*, p. 45.
40 Nichols, *Leicestershire*, 2 pt 1, p. 269.

No one who knows the site today would deny the enlivening qualities of the air, especially in winter, but it is the local water which over the years has received a greater degree of attention both from Nichols and others.

In 1567 Sir William Cecil wrote to Robert Dudley, earl of Leicester, 'wishing myself to be with your lordship at Burton . . . where I am informed this may to grow a sovereign medicine for my gout'. The compiler of the old index of the Pepys Manuscripts, from which this quotation is taken, believed that the location referred to was Burton-on-Trent, Staffordshire, but the new index states Burton Lazars, and this is quite possibly correct since both Cecil and Dudley had claims to land there.[41] If Burton Lazars is indeed the place referred to, it is the earliest surviving reference to the curative power of the water. Two hundred years later Nichols stated, 'The waters are foetid and saline without any mineral taste, but are esteemed pure in the highest degree, and create an appetite. They brace and invigorate weak constitutions and render all less liable to colds and the inclemencies of the weather.'[42] Statements such as these correspond closely to descriptions of the leper hospital at Harbledown and also Satchell's comments about the importance of hydrotherapy in the treatment of the disease.[43]

According to Nichols, there was a spring at Burton, known as St Augustine's Well, which had a 'high reputation' during the medieval period and which was associated with 'an ancient stone cross'. However, having become neglected, the structure was dismantled in about 1740 and the stonework was applied to the repair of the parish church, where some of it may yet survive. In 1760, when the Georgian interest in spas was at its peak, the spring was reopened and a bath and 'drinking-room' established in the village.[44] Anxious to encourage customers, the proprietors of the spa distributed broadsheets advertising its benefits, which, they said, rested on the fact that Burton Lazars had stood in 'high repute' for the cure of leprosy since the twelfth century. The spa was advertised as a 'cold bath of most remarkable healing quality in all sores, scorbutic and cutaneous disorders', and several case histories were recited of sufferers who attributed miraculous recoveries to 'Burton-waters'.[45] For example, Sarah Ward, aged twelve, was brought to the spa soon after it opened because:

> for ten years [she] had laboured under a most inveterate scurvy, her head was one entire scab, her body much blotched whose mother after all the advice she could procure and her being pronounced incurable, brought her to bath in and drink this water, which without any other application in about three months wrought an entire cure. Her skin is quite clear and sound and she in perfect health.[46]

---

41 E.K. Purnell (ed.), *Pepys Mss*, HMC (1911), p. 103. For the interest of Cecil and Dudley in Burton Lazars, see Chapter 7, p. 236.

42 Nichols, *Leicestershire*, 2 pt 1, p. 269.

43 Satchell, 'Leper Houses', pp. 145–7.

44 Nichols, *Leicestershire*, 2 pt 1, p. 269. The name 'St Augustine's Well' is given in LRO, 25D55 on which Nichols relied heavily for his information. What may be the base of a cross and a portion of a canopy are in Burton Lazars churchyard.

45 LRO, 25D55; Throsby, *Leicestershire Views*, pp. 177–81. Complaints included scurvy, ulcers, swellings in the throat and 'blotches and sores'. Cures could be effected by bathing or drinking.

46 *The Leicester and Nottingham Journal*, 10 May 1760.

Nichols, evidently impressed, commented that 'The sores in healing died upon the skin, which peeled off in a white scurf.'[47]

Because of successes such as these, the original spa, which had been hastily constructed, was taken down in 1794 and rebuilt 'on a larger and more commodious plan'. This new bath-house was probably the one stated to have been built in pseudo-ecclesiastical style, having 'church like windows' and 'compartments resembling the old fashioned high church pews'. In fact, 'excepting for the water, the place looked like a church'.[48] Despite this impressive rebuilding, Burton Lazars spa did not have a long life. By 1849 the enterprise had come to an end and the last remains of the bath-house were taken down and the spring covered over.[49] The successive buildings were located on the Melton–Oakham road, opposite Lime Street, where a distinct hump in a paddock still hints at their presence. The existence of a healing spa at Burton Lazars between 1760 and 1849 is therefore beyond dispute and, given the attempt to exploit the history of the place as part of its appeal, it is possible that materials were shifted from the old hospital site to construct the new 'church like' bath-house in 1794. However, the eighteenth-century commentators were on very insecure ground when it came to forging links between 'St Augustine's Well' and medieval leprosy cures. Indeed, it is not clear on what evidence their claims rested, other than the writings of Burton.

An attempt to revive the spa was made by Miss Hartopp of Dalby Hall in 1889 when hydrotherapy was again fashionable because of its reported successes at centres such as Harrogate and Buxton.[50] Again she reverted to what was popularly believed to be the historical tradition, emphasising the 'Rediscovery of the famous Leper Spa celebrated throughout the Middle Ages for its extraordinary cures of leprosy and skin diseases generally', adding, as an afterthought, that in the eighteenth century it had also been found beneficial for 'dyspepsia and general ailments'. In line with the scientific preoccupations of the day, she called in an 'eminent chemist', John Attfield, Professor of Chemistry to the Pharmaceutical Society of Great Britain, to provide supporting evidence, and in a written report he concluded that the spring produced 'a valuable saline and alkaline or anti-acid mineral water of great purity', similar to Appollinaris Water or Lippick Water. 'Aereated and bottled in the usual way it would form a pure and useful table water, especially for persons liable to dyspepsia and various hepatic and gastric troubles.' Interestingly, Attfield made no suggestion that the water might be beneficial for skin disorders, and there is confusion about where exactly his sample originated from. Did it come from 'the original spring of the leper hospital' (presumably the old spa opposite Lime Street); or from another 'more powerful' spring on a different part of the estate (the location of which was not disclosed)? Since Miss Hartopp appears to have been thinking in terms of

47 Nichols, *Leicestershire*, 2 pt 2, p. 269.
48 *Ibid*; LRO, *Leicestershire Villages*, p. 95.
49 P.E. Hunt, *The Story of Melton Mowbray* (1957, 2nd edition Grantham, 1979), p. 44; Rothery, *Burton Lazars*, pp. 30–2.
50 Burton Lazars Church, *Burton Lazars Spa, near to Melton Mowbray, Leicestershire* (including an Analysis and Report by J. Attfield, 1889).

cashing in on bottled mineral water, the new, 'more powerful' spring might be the more likely contender, and if this was indeed the case the link with the village of Burton Lazars, let alone the hospital site, is non-proven.[51] In any event, the plan came to nothing and its only known record is in the form of a distressed advertising brochure propped up in Burton Lazars church.

Much hangs on the question of whether or not the Lazarites had access to, or control of, the health-giving spring opposite Lime Street. Twentieth-century reports describe it as 'chalybeate' (1909) and 'impregnated with sodium chloride and sulphuretted hydrogen' (1931), the latter fitting reasonably well with Attfield's analysis of 1889.[52] Although it was described as St Augustine's Well in the eighteenth century (creating a tentative link with the order), the problem is that it lies well outside the bounds of the hospital, and if it *was* used in the treatment of leprosy the lepers would have to have been taken to the spring or the spring water transported to the lepers. The British Geological Survey reports that the only water on the hospital site, which still fills the moats and fishponds at certain times of the year, is seepage water replenished by surface drainage from rainfall and water percolation from below. Since 'high concentrations of iron, sulphate and chloride are known to occur in ground waters in both the boulder clay and the lias', this seepage water also has a mineral content and therefore, just like the spring water, could be deemed beneficial in terms of hydrotherapy.[53] Even without the spring, the benefits of water to the medieval Lazarites cannot wholly be discounted; with the spring, they stood in control of a remarkable therapeutic asset. Satchell comments that very few samples of water from leper hospitals have been subjected to chemical analysis, and in this context Burton Lazars seems to have fared better than most. Moreover, though 'some of the traditions were probably invented by antiquarians', like Nichols, 'it seems difficult to discount them all'.[54]

Turning to natural features other than water, a botanical survey of the hospital site undertaken in the 1980s revealed little that was unexpected. Only *Euphrasia officinalis* (eyebright) seemed to be out of its usual context, a plant much esteemed in the treatment of colds, sore throats, catarrh and especially complaints of the eye.[55] Another plant, not evident on site today but clearly valued by the order, was *Cuminum cyminum* (cumin). Charters enrolled in the Cartulary indicate an interest in obtaining supplies of cumin seed, which, along with black pepper, was strongly recommended in the *Macer Floridus de Viribus Herbarum* as one of the most useful of all medicinal plants, efficacious in a large number of complaints from aches and pains to cholera and liver and kidney

51 But see L. Richardson, *Wells and Springs of Leicestershire*, Memoirs of the Geological Survey (1931), p. 85, which, similarly, places emphasis on 'sodium chloride and sulphuretted hydrogen' Did Richardson do his own sampling or did he rely on Attfield, perhaps getting the wrong spring as a result?

52 G.W. Lamplugh *et al.*, *The Geology of the Melton Mowbray District and South-East Nottinghamshire (Sheet 142)*, Memoirs of the Geological Survey (1909), p. 35; Richardson, *Wells and Springs*, p. 85.

53 UNCLH, letter from R.A. Monkhouse, British Geological Survey, to J.M. Allsop, 8 December 1986.

54 Satchell, 'Leper-Houses', p. 146.

55 B. Moffat *et al.* (eds), *Sharp Practice. Reports on Researches into the Medieval Hospital at Soutra, Lothian Region*, Soutra Hospital Archaeoethnopharmacological Research Project, 1 (Edinburgh, 1986), 2 (Edinburgh, 1988); Phillips and Foy, *Herbs*, pp. 140–1. The survey was undertaken by Jean Nicholson.

disorders.[56] However, the evidence in both cases is no more than slight. Rents were often paid in cumin in the Middle Ages, and certainly neither plant was valued in the treatment of leprosy. Moreover, religious orders that made no contribution to the care of the sick were just as likely to maintain supplies of medicines such as these for the treatment of their own brethren who would inevitably fall sick from time to time.

Given the consistent reports of the sulphurous nature of Burton's water, it is difficult to believe that Roger de Mowbray was not aware of this in the twelfth century and that this knowledge did not contribute to his decision to give these particular lands to the Lazarites. After all, he was acting in support of what was probably the major foundation for lepers in the Christian world. There may even have been a small, informal community of lepers already there, drawn to the place by the acknowledged qualities of the water.[57] It was not unreasonable for him to suppose that, once the site was given to the order, it may have been developed into something resembling the leper hospital in Jerusalem, with which he must have been familiar. He was not to know how things were to develop over the forthcoming years. In other words, Mowbray's grant of land, which, like Harbledown, may have been uniquely suitable for a leper hospital in topographical terms, did not mean that it was inevitable that a leper hospital was going to develop there. This is an important point, which helps to explain much of the confusion that was to develop around the site in later years.

Little remains at Burton today except for a fairly extensive series of earthworks, mapped by Brown and a team from the University of Leicester in the 1980s and published in *Landscape History* (Plan 3).[58] This has been improved by the addition of parchmarks plotted by Allsop and Hatton during the dry summer of 1996.[59] The parallels against which these earthworks can be evaluated are the hospital and preceptory plans derived from the work of Gilchrist, though she would be the first to concede that these were a complex set of institutions with few unifying features and little excavation work to provide clear comparison. Large hospitals, following the Augustinian rule, tended to be urban and to adopt the 'double courtyard' plan – as at St Cross, Winchester, or St Leonard's, York – having an 'inner court' for the use of professed brethren and an 'outer court' for service buildings.[60] Smaller hospitals – and these were the clear majority – were much more variable. Leper hospitals were often positioned on the outskirts of major towns and had their own chapels and burial grounds, signalling 'the journeying point at which the town met its surroundings, and at which the traveller or pilgrim passed from one territory into another'.[61] Satchell

---

56 G. Frisk (ed.), *A Middle English Translation of Macer Floridus de Viribus Herbarum* (Upsala, 1949), pp. 75–6, 177–8. For grants of cumin at Burton Lazars, see, for example, BL, Cart, ff. 97, 107, 142; and at St Giles's BL, Harl Mss, 4015, ff. 129, 131; Williams, *Early Holborn*, 2, no. 1642.

57 Many leper hospitals developed in this way. Satchell, 'Leper-Houses', pp. 142–5.

58 For the surviving earthworks at Burton, and the difficulties of interpretation, see Brown, 'Burton Lazars', pp. 31–45.

59 UNCLH, J.M. Allsop and M. Hatton, 'A ground survey of crop (parch) marks on the earthwork site of the medieval order of St Lazarus at Burton Lazars near Melton Mowbray, Leicestershire, with a reappraisal of the earthwork map in the light of this new evidence', MFR, 96/10 (1996).

60 Cullum, *Cremetts and Corrodies*, p. 8; Rawcliffe, *Medicine for the Soul*, pp. 34–64.

61 Gilchrist, *Contemplation and Action*, p. 40; Orme and Webster, *English Hospital*, pp. 87–8.

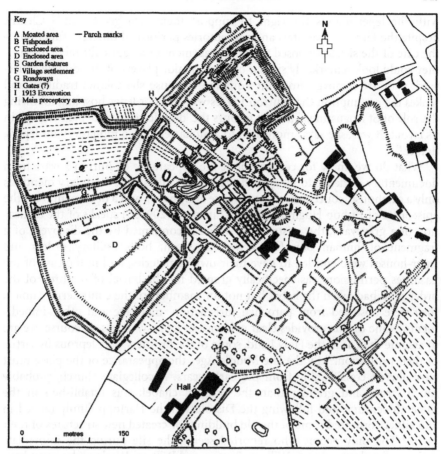

Key

A Moated area   — Parch marks
B Fishponds
C Enclosed area
D Enclosed area
E Garden features
F Village settlement
G Roadways
H Gates (?)
I 1913 Excavation
J Main preceptory area

N

0   metres   150

Plan 3: Burton Lazars Preceptory.

suggests that these relatively high-profile locations were designed to be advantageous in the collection of alms on which the hospitals depended heavily.[62]

The preceptories of the military orders, on the other hand, were buried deep in the countryside following the example of the Templar house at South Witham, Lincolnshire, excavated during the 1960s.[63] Although this was a minor house, having none of the impressive architecture of its near neighbour, Temple Bruer, it demonstrates well the emphasis on agricultural production, with features such as fishponds, workshops and barns assuming prominence. These were rural sites with a 'limited religious function', characterised by dispersed buildings clustered around small chapels such as survive for the Lazarites at Grattemont and Pastoral in France.[64] Gilchrist concludes that 'they may have resembled the larger colleges of secular canons or hospitals', though they shared

62 Satchell, 'Leper-Houses', pp. 173–5, 227–32.
63 'South Witham', pp. 232–7; Gilchrist, *Contemplation and Action*, pp. 69, 81–6.
64 Gilchrist, *Contemplation and Action*, pp. 74–80, 103.

with the leper-houses the right to support their own graveyards.[65] Clearly, despite the fact that hospitals and preceptories performed different functions – the care of the sick as opposed to the management of an agricultural demesne – they could look remarkably similar once the major players of the 'double court-yard' plan are removed from the equation. Because she follows tradition and makes the assumption that Burton Lazars was a major leper hospital, following the rule of St Augustine, Gilchrist favours the 'double courtyard' plan to explain its layout. It was, she says, 'more akin to a monastery' . . . a monastery for lepers, in fact.[66]

What do we know for certain about the appearance of Burton Lazars from documentary evidence to set against these generalities? The Cartulary mentions only a gatehouse, courtyard, chapter house and chapel, and a document from the episcopate of Bishop Hugh de Wells of Lincoln (1209–35) speaks of the dedica-tion of a graveyard, the existence of which is confirmed by the discovery of a fragment of human bone.[67] As we have seen, both military orders and leper-houses were entitled to have their own cemeteries, and in the case of the Lazarites permission was specifically granted for the burial of brethren of the order, who had taken the habit, but not for members of the confraternity unless they were absolved from parochial jurisdiction, marriage and other impedi-ments. None of this provides clear evidence of leprosy, unless, of course, we are to assume that, as in the Holy Land, some of the brothers were leprous by virtue of their profession.[68] By the late Middle Ages the appearance of the place must have altered considerably from the early years. A collegiate church, probably much larger and grander than the original chapel, was established in the fifteenth century; and following the Dissolution the Hartopp family moved in and either converted some of the old buildings or created new structures of their own.[69] The only people who reported seeing the site during the immediate post-medieval period were William Burton and William Wyrley, who must have visited some time between 1598 and 1609.[70] Burton noted the existence of a chapel (almost certainly the new church of the fifteenth century) and Wyrley commented that the 'monastery' stood adjacent to its south wall.[71] Whether he meant by this a set of new buildings associated with the college, or something older, cannot be determined.

The evidence from Brown's landscape plan is even more sketchy. It is clear that some of the complex was constructed over the top of pre-existing ridge and furrow, and there is a moated area and a series of fishponds, both of which still retain some water. A prominent 'T' feature is probably associated with a

65 *Ibid*, pp. 67, 103.

66 *Ibid*, p. 45.

67 BL, Cart, ff. 18, 22, 53, 70; *DCAD*, 5, p. 100 The fragment of human bone, identified by Manchester as a piece of jaw, displays no signs of leprosy, though this is a part of the body where degeneration is unlikely to have occurred.

68 See Chapter 1, p. 8.

69 See Chapter 3, pp. 92–9; Chapter 7, pp. 236–7.

70 L. Campbell and F. Steer, *A Catalogue of Manuscripts in the College of Arms Collections*, 1 (London, 1988), p. 352.

71 Burton, *Leicestershire*, p. 64; CA, Vincent Mss, 197, f. 39v.

sixteenth- or seventeenth-century garden, since comparisons have been discovered elsewhere, and the whole of the settled area is enclosed on three sides by a clearly defined ditch and bank boundary.[72] Outside of this area there are the probable remains of a shifted medieval village to the west; some enclosures probably associated with the management of livestock; and a system of trackways connecting up the site with major roads in the vicinity. Unfortunately, the earthworks and parchmarks within the main settled area are not of sufficient clarity to enable a coherent picture to emerge, the confusion being created by the multi-generational nature of the site and localised disruption caused by the excavations of 1913.[73] Nor has it been possible to employ the technique of fieldwalking to discover more about the site by an assessment of small finds. Though occasional fragments of medieval pottery and other objects have come to light, these have not been on the scale to enable any firm conclusions about dating or function to be reached. The reason for this dearth is that the hospital site and surrounding fields are virtually all under pasture. Moreover, the Scheduled status of the monument is likely to preclude excavation for the foreseeable future.

It has been suggested by Allsop, independent of Gilchrist, that concealed within this confusion there is the suggestion of a 'double courtyard' plan, with an 'inner court' occupying the southern area (church, chapter house and cloister) and an 'outer court' to the north (Plan 4). It is argued that this plan fits well with the topography of the site and practical issues such as drainage.[74] However, if such a plan is evident from the surviving landscape features, it is not clear whether it applies to the pre- or post-collegiate phase, and the theory would need to be tested by excavation before it is finally confirmed.[75] One of the strongest arguments against it is that it conflicts with the observation of Wyrley, who suggests that the monastic buildings were on the south of the church, not the north as argued by Allsop. Basically, given our present state of knowledge, it is not possible to make a definitive statement about the function of Burton Lazars based on its surviving form. The few features that can be diagnosed with any certainty (boundaries, fishponds, a moated enclosure, stock pens, trackways and a garden feature) are more secular than ecclesiastical and could relate equally well to the activities of a medieval preceptory, a hospital or a post-Dissolution estate. Its location does not help much either, since its position, about a mile away from a small town, Melton Mowbray, makes it neither suburban nor rural in the true sense of the word. Certainly there is no clear evidence of Gilchrist's *leprosarium*, and her 'monastery' must be treated with equal caution.

If evidence derived from the site is tenuous in establishing the presence of a

---

[72] For a comparable garden feature, see R.F. Hartley, *The Medieval Earthworks of Central Leicestershire*, Leicestershire Museums Publication, no. 103 (Leicester, 1989), pp. 8–9, 19.

[73] See UNCLH, Allsop and Hatton, 'Crop Marks'; J.M. Allsop, M.J. Allsop and M. Hatton, 'Service trenches adjacent to the SE of the hospital site at Burton Lazars', MFR, 99/7 (1999).

[74] UNCLH, J.M. Allsop, 'The interpretation of the earthwork site of the order of St Lazarus at Burton Lazars', MFR, 01/10 (2001).

[75] Rawcliffe points out that the new colleges of the fifteenth century were great favourers of cloisters and quadrangles. 'The layout enabled priests and choristers to process into churches which . . . were growing larger and increasingly ornate'. Rawcliffe, *Medicine for the Soul*, p. 61.

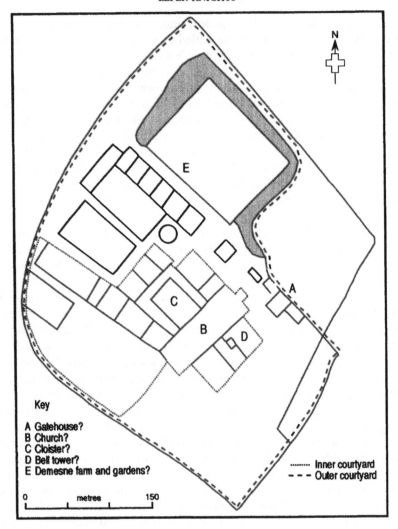

Key

A Gatehouse?
B Church?
C Cloister?
D Bell tower?
E Demesne farm and gardens?

········· Inner courtyard
‒ ‒ ‒ Outer courtyard

0   metres   150

Plan 4: Burton Lazars preceptory: a possible interpretation.

leprosarium at Burton, there is a further clue that needs to be considered before the notion is abandoned altogether. This is the so-called 'leper head', now preserved in Burton Lazars church but believed to originate from the hospital (Plate 25).[76] The 'leper head' is a stone corbel, which has been dated to *c.*1250–1350 and shows an individual with staring eyes, a collapsed nose and wide, gaping mouth. Manchester regards it as a classic portrayal of someone suffering from lepromatous leprosy and it certainly has clear parallels with the corbel, discussed above, on the north side of the Angel Choir in Lincoln Cathedral: 'The orbital, nasal and oral changes portrayed by the "leper head" sculpture indicate that the carving is of the head of a person with advanced

76 D. Marcombe and K. Manchester, 'The Melton Mowbray "Leper Head": an historical and medical investigation', *MH*, 34 (1990), pp. 86–91.

Plate 25: The 'leper head' from Burton Lazars
church. A thirteenth/fourteenth-century sculpture
believed to have come from the preceptory of
Burton Lazars.

lepromatous leprosy.'[77] Who was this unfortunate person? Rawcliffe has pointed
out that medieval hospitals sometimes incorporated imagery relating to their
foundation, and it is just possible that the 'leper head' is intended to be a representation of one of the saints venerated by the order.[78] The unusual headgear,
reminiscent of the folds of a shroud, could conceivably relate to either of the two
Lazaruses on the basis that in both cases death was a significant element in their
legends.[79] Indeed, the Burton Lazars corbel has marked similarities with Giotto's
fresco in the Arena Chapel, Padua, showing St Lazarus of Bethany, with the
obvious qualification that the English representation is leprous and the Italian
one is not (Plate 2 above).[80] If a shroud was a significant feature in the iconography of Lazarus of Bethany, and if at Burton Lazars we have a shrouded leper, it

---

[77] *Ibid*, pp. 89–90.
[78] Rawcliffe, *Medicine for the Soul*, p. 63.
[79] See Chapter 1, pp. 3–6.
[80] G. Duby (ed.), *A History of Private Life, 2, Revelations of the Medieval World*, translated by A.
     Goldhammer (Cambridge, Massachusetts and London, 1988), p. 513.

would seem to give support to the hybrid Lazarus featured in *The Cyrurgie of Guy de Chauliac* as being in some way special to the order.[81]

But whether the corbel represented St Lazarus or simply a generic leper (projecting the idea of the living dead, perhaps?), its presence at Burton Lazars does not take us on much further with regard to the function of the place. Assuming that the 'leper head' did indeed originate from the hospital, which on balance seems likely, it still does not prove that lepers were being treated there, simply that lip-service was being paid to some received ideology concerning lepers. Indeed, it may be that the inclusion of this sort of sculpture in the fabric of the building was no more than an attempt to use art to compensate for a life-style that had, actually, become largely detached from the subject matter of the imagery. If this was the case, the 'leper head' could be seen as yet another example of the exploitation of the *image* of leprosy rather than a determined purpose to do anything about it.

But possibly the clearest evidence concerning the nature of the house at Burton comes from the charters enrolled in the Cartulary, most of them dating from the period *c*.1190–1250 when lepromatous leprosy was perceived to be a major social problem in England and elsewhere. Out of 356 charters providing some sort of description of the order, 48 (13 per cent) simply refer to the lepers of Jerusalem – and these are usually the earliest – while 42 (12 per cent) specify the lepers of Jerusalem and their brethren in England. The largest number of grants, 147 (41 per cent), are made simply to the brethren of the order at Burton. However, the most interesting section of charters, totalling 115 (32 per cent), makes reference to the lepers of Jerusalem along with their *healthy* brethren in England. A typical form of words is 'Gift . . . to God, St Mary, the leprous brethren of St Lazarus of Jerusalem and their healthy brethren dwelling in England'.[82] Thus, a clear distinction is drawn between the leprous section of the order, based in Jerusalem, and the healthy brethren in England, or at Burton as is sometimes more specifically stated.[83]

This pattern is complicated by four charters (1 per cent) that mention the lepers of Jerusalem in conjunction with *leprous* brethren at Burton. For example, 'the leprous brethren dwelling in England at Burton' or 'the leprous brethren of St Lazarus of Burton serving God therein'.[84] These individuals must have been an English branch of the leper brothers recruited in the Holy Land, and their presence at Burton proves that in the mid-twelfth century, at least, the nature of the operation in England matched that in Jerusalem. However, this pristine ideology probably lasted little longer than 20 years. In 1184 William Burdet granted Tilton hospital and its property to the 'infirm' brethren of St Lazarus, the charter being witnessed by Arnald, 'prior of the infirm'.[85] Arnald, of course, raises the possibility that other officers of the order described as priors before 1208 were, like him, bearing special responsibility for the leper brothers and were, possibly,

---

[81] See Chapter 1, pp. 5–6.
[82] BL, Cart, f. 12. For other examples of this form of words see ff. 2, 3, 8, 11, 14, 19, 20, 23–30.
[83] *Ibid*, f. 8.
[84] *Ibid*, ff. 3, 105.
[85] *Ibid*, f. 203.

lepers themselves.[86] Was Burdet's grant of Tilton a move to separate the healthy and leprous sections of the order, with the uninfected brothers remaining at Burton Lazars and the lepers being shipped off to Tilton? This theory would help to explain why Tilton became gradually marginalised and eventually closed down in the thirteenth century, in line with the decline of the disease and the changing attitudes of the order.

If Burton Lazars had been a conventional *leprosarium*, such as those studied by Satchell, it would have been much more direct when it came to spelling out the details of its incorporation and would have used descriptions similar to other hospitals – 'the lepers of the hospital of St Bartholomew without Oxford' or 'the master and lepers of St Leonard, Nottingham', for example.[87] The Burton charters are equally ambiguous when it comes to determining whether or not the grantees of land to the order were making their gifts in return for some sort of service offered to them by the institution. Generally no *quid pro quo* is stated, though the lack of such a statement does not necessarily mean that no arrangement between grantee and grantor existed.[88] Satchell has argued that such gifts were probably quite common, but tended to be disguised because of fears of accusations of simony.[89] At Burton only William, son of Roger Wisman of Kirkeby, noted that he had a claim to sustenance from the master and brethren in return for a virgate of land.[90] This is the only documentary evidence from the Cartulary (or indeed from any other early source) that might hint at some sort of institutional placement, even for a corrodian, apart from one brought about by very unusual circumstances. In 1319 Thomas de Standen, a former Templar, selected Burton Lazars as the place of his enforced retirement following the suppression of his order. Bishop John Dalderby of Lincoln (1299–1320) duly wrote to the master and brethren asking them to accept him and also to the prior of the Hospitallers requesting that his stipend be paid.[91] It was an incident that, significantly, bound the place into the traditions of the military orders rather than the care of the sick.

The conclusion must be that the reputation of Burton Lazars as a major *leprosarium* is much exaggerated, and is based on a misunderstanding of the activities of the order in the Holy Land in relation to its role in England. It is borne out by neither documentary nor archaeological evidence. In the historical tradition, the myth began with William Burton in the seventeenth century and was amplified in the eighteenth and nineteenth centuries when Burton Lazars was developed, unsuccessfully, as a spa.[92] Indeed, it could be suggested that a

---

86 These were Robert, son of Hugh (mid- to late twelfth century) and William (oc.1204, 1208). PRO, CP 25/1/121/6; Farnham, 1, p. 252; LRO, DE2242/5. Thereafter the term 'prior' does not occur.

87 *CPR, 1266–72*, pp. 27, 255.

88 See, for example, the case of Elias de Amundeville at Carlton-le-Moorland cited below. Elias attached no conditions to his charters, yet it is plain from the Hundred Rolls (1274) that his grants made provision for a leprous daughter. BL, Cart, ff. 247–8; *Rot Hund*, 1, p. 284.

89 Satchell, 'Leper-Houses', p. 235.

90 BL, Cart, f. 209.

91 LAO, Dalderby Memoranda, p. 986.

92 Burton, however, does note the continued prevalence of leprosy in Cornwall 'occasioned most by the disorderly eating of sea fish, newly taken, and principally the livers of them, not well prepared, soused,

piece of creative image building on the part of the order in England misled historians for 400 years after the Reformation. Given the circumstances of the foundation of the hospital in the Holy Land, incorporating both healthy and leprous brethren, it would be unlikely, perhaps, if some reflection of this did not percolate through to England in the early years. That may be sufficient to explain the very few charters in the Cartulary mentioning leprous brethren at Burton. However, it probably soon became apparent that the presence of leper brothers was incompatible with the demands of the master-general that Burton Lazars should return ever greater profits.

The solution seems to have been to marginalise the lepers to a separate institution, Tilton, with its own rules and endowments, leaving Burton to concentrate on money-raising activities. The fact that the topographical advantages of Burton Lazars in the treatment of leprosy were squandered by this separation does not seem to have figured largely in the decision-making process. It was the bigger, wealthier estate and that was what counted. Even after the abandonment of Burton by the leper brothers it would have been difficult to have refused sustenance to an itinerant leper who turned up unannounced at the gatehouse or even a *nuntius* from a smaller institution.[93] Cullum has underlined the importance of casual relief distributed to the poor and needy at the hospital gate of St Leonard's, York, and these spontaneous acts of charity went without saying in the world of the medieval hospital.[94] But the presence of the occasional leper soliciting alms is not sufficient to justify the very substantial reputation that has grown up around this place over the years. The emphasis of the charters is very much on *healthy* brethren who were in England to do the practical work of raising money for the Crusade. For this they needed a base that was, essentially, a preceptory rather than a refuge for the sick, an institution to support the work of the leper hospital at Jerusalem rather than to replicate it. This important change of emphasis may not at first have been as clearly understood by English founders and benefactors as it was by successive masters-general of the order. Indeed, the distinction may have been deliberately clouded, even after the first leper brothers were packed off to Tilton.

The daughter houses

The conflict between image and reality, evident at Burton Lazars, also characterised the relationship between the English mother house and some of her original dependencies. The word 'hospital' is often encountered in the context of the preceptory at Burton, even though it only had a very indirect role in the treatment of the sick. The same word was also applied to the subsidiary houses with equal ambiguity, since sometimes we are dealing with a place for the care of the sick and sometimes with a preceptory or grange, a smaller version of the

---

pickled or seasoned'; Burton, *Leicestershire*, p. 64. Other contemporaries were aware of this same phenomenon. C. Creighton, *A History of Epidemics in Britain*, 1 (London, 1965), p. 82.

93   For *nuntii*, see Satchell, 'Leper-Houses', p. 168.

94   Cullum, *Cremetts and Corrodies*, p. 30.

'hospital' at Burton.[95] As Satchell has commented, 'Though some of these [Lazarite] houses catered in part for lepers, they were institutionally different from ordinary leper-houses.'[96]

This confused state of affairs was caused by the fact that twelfth-century patrons, who had already established small local foundations for lepers, sometimes felt that it was in the best interests of the institution, and of their soul's health, to hand over management and control to the order of St Lazarus, a trend legitimised by Clement IV's bull of 1265.[97] These small leper-houses were often set up with minimal endowments and tended to be based on spiritual *foci* such as hermitages or holy wells; often they were designed principally to cater for leprous relatives of the founder.[98] Some became placed on a more formal footing as time went on, and the gift of such an institution to the order of St Lazarus must have been designed to do just that. The order invariably accepted these hospitals, not so much from a desire to nurse the sick, it seems, but because of the endowments they brought with them, funding which could eventually be diverted away from the localities towards the main priorities of the order in the Latin kingdom. The order of St Thomas of Acre, which similarly received gifts of working hospitals, found itself in exactly the same position. According to Forey, 'once the military orders had dependencies in the West, patrons expected them to perform the same functions as other religious houses; establishments in western Europe were not viewed merely as administrative centres for the collection of revenues'.[99] Yet that is exactly what the military orders wanted them to be, and several of the smaller hospitals of the order of St Thomas, such as those at Doncaster and Buckingham, were closed down to enable more money to be sent to the East.

Gilchrist suggests that Burton Lazars had the supervision of 12 smaller leper hospitals, but in reality the number of unambiguous foundations was much fewer.[100] Of the subsidiary houses only Harehope, Foulsnape and Tilton probably began life with some sort of caring role, Tilton being granted by William Burdet in 1184 on the specific understanding that 'the brethren will hold the hospital according to the rules of the house'.[101] Locko and Threckingham are more difficult cases. At Locko, although no hospital function is spelt out, the unusual place name (indicating a sealed enclosure) and the presence of a holy well and chapel (possibly with a burial ground attached) imply that lepers may well have been present, at least in the early years of its existence.[102]

---

95   There is no evidence, for example, that Choseley was ever anything more than a preceptory. Knowles and Hadcock, *Medieval Religious Houses*, p. 352; NRO, Norwich Consistory Court, Will Register 1370–1383, Heydon, f. 155 (MF 22).

96   Satchell, 'Leper-Houses', p. 75.

97   See Chapter 1, pp. 15–16.

98   Satchell, 'Leper-Houses', pp. vii, 142–5, 150–1, 222.

99   Forey, 'St Thomas of Acre', p. 493.

100 Gilchrist, *Contemplation and Action*, p. 61.

101 BL, Cart. f. 203; Hodgson, 'Hospital of St Lazarus', pp. 76–9; M.H. Dodds (ed.), *A History of Northumberland*, 14 (Newcastle-upon-Tyne, 1935), pp. 417–22; R. Holmes, 'The Hospital of Foulsnape in the West Riding', *Yorkshire Archaeological and Topographical Journal*, 10 (1889), pp. 543–53.

102 Marcombe, 'Locko', pp. 51–63.

Threckingham was stated to have a 'St Lazarus hospital' for a short period in the late thirteenth and early fourteenth centuries. In 1292 and 1299 unbeneficed priests were appointed to serve in it, and in 1319 there is mention of a master, James.[103] Chaplains are unlikely to have been a priority if Threckingham had been only a preceptory, so there must be a possibility that it too, like Locko, for a while catered for lepers. But the clearest early examples are of working leper hospitals being handed over to the order as going concerns, which happened at Harting, founded by Henry Hussey early in the reign of Henry II, and at Carlton-le-Moorland where the Amundevilles endowed a small institution in the second half of the twelfth century. In 1180 Ralph de Amundeville gave the hospital to the order on condition it provided food and clothing for four lepers there, and a little later Elias de Amundeville added to the endowment 'because a certain daughter of his was a leper'.[104] Ignoring St Giles's, Holborn, and Holy Innocents', Lincoln, which in terms of their leper hospital status were in a category of their own, the order supervised two (certain), three (probable) and two (possible) smaller leper-houses. Moreover, none of these seven endured for more than a short period of time with a caring function.

There may have been unfulfilled intentions of establishing leper hospitals at other locations, reflecting the case of Burton Lazars itself. At Braceborough, Lincolnshire, the rectory had fallen into the hands of the order by 1221, though there is no evidence that any lands in the area ever followed. What made the village attractive was the fact that it had a powerful spring with a reputation for healing qualities, especially for eczema and skin disorders.[105] Similarly, the order's land on Dampgate, Kings Lynn, was in a classic liminal spot, the sort of place often colonised by leper hospitals. It was situated on the margins of the town, between Bishop's Bridge and the drawbridge, and close to the hospital of St John the Baptist. Even if a hospital was never established there, it was an excellent position from which to solicit alms, being situated on one of the major thoroughfares in and out of this bustling seaport.[106] Braceborough and Kings Lynn may have been potential hospital sites that came to nothing, perhaps because of the order's lack of enthusiasm or resources to develop them.

The case of Harehope is relatively well documented but with the usual frustrating gaps in the evidence. The date of the foundation of the hospital is not clear and, according to Dodds, the early history of the township is 'somewhat confused'.[107] It was granted to Gospatric, first earl of Dunbar, by Henry I as part of the lordship of Beanley, but Tynemouth Priory also had an interest by virtue of another grant to St Alban's Abbey, Tynemouth's mother house, by Queen

103 R.M.T. Hill (ed.), *Rolls and Registers of Bishop Oliver Sutton*, 7, LRS, 69 (1975), pp. 24, 119–20; *CPR, 1317–21*, p. 378. The priests were Richard de Kirkeby (1292) and Thomas de Chalcombe (1299).

104 BL, Cart, ff. 245–6; *Rot Hund*, 1, p. 284; *VCH, Sussex*, 2, p. 103. In 1162 Henry II granted the lepers of Harting a fair on St John's day and its eve and morrow.

105 *Kelly's Directory of Lincolnshire, 1905* (London, 1905), p. 101. In 1905 Braceborough Spa was said to produce 1,500,000 gallons of water per day. Francis Willis MD had established a bath-house there for the treatment of the sick.

106 Rutledge, 'Kings Lynn', pp. 94, 108.

107 Dodds, *Northumberland*, 14, p. 419.

Matilda.[108] Tynemouth, indeed, came to have a major stake in the area because of a further grant from Richard de Marisco, bishop of Durham (1217–26). This was of the church of Eglingham, in which parish Harehope is situated, given to improve the quality of the beer consumed by the St Albans monks.[109] Between 1138 and 1166 Gospatric, second earl of Dunbar, granted Harehope to his younger brother, Edward, who was succeeded by his son, Waldeve, after 1178.[110] It was probably Waldeve who founded the hospital at Harehope, presumably for lepers, some time in the late twelfth century. The first reference relates to a master, Walter de Novo Castro, in 1189, and either then or soon after that date the institution was handed over to the order of St Lazarus by Waldeve.[111] The order was almost certainly in possession by 1230, and in 1247 the gift was recorded in an inquest before the *Curia Regis*.

Difficulties with Tynemouth Priory were evidently ongoing and may have been one of the reasons for Waldeve wanting to be rid of the place. In the early thirteenth century German, prior of Tynemouth, and Osbert, master of Harehope, reached an agreement over 30 acres of land in Horshalewes, but by 1235 the compact had broken down and the two sides were at odds again.[112] Whereas in 1235 the master of Harehope, Thomas, was pleading in his own right, by 1292 his successor, John de Horbling, was clearly described as 'master of the hospital of St Lazarus of Harehope'.[113] The assumption that Tilton and Harehope were leper hospitals is not made because lepers are specifically mentioned in either case, but because their secular founders believed that the order of St Lazarus was the right organisation to entrust with their management. Only at Harting and Carlton-le-Moorland is the documentary evidence beyond dispute.

Of these six early institutions (at the most) that probably catered for lepers, Harehope and Tilton have both left evidence on the landscape in terms of earthworks. Neither conforms to the classic leper hospital plan of being on the edge of a town, since both occupy isolated rural positions, Harehope especially so. Situated in the midst of a prehistoric highland landscape in the parish of Eglingham, the area is pock-marked with hill forts, cyst burials and ring-and-cup marks on rock outcrops (Plan 5).[114] A circular feature, of quite considerable size, is located near the hospital on the edge of an enclosure remarkably similar in shape to that

---

108 *Ibid*; Hodgson, 'Hospital of St Lazarus', pp. 76–7. H.T. Riley (ed.), *Gesta Abbatum Monasterii Sancti Albani, 1, Chronico Monasterii S. Albani*, Rolls Series, 28 (1867), pp. 67–8. A curious notion grew up that Harehope was actually in the parish of Eddleston, Peebleshire. It began in G. Chalmers, *Caledonia*, 4 (Paisley, 1889), p. 943, and was perpetuated in R.N. Hadcock, 'A Map of Medieval Northumberland and Durham', *AA*, 4th series, 16 (1939), p. 166. The confusion is set to rest by Barrow in *Regesta Regum Scottorum*, 2, pp. 162–3, who states that the belief is 'erroneous'.

109 Riley, *Gesta Abbatum*, 1, pp. 320–1; H.H.E. Craster, *A History of Northumberland*, 8 (Newcastle-upon-Tyne, 1907), p. 74.

110 Hodgson, 'Harehope', p. 77; Dodds, *Northumberland*, p. 419; *CDS*, 1, pp. 316–7.

111 D.S. Boutflower (ed.), *Fasti Dunelmensis*, SurS, 139 (1926), p. 195.

112 *Northumberland Pleas, 1198–1272*, Newcastle-upon-Tyne Records Committee, 2 (1922), pp. 115–16; *Curia Regis Rolls, 15, 1233–37*, pp. 443–4. It is possible that this master is Osbert de Stanford, subsequently master of Burton Lazars. See Appendix 1.

113 PRO, KB 27/129, m.69. See also AC, Archives of the duke of Northumberland, Northumberland Collections, 23, p. 428.

114 Allsop, 'Harehope Hospital'.

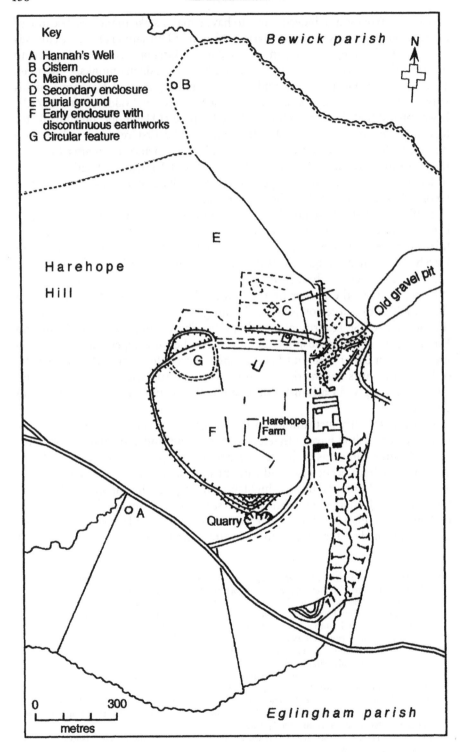

Key

A Hannah's Well
B Cistern
C Main enclosure
D Secondary enclosure
E Burial ground
F Early enclosure with
    discontinuous earthworks
G Circular feature

Bewick parish

N

o B

E

H a r e h o p e

H i l l

Old gravel pit

C

D

G

Harehope
Farm

F

o A

Quarry

0   300

metres

Eglingham parish

Plan 5: Harehope hospital.

at Tilton.[115] Though this area is bounded in part with linear banks and contains fragmentary earthworks, the main focus of the hospital was to the north. In 1308 Sir Adam Veau spoke of 'the houses in our courtyard of Harehope', suggesting a fairly random and dispersed settlement.[116] Two enclosures have been located, one of them, no doubt, Veau's 'courtyard' of 1308: first, a large rectangular enclosure (about 200 x 115m) surrounded by linear mounds, and second, a smaller, less regular one, with discontinuous earthworks. It was in this second enclosure that the remains of a building were shown to the county archaeologist in 1955.[117] At the time of this visit, the farmer pointed out an area to the west, below the cistern on the hillside, which he said was the burial ground, but no evidence of this can be discerned from the earthworks. Beyond the enclosures, an area of disturbance near the stream may point to the existence of a watermill.

Tilton, in the parish of Cold Newton, provides evidence of a clear ditch and bank boundary, similar to that at Burton Lazars, with evidence of rectangular structures and a prominent 'U' feature within it (Plan 6). There is one building that is outside the boundary and another that crosses it, suggestive of functions that were shared between the institution and the world outside its walls. These may possibly be identified with a chantry chapel and smithy, which documentary sources confirm to have existed at Tilton in the thirteenth century.[118] Though both Harehope and Tilton provide evidence of enclosed areas and structures, which would have been common to both hospital and preceptory-style institutions, like Burton Lazars the archaeology of neither provides definitive evidence of function. In both cases their possible leper hospital status is to be inferred from documentary evidence alone. However, what does survive fits well with their small-scale and informal beginnings, which may have been no more than a series of simple structures within an enclosure.

There was no avoiding the responsibility to manage and maintain these places in the years immediately after their donation, especially when the relatives of founders and benefactors were living there, but over the longer term it was the clear policy of the order to abandon these small outposts and develop them simply as granges, or working farms, with no clearly defined charitable provision. Harting was sold to Dureford Abbey in about 1248, the last reference to Harehope is in 1334/5 and Locko disappears from the records after 1347.[119] Foulsnape and Carlton-le-Moorland appear to have been similarly short-lived, though at Foulsnape the master of St Nicholas's hospital, Pontefract, had to find a chaplain to do service there three days a week in 1357; and as late as 1507 a John Bule described himself as 'of the hospital of St Michael the Archangel, Pontefract' (i.e. Foulsnape).[120]

---

115 It is suggested that both of these may represent early field boundaries, prior to the respective institutions being established.

116 GRO, J7/67/02/001/00/00 (MF 1354).

117 Northumberland County Council, SMR ID 3618.

118 UNCLH, J.M. Allsop, 'Preliminary notes on Tilton Hospital', MFR (2001).

119 J.C. Hodgson (ed.), *A History of Northumberland*, 7 (Newcastle-upon-Tyne, 1904), pp. 56–7; M.T. Martin (ed.), *The Percy Chartulary*, SurS, 117 (1909), p. 303; Knowles and Hadcock, *Medieval Religious Houses*, p. 362.

120 Holmes, 'The Hospital of Foulsnape', p. 552; J. Raine (ed.), *Testamenta Eboracensia*, 4, SurS, 53 (1868), p. 93.

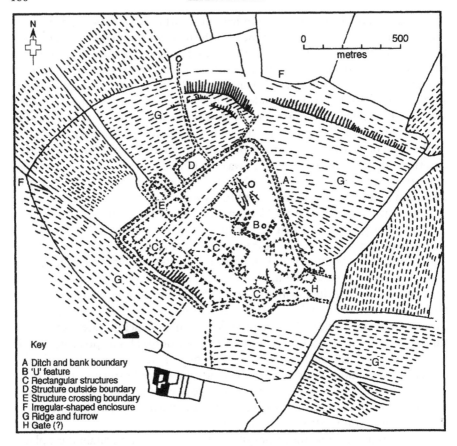

Key

A Ditch and bank boundary
B 'U' feature
C Rectangular structures
D Structure outside boundary
E Structure crossing boundary
F Irregular-shaped enclosure
G Ridge and furrow
H Gate (?)

Plan 6: Tilton hospital.

At Tilton, where the Lazarites had specifically promised to honour the statutes of the house, it was stated that in about 1290 they had withdrawn the services of a chaplain 'to celebrate divine service for the king's ancestors and for all the faithful departed' and also of a smith 'to stay continually in a smithy there to shoe the horses of those coming at the cost of the master and brethren'.[121] Complaints about this last economy led to the seizure of lands in Tilton and Cold Newton in 1336 by John de Windsor, escheator of Warwickshire and Leicestershire, but after an inquiry the rights of the order were upheld and the escheator was commanded 'not to meddle thereon'.[122] The incident, which was hailed as a victory and recorded meticulously in the Cartulary, seemed to vindicate the policy of asset stripping imposed upon the dependant houses. For those founded with the support of lepers specifically in mind the decline of the disease could always be cited as justification, requiring rationalisation and reorganisation in changing times. Tilton, indeed, was a particularly difficult case since it was too close to Burton to be kept open even as a preceptory when its hospital

121 *CCR, 1343–46*, p. 631.
122 BL, Cart, ff. 209–11.

role had lapsed. Its closure symbolised the fact that the founding ideology of the order, imported to England by Roger de Mowbray, was dead and buried.

Orme has highlighted a similar conflict of interest in the case of the Hospitallers who were given the hospital of St Cross, Winchester, by the bishop in 1151, but gave it back to him in 1185 'suggesting that their hospital work for the public did not develop successfully'.[123] This is hardly surprising, since 'Most of their members' time was spent administering property and supporting crusades, and their hospital work was less prominent.'[124] Indeed, Orme has concluded, of the military orders in general, that they 'lacked the dynamic and resources to make much impact' in the hospital sector, and this statement is confirmed by the record of the order of St Lazarus.[125] The basic problem was that investing in good deeds by way of a hospital network in western Europe cost money and inevitably detracted from the contributions that could be sent to the Latin kingdom. As pressure for increased funding grew in the thirteenth century, owing to the worsening state of the finances of the military orders, a cutback on charitable activities in the West must have seemed inevitable.

St Giles's, Holborn, and Holy Innocents', Lincoln

For the Lazarites the most startling reminder of changing times came in 1291 with the fall of Acre. Since the order in England now had no clear part to play in the Crusade, Edward I determined to resolve the problem by doing exactly what lesser patrons, such as the Burdets and Amundevilles, had done a hundred years earlier, but now with the added authority of papal approval. Accordingly, in 1299 he handed over the 'royal' leper hospital of St Giles-in-the-Fields, Holborn, a deft move on the part of the king because, he believed, it would have the effect of resolving a number of difficulties. Since St Giles's was a major foundation, theoretically established for 40 lepers, the English Lazarites might actually be given something useful to do. Moreover, the gift absolved the Exchequer from the need to pay them an annual pension, then badly in arrears, and the king was also able to dissociate himself from the growing conflict with the city of London over the appointment of wardens, which had been brewing up since 1250.[126]

St Giles's was indeed a house with an illustrious history. Founded by the pious Queen Matilda in the early twelfth century, it was a royal free chapel, exempt from episcopal visitation and generously endowed by English kings and the citizens of London in the expectation that it would help relieve the considerable problem of leprosy with which the capital was beset. It would appear that the king anticipated that the Lazarites would develop a hospitaller role, using St Giles's as the base from which their rebirth would begin. The difficulty was that the brethren of St Lazarus took to St Giles's exactly the same attitudes that had characterised their management of the earliest daughter houses. They were to discover, to their cost, that tactics that might have been effective in the back-

123 Orme and Webster, *English Hospital*, p. 72.
124 *Ibid.*
125 *Ibid*, p. 74.
126 Honeybourne, 'Leper Hospitals', pp. 21–2.

woods of Northumberland and Lincolnshire were not necessarily going to be so successful under the watchful eye of the royal Chancery and the corporation of London.

When the order took over the management of St Giles's there were undoubtedly leprous persons still in residence. Indeed, in 1315 'as it is not fit that healthy men should be lodged with lepers' the master of Burton petitioned Parliament that the hospital should be exempt from granting liveries to the king's officers 'whilst any lepers make their stay therein'. In this he was successful, and the verdict in favour of the hospital was included in a new charter recorded on the Patent Rolls.[127] However, that the master's action was far from altruistic is indicated by another petition to Parliament, this time from the mayor and corporation in 1327, stating that the Lazarites were rejecting other claimants for support (and this included royal servants as well as the citizenry of London) in favour of their own brethren. By 1327 there were 10 of these 'brothers of Burton' in residence, who had overthrown the ancient tradition of caring for the sick 'and there ordained a different order . . . and destroyed and removed the goods of the said hospital to the great slander of holy church'. The petitioners requested that the offending Lazarites be removed 'so that the wishes of those who gave to the said hospital their lands and rents may be performed'.[128]

A key question is to try to assess what exactly these 'brothers of Burton' were doing at St Giles's, since the sources are silent on the matter. If they were leper brothers then the master could reasonably claim to be fulfilling the spirit of the statutes, even though the customary means of selection might have been altered. If, on the other hand, they were non-leprous individuals, then the break with traditional practice could be seen as both sudden and profound. The suggestion on the part of the mayor that the old order had been 'overthrown' seems to point to the latter. Perhaps the preferred scenario for St Giles's under the early years of Lazarite management was for an expanded community of 'brothers of Burton' – possibly comprising a mixture of younger healthy brethren and older corrodians – to serve a diminished community of lepers recruited from the city. This would have been sufficient to launch the institution on a new path and in so doing upset the sensitivities of traditionalists.

This simmering resentment on the part of the city was not resolved, and it erupted again in 1348 against the backdrop of the Black Death when the perceived inadequacies of the order may once again have been exposed. The Londoners renewed their complaints to the king and managed to initiate an inquiry into the conduct of the hospital.[129] Eventually, in 1354, new rules of management were drawn up by the Chancellor, John de Offord, dean of Lincoln (1344–48), and, although a text of these has not survived, a fairly clear picture of his arbitration can be reconstructed from other sources.[130] The hospital was to be staffed by a warden, three brothers, two sisters and two secular chaplains

127 CPR, 1313–17, p. 300; Rot Parl, 1, p. 310.
128 H.G. Richardson and G. Sayles (eds), Rotuli Parliamentorum Anglie Hactenus Inediti MCCLXXIX–MCCCLXXIII, CS, 3rd series, 51 (1935), p. 135.
129 Honeybourne, 'Leper Hospitals', p. 23; J. Stow, A Survey of London (London, 1598), p. 364.
130 Offord died as archbishop-elect of Canterbury. DNB, 14, pp. 901–2.

'according to the disposition of the master of Burton St Lazarus, master of the order in England'. These ecclesiastics were to serve a greatly reduced community of 14 lepers nominated by the corporation of London and drawn from the city and suburbs, or, if there were insufficient there, from the county of Middlesex. If in future the hospital received additional endowments, the number of lepers might be increased.[131]

As early as 1355 the order was complaining that the support of even 14 lepers was beyond its means (or, more truthfully, perhaps, its inclination), and this became a continuing grievance as the century progressed. During the quarrel with the abbot of St Mary Graces in the 1390s Walter de Lynton was accused of reducing the number of lepers who stood 'in want of maintenance' and replacing them with sisters of his order, contrary to the foundation. By 1401 the situation was so dire that Henry IV was obliged to order the mayor to make a special collection of £5 0s 0d from hospital tenants in the city for division among five male lepers at St Giles's, and a few months later a similar collection and distribution was enjoined.[132] In 1402 a new enquiry into the state of the hospital revealed that the number of lepers supported there had been reduced by five or more owing to the parlous state of the revenues.[133]

Although the Lazarites were less than enthusiastic about the support of lepers at St Giles's, just as they had been at some of the smaller houses, there was, nevertheless, some truth in their claim that the years after 1350 were extremely difficult ones for them. Not only were they beset by serious internal rivalries, they also suffered because of economic depression, fire, and the inability to administer the St Giles's lands effectively because of difficulties with the crown and corporation.[134] The sale of corrodies to wealthy people who required a comfortable place of retirement in old age was one way out of this financial *impasse*, and this was a market that was particularly buoyant in London with its proliferation of royal civil servants and wealthy city merchants. However, the business needed to be carefully monitored, since the sum charged had to take account of life expectancy so that the institution did not end up out of pocket at the end of the day. Alternatively, because this was a royal foundation, a corrodian might be imposed on the house by order of the crown to reward a loyal servant, thus deepening its financial plight still further.

This may have been the case with John Plompton, clerk, awarded a corrody at St Giles's, 'with the assent of the master of Burton', in 1372. Plompton was to be provided with 2d per day for three years, payable annually, and then a corrody for life comprising 'bread, ale, flesh, fish and other viands at the table of the brethren, if he be in health, and if he be ill there shall be ministered to him in his chamber such viands as the master and his *confrères* have, with a chamber with a chimney and a wardrobe'.[135] In an agreement of 1342 the sustenance offered to

---

131 CLBCL, G, pp. 28–9, 30–1; CPapR, Petitions 1342–1419, p. 270.
132 Honeybourne, 'Leper Hospitals', p. 24; CLBCL, I, pp. 13–44.
133 Honeybourne, 'Leper Hospitals', p. 25.
134 See Chapter 2, pp. 51–3; Chapter 4, pp. 123–4.
135 CPR, 1370–74, p. 358. If the master and brethren were 'not willing' to support Plompton in this way

Sarah, widow of John de Baillol, was spelt out in more detail. Each week she was to be given seven white loaves, four black loaves (such as the sisters of the order received for their maids), and 1s for 'ale and kitchen'. Every year she was to receive a bushel of peas, a bushel of salt and a bushel of oatmeal for porridge. She was also to be allowed 52 faggots and a quarter of coals for heating, 14s 4d for clothing, £1 'for chamber' and 1s for lighting.[136] The most outstanding corrodian to obtain residence at St Giles's was Nicholas de Exton, fishmonger, who in 1375 paid £40 for the use of a house, garden and curtilage for life in the hospital for the use of himself, his wife, Katherine, and his brother, Richard.[137] He seems to have retained it at least until 1381.[138] Exton was a leading figure in London politics, and as early as 1365 was part of a group of fishmongers who instigated a murderous attack on one Giles Pykeman.[139] The underlying issue in his turbulent political career was tension between the victualling and non-victualling guilds, and during this conflict Exton became a notable champion of the victuallers and a fierce opponent of the non-victualler mayor, John de Northampton. In 1377/78 he was suspended as an alderman and in 1382 lost his citizenship altogether 'for opprobrious words to John of Northampton, then mayor'.[140] Because of these disagreements there were times when Exton was forced to leave the city, and on one occasion Northampton was reported to have boasted that if he caught up with him 'he would have led him through Chepe like a robber and a cut-purse'.[141]

In these tense circumstances it is not difficult to see why Exton regarded St Giles's as a safe bolt hole for himself and his family. Holborn was outside of the jurisdiction of the city and, moreover, the hospital offered the extra protection of being a peculiar with royal associations, somewhere the mayor would think twice about invading. For a man with almost unlimited resources this was £40 well worth spending.[142] Exton himself became mayor in 1386/87 and won some notoriety because of his betrayal of his predecessor, Sir Nicholas Brembre, a grocer and fellow victualler, to the Lords Appellant.[143] It has been argued that by abandoning Brembre, a notable supporter of Richard II, Exton saved London from the vengeance of the Appellants, and he may well also have used his influence in support of the Lazarites during a period that was equally difficult for them, though for different reasons.[144] He was certainly the most influential figure to be associated with St Giles's during its period of management by the order.

As the case of Nicholas de Exton demonstrates, the corrody was a very flexible

---

he was to receive 12d per week in lieu. They were bound in £40 to observe the contract, which was enrolled on the Patent Rolls in 1373.

136 Williams, *Early Holborn*, no. 1615.
137 *Ibid*, nos. 1617, 1618, 1661.
138 Honeybourne, 'Leper Hospitals', p. 29.
139 A.R. Myers, *London in the Age of Chaucer* (London, 1972), p. 209.
140 C. Pendrill, *London Life in the 14th Century* (1925, reprinted London, 1971), p. 156; R. Bird, *The Turbulent London of Richard II* (London, 1949), p. 34.
141 Pendrill, *London Life*, p. 158.
142 Exton was capable of extending a loan of £1,000 to the king. Bird, *Turbulent London*, p. 97.
143 *Ibid*, pp. 96–9; Sheppard, *London*, p. 97.
144 See Chapter 3, pp. 83–5.

tum:vt fitis noua confperfio. ficut eftis
azimi. Etenim pafcha noftrum:immo=
tus eft chziftus. Itaqz epulemur. Nõ in
fermento veteri:neqz in fermento mali=
tie et nequitie. Sed in azimis fincerita=
tis et veritatis. Grad. Hec dies quam fecit
dñs:exultemus et letemur in ea. y. Confitemi=
ni dño quoniam bonus:quoniam in feculũ mi=
fericozdia eius. A lleluya. y⁹. Pafcha noftrũ
immolatus eft chziftus.   Sequentia.
Vlgens pzeclara rutilat per ozbẽ
hodie dies. in qua chzifti lucida.
narrantur ouanter pzelia. Oc hofte fup
bo quem iefus triumphanit.pulchze ca
ftra illius perimens teterrima. Vnfelir
culpa eue. qua caruimus oẽs vita. B
                          N. iii.

Plate 26: Sir Richard Sutton, squire steward of Syon Abbey, and a close associate
of the order of St Lazars who probably resided at St Giles's prior to his death in
1524. From a missal of *c.*1520.

device, which could be tailored to suit individual needs and which by shrewd
management should not have acted too much to the detriment of the house.
Although the examples quoted above are all of outsiders who bought their way
into the system, the Templars and Hospitallers were well known for providing
corrodies for former servants, and the Lazarites may well have followed a similar
practice.[145] Another influential individual who probably resided at St Giles's was
Sir Richard Sutton, a Tudor privy councillor and steward of Syon Abbey
(Plate 26). Though no formal purchase of a corrody survives, as in the case of
Exton, Sutton had family ties with the ruling hierarchy of the order, and the fact

---

[145] Gilchrist, *Contemplation and Action*, pp. 67–8. For a comparison, see A.G. Little, 'The Corrodies of
the Carmelite Friary of Lynn', *Journal of Ecclesiastical History*, 9 (1958), pp. 8–29.

that he had bedding and household goods at the hospital when he drew up his will in 1524, as well as leaving £2 to the repair of the highways around St Giles's, suggests close, and possibly uncomfortable, associations with the place.[146]

Though these residents are unlikely to have been leprous, their stay in the hospital might have taxed the nursing skills of the brethren and sisters when they became too old and feeble to fend for themselves. Indeed, members of the order might well have regarded their own positions as being, in part, an insurance policy against old age and helplessness. We know little of the sisterhood of St Lazarus, for example, except that they were wealthy ladies able to support maids who ate black bread. Rawcliffe has pointed out the important part played by women in the care of the sick and disadvantaged, and 'sisters' are consistently spoken of in the context of St Giles's.[147] As Honeybourne has observed, 'The few leper patients mentioned by name are never women', so it could well be that they had some sort of caring or quasi-religious purpose.[148] Possibly they had something in common with the vowess who traditionally adopted a religious habit and took a vow of chastity in her widowhood. In the spiritual environment of a hospital, performing the Comfortable Works so long as they were able, these Margery Kempes of the capital might live out their last days with privileges very similar to those of a corrodian, but with a higher status in the eyes of God and man.

As leprosy declined even further in the fifteenth century the emphasis of charitable provision at St Giles's shifted decisively in favour of the poor and aged. Yet when in 1457 the order received the gift of Holy Innocents' Hospital, Lincoln, from the crown, the grant was expressed in terms that suggested the disease was still rife:

> On showing of the king's household servants that many of them heretofore have been smitten with leprosy and some now are so smitten and have no place for their relief [the master was ordered] to sustain yearly for ever three lepers from the servants of the household to be nominated by letters patent, under the great seal, or if so many cannot be found in the household, three lepers from the king's tenants.[149]

By this time 'leprosy' had become a catch-all for virtually any ailment that appeared infectious or unpleasant. The Lincoln hospital brought with it a useful endowment, though not on the same scale as St Giles's, and like the London hospital, Queen Matilda had played a leading role in its foundation.[150] Originally Holy Innocents', known locally as the Malandry, had supported 10 lepers, 'outcasts from the city of Lincoln', appointed by the mayor or the king, but by the

146 PRO, PROB 11/21, ff. 209–10 (Sir Richard Sutton, 1524).
147 Rawcliffe, *Medicine for the Soul*, p. 193; Honeybourne, 'Leper Hospitals', pp. 23, 25.
148 Honeybourne, 'Leper Hospitals', p. 29.
149 *CPR, 1452–61*, p. 359; *1461–67*, p. 123.
150 W.D. Cookson, 'On the Hospital of the Holy Innocents, called *Le Malardri*, at Lincoln: with some account of ancient customs and usages touching leprosy', in *A Selection of Papers relative to the County of Lincoln, read before the Lincolnshire Topographical Society, 1841, 1842* (Lincoln, 1843), pp. 29–66; Brooks, 'Holy Innocents', pp. 157–88; Satchell, 'Leper Houses', pp. 132–3.

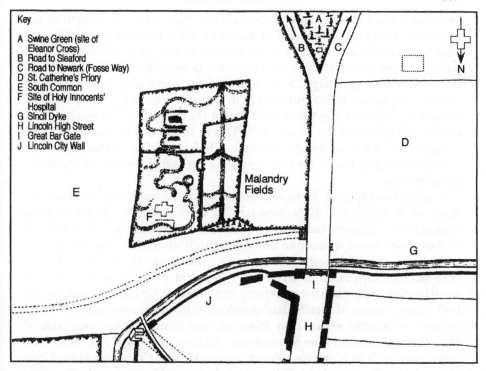

Key

A Swine Green (site of Eleanor Cross)
B Road to Sleaford
C Road to Newark (Fosse Way)
D St. Catherine's Priory
E South Common
F Site of Holy Innocents' Hospital
G Sincil Dyke
H Lincoln High Street
I Great Bar Gate
J Lincoln City Wall

Malandry Fields

Plan 7: Holy Innocents' hospital, Lincoln.

fourteenth century its administration had become scandalous.[151] Visitations revealed that virtually no lepers were in residence, that the endowments were consumed by healthy people – some of them merchants – and that the warden was invariably a non-resident royal servant, often a Chancery clerk, who exploited the position for his own profit.[152]

The grant to Burton Lazars was seen as an opportunity to reform this disorder, especially since the master was now emerging as a man with a significant role to play in local affairs, in need of the sort of support previously offered to royal civil servants as a matter of course. The reduction of the number of lepers to three represented a drastic curtailment of the original foundation, and the 1457 grant made it clear that these need not even be supported at Holy Innocents'.[153] The gift is therefore best seen, perhaps, as a means of bolstering up the weak position of St Giles's, because now the king could command at least three

---

151 There is some doubt as to whether 10 or 20 lepers were actually supported. The former seems more likely. Brooks, 'Holy Innocents', p. 164. For early examples of royal admissions to the hospital, see CCR, 1296–1302, p. 353; CPR, 1281–92, p. 389; 1301–07, pp. 531–2.

152 Brooks, 'Holy Innocents', pp. 169–70, 173.

153 This reduction was not unique and could be seen as quite modest. In 1434 Thomas Langley's new statutes for Sherburn reduced the number of lepers from 65 to two 'if they could be found', but enjoined that 13 poor men should also be supported. Boyle, Durham, p. 471; R. Surtees, The History and Antiquities of the County Palatine of Durham, 1 (1816, reprinted Wakefield, 1972), pp. 129–30. St John's Hospital, Blyth, was virtually derelict in 1446 when its provision was shifted from lepers to poor strangers and pregnant women. J. Raine, History of Blyth (Westminster, 1860), pp. 148–9.

placements there for his household servants or tenants on the strength of the Lincoln revenues without dissent or acrimony. What happened to Holy Innocents' is not at all clear. Whether or not the sick were supported there, its chapel remained open to receive the offerings of passers-by, which in 1535 came to £2, the whole site being managed by a warden, Gilbert Thimbleby.[154] A hint that the Lazarites might have been aiming at a fresh start at Lincoln is provided by the information, given in a deposition of 1672, that the hospital was known locally as 'St Mary Magdalen of the Malandry'.[155] This dedication, of course, would have brought the institution closer to the cult of St Lazarus, but whether there was indeed a 'refoundation', or the later deponents were simply misinformed, cannot be ascertained.

Unlike places such as Tilton and Harehope, there was no doubt about the status of St Giles's and Holy Innocents' as leper hospitals. They were both substantial foundations, independent of the order of St Lazarus, which reflected in their location and appearance features normally associated with such institutions. Both were highly visible, close to main roads and on the outskirts of cities; both had their own institutional seals; and both had ground plans typical of the small hospital rather than the preceptory or monastery. We know of the layout of both places because of sketch plans drawn up before their sites were enveloped by modern building works. Holy Innocents' was located on the south side of Lincoln where the road from Sleaford joins the Fosse Way (Plan 7). It was a busy area shared with St Katherine's Priory and an Eleanor Cross on nearby Swine Green. A plan drawn up in 1841 shows Holy Innocents' occupying a large rectangular space on the South Common, but it is likely that the hospital buildings occupied only a small part of this area, most of the site being taken up by gardens and orchards. One of the surviving earthworks was cruciform, suggesting the site of the parochial chapel; another was rectangular and labelled 'cow shed . . . apparently built out of the ruins of the ancient hospital'.[156]

St Giles's proximity to the suburb of Holborn and the city gallows at Tyburn would have given it a similarly busy and cosmopolitan feel (Plan 8). Here the site was roughly triangular, being bounded by three roads, one of them being the old Roman road to Oxford.[157] Matthew Paris sketched the hospital in the thirteenth century to illustrate his *Chronica Majora*, but the illustration is schematic and not designed to convey a picture of architectural detail other than saying that this was a substantial foundation and a worthy 'memorial' to Queen Matilda (Plate 27).[158] A plan of 1585 is more accurate, and shows a walled precinct, which was entered by way of a gatehouse wide enough to give access to a cart.[159] As with Holy Innocents', the enclosed area was sparsely populated, with the paro-

154 *Valor*, 4, p. 29.
155 PRO, E 134/24 Chas 2/Trin 8.
156 Cookson, 'Holy Innocents', between pp. 28 and 29.
157 Honeybourne, 'Leper Hospitals', p. 20.
158 CCC, Ms 26, f. 110v. Reproduced in R. Vaughan (ed.), *The Illustrated Chronicle of Matthew Paris: Observations of Thirteenth Century life* (Stroud, 1993), p. 103.
159 Clay, *Medieval Hospitals*, opposite p. 117; Honeybourne, 'Leper Hospitals', pp. 21–30; 'A Map drawn in 1585 to illustrate a lawsuit concerning Geldings Close', *London Topographical Society*, Publication 54 (London, 1925).

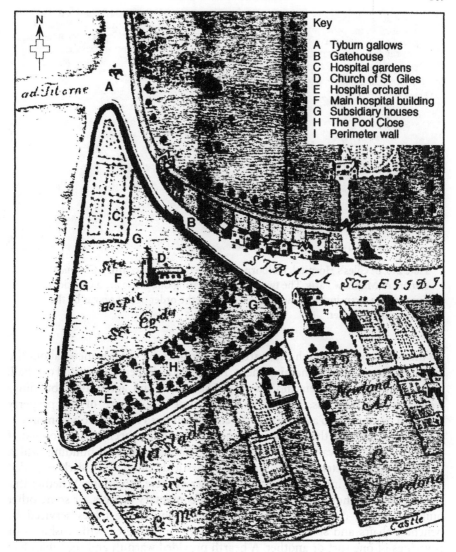

Plan 8: St Giles's hospital, Holborn.

chial chapel of St Michael near the centre and four sets of dispersed buildings surrounded by gardens and orchards. There are documentary references to a master's house (providing rooms for a chaplain, clerk and a messenger or servant); leper-houses; and a chapter house, which was newly constructed in the early fourteenth century, soon after the Lazarites took over control.[160]

For St Giles's this topographical picture can be enhanced by details extracted from the inventories of 1371 and 1391.[161] Both documents appear to be agreed

---

[160] Honeybourne, 'Leper Hospitals', pp. 21, 25.
[161] PRO, E 326/12434 (1371); E 315/38 (1391). For a discussion of the reliability of these documents, see Chapter 4, pp. 120–2.

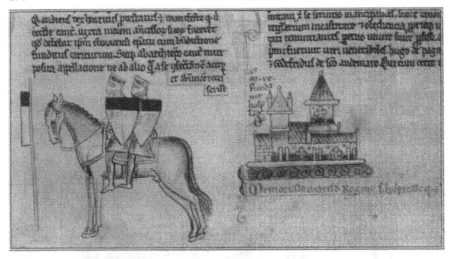

Plate 27: St Giles's Hospital, Holborn, from the thirteenth-century *Chronica Majora* of Matthew Paris. The two Templars sharing one horse are a coincidence but they are a reminder of the support given to the order of St Lazarus by the larger military order.

on the basic layout, though there are quite considerable discrepancies about the extent of the property remaining there. The hospital, it seems, consisted of a hall, chamber, buttery, kitchen and brewery. The chapel and agricultural buildings were additional to this, and, given the volume and nature of the property recorded, we must also assume that the corrodians lived in separate accommodation, not included in these surveys. Some of it must have been well appointed, if Nicholas de Exton was living true to form. The main hospital building, which has all of the characteristics of a modest domestic dwelling, was clearly regarded as the heart of the institution for the purposes of these valuations. Whether this was the master's house, referred to in the documentary sources, or some other building, is not clear. In the hall there were long trestle tables serviced by benches, chairs and stools. Most of these were upholstered with cushions or coverings of one sort or another. A hearth provided warmth and the tables had basins and water jugs on them for communal meals. In the buttery, adjacent to the hall, were stored those items required to sustain the feasting – table cloths, towels, pewter salts, bronze candelabra – and some prestigious items, four mazers bound with silver and a set of silver spoons.

The kitchen and brewery were purely utilitarian spaces, full of pots, pans, barrels and vats, but the chamber (presumably an upstairs room) offers further clues about the quality of life of those connected with the institution. Though the number of mattresses and featherbeds (three in 1371 and seven in 1391) is small, the amount of bed linen and blankets is much more plentiful, raising questions about the number of persons supported in the institution. Did the mattresses accommodate one or two people? Illustrations of bed sharing are common enough in medieval sources, even in a hospital context, though this may not have been the case in leper hospitals where there is evidence of a trend towards individual accommodation in the fourteenth century, not least at St Giles's.[162] And what of the lack of beds? Are we to assume they were fixtures, and therefore not included in the inventories, or that the hospital followed contemporary continental practice? Duby notes that 'Patients' beds in mid-fourteenth-century *leprosariums* and hospitals in the diocese of Paris apparently had neither frame nor curtains, just a mattress, a pillow, a pair of sheets and a cover.'[163]

The apparent lack of consistency in the relationship between mattresses and bed linen raises questions about how the hospital was being run. In 1391, for example, there were 20 pairs of linen sheets, 24 blankets and 'a set of bedcloths decorated with butterflies'. Were the lepers living in old-fashioned, relatively sparse accommodation; was the linen a left over from an earlier, busier, age; was the chamber a store room, distributing bedding to people who were sleeping elsewhere; and who used that special set 'decorated with butterflies'? Numbers were certainly well down at this period compared with earlier years. In 1381 there were two brothers at St Giles's (including the warden) and a number of lepers that was fewer than the 14 specified in 1355 – in 1401 there were only five.[164] On the basis of one person per mattress, the institution was more or less in line with these reduced circumstances; if it was two to a bed, it came close to the quota of 1355. The inventories provide us with a tantalising glimpse of a Lazarite leper hospital in the late fourteenth century, but, as ever, they raise more questions than they answer.

Provision for the poor

By the late fifteenth century the master of Burton commanded a certain revenue, some of it derived from well-established leper hospitals, to fulfil the charitable duties of his order. In 1479 Sir William Sutton recorded this obligation as being the need to support 14 'poor lepers', the St Giles's complement, making no mention of any provision resting on the endowments of Holy Innocents' or Burton Lazars. However, by then the principle of out-relief was already well established, since he added that if these individuals did not have hospital placements he was to 'pay them a weekly sum of money for the necessities of life', a statement that tends to contradict the idea that these pensioners were, in fact, leprous and in need of institutional care.[165] When the *Valor Ecclesiasticus* of 1535 made a survey of the alms payable by Sir Thomas Ratcliffe, the 14 pensioners of St Giles's appeared again, this time described as 'paupers' in receipt of 2d per day, 'according to the meaning and purpose of the foundation'. In addition to this, Burton Lazars was stated to be supporting a single pauper, 'from an old foundation', at 3d per day.[166] This raises the question of what had happened to the three

---

162 Duby, *Private Life*, p. 498, showing fifteenth-century bed sharing at the Hôtel-Dieu, Paris.
163 *Ibid*, pp. 493–4.
164 McHardy, *Church in London*, p. 38. In addition, there were two 'celebrants' who, given their parochial function, may well have dwelt elsewhere. Honeybourne, 'Leper Hospitals', p. 24.
165 *CPapR, Letters 13 pt 1, 1471–84*, p. 3. In about 1500 the master was required to review his agreement with the city concerning the number of 'lepers' to be supported at St Giles's. Honeybourne, 'Leper Hospitals', p. 30.
166 *Valor*, 4, p. 153. At Sherburn the out-relief payments established in 1434 were 10d per week and 6s 8d

'lepers' who were supposed to be maintained out of the Lincoln revenues. The most likely explanation is that these were subsumed in the 'old foundation' that was noted at Burton, charitable relief having shifted once and for all away from Lincoln. Whether 3d per day represented the three Lincoln placements merged into one, or whether two nominations had permanently lapsed because of the deterioration of the revenues, is impossible to say.

The *Valor* also enables us to assess what proportion of the order's wealth was bestowed on the poor, a particularly relevant question in view of the various pleas of poverty that had characterised the years after 1350.[167] The total charitable provision for 15 paupers in 1535 came to £47 2s 11d, though there may have been occasional, unrecorded, payments of alms in addition to this. With a total income of over £336, before deductions, this means that 14 per cent of revenue was directed to charitable work, a figure that compares very favourably with similar calculations made by Rawcliffe for East Anglian religious houses. In 1534, for example, Norwich Priory bestowed three per cent of its annual expenditure on alms giving, and at about the same time Carrow Priory spent only one per cent of its disposal income on alms.[168] These were, of course, monasteries rather than hospitals, but, nevertheless, their recorded charitable activities fell well below the 10 per cent of disposable income that churchmen generally felt was a fair measure of income to go to the poor. In this context the Lazarites were not performing too badly, but it must be said that virtually all of that charitable provision rested on the endowments of the institutions given to the order by the crown after 1299, St Giles's and Holy Innocents' – in other words, the *real* leper hospitals. If we consider the original estate of the order, prior to the gift of St Giles's, then nothing was earmarked for charitable relief at all, except perhaps the single placement at Burton Lazars, which may well rest on a post-1299 endowment in any case.

This was the sort of indictment of traditional religious practice that the Protestant reformers of the sixteenth century viewed with some relish and that had been criticised even by Catholics, such as John Bromyard, as early as the fourteenth century.[169] The complaint, which was repeated over and over again in the early sixteenth century, was that the resources of the hospitals were being consumed by the clergy who administered them, not by the poor, and were often misdirected to theologically dubious prayers for the dead.[170] Simon Fish, in *A Supplicacyon for the Beggers*, one of the most hard-hitting Reformation tracts, published in about 1529 and directed to Henry VIII, asked 'But what remedy to relieve us: your poor, sick, lame and sore bedemen? To make many hospitals for the relief of poor people? Nay, truly. The more the worse, for ever the fat of the whole foundation hangeth on the priests' beards.'[171] A little later, in 1542, Henry

---

per annum for fuel and clothing; this made the St Giles's and Burton Lazars pensioners appreciably better off.

167 See Chapter 4, p. 130; Chapter 5, p. 163.
168 Rawcliffe, *Medicine for the Soul*, p. 195.
169 *Ibid*, p. 191.
170 Orme and Webster, *English Hospital*, pp. 150–1, 155.
171 F.J. Furnival (ed.), *Simon Fish, A Supplicacyon for the Beggers*, EETS, extra series, 13 (1871), pp. 13–14.

Brinklow addressed the king in similar terms in the *Complaynt of Roderyck Mors*. 'And for Christ's sake, ye rulers, look upon your hospitals, whether the poor have their right there or no. I hear that the masters of your hospitals be so fat that the poor be kept lean and bare enough; the cry of the people is heard unto the Lord, though ye will not hear.'[172] As a new age of Christian humanism dawned and politicians began to explore notions of the 'godly commonwealth', traditional religious and charitable practice was to be subjected to very close scrutiny.

Jordan had comments such as these ringing in his ears when he criticised late-medieval religious institutions for failing to match up to their aspirations in terms of charitable relief.[173] Despite a reassessment of his work by Hadwin, and considerable supporting information from the localities from the likes of Rawcliffe, it is, nevertheless, still difficult to see the order of St Lazarus making a very committed contribution to the care of the sick or the support of the poor.[174] Harper-Bill, who speaks of 'a tendency to disinvestment in charity' and a concentration on church building instead, sums up a set of priorities that would have been instantly recognisable to Sir William Sutton and his contemporaries.[175] Those with a sense of history might well have asked if the situation had ever been significantly different or, indeed, if charity was the principal purpose of the order in England in any case. In the Holy Land the leper knights were few in number and a relatively short-lived phenomenon. Nevertheless, their support, and that of the healthy knights who replaced them, was the principal claim on the estates of the order in the early years of its existence. Despite persistent misconceptions, Burton Lazars was a preceptory for the management of land, not a hospital for the care of the sick. Contemporaries were confused by all of this, believing that the order had a deep-rooted and altruistic concern for the welfare of lepers, even when, time and time again, this was proved not to be the case.

This double agenda meant that institutions that were donated on condition they supported lepers became viewed by the Lazarites as an embarrassing distraction. From the thirteenth century onwards their 'hospital' establishments in England were closed or curtailed, leading to conflicts with the Burdets over Tilton and with the citizens of London over St Giles's. Until 1291 this policy could be justified by the need to support the Crusade, and after that date by the difficulties in finding sufficient numbers of lepers to fill the places available, but the attitude was consistent and remained with the order up to the time of its suppression. The confusing exploitation of the *image* of leprosy, and particularly the potent symbol of the leper knight, also survived, but this was not quite the same as working with the sick and deprived in the fashion of true hospitallers. Inevitably it gave rise to charges of hypocrisy that were well established by the

---

172 J.M. Cowper (ed.), *Henry Brinklow's Complaynt of Roderyck Mors*, EETS, extra series, 22 (1874), p. 52.
173 W.K. Jordan, *Philanthropy in England, 1480–1660: a study of the changing patterns of English social aspirations* (London,1959), pp. 58–9, 114–15.
174 J.H. Hadwin, 'Deflating Philanthropy', *Economic History Review*, 2nd series, 31 (1978), pp. 105–17; Rawcliffe, *Medicine for the Soul*, pp. 194–5.
175 Harper-Bill, 'English Church', p. 121.

sixteenth century. Although some members of the order were no doubt motivated by genuine charitable feelings and were sometimes provided with opportunities to care for the sick and aged, for the majority leprosy was best viewed at a distance and was only reluctantly grappled with at first hand.

6

Privileges, Pardons and Parishes

receive them kindly and treat them honorably
(Bull of Clement IV, 1265)

Spiritual privileges

Because of its origins and self-conscious perception of its role in the Crusade and provision for the sick, the order of St Lazarus enjoyed certain significant privileges in the sphere of its ecclesiastical activities. These included exemption from clerical taxation and the right to gather alms and sell indulgences, concessions that were not universally popular. In terms of its overall income, Orme has commented on the extent to which the order was dependent on tithes (a form of support unusual for leper-houses), and this proved to be another controversial issue since by collecting and spending this parochial income local communities were being deprived of resources that were, arguably, theirs.[1] 'The appropriation of parish churches has often been regarded as one of the great evils of the late-medieval church.'[2] Between them these issues were to raise the hackles of both clergy and laity in medieval England.

The extent to which all of this posed a difficulty for the order, especially in the more spiritually aware environment of the late Middle Ages, is the theme of this chapter. In this context it is important not to embrace too readily the seductive rhetoric of the Lollards and see medieval spirituality merely as a prelude to an inevitable Reformation. Many aspects of popular piety, such as the successful confraternity of St Lazarus, integrated well with the spiritual preoccupations of the age, and Harper-Bill has concluded, along with Duffy, that the people of late-medieval England enjoyed 'a vibrant faith which satisfied all levels of society'.[3] Nevertheless, it is equally relevant to observe, perhaps, that when the day of reckoning came the order of St Lazarus had virtually no one to stand up for it, not even its knightly master, bred on a legend of chivalry and the gallant deeds of the past.

The clearest early pronouncement of the spiritual privileges of the order came under Innocent III in the bull *Licet Universorum Fidelium*, which permitted it

---

[1] Orme and Webster, *English Hospital*, p. 93; Satchell, 'Leper-Houses', pp. 162–3.
[2] Harper-Bill, 'English Church', p. 94.
[3] *Ibid*, p. 122.

rights of burial for its own members and exempted it from the payment of tithe on trees and animals.[4] In addition, the Lazarites were permitted to receive 'men fleeing from the world . . . and to retain [them] without contradiction', in other words, a right of sanctuary for those who agreed to commit themselves to the objectives of the order. Moreover, during an interdict, divine service was permitted to continue, but 'in a low voice having closed doors . . . and without ringing bells'.[5] Of more practical benefit was the exemption from clerical taxation, though this often gave rise to controversy. As Lunt has shown, the taxation of the clergy in England dated from the twelfth century and was initially levied under the pretext of supporting the Crusade.[6] Since the Lazarites were dedicated to this goal in any case, and in theory were also devoted to the care of lepers, it made sense that they should be exempt. They were accordingly excluded from the Valuation of Norwich in 1254, and in 1290 the Pope ordered the collectors of the tenth in England to observe the privileges of all lazar-houses, hospitals and military orders.[7]

The warning was timely, because in 1291 the *Taxatio* of Pope Nicholas IV (1288–92) sought to place clerical taxation on a more effective footing, and this time most of the property of the order was included. The new assessments were unpopular with the clergy, but since the king was invariably the recipient of the tenth, by grant of Convocation, the Exchequer did not discourage the development. The zeal in collecting the tax, combined with the political problems of Edward I and Edward II in Scotland, meant that old exemptions were brought under close scrutiny and several priests serving the order's livings were excommunicated for non-payment in 1296.[8] When the Lazarites brought their immunities to the attention of the treasurer and the barons of the Exchequer, they replied, cryptically, that 'the liberties that they hoped would be granted had not been written as clearly as they should have been'.[9] In 1315 the order petitioned the king to inspect the controversial charters, and in 1319 Edward II ruled that it was lawfully exempt from the tenth and in future was to be acquitted 'by reason of their order and by virtue of papal bulls and other muniments . . . especially as it behoves them to be in the front rank against the enemies of the cross in the Holy Land'.[10]

Although this was an important judgment, some royal officials clearly viewed the privileges as anachronistic since very little crusading was going on in the

---

4   For a possible example of this privilege in operation, see the agreement made between the master and the prior of Chacombe, Northamptonshire, in 1229 over the tithes of Great Dalby. Madox, *Formulare Anglicanicum*, p. 30; BL, Cart, f. 81.

5   C.R. Cheney and M.G. Cheney, *The Letters of Innocent III (1198–1216) concerning England and Wales* (Oxford, 1967), p. 278; BL, Cart, ff. 205–6.

6   Lunt, *Financial Relations*, pp. 387, 413.

7   *CPapR, Letters, 1, 1198–1304*, p. 527; *CChanR, 1277–1326*, p. 269; *CCR, 1279–88*, p. 12. For a discussion of the position of hospitals in relation to the clerical taxation of the thirteenth century, see Orme and Webster, *English Hospital*, pp. 95–7.

8   The vicars of Lowesby and Threckingham, for example, for whom see below, pp. 202, 207. The master was under sentence of excommunication in 1321, but whether this was connected with the issue of tax payments is not clear. N. Bennett (ed.), *The Registers of Bishop Henry Berghersh, 1320–1342*, 1, LRS, 87 (1999), p. 5.

9   *Rot Parl*, 1, p. 343.

10   *CCR, 1318–23*, p. 71.

fourteenth century (none involving the Lazarites) and the problem of leprosy was visibly receding. It is also not clear whether the privileges applied only to the immediate possessions of the order or parishes in which it owned the tithes and/or advowson. Under Edward III fresh attempts were made to collect money, by which the master and brethren were said to be 'much disquieted and aggrieved'. In response to repeated complaints, the king directed orders to the Treasurer (1333) and the papal nuncio in England (1337) ordering them to uphold his father's acquittance, a loss of £8 2s 2½d to the Exchequer in the diocese of Lincoln and £3 6s 8d in Coventry and Lichfield.[11] But although these sums were more than compensated for by 'loans' extracted from the master and the seizure of temporalities because of the war with France, the battle over tenths continued, and in 1344 and 1387 fresh rulings in favour of the order were recorded.[12] As late as 1453 the Lazarites, along with the Carthusians, the Augustinians of Syon and certain collegiate foundations, were recorded as being exempt from a clerical tenth granted to Henry VI by the Convocation of Canterbury.[13] It was an important privilege sustained only by continued watchfulness, but increasingly a backward-looking concession to the past rather than a true reflection of contemporary realities.

The order was also exempt from episcopal visitation because after 1262 it fell under the jurisdiction of the Patriarch of Jerusalem and later the Pope. Popes were occasionally prepared to exercise their right of direct intervention, as Urban IV did in 1263 when he ordered the abbot of North Creake, Norfolk, to see to it that property illegally taken away from the order was restored.[14] The royal free chapel of St Giles, held after 1299, represented a chink in this armour of privilege. Although the warden had control over the hospital precinct and adjoining parish as a peculiar, the king's chancellor, or his deputed clerks, retained rights of visitation and correction.[15] This was accepted as part of the price paid for the gift of the hospital, but there was an ongoing conflict with the bishops of London dating back to a 'usurped' visitation by Bishop Fulk Basset (1241–59) in 1259.[16] Although it was prepared to accept the visitational rights of the bishop over its Middlesex vicarage of Feltham, the position of the order was that it was not prepared to see them extended to the hospital or parish of St Giles.[17]

The Lazarites had only been in possession of St Giles's for four years when the warden, John Crispin, was confronted with a metropolitan visitation by Robert de Winchelsey, archbishop of Canterbury (1294–1313), when 'some malefactors broke the locks of the gates of the hospital . . . and opened the gates for him to

11 PRO, E 359/3; E 159/109, m.120; CCR, 1330–33, p. 187; 1333–37, pp. 32, 44; 1337–39, p. 34.
12 CPR, 1343–45, p. 224; CCR, 1385–89, pp. 218–19; BL, Add Chart, 63677.
13 CCR, 1447–54, p. 449; CFR, 1452–61, pp. 37–40.
14 J.E. Sayers, Original Papal Documents in England and Wales from the Accession of Pope Innocent III to the Death of Pope Benedict XI (1198–1304) (Oxford, 1999), p. 309. The order probably relates to Choseley.
15 CPR, 1381–85, p. 596.
16 It was alleged that Basset had visited not by right, but by virtue of a commission from the king when the hospital was in the hands of the citizens of London.
17 CPR, 1388–92, p. 458.

exercise the office of visitation, and carried away some papal letters, charters, writings and muniments, as well of privileges as others touching the rights and possessions of the hospital'.[18] Although the order had its protest recorded on the Patent Rolls, the problem continued and in 1391 Robert Braybroke, bishop of London (1381–1404), was admitted by Richard de Kynbele, sometime brother of the hospital, and his brother Hugh.[19] The warden, John Macclesfield, opposed the visitation, and, once more, had his dissent recorded on the Patent Rolls. Thereafter the problem does not appear to have recurred.

It is significant that the visitations of Winchelsey and Braybroke were both undertaken with internal collusion at times when the order was perceived to be weak, in 1303 after the hospital had just come into its hands and in 1391 when it was undergoing a challenge from the crown over the question of the mastership. On the latter occasion the intrusion was resisted not by the 'traditional' master of Burton but by Macclesfield, a royal clerk, appointed to St Giles's against the wishes of the order. A bone of contention, implicit in all these exemptions, was their unpopularity amongst fellow churchmen who did not have such privileges or who felt that their interests might be damaged by their operation. Consequently, as the thirteenth century progressed, there were those, 'inflamed by the heat of avarice', who were believed to be undermining the work of the order because of jealousy and mistrust. The bishops were considered the major culprits. Some of them were providing little help with the apprehension of apostates; discouraging priests who wanted to join the order for short periods of time; and creating obstacles when it came to the dedication of chapels and oratories.[20] Support from the papacy was considered vital to keep these local vested interests in check.

Alms gathering

Another vexatious privilege, shared with the friars and many other hospital foundations, was soliciting for alms.[21] This was a practice particularly common in leper-houses, where Satchell has argued that these 'countless gifts of casual alms' comprised a major source of income.[22] Indeed, some of the properties of the order seem to have been deliberately selected with this objective in view, and at Westwade, Norfolk, where the Lazarites had a chapel and hermitage from the mid-twelfth century, this sort of alms gathering had developed into a fine art. The chapel was built on a bridge over the river Tiffey, adjacent to a crossroads, on the route from Wymondham to Dereham. The position of the building allowed only a narrow walkway for the use of travellers, and the brothers who were based there were vigilant 'to get what they could of the passengers that went by'.[23] A drawing of this establishment, as it was in about 1730, survives among Martin's

18 CPR, 1301–7, p. 189.
19 CPR, 1388–92, p. 458.
20 Barber, 'Order of St Lazarus', pp. 453–4.
21 Orme and Webster, English Hospital, p. 47.
22 Satchell, 'Leper-Houses', pp. 175, 166–9.
23 Blomefield, Norfolk, 2, pp. 504–5; VCH, Norfolk, 2 (1906, reprinted London, 1975), p. 453; N. Salmon, Roman Stations in Britain (London, 1726), p. 8.

Plate 28: The bridge-chapel at Westwade, Norfolk. Although the chapel was in a ruined state by the eighteenth century, this pictorial record of its survival is unique in the context of buildings of the order.

Church Notes in the Norfolk Record Office (Plate 28).[24] It is a considerable rarity since it is the only record of a building associated with the order in England other than an extant parish church. Nothing survives above ground today, though in 1986, when roadworks were in progress, it was reported that stone and flint foundations were to be seen.[25] The chapel was evidently a substantial building with stone quoins and two pointed windows, one of them with a hood moulding. Though a good deal of erosion had taken place by the eighteenth century, a collapsed section of wall may indicate where once there had been a doorway. These bridge-chapels were full of spiritual symbolism and their support was generally regarded as a means of speeding the journey of the soul through purgatory, 'converting the roadway into a sacred passage'.[26]

If escape was virtually impossible from the clutches of the brethren of Westwade, it is perhaps significant that other houses, notably Burton Lazars, St Giles's, Locko, Harehope, Threckingham and Choseley, were all similarly located on or near major routes or crossroads, which would make this sort of soliciting upon travellers quite straightforward. Threckingham, indeed, enjoyed a very remarkable position. Although the village possessed a market at the time of Domesday, it rose to even greater prominence after 1268 because of a grant by Henry III establishing Stow Green Fair, under the control of Sempringham Priory, at a nearby location. This fair, which met on the vigil, feast and morrow of St John the Baptist (23–25 June), was to develop into one of the most important social and trading events in Lincolnshire.[27] There were, no doubt, ways in which the order learned to exploit it. It is perhaps no coincidence that the brief flourishing of 'St Lazarus hospital' at Threckingham was during the early years of Stow Green Fair. It is possible that it had more in common with Westwade, in

24 NRO, Rye Mss, 4, Collection of Church Notes by Thomas Martin and others (Westwade chapel).
25 Norfolk Landscape Archaeology, SMR 8923 (Westwade Hospital, Chapel Bridge).
26 Duffy, *Stripping of the Altars*, pp. 367–8; Rawcliffe, *Medicine for the Soul*, p. 35; Satchell, 'Leper-Houses', pp. 173–4.
27 A. White, *Stow Green Fair*, Lincolnshire Museums Information Sheet, Archaeology Series, no. 16 (1979).

other words, a base from which to solicit alms, than with either a preceptory or hospital in the true sense of the word.

More important than these localised initiatives was a papal privilege that allowed admission into churches once a year to collect alms 'for the maintenance of the standard of St Lazarus against the enemies of the cross', the collection being carried out by a brother known variously as the messenger (*nuntius*), general attorney or proctor.[28] This important concession was first mentioned by the curia in 1265, when it was said to rest on a grant of 'Pope Innocent'. Although no such privilege is mentioned in *Licet Universorum Fidelium*, it was probably Innocent III who granted it since, as early as 1216, Henry III appears to have issued Letters Patent ordering that these collections be made without impediment. Although its origins are not clear, this privilege appears to have been similar to the one enjoyed by the other military orders allowing admission to churches once a year to collect benefactions from members of their confraternities. On these occasions churches under interdict were to be opened and members of the confraternities were not to be denied burial unless they were personally excommunicated.[29]

A confirmation of the order's privileges by the bishop of Jerusalem in 1323, which is much preoccupied with the question of spiritual benefits for supporters, provides a tantalising glimpse of this process in action. The representatives of the order not only went into parish churches; they also appear to have targeted gatherings where large numbers of clergy and laity were likely to be present, perhaps local synods, meetings of courts, markets or fairs. And it was not just money they were interested in. People contributed horses, weapons, jewellery, even their very persons, to join in the fight against the Infidel. In the latter case, the most dramatic manifestation of support that could be expected, new recruits joining the crusader armies were promised eternal life in the event of death or capture – they had the bishop's guarantee that they were 'the heirs of Christ'. Most people will have been content with more mundane spiritual fare, such as remission of penance, and in its last sentence the document proudly announces that the sum of the indulgences to benefactors was no less than 320 years.[30]

Despite their worthy objectives, it is clear that the collectors suffered obstruction, not so much from the bishops in this instance as from local clergy who feared that their activities would detract from their own parish offerings, and, at worst, diminish the number of tithe-paying parishioners. The upshot of this concern was Clement IV's bull of 1265, summarising the privileges of the order, in which the Pope particularly emphasised the importance of itinerant alms collection, requesting the clergy to 'receive them kindly and treat them honourably' during such expeditions. Soon after this royal protections begin to appear on the Patent Rolls, often with a clause *rogamus* directed to the ecclesiastical authorities urging them to assist. These documents run from 1271 to 1356 but

---

28 *CPR, 1281–92*, p. 137. *Nuntii* were an important feature of leper-houses. See Satchell, 'Leper-Houses', p. 168.
29 Forey, 'St Thomas of Acre', p. 491.
30 GRO, Berkeley Castle Muniments, J7/67/02/002/00/00 (MF 1297).

are clustered into three main phases, representing peaks of alms gathering activity.[31] Between 1271 and 1291 there are four grants, mostly for unspecified periods of time; between 1311 and 1322 there are 10, usually for three years; and between 1347 and 1356 there are five, all for a year.[32] In obedience to the king's wishes, bishops generally lent their support, and on four occasions between 1313 and 1318 Bishop John Dalderby of Lincoln wrote to his officials commending such initiatives.[33]

The main problem, addressed in almost all the grants up to 1332, appears to have been to forestall impostors who were turning up at remote churches claiming to be the proctor of St Lazarus and absconding with the donations of the parishioners. But people were probably equally confused by the order's own internal squabbles. Until 1291 collection seems to have been managed exclusively by agents sent from the Holy Land. Following the fall of Acre, the second phase (1311–32) is characterised by some confusion during which proctors from Boigny and those appointed by the order in England appear to have been vying with one another prior to the eventual triumph of the English faction in about 1325. There is no way of knowing the extent of the prize for which they were in competition. It is significant that the peak of alms gathering activity, between 1311 and 1322, corresponds almost exactly with the period of deepest economic depression, during which other hospitals, with similar privileges, must have been just as active in pursuit of the offerings of the faithful.[34] It seems clear that a law of diminishing returns was taking hold and that the collections were, increasingly, desperate measures designed to stave off financial disaster. The fact that the last protection is dated 1356 might imply a total collapse of benevolence following on from the Black Death. Certainly there would come a point when the costs and risks of such expeditions began to outstrip their benefits.

Indulgences

The Black Death was to have a profound effect on many aspects of English spirituality, not least the personalisation and quantification of benefits anticipated in the next life for good deeds done on earth. As Harper-Bill comments, 'The general commemoration of the faithful departed was hardly sufficient, for it was the popular belief that the benefit accruing to an individual soul decreased in proportion to the number of dead for whom prayers were offered.'[35] Just as the traditional mode of alms collection was winding down, papal bulls of 1347 (*Quam Amabile Deo*) and 1414 *(Meritis Vestre Devotionis)* – and a general confir-

---

31 BN, Mss Francais 203. Barber, 'Order of St Lazarus', pp. 453–4. For the Patent Rolls record see, for example, CPR, 1266–72, p. 526; 1281–92, pp. 113, 137, 431; 1317–21, pp. 131, 571; 1348–50, pp. 108, 203. The clause *rogamus* requested the ecclesiastical authorities to permit the order freely to seek alms in their churches.

32 CPR, 1266–72, p. 526; 1281–92, pp. 113, 137, 431; 1307–13, p. 344; 1313–17, pp. 1, 214, 394; 1317–21, pp. 131, 571; 1324–27, p. 126; 1327–30, pp. 238, 412; 1330–34, p. 242; 1345–48, p. 284; 1348–50, pp. 108, 203; 1354–58, pp. 284, 352.

33 LAO, Dalderby Memoranda, pp. 548, 837, 889, 917.

34 Rawcliffe, *Medicine for the Soul*, pp. 65, 84.

35 Harper-Bill, 'English Church', p. 111.

mation in 1480 – granted very specific indulgences to those who contributed to
the order. In special cases (such as the financial problems facing St Giles's in the
1350s) additional grants might be made for limited periods of time.[36] In other
words, alms giving was now associated with specifically targeted and quantifiable
benefits to the donor, over and above the general sense of well-being that must
have accompanied the earlier gifts. As a concession to the increasingly legalistic
spirit of the age, these benefits began to be written down in the form of a
contract, an indisputable guarantee of their efficacy as the Day of Judgement
loomed. Duffy has pointed out that these indulgences did not so much offer
remission of sin, as commutations of temporal penance imposed for sin. Nevertheless, they came to offer a wide range of benefits and, 'there is abundant
evidence that they were eagerly sought by every class in English society in the
later Middle Ages'.[37]

By the fifteenth century the standard Lazarite indulgence had come to include
a range of privileges deliberately designed to appeal to the average lay person,
including the benefit of 'all masses and other devotions to be offered to God in
all churches throughout the whole world'. More specifically, vows of abstinence
and pilgrimage might be commuted, sins remitted at the hour of death and
burial allowed even if a church was under interdict, 'unless [the donor] shall
have been excommunicated by name'.[38] On Good Friday penitents could go to
their parish priest and be absolved from their sins with these words:

> By the authority of our Lord Jesus Christ and of St Peter and St Paul the Apostles
> and of a papal bull of indulgence, I absolve thee from all thy sins confessed to me
> and repented of and of which thou wishest to confess if they occur to thy memory
> and I restore thee to the unity of the faithful in the sacraments of the church. In the
> name of the Father etc.[39]

In addition to this, special privileges were devised for members of the clergy.
A priest might be granted absolution for not reciting the canonical hours, for
example, or failing to travel to Rome to seek absolution for 'notorious irregular-
ity'.[40] The increasing emphasis on contractual spiritual privileges such as these is
to be set against the backdrop of the new collegiate church at Burton which
became the focus of the order's activities in the fifteenth century. In an age when
plague was endemic, 'The most obvious psychological consequence of greatly
increased and sudden mortality was an almost desperate fear of oblivion after
death', and to counteract this people did their very best to be associated with

---

36 *CPapR, Letters 13 pt 1, 1471–84*, p. 263; *Petitions 1, 1342–1419*, p. 270.
37 Duffy, *Stripping of the Altars*, p. 288.
38 See, for example, SRO, Sutherland Collection, D 593/A/1/32/1.
39 MUOL, 7527. Lunt states that an indulgence could be obtained by all those who visited the hospital on
    Good Friday, but he may be confusing this with the general privilege extended to the parish priests of
    penitents on Good Friday. Lunt, *Financial Relations*, 2, p. 502; PRO, E 135/21/72, 73.
40 See, for example, LRO, BR11/19/2. This indulgence, to Robert Bostock and his family in 1473, has been
    printed in M. Bateson (ed.), *Records of the Borough of Leicester, 1327–1509*, 2 (London, 1901), pp.
    386–7. It proves, like others of its type, that an individual did not have to be a priest to obtain an
    indulgence granting privileges especially directed to the clergy. Indulgences seem to have been issued
    with little attention to the detail of their content.

religious orders and what they stood for.[41] As one contemporary cleric put it, 'Amongst the different works of piety and services of divine majesty . . . solemn masses shine forth as Lucifer amongst the stars'.[42]

The growing popularity of masses and indulgences to speed the passage of the soul through purgatory had the effect of encouraging the Lazarites to package and manage their privileges in a different fashion in line with the changing attitudes of the laity in the late Middle Ages. Rather than a member of the order travelling around the country soliciting donations as he went, these written indulgences were now trafficked by freelance collectors, often termed pardoners or proctors, licenced by the diocesan authorities. Eight of these individuals have been traced working in the dioceses of Lincoln, Hereford and Durham between 1481 and 1533, and as late as 1535 a 'feigned proctor of St Lazar' was operating in the diocese of Bangor.[43] These pardoners did not always work exclusively for the order. John Bell, licensed to sell indulgences in Hereford in 1519, was also employed by the hospitals of St Anthony, London, and St Thomas, Rome.[44] Five indulgences bearing the confraternity seal of the order have been located and, of these, two have the space for the name of the recipient left blank despite being sealed and dated, suggesting that the travelling pardoners were sometimes armed with fully authenticated 'open' indulgences.[45] On the other hand, the discovery in the early 1990s of a version of the Burton Lazars confraternity seal matrix at Robertsbridge, near Lewes, Sussex, might imply that the itinerant pardoners were also let loose with seals of their own.[46]

The profit derived from this exercise by issuer and agent is not clear. Endorsements of 1d or 2d on three surviving documents might suggest the pardoner's fee. When the pardoner of St Lazarus visited Sir Francis Willoughby's household at Wollaton, near Nottingham, in 1509 and 1522 he received 4d on each occasion.[47] Similarly, in his will of 1522, Thomas Sturston of Foulsham, Norfolk, left 4d to the pardoners of the Trinity at Ingham, St Thomas of Rome, Our Lady of the Sea, Burton Lazars and Our Lady of Bedlam. By contrast, the pardoners of Jesus, the Five Wounds, Our Lady of Rouncivall and St John's Friary, Norwich, received only 2d, suggesting a clear pecking order in the purchase of salvation.[48] It is not clear whether or not the 4d paid by Willoughby and Sturston actually

---

41 Harper-Bill, 'English Church', p. 110.

42 Rawcliffe, Medicine for the Soul, p. 107.

43 M.P. Howden (ed.), The Register of Richard Fox, 1494–1507, SurS, 147 (1932), pp. 46, 73; A.T. Bannister (ed.), Hereford Diocese, Register of Thomas Myllyng, CYS, 26 (1920), p. 74; A.T. Bannister (ed.), Hereford Diocese, Register of Richard Mayew, CYS, 27 (1921), p. 53; K. Major, A Handlist of the Records of the Bishop of Lincoln and the Archdeacons of Lincoln and Stow (London, 1953), p. 42; A.T. Bannister (ed.), Hereford Diocese, Registers of Bothe, Foxe and Boner, CYS, 28 (1921), pp. 355–60; LP, 8, 1535, pp. 242–3.

44 Bannister, Registers of Bothe, Foxe and Boner, p. 355.

45 SRO, Sutherland Collection, D 593/A/1/32/1; D 593/A/1/33/2; BL, Wolley Mss, Charter viii, 13 (blank); Add Chart, 37362 (blank); SRRS, 6000/2623.

46 A more likely interpretation is that this matrix was a prototype. See, D. Marcombe 'The Confraternity Seals of Burton Lazars Hospital and a newly discovered Matrix from Robertsbridge, Sussex', TLAHS, 76 (2002), pp. 51–62.

47 Stevenson, Middleton Mss, pp. 327, 348. Sir Francis gave the same sum to wandering friars and 'a blind minstrel', perhaps suggesting it was a gift of charity rather than payment for an indulgence.

48 H. Harrod, 'Extracts from early Norfolk wills', Norfolk Archaeology, 1 (1847), p. 271.

constituted the price of a St Lazarus indulgence. If it did, it indicates that the service was competitively priced and not beyond the means of even the relatively poor in late-medieval England. Certainly, one of the big problems for all of the institutions who shared these privileges was competition, because, as with the earlier alms gathering activities, too many people ended up chasing after the same finite resources.[49]

Given its long life, in a variety of forms, it is likely that the indulgence was always an important factor in the spiritual life of the order and one that gave it long-term exposure before a very wide cross-section of the population of the British Isles. Whether this exposure was ultimately beneficial is another question altogether. The parody of the pardoner in the *Canterbury Tales* is worthy of close attention because, although he is 'of Rouncivale', he must bear many similarities to the pardoner of St Lazarus. Indeed, Chaucer quite probably incorporated well-known characteristics to please his patron, John of Gaunt, who had differences of opinion with the order. The caricature, which pillories the greed and cynicism of the pardoner, no doubt met with his approval, and despite what Harper-Bill says about the 'conviviality and communal endeavour' evident in the *Canterbury Tales*, it is not an attractive picture:[50]

> But let me briefly make my purpose plain;
> I preach for nothing but for greed of gain
> And use the same old text, as bold as brass
> *Radix malorum est cupiditas.*
> And thus I preach against the very vice
> I make my living out of – avarice.[51]

The image struck a chord, and in the sixteenth century it became even more pointedly targeted. In 1567 William Bowyer presented a manuscript volume illustrated with colour plates to Robert Dudley, earl of Leicester. The pictures and the text were designed to appeal to Dudley's puritan sentiments since they are vehemently anti-clerical, one of the sections being entitled 'On the Hypocrite Brother' and featuring a Lazarite throwing down his habit to reveal a well-dressed, courtly gentleman (Plate 29). In the foreground stands the same brother in a grey habit holding a leper's clapper, the implication being that an exploitation of its privileges had made the order rich.[52] Bowyer was keeper of the muniments in the Tower of London, so he will have been more knowledgeable than most about the privileges enjoyed by the order. His poem is important enough to deserve a fairly lengthy quotation:

> Pious minds pity the needy man
> And deny no gifts to those who live under affliction.
> Although the worthless miser, whose mind is satisfied by no good deeds,

---

[49] Orme and Webster, *English Hospital*, p. 98.

[50] Harper-Bill, 'English Church', p. 119.

[51] G. Chaucer, *The Canterbury Tales*, translated into modern English by N. Coghill (1951, reprinted Harmondsworth, 1972), p. 261.

[52] HL, HM 160, f. 129. The section also contains a series of transcriptions of grants and confirmations relating to the order, ff. 129–34.

Gives nothing to the poor,
It is only shame and fear which will make him give abundantly
Since the work of piety moves him not at all.
With this hope aroused, which it is agreed rarely deceives,
Instantly we pretended to be men without means.
Wherefore nobles granted us lands and houses
And rural people gave us large gifts . . .
At last we pretended to be the unworthy brethren
Taking the name which poor Lazarus holds.
This sad tale was a source of terror to the rich.
How wonderfully it terrified those wicked men,
Everyone who tried to seek money by usury,
So that each man might bestow gifts more abundantly on us!
By this trickery we have misled the whole world.
Our intention had been to despoil wretched men.
By these spoils our pride is grown,
False superstition is increased far and wide.[53]

The argument clearly expressed here is that the order unscrupulously preyed on the consciences of the rich, exploiting the stories of Lazarus to convey the notion that if people did not give alms they would pay a heavy price for their lack of charity. Unfortunately, the 'poor Lazarus' of Bowyer's poem takes us no closer to the true identity of the patron saint of the order. On the surface, it might be taken to refer to Lazarus the beggar, until it is remembered that Lazarus of Bethany also had some alarming other-worldly tales to tell. In the *Kalender of Shepherdes* and *The Arte or Crafte to Lyve Well and to Dye Well*, popular devotional tracts on the eve of the Reformation, Lazarus, newly risen from the grave, is commanded by Jesus to provide detailed descriptions of the torments of hell.[54] Many of these, which became collectively known as the *Vision of Lazarus*, are punishments for the sins of the rich:

> The usurous are boiled in molten gold, the gluttonous fed with, and fed on by toads and serpents, and, perhaps most vividly, the proud are bound to great iron wheels, covered with burning hooks. The restless revolution of the wheels, endlessly raising and lowering the souls of the proud, is a gruesome metaphor of their sin.[55]

The message from both Lazarus the beggar and Lazarus of Bethany was clear – amend your behaviour on earth (and this could be assisted hugely by giving money to poor religious orders), or suffer an eternity of torment in hell. Much of this 'trickery' and 'false superstition', as Bowyer would have it, must have stemmed from the sale of indulgences. And it would not have escaped people's attention that this order, which exploited its supposed poverty and the fear of everlasting damnation to procure these donations, was in the process of building a new and impressive church, an objective which, to some, at least, must have

[53] *Ibid*, f. 129.
[54] The *Kalender* was first published in France in 1493 and by Wynkyn de Worde in 1508. *The Arte or Crafte* was published by Wynkyn de Worde in 1505. Duffy, *Stripping of the Altars*, pp. 50, 81–2, 340–1.
[55] *Ibid*, p. 340.

Plate 29: William Bowyer's painting of the 'hypocrite brother' from the 1560s.
A brother of St Lazarus with a disturbing double *persona* – on the left a poor,
begging friar; on the right a fashionable country gentleman.

seemed incompatible with what the Lazarites professed. If Bowyer's testimony is
to be believed, greed, deceit and hypocrisy were what stuck in people's throats
about these 'poor' friars.

The confraternity

Indulgences were all well and good, but the St Lazarus pardoner had a further
trick up his sleeve that gave him the edge over some of his competitors and
neatly linked up the old privileges from the crusading era with the new collegiate
status of Burton in the fifteenth century. This was the order's confraternity,
which became inseparably merged with its indulgence activities as time went on.
The confraternity in all probability was not a product of the late Middle Ages,
though it reached its peak then and probably underwent a fundamental reorganisation. Both the Templars and Hospitallers conducted confraternities in the
thirteenth century by which lay people were affiliated to their orders in return
for monetary payments, and it is likely that the Lazarites followed a similar

practice.[56] There is certainly evidence that the order enjoyed a special relationship with particular families, which probably stemmed from this sort of ongoing involvement. The fifteenth-century Sutton masters, for example, may have been related to Thomas de Sutton, an officer of the order in 1318; and Sir Thomas Norton was possibly connected with the renegade brother Robert Norton, alias Thomas Poutrell, of 1428.[57]

But the clearest case involves the Lincolnshire family of Trickingham, lords of Threckingham, where the order owned estates and the rectory (Plate 30). In the thirteenth century at least five individuals of this name had close connections with the Lazarites: Alexander, an attorney of the master in 1254, Hugh, a witness to a charter in 1264, and Reginald, John and Thomas who were parish priests.[58] It was by fostering such links with the secular gentry that the order helped safeguard its influence and future. Alongside this there is evidence of patrons and benefactors being included on the hospital's bederoll. William de Ferrers, fifth earl of Derby, and Edmund 'Crouchback', first earl of Lancaster, both enjoyed this privilege, for example.[59] There was nothing to stop these two practices – secular support and masses for the dead – being merged, blended with the papal privileges and a confraternity formed that might be both remunerative and generally supportive of the interests of the house. Confraternities were enjoying a huge growth in popularity in the late Middle Ages since 'their core and essence was that they were communal chantries designed to unite their brethren in prayer for the souls of deceased members'.[60] They were a way of involving everyone, and especially the relatively poor who could not afford a personal chantry, in the great spiritual preoccupation of the age.

When exactly the confraternity of St Lazarus took off is not clear, but between 1455 and 1526 there are 26 extant grants of confraternity and indulgence, compared with the five grants specifically of indulgences noted above (Appendix 2).[61] The grants are spread over the masterships of Sir William Sutton, Sir George Sutton and Sir Thomas Norton and are remarkably evenly spaced, suggesting a consistent popularity for the product from the mid-fifteenth century to the eve of the Reformation. These dates tie in conveniently with the building of the collegiate church, and it is likely that the growth of the confraternity was, on the one hand, inspired by this development and, on the other,

---

56 Gilchrist, *Contemplation and Action*, pp. 64–5.
57 *CPR, 1317–21*, p. 131; PRO, CP 40/675, m.505d (Farnham, 1, p. 262).
58 BL, Cart, f. 61; PRO, KB 26/154, m.20d (Farnham, 1, p. 254); F.N. Davis (ed.), *Rotuli Hugonis de Welles*, 3, LRS, 9 (1914), p. 91; R.M.T. Hill (ed.), *Rolls and Registers of Bishop Oliver Sutton*, 1, LRS, 39 (1948), p. 153; R.M.T. Hill (ed.), *Rolls and Registers of Bishop Oliver Sutton*, 7, LRS, 69 (1975), pp. 11, 16, 24; F.N. Davis (ed.), Lincoln Diocese, *Register of Richard Gravesend*, CYS, 31 (1925), p. 12.
59 W.H. Hart (ed.), 'Calendar of Fines for the County of Derby', *JDANHS*, 8 (1886), pp. 55–6; 13 (1891), p. 18.
60 Harper-Bill, 'English Church', p. 113.
61 BL, Add Chart, 19864; 47555; 66397; 53492; 53710; Harl Mss, Charter 43 A 13; 2077, f. 33; c 18 e2 (7); Stowe Mss, Charter 619; 620; PRO, C 270/32/5; E 135/21/72; E 135/21/73; Bod Lib, Ms Ch Leicester a 1, f. 21; Ms Barlow 1, pp. v–vi; Top gen C 23, f. 22; SRO, Sutherland Collection, D 593/A/1/32/14; 15; LRO, DE2242/6/7; BR11/19/2; WAM, 6660; DRO, D/2977/2/37; CRO, Shakerley Collection, DSS 3991, Drawer 2/1, ex Bundle 2; MUOL, 7527; UNMD, Middleton Mss, MiF 1/6; W. Beaumont, 'Original Documents', *Archaeological Journal*, 24 (1867), p. 265. See Appendix 2.

Plate 30: Tomb effigies taken to be those of Sir Lambert de Trickingham and his wife (*c.*1280) from the church of Threckingham, Lincolnshire. The Trickinghams had close associations with the order in the thirteenth century.

helped to fund it. Confraternities and indulgences were very often linked to church-building programmes.[62]

With the exception of those grants that have turned up in national repositories, such as the Public Record Office and the British Library, the remainder have come from archive offices in Leicestershire, Nottinghamshire, Derbyshire, Staffordshire, Shropshire and Cheshire, suggesting that the confraternity was most popular in midland England. Moreover, a total of 31 extant grants of confraternity and/or indulgence must represent only the smallest tip of a very considerable iceberg. These were ephemeral documents, many of which must have perished at the Reformation, and the fact that a relatively large number has survived indicates that this must once have been an extensive operation. The popularity of the confraternity, certainly up to the 1520s, suggests a different story to Bowyer's, retrospective, criticisms. Why should people so readily have identified with an organisation noted for its fraud and deception? The *Vision of Lazarus*, for all its harrowing images of hell, does not provide an entirely satisfactory answer. This flourishing confraternity must have had a more positive side too.

What can we learn of the confraternity from its surviving documentation? As Harper-Bill has stated, 'the size and status of the membership varied according to the nature and function of each particular confraternity. The greatest enjoyed nationwide prestige and attracted distinguished brethren from far beyond their own region.'[63] It certainly appears that the confraternity of St Lazarus aspired to such 'nationwide prestige' and broad-based membership. The letters of confraternity themselves vary greatly in quality from the attractively produced document, with coloured initial capitals, given to James Layton and Eleanor his wife in 1486 (Plate 31),[64] to the workaday piece of parchment issued to Robert Oldver and his family in 1484.[65] In one grant, to Margaret Bowis in 1497, the words of the absolutions to be used on Good Friday and 'In the article of Death' are transcribed on the reverse, no doubt for the guidance of her parish priest who would have to perform these rites.[66] There is one example of a printed grant, that to Thomas West and Joan his wife in 1510, decorated with a woodcut of Christ arising from the tomb as a soldier looks on (Plate 32).[67] The fact that it was worthwhile printing letters of confraternity by the early sixteenth century, as both St Thomas of Acre and St Katherine's, Lincoln, did, once more points to a buoyant demand for the product on offer.[68] But most documents up to and including the last in 1526 were handwritten and were stated to be 'signed with our seal of the confraternity at Burton aforesaid in our chapter house'.

The confraternity seal, which survives in many forms and for which at least two bronze matrices still exist, is a vesica showing the figure of a bishop beneath

---

62 Duffy, *Stripping of the Altars*, p. 289; Rawcliffe, *Medicine for the Soul*, pp. 106–7; Orme and Webster, *English Hospital*, p. 97.
63 Harper-Bill, 'English Church', p. 113.
64 CRO, Shakerley Collection, DSS 3991, Drawer 2/1, ex Bundle 2.
65 DRO, D/2977/2/37.
66 MUOL, 7527.
67 BL, c 18 e2 (7).
68 Orme and Webster, *English Hospital*, pp. 60–1, 98.

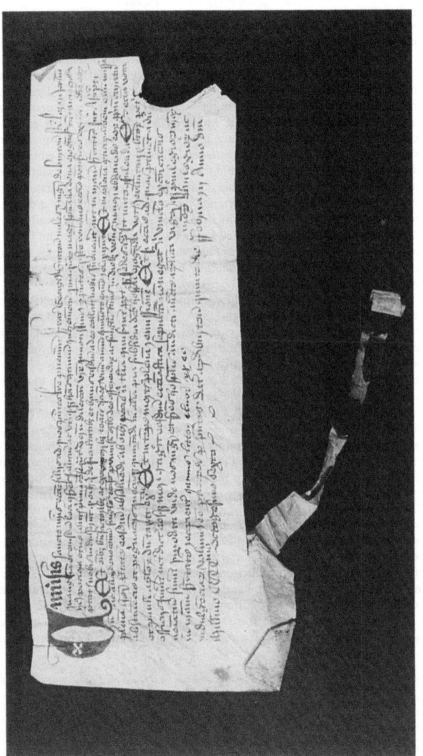

Plate 31: Letter of confraternity (1486) from Sir George Sutton to James Layton and Eleanor, his wife.

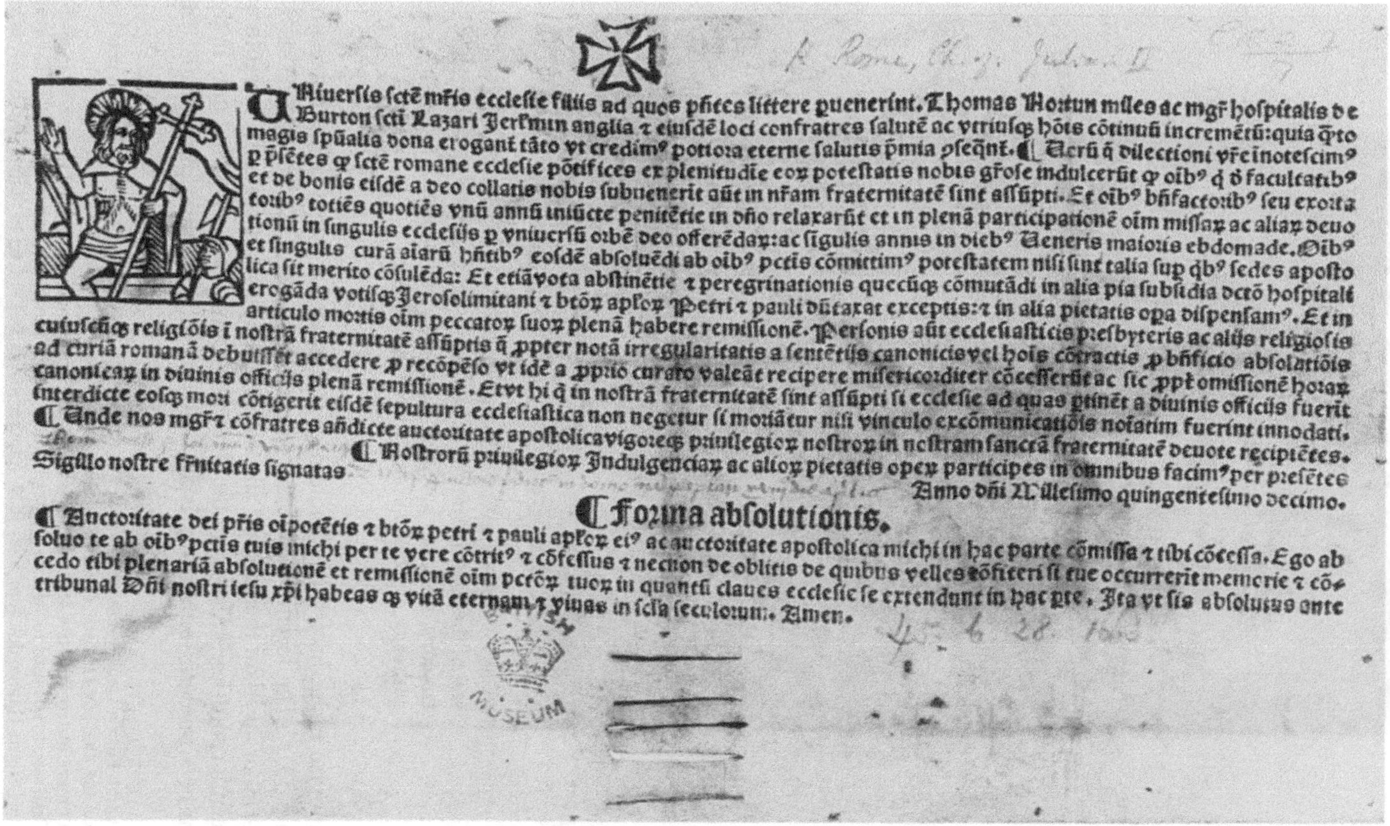

Uniuersis sctē mřis ecclesie filiis ad quos p̄ntes littere puenerint. Thomas Norton miles ac mgř hospitalis de Burton scti Lazari Jerl'm in anglia ⁊ eiusdē loci confratres salutē ac vtriusq̧ hōis cōtinuū incremētū: quia q̄to magis spūalia dona erogant tāto vt credim⁹ pottora eterne salutis p̄mia ꝯseq̄nt. ¶ Uerū q̄ dilectioni vr̄e inotescim⁹ ꝙ p̄sētes ꝙ sctē romane ecclesie pōtifices ex plenitudīe eoꝝ potestatis nobis g̃rose indulcerūt ꝙ oib⁹ q̄ d̄ facultatib⁹ et de bonis eisdē a deo collatis nobis subuenerit aūt in nr̄am fraternitatē sint assūpti. Et oib⁹ bn̄factorib⁹ seu exorta torib⁹ totiēs quotiēs vnū annū iniūcte penitētie in dn̄o relaxarūt et in plenā participationē oīm missaꝝ ac aliaꝝ deuotionū in singulis ecclesiis ꝑ vniuersū orbē deo offerēdaꝝ: ac sīgulis annis in dieb⁹ Ueneris maioris ebdomade. Oib⁹ et singulis curā aiarū h̄ntib⁹ eosdē absoluēdi ab oib⁹ pctis cōmittim⁹ potestatem nisi sint talia sup q̄b⁹ sedes apostolica sit merito cōsulēda: Et etiā vota abstinētie ⁊ peregrinationis quecūq̧ cōmutādi in alia pia subsidia dctō hospitali erogāda votis q̧ Jerosolimitani ⁊ btōꝝ aplōꝝ Petri ⁊ pauli dūtaxat exceptis: ⁊ in alia pietatis opa dispensam⁹. Et in articulo mortis oīm peccatoꝝ suoꝝ plenā habere remissionē. Personis aūt ecclesiasticis presbyteris ac aliis religiosis cuiuscūq̧ religiōis ī nostrā fraternitatē assūptis q̄ ꝓpter notā irregularitatis a sentētiis canonicis vel hois cōtractis ꝓ bn̄ficio absolutiōis ad curiā romanā debuissēt accedere ꝓ recōpēso vt idē a ꝓprio curato valeāt recipere misericorditer cōcesserūt ac sic ꝓpt omissionē horaꝝ canonicaꝝ in diuinis officiis plenā remissionē. Et vt hi q̄ in nostrā fraternitatē sint assūpti si ecclesie ad quas ꝑtinēt a diuinis officiis fuerit interdicte eosq̧ mori cōtigerit eisdē sepultura ecclesiastica non negetur si moriātur nisi vinculo excōmunicatiōis noīatim fuerint innodati. ¶ Unde nos mgř ⁊ cōfratres an̄dicte auctoritate apostolica vigoreq̧ priuilegioꝝ nostroꝝ in nostram sanctā fraternitatē deuote recipiētes. ¶ Nostrorū priuilegioꝝ Indulgenciaꝝ ac alioꝝ pietatis opeꝝ participes in omnibus facim⁹ per presētes Sigillo nostre fr̄nitatis signatas

Anno dn̄i Millesimo quingentesimo decimo.

¶ Forma absolutionis.

¶ Auctoritate dei pr̄is oīpotētis ⁊ btōꝝ petri ⁊ pauli aplōꝝ ei⁹ ac auctoritate apostolica michi in hac parte cōmissa ⁊ tibi cōcessa. Ego absoluo te ab oib⁹ pctis tuis michi per te vere cōtrit⁹ ⁊ cōfessus ⁊ necnon de oblitis de quibus velles cōfiteri si tue occurrerit memorie ⁊ cōcedo tibi plenariā absolutionē et remissionē oīm pctōꝝ tuoꝝ in quantū claues ecclesie se extendunt in hac pte. Jta vt sis absolutus ante tribunal Dn̄i nostri iesu xp̄i habeas q̧ vitā eternam ⁊ viuas in scl'a seculorum. Amen.

Plate 32: Printed letter of confraternity (1510) from Sir Thomas Norton to Thomas West and Joan, his wife.

Plate 33: One of several fifteenth-century versions of the
seal of the confraternity of St Lazarus. Its resemblance to
episcopal seals may have been designed to give it added
authority, especially in the issue of indulgences.

a canopied niche, his left hand holding a crozier and his right raised in blessing
(Plate 33).[69] The legend is SIGILLU: FRATERNITAS: SCI: LACIRI: IERUSALEM: IN:
ANGLIA, or a variant thereof, and all existing examples date from the fifteenth or
sixteenth centuries.[70] Also from the sixteenth century, but surviving only in the
form of a modern impression, is an oval seal with the inscription SIGILL: DE:

[69] LCCM, Burton Lazars Confraternity Seal; FM, Seals, Waldon 37; A Way 54.1890–1; BL, Seal xxxv 169;
lxvi 48a, 48b; lxix 43; Birch, *Catalogue of Seals*, 1, nos. 2790–3.

[70] A bronze matrix (Seal lxvi 48a) survives in the British Museum, corresponding to no. 2791 in Birch's
Catalogue. It was used to validate grants of probate in the Lincoln Cathedral prebendal peculiar of
Long Stowe, Huntingdonshire, until 1837. Another matrix was dug up in Suffolk in the early nine-
teenth century, but its whereabouts is now unknown. See, 'An Inedited Seal of Burton Lazars',
Archaeologia, 18 (1817), p. 425; W.S. Walford, 'A Discussion Paper on Seals', *Proceedings of the Society of
Antiquaries*, 1st series, 4 (1859), p. 274; A.B. Tonnochy, *Catalogue of British Seal-Dies in the British
Museum* (London, 1952), p. 152. For a full discussion, see Marcombe, 'Confraternity Seals'.

INDULGENCIA: DE: BURTO: SCI: LAZARI: IRL'Y.[71] This suggests that it was designed specifically to validate indulgences, though, in practice, the confraternity seal is invariably encountered fulfilling this function. Despite the fact that the style of engraving on the indulgence seal is crude and far inferior to the highly competent workmanship of most of the confraternity seals, it does bear some significant iconographical details. Its central figure shows a bishop standing under a baldachin supported by two poles. In his left hand he holds a crozier, in his right a highly pronounced leper's clapper. The clapper is always absent from the confraternity seals, but its presence, in the context of a bishop, on the indulgence seal, suggests that the individual depicted is none other than St Lazarus of Bethany.[72]

The use of the image of St Lazarus of Bethany on the indulgence seal and the more commonly encountered confraternity seals suggests that the order was striving to achieve the 'authority' of episcopal imagery in its issue of indulgences. After all, who, in the later Middle Ages, would have had much faith in a seal adorned with a beggar? The duplication of 'spiritual' seals, numerically and geographically, is puzzling and goes against the frequently encountered statement that indulgences and letters of confraternity were being sealed in the chapter house at Burton. If so, why did the order need so many matrices; why was one found in Sussex; and why was it necessary to seal blank documents? Had there been a single matrix held at Burton and a policy of central production and validation there would have been no need for any of this. The pattern of documentary survival suggests that either additional matrices were issued to local agents or that the order suffered widespread problems of forgery, which is quite feasible given the far-flung nature of its operation, which must have been exceedingly difficult to monitor and regulate effectively.

Members of the confraternity came from all social classes. In one document dated 1465 Sir Henry Stafford is named along with his wife, Lady Margaret Beaufort, and her son Henry, Lord Richmond, the future Henry VII;[73] in another, of 1479, Elizabeth Hesilrige, a future prioress of Nuneaton, is the grantee.[74] But the majority of confrères are not so easily identified, and it is quite common for husbands and wives, and whole families, to be united in a single grant.[75] Indeed, on two occasions entire parishes joined – East and West Hagbourne, Oxfordshire, in 1463 and Tredington, Gloucestershire, in 1504.[76] The service that these 'sharers of our privileges, indulgences and other works of piety' coveted most was the addition of their names to the bederoll of the collegiate church at Burton. The continual round of prayer and intercession maintained there by the priests of the college would ensure that the souls of members of the confraternity would make a hasty passage through the gloomy realms of purgatory and be born again to the joys of eternal life. James Breton, rector of

---

71 BL, Seal xxxv 169; Birch, *Catalogue of Seals*, 1, no. 2794.
72 For a discussion of the iconography of St Lazarus, see Chapter 1, pp. 5–6; and for the 'secular' seals of the order, see Chapter 4, pp. 111–14.
73 WAM, 6660.
74 BL, Add Chart, 47555.
75 As in the case of the Bostocks, above. LRO, BR11/19/2.
76 PRO, C 270/32/5; Bod Lib, Ms Barlow 1, pp. v–vi.

Bulphan, Essex, summed up this pervasive preoccupation in his will of 1517. Leaving 1s 8d each to three confraternities – St Thomas at Rome, 'St Lasery of Burton' and the Holy Trinity at Mundon, Essex – he requested 'that the said fraternities pray for me as they be accustomed to pray for brethren and sisters having letters of them'.[77]

Satisfying this demand of brethren with 'letters' was undoubtedly the main spiritual preoccupation of the order in the late Middle Ages. Whether the confraternity also incorporated a social function, as did the Corpus Christi guilds in the towns, is not evident from the surviving documentation, but Burton Lazars, with its splendid new church and image of St Lazarus, would certainly have provided a natural focus for processions, pilgrimages and pageants. Evidence of pilgrimage to Burton is no more than slight. Two pilgrim badges have been found close to the village (one of them a Canterbury bell), and in 1980 a late-medieval lead ampulla was discovered at Kirby Bellars bearing a cross *patée*, a device often associated with crusading orders and precisely the same as the cross illustrated at the top of the printed letter of confraternity of 1510 (see Plate 32). Though, as Spencer states, it is 'too cryptic to convey any certain meaning to us now', it is possible that it was a pilgrim souvenir taken away from the collegiate church on just such an occasion.[78]

Support from the laity

Other individuals, who may or may not have been members of the confraternity, also left endowments to Burton Lazars to pray for their souls, especially after the advent of the collegiate church. William Sutton, rector of St Stephen, Walbrook, who died in 1503, left £1 to the college 'to pray for my soul'; and in 1522 Maurice Berkeley of Wymondham bequeathed to the brethren of Burton, and others, a sum of money 'to have a solemn *obit* kept . . . with ringers of bells and to have a hearse and tapers set after the manner of their solemn *obits* kept within their said monasteries'. Berkeley, who along with Sutton is likely to have been a *confrère*, left legacies of 1s to 'all my brethren of Burton Lazars . . . to any of them' and nominated Sir Thomas Norton as his supervisor.[79] From this bequest it is not clear if Berkeley is referring to the professed brethren of the college or the brethren of the wider confraternity. Since he was a kinsman of the founder he probably felt an obligation to be magnanimous, and the comparatively small legacy, coupled with the words 'to any of them', may suggest the confraternity. We might expect that the support of such people could be taken for granted, yet the wills of other key individuals do not always reflect this same sense of generosity. Maurice, fourth Lord Berkeley (1523), Thomas Howard, seventh duke of Norfolk (1524)

---

[77] I. Darlington (ed.), *London Consistory Court Wills, 1492–1547*, LonRS, 3 (1967), p. 34.

[78] B. Spencer, 'Two Leaden Ampullae from Leicestershire', in 'Archaeology in Leicestershire and Rutland', *TLAHS*, 55 (1979/80), p. 89; Leicestershire County Council, SMR ID M9912, unspecified (Sandy Lane, MM SK756). The discovery of a shell-shaped ampulla between Burton Lazars and Melton Mowbray has also been reported by a metal detectorist, though this is not officially recorded.

[79] CCA, Dcc, Reg F, f. 198 (William Sutton, 1503); Taylor, *Berkeleys of Wymondham*, p. 29.

and Thomas, fifth Lord Berkeley (1533) – all of whom are likely to have had close associations with the house – are silent on the matter.[80]

Most remarkable, perhaps, is the will of Sir Richard Sutton (1524), a notably pious and charitable man, who had family connections with the order and may have ended his days as a corrodian at St Giles's. Yet, like Norfolk and the Lords Berkeley, he also chose to commission prayers for his soul from other providers.[81] It could be that as probable members of the confraternity these individuals expected such *obits* to be carried out as a matter of course, making William Sutton and Maurice Berkeley exceptional simply because they were asking for something over and above the ordinary. Outside of this immediate circle of aristocratic supporters, breaking through to new markets seeking intercession cannot always have been easy. Harper-Bill has made the intriguing suggestion that some of the papal indults for portable altars may be linked with masses for the dead, enabling priests to travel around and set up for a mass, literally, on the tomb chest of a deceased patron. If he is correct, then the indult granted to Sir William Sutton in 1450 may have enabled priests of the order to fulfil just such a function.[82]

Support also came from lesser people, though on a more limited scale. Robert Rowe of Burton Lazars, who died in 1521, requested burial in 'the cemetery of Burton St Lazarus', probably the burial ground of the collegiate church, and he appointed Rawcliff Blake, 'priest of the place of St Lazarus', as one of his executors.[83] These requests suggest a relatively close association with the house and Rowe may have been a tenant or secular servant of the college. Isabella Gillot of Leicester, a notable patron of religious causes, left her smallest legacy, 3s 4d, 'to the house of Burton Lazars', placing it in importance after St Katherine's Priory, Lincoln, and the shrines of Our Lady at Walsingham and Ipswich. Out of 10 testators traced for the village of Burton before the dissolution of the house only one, John Deychen in 1533, looked to the order to intercede for the salvation of his soul. He stated, 'I bequeath to the master of Burton Lazars 2s 4d, also to the brother of the same place to say for a *trental*, 10s.'[84] It is likely that one of the priests of the house was customarily engaged by the vicar of Melton Mowbray to serve the parochial chapel of St Margaret at Burton Lazars, which was quite separate from the college, since in 1521 the job was being done by a Brother Ralph Blake, and in 1535 payment of £5 was made 'to a monk of Burton' for the same service.[85] This was possibly 'the brother of the same place' referred to by Deychen. It is also possible that two of the last priests of the collegiate foundation, William Frankis and Robert Coke, were members of local yeoman families of the same name.[86] A similar pattern is encountered at Spondon where the order was also a major landowner. Out of 16 wills dating between 1534 and 1545

---

80 PRO, PROB 11/21, ff. 108–10 (Maurice, fourth Lord Berkeley, 1523); ff. 176–7 (Thomas Howard, seventh duke of Norfolk, 1524); 11/25, ff. 3–6 (Thomas, fifth Lord Berkeley, 1533).
81 PRO, PROB 11/21, ff. 209–10 (Sir Richard Sutton, 1524).
82 Harper-Bill, 'English Church', p. 112; *CPapR, Letters 10, 1447–55*, p. 93.
83 LRO, PR, Reg I (1515–26), f. 233 (Robert Rowe, 1521).
84 LRO, PR, Reg II (1526–33), f. 68 (John Deychen, 1533).
85 Nichols, *Leicestershire*, 2 pt 1, p. 250; LRO, PR, Reg I (1515–26), f. 233 (Robert Rowe, 1521).
86 For other members of these families, see LRO, 10D41/13/2, ff. 45, 52, 67.

only that of John Brownell, yeoman, who died in 1543, set aside 6s 8d for an *obit* in the college of Burton.[87]

The order did slightly better in London. According to the 1548 Chantry Certificate, 12 benefactors in city parishes had bequeathed money to Burton Lazars or St Giles's for prayers for their souls.[88] Though one of these was Thomas More, dean of St Paul's (1406–21), the majority appear to have been merchants or tradesmen and none of the sums involved exceeded 10s *per annum*. In all, London brought in about £3 10s 4½d in terms of prayers for the dead.[89] Although this is not a large sum, it must be set alongside similar small endowments that came from Burton Lazars and Spondon and may well have been replicated in other parts of the country. Whether these local benefactors were also members of the confraternity is not evident, since no case has yet come to light to confirm the connection. What is clear from this evidence, however, is that enthusiasm for the order of St Lazarus was far from overwhelming among the people of late-medieval England. The order certainly engendered less popular support in wills than was received by the friars and the parochial guilds, and the fact that the image of St Lazarus at Burton received offerings of only 3s 4d in 'normal years' is another indication of relatively low levels of popular devotion to the cult.[90] A place on the bederoll at Burton Lazars was evidence of a more rarefied spiritual interest, probably triggered by personal association or specifically targeted religious enthusiasms.

Certainly the messages are contradictory. On the one hand a confraternity that appears to have been well dispersed, large and successful; yet on the other, little evidence of widespread popular support and some sharp criticism from reformers in the 1560s. Perhaps the answer lies in the fact that the reservations expressed by Bowyer were most evident among poorer people, rather than the more substantial individuals who joined the confraternity and who could well afford religious insurance policies, often taken from a number of different institutions and approached in a pragmatic, matter-of-fact fashion. Such polarisation was certainly a factor of late-medieval religious life. Orme has pointed out how instances of animosity often ran alongside evidence of co-operation, and Richmond has argued that the gentry, increasingly, were withdrawing into a spiritual world of their own.[91] The experience of Burton Lazars may well be providing further evidence of such religious schizophrenia.

[87] LJRO, B/C/11 (John Brownell, 1543).

[88] C.J. Kitching (ed.), *London and Middlesex Chantry Certificate 1548*, LonRS, 16 (1980), pp. 1, 11, 38, 48, 51, 52, 53, 56.

[89] The calculation includes 16s from John Tripley to St Nicholas's, Cole Abbey, to be shared between Burton Lazars and 'Christchurch'. Half has been accounted to Burton. Kitching, *London Chantry Certificate*, p. 11. For More, see *Fasti, 5, St Paul's London*, p. 6.

[90] *Valor*, 4, p. 152. The image might once have received more than this. Payments of this sort were generally falling off in the early sixteenth century, or perhaps, were deliberately under-rated for the *Valor*.

[91] Orme and Webster, *English Hospital*, pp. 103–6; Harper-Bill, 'English Church', p. 119.

Parish churches

Apart from centrally managed initiatives, such as alms gathering and the confraternity, spiritual influence spread into the community most persistently by way of the order's parish churches. Originally there were 12 of these, but by the time of the Dissolution only seven survived, the high level of loss being caused by legal difficulties rather than the desire of the Lazarites to alienate these potentially valuable assets (Map 7). During the reign of Henry II William Burdet granted the Leicestershire churches of Gaulby and Lowesby (part of the properties of Tilton hospital) and also the reversion of Haselbech, Northamptonshire, on the death of his son.[92] At the same time Simon de St Liz, earl of Huntingdon, and his wife, Alice de Gant, made a gift of three important Lincolnshire churches: Hale, Heckington and Threckingham.[93] The church of St Giles, Edinburgh, was one of the earliest and most prestigious grants of all since it was made by David I, king of Scotland and brother of Queen Matilda, before 1153; and prior to 1200 William de Ferrers, third earl of Derby, had added Spondon, Derbyshire, and Henry de Lacy, Castleford, Yorkshire.[94] All of these churches, with the exception of St Giles's, Edinburgh, were mentioned in confirmations granted by Henry II between 1178 and 1184 and John in 1200.[95]

Braceborough, Lincolnshire, had fallen into the hands of the order by 1221, though it is not noted in any of the early grants or confirmations, and a pension of £1 0s 0d from the church of Briston, Norfolk, appears in 1291.[96] St Giles's, Holborn, and Feltham, Middlesex, the last spiritualities to be granted, came as part of the London possessions in 1299.[97] Some of these grantees, particularly the Lacys and Gants, were part of Roger de Mowbray's extended family grouping, but the relationships were not always harmonious, as the dispute between Gilbert de Gant and Henry de Lacy over the Pontefract lands was to prove.[98] Moreover, the pious intentions of some of these noble benefactors were to be blighted by the lack of a proper legal title to their gifts or the desire of their descendants to undo the good works of earlier generations.

The block of Lincolnshire churches given by Earl Simon posed a particular problem because Hale and Heckington had already been granted to Bardney Abbey by Gilbert de Gant, earl of Lincoln, though, strangely, they did not appear on the papal bulls of confirmation in the hands of the Bardney monks. By 1195 a

---

[92] BL, Cart, ff. 203–5, 207. Gaulby had a chapel at Frisby to be served three days a week from the mother church. Nichols, *Leicestershire*, 2 pt 2 (London, 1798), p. 570; W.P.W. Phillimore (ed.), *Rotuli Hugonis de Welles*, 1, LRS, 3 (1912), p. 264; F.N. Davis (ed.), *Rotuli Roberti Grosseteste*, LRS, 11 (1914), p. 400. Lowesby had a chapel at Cold Newton served daily from the mother church. Phillimore, *Rotuli Hugonis de Welles*, 2, p. 232.

[93] BL, Cart, p. 205.

[94] *Ibid*; Barrow, *Regista Regum Scottorum*, 2, pp. 116–17; BL, Harl Ms, 3868, f. 15. Spondon was responsible for chapelries of Stanley and Chaddesden. O. Mosley, *History of the Castle, Priory and Town of Tutbury* (London, 1832), pp. 235–9.

[95] BL, Cart, ff. 204–5; *CChartR, 1327–41*, pp. 76–7; *Rot Chart*, 1, p. 67; Nichols, *Leicestershire*, 2, Appendix xvi, Charters 7, 10.

[96] *Rotuli Hugonis de Welles*, 2, p. 112; *CCR, 1399–1402*, pp. 450–1.

[97] *CCR, 1399–1402*, pp. 450–1.

[98] *VCH, Yorkshire*, 2, p. 161.

Map 7: Distribution of spiritualities.

suit between Burton Lazars and Bardney was under way before the *Curia Regis*, but the monks prevailed and in 1204 the prior of Burton reached a final concord with Earl Gilbert over the third church in the group, Threckingham.[99] In it Gilbert released all claim to the prior and 'for this quit-claim, fine and concord the said prior received Gilbert into all benefits and prayers of his house'.[100] It is possible that Braceborough was obtained at about this time as some sort of compensation for the loss of Hale and Heckington, the latter, in particular, being an important church by any standard.[101] Similarly, the grants of Edinburgh and Castleford do not appear to have had long-standing effect, but when exactly they were lost is not clear. Although both are mentioned in the confirmations of King John (1200) and Innocent III (1198–1216), there is no hint that Castleford was still Lazarite property at the time of the 1291 *Taxatio*, and when Robert II expropriated the properties of the order in Scotland in 1376 no mention was made of the rectory of St Giles, suggesting that by then it was already in Scottish hands.[102]

Haselbech was confirmed by William Burdet in 1298 though the advowson of the church was this time specifically excluded from the grant.[103] Nevertheless, in 1319 the patronage was in dispute between Roger de Lyle, Roger de Hanlo and Isabella, his wife, and the master of Burton Lazars, but the claim of the order appears to have been extinguished since never again does it appear in the list of patrons.[104] Certainly by the time of the *Valor Ecclesiasticus* Haselbech was not noted amongst the Northamptonshire properties of the order.[105] Indeed, by the early sixteenth century the surviving parish churches were Gaulby, Lowesby, Threckingham, Spondon, Braceborough, St Giles's, Holborn, and Feltham, just over half of the number originally granted. To this list should be added Holy Innocents', Lincoln, granted as late as 1457, which, like St Giles's, Holborn, had once doubled up as a parish church and hospital chapel.[106] Whether it still fulfilled its parochial function in the sixteenth century is extremely doubtful, however.

The management of these spiritualities raises important questions about the religious priorities of the Lazarites and the extent to which they conformed to generally accepted standards of behaviour. Did they regard their parishes as areas in which they had a special pastoral responsibility, as the Augustinian and Premonstratensian canons did, or were they merely looked on as sources of income and patronage akin to the temporal estate? One of the principal problems for the early grantees was what exactly was meant by the gift of a 'church'. Much was uncertain. What precisely was included in the rectory, was the

99 F. Palgrave (ed.), *Rotuli Curia Regis*, 1 (London, 1835), pp. 9–11, 102; A.H. Thompson, 'Notes on the History of Bardney Abbey', *Lincolnshire Architectural and Archaeological Society, AASRP*, 32, pt 1 (1913), pp. 63–7.

100 *Feet of Fines, Lincolnshire*, PRS, p. 92. Further early evidence for the confraternity, perhaps, for which see above, pp. 186–94.

101 Heckington is one of the finest examples of fourteenth-century church architecture in Lincolnshire.

102 Easson, *Medieval Religious Houses. Scotland*, pp. 162–3; R. Holmes (ed.), *The Chartulary of St John of Pontefract*, 1, Yorkshire Archaeological Society, Record Series, 25 (1899), p. 130.

103 BL, Cart, f. 207; *Taxatio*, p. 39.

104 P. Whalley (ed.), J. Bridges, *The History and Antiquities of Northamptonshire*, 2 (Oxford, 1791), p. 37.

105 *Valor*, 4, p. 152.

106 Orme and Webster, *English Hospital*, p. 55.

advowson the subject of a separate grant and to what extent did the privileges of the order extend to its dependent clergy? In her study of the Honour of Mowbray, Greenway highlighted this as a particular difficulty in the twelfth and thirteenth centuries: 'Problems and disputes arose from the fact that portions of tithe in many places had been alienated earlier. In some cases lay patronage may have been maintained even after churches had ostensibly been given away.'[107] The extent of all this was a notable bone of contention at Gaulby. In 1221 the rector, Thomas de Loddington, became involved in a dispute with Thomas Mause over whether property at Gaulby, Kings Norton and Frisby was part of the rectory. Mause, surprisingly, looked to the master of Burton for support, but he failed to appear in court on the appointed day and judgment was given for the rector.[108] The decision is unlikely to have solved the underlying problem, since later rectors were obliged to prosecute similar suits to clarify their rights; first against the master of the hospital of St John, Leicester, for riotously pulling down and removing a house in Frisby (1260), and second against Robert de Norton for a messuage and virgate in West Norton (1284).[109]

A more serious problem was brewing over the advowson of Gaulby, given to the order by Alexander IV in 1255 because of reverses suffered in the Crusade.[110] Unfortunately, the papal grant, well intentioned though it was, did not take account of the claims of the abbot and convent of St Mary's, Leicester, or of the Burdets, who had given the church to the order in the first place, and the matter proved to be an ongoing cause of friction. In 1274 the prior of St Mary's claimed a fourth part of the advowson, but he failed to appear in court to answer the complaint of the master of Burton and his abbot was ordered to compel him to attend.[111] Although the outcome of this controversy is not known, another dispute broke out in the 1290s when the Lazarites presented a fresh candidate to the rectory, John de Staunton, in view of the pluralism of the sitting incumbent, Henry de Merston. Merston, who had been rector since 1280 and had defended his rights in 1284, was possibly a candidate of the Burdets and hence resisted by the master of Burton. In any event, Bishop Oliver Sutton of Lincoln (1280–99) was obliged to issue two orders for the dispute to be settled by commissaries, as a result of which Merston resigned in favour of Staunton in 1297 and Sir Robert Burdet agreed not to proceed with his attempt to present another candidate.[112] Nevertheless, when the rector received permission to be absent for two years of study in 1300, 'intruders' entered upon his property and stole wool and other commodities and Bishop John Dalderby issued an order for their excommunica-

107 Greenway, *Mowbray Charters*, p. xliii.
108 PRO, JUST 1/948, m.14d; CP 25/1/121/9 (Farnham, 2, p. 270); D.M. Stenton (ed.), *Rolls of the Justices in Eyre*, SS, 59 (1940), pp. 161–2, 324–5, 572–3.
109 PRO, JUST 1/457, m.8 (Farnham, 2, p. 271).
110 Bourel, *Registres d'Alexandre IV*, no. 404, p. 122.
111 PRO, CP 40/5, m.5 (Farnham, 1, p. 254).
112 R.M.T. Hill (ed.), *Rolls and Registers of Bishop Oliver Sutton*, 5, LRS, 60 (1965), pp. 19, 28, 161; R.M.T. Hill (ed.), *Rolls and Registers of Bishop Oliver Sutton*, 8, LRS, 76 (1986), p. 67. The commissioners were Henry de Nassington and Walter de Wooton, canons of Lincoln, and the official of the archdeacon of Northampton. Nassington sequestered the revenues of the church in 1294 because it was feared that they would be dissipated by Merston.

tion.[113] Despite a further controversy over the advowson in 1417, the situation at Gaulby was generally calmer after 1301.[114] Another dispute over the appointment of clergy broke out soon after this at Braceborough where the order was obliged to go to court to uphold its rights against the Wasteneys family.[115] The ongoing uncertainties as to the ownership of ecclesiastical rights at Gaulby and Braceborough probably dissuaded the brethren from attempting to appropriate their rectories, since by so doing they might have brought down on their heads more problems than they cared to endure.

Appropriation of tithes

Although these were difficult cases, the appropriation of tithes was an important feature of the thirteenth century and the order of St Lazarus did not prove itself to be backward in this respect. This practice involved religious institutions, such as monasteries and hospitals, setting aside a portion of the parochial tithe for their own use. When the greater tithes were taken over in this fashion, a vicar, supported by the lesser tithes, might be installed with cure of souls in the parish; when all of the tithes, greater and lesser, were appropriated, a stipendiary curate or parish priest, paid by the appropriator, was put in place to care for the spiritual needs of local people. Appropriation was invariably a controversial issue. Though it worked to the financial benefit of the institution carrying it out, vicars and curates were not generally deemed to possess the same pastoral qualities as the better-paid rectors who disappeared from the parishes as a result of the process.[116]

The most valuable living owned by the order was Spondon, and here too there was some disagreement over whether the original grant had included the advowson. In 1251 William de Ferrers, fifth earl of Derby, and Philip de Insula, master of Burton, reached an agreement that the advowson was in the right of the hospital, but this was thrown into doubt by the eclipse of the Ferrers family in 1266 following their support for Simon de Montfort.[117] However, with the backing of Edmund 'Crouchback', first earl of Lancaster and second son of Henry III, who succeeded to the Ferrers estates, the new master of Burton, Robert de Dalby, determined not only to clarify the issue of the advowson but also to appropriate the greater tithes for the long-term benefit of the order, a scheme with which the earl is likely to have colluded since he himself had been a crusader in 1271.

It appears that in 1286 Dalby paid Lancaster 60 marks [£40] for the advowson of Spondon, despite the earlier agreement with William de Ferrers, and he also obtained a licence from Roger de Longespee, bishop of Coventry and Lichfield

---

113 LAO, Dalderby Memoranda, pp. 8, 74.

114 PRO, CP 40/626, m.340 (Farnham, 1, p. 262). In 1417 John Mowbray, earl of Nottingham, proceeded against Walter de Lynton and John White, clerk, because they had blocked his alleged right of presentation to the rectory. He was the guardian of the lands of John Beler, who may have had a grant of the advowson for a turn from Burton Lazars.

115 Bennett, Registers of Berghersh, 1, p. 41.

116 Orme and Webster, English Hospital, p. 93.

117 Hart, 'Calendar of Fines', pp. 55–6; BL, Harl Mss, 3868, f. 15.

(1257–95), for the appropriation of the rectory and the creation of a vicarage.[118] The existing rector, Hugh de Vienne, was a king's clerk and a prominent household official of the earl who needed to be compensated for his resignation, and Dalby agreed to pay him 120 marks [£80] *per annum* for life, a considerable sum, which was probably only offered on the assumption that the rector would not live very long.[119] Certainly Hugh de Vienne ceased to be active in Lancaster's household in 1284, two years before the grant, but the date of his death is unknown. As security for these lavish payments Dalby pledged the entire lands and moveable goods of the order, but by the time of Lancaster's death in 1296 the rector had not been paid in full and the order was requesting some less onerous form of surety.[120] Nevertheless, the tithes were a sound investment, and the size of the settlement with Hugh de Vienne reflected the sort of income the order could anticipate from the appropriation in the future.

At Lowesby a similar tactic was attempted, but without the influential lay support enjoyed at Spondon. In 1260 when the master exercised his right of presentation his candidate was opposed by William Burdet, lord of Lowesby, who put forward 'another chaplain of his own' but later withdrew and admitted 'that he had no right of presentation'.[121] In about 1290 the tithes of the parish were appropriated to Burton Lazars, without any of the surviving documentation generated at Spondon, a move that triggered a hostile reaction. Riots broke out in 1294, instigated by those attempting to prevent the collection of tithes; in 1296 the arrest of the rector was requested because he had remained excommunicate for more than 40 days having failed to contribute to the clerical subsidy; and in 1297 the churchyard required reconsecration since it had been 'polluted by bloodshed' by the actions of Sir William Burdet.[122] The crisis was resolved when Burdet agreed to pay the expenses incurred in the reconsecration and issued a confirmation of his family's grants to the order in 1298.[123] But the appropriation, if that had been the underlying issue, was upheld. Despite his promise, Burdet had still not carried out the reconsecration by 1311, though in that year Bishop John Dalderby issued a licence to allow it to go ahead, which suggests it may have been imminent.[124]

The breakdown in relations between the Lazarites and the Burdets, evident at Gaulby and Lowesby, was an unedifying spectacle in view of the crusading proclivities of the first William Burdet who made the initial grants to the order

---

118 *CCR, 1279–88*, p. 418; *CPR, 1422–29*, pp. 268–9; *1461–67*, pp. 136–7; *CChartR, 1327–41*, p. 77; I.H. Jeayes, *Descriptive Catalogue of Derbyshire Charters* (London and Derby, 1906), p. 275; Hart, 'Calendar of Fines', pp. 17–18; BL, Harl Mss, 3868, ff. 15–18.

119 Somerville, *Duchy of Lancaster*, 1, pp. 13, 74, 79, 83–4, 349. Vienne was a prebendary of Dublin and provided the house in London which Lancaster used for his Wardrobe.

120 Cox, 'Calendar of Fines', pp. 17–18; PRO, C 49/2/23.

121 Davis, *Register of Gravesend*, p. 139.

122 Hill, *Registers of Sutton*, 5, p. 149; R.M.T. Hill (ed.), *Rolls and Registers of Bishop Oliver Sutton*, 6, LRS, 64 (1969), pp. 32, 75. It is not certain which William Burdet is intended here since at least two were near contemporaries. However, it may have been the same Sir William Burdet who obtained a charter for a market and two fairs at Lowesby and who was killed at Dundee in 1308. Nichols, *Leicestershire*, 3 pt 1 (London, 1800), pp. 337–8.

123 BL, Cart, f. 207; Hill, *Registers of Sutton*, 6, p. 75.

124 LAO, Dalderby Memoranda, p. 424.

Table 7: Spiritualities according to the *Taxatio*

Parish	County	Rectory £	s	d	Vicarage £	s	d	Pension £	s	d
Braceborough	Lincolnshire	12	0	0	–			1 to OSL	6	8
Briston	Norfolk	–			–			1 to OSL	0	0
Gaulby	Leicestershire	16	0	0	–			–		
Haselbech	Northamptonshire	6	13	4	–			–		
Lowesby	Leicestershire	14 appropriated to OSL	13	4	4	13	4	–		
Spondon with chapel	Derbyshire	33 [appropriated to OSL]	6	8	6	13	4	–		
Threckingham	Lincolnshire	20 appropriated to OSL	0	0	5	6	8	–		

Source: *Taxatio*, pp. 39, 61, 62, 63, 64, 81, 246.
Although the *Taxatio* does not state that the rectory of Spondon was appropriated to the order, other documentary sources clearly indicate that it was.

in the twelfth century. Quite why his descendants failed to share his supportive attitude is not entirely clear. It might simply have been an attempt to tighten their grip on communities where they possessed the lordship but lacked influence over ecclesiastical affairs, or it could be that they perceived a change in the priorities of the Lazarites since the pioneer days of the Jerusalem hospital. At about this time the masters John de Horbling and Robert de Dalby were flexing their muscles as feudal overlords in nearby Cold Newton, which might have caused some alarm to the Burdets who were the ancient owners of the fief. More specifically, the livings of Gaulby and Lowesby had been annexed to Tilton hospital, another Burdet property handed over to the Lazarites, but by 1290 it was being run down (if not actually abandoned) and the order was making moves to appropriate the tithe income to purposes that might have been regarded as less worthy and were certainly less local. Possibly it was felt that if the intentions of founders and benefactors were being ignored in this fashion, these were assets that might as well remain with the family, and the local community, than with an increasingly remote and detached religious order. By contrast, the tithes of Threckingham appear to have been appropriated without visible upheaval and, as at Spondon, this might be accounted for by a harmonious relationship with the Trickinghams, the leading secular family of the parish. The extent of these appropriations by 1291, along with the values of the rectories and vicarages of the order, is presented in Table 7.

The importance of spiritual income

What was this controversial parochial income worth to the order? For valuations we rely heavily on the *Taxatio* of 1291 and the *Valor Ecclesiasticus* of 1535, the two most important assessments of ecclesiastical income in England in medieval

Graph 2: Spiritualities according to the *Taxatio* and the *Valor Ecclesiasticus*

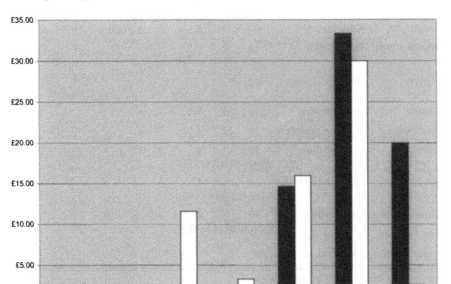

Source: *Taxatio*, pp. 39, 61, 81, 246; *Valor*, 4, pp. 152–3.

and early modern times. For the diocese of Lincoln there are also the printed returns for Cardinal Wolsey's survey of 1526, a useful addition to the information provided by the major sources. The problem with both the *Taxatio* and the *Valor* is that they are both likely to underestimate the real value of livings. Indeed, for the *Taxatio* the Pope declared that the new tax should be borne 'without grave inconvenience', a statement that encouraged clergy and assessors to agree on the lowest acceptable assessments.[125] Graph 2 illustrates how spiritual income had changed between 1291 and 1535.

Of the rectories, Braceborough was already charged with a pension of £1 6s 8d to the order in 1291, which remained unaltered until 1535. Gaulby was free of any pensions in 1291, but by 1526 an annual payment of £3 6s 8d had been imposed, a sum that is the same in the *Valor*.[126] In 1291 the appropriated rectories of Lowesby, Threckingham and Spondon were deemed to be worth £68 *per annum*, yet by 1535 the combined income was alleged to be only £48 6s 8d. Spondon and Lowesby were more or less unchanged from their *Taxatio* values, but Threckingham had collapsed from £20 (1291) to £2 6s 8d (1535). Feltham rectory, which had not been in the hands of the order in 1291, brought in £11 12s

---

[125] Robinson, *Geography of Augustinian Settlement*, pp. 110–13. Archbishop Winchelsey and Bishop Sutton of Lincoln were notable opponents of the tax.

[126] *Taxatio*, pp. 60, 64; *Valor*, 4, p. 152; Salter, *Lincoln Subsidy*, pp. 59, 119. The Gaulby pension later provoked litigation. See PRO, E 134/1655/East 21.

Table 8: Spiritualities according to the *Valor Ecclesiasticus*

Parish	County	Rectory £	s	d	Vicarage £	s	d	Pension £	s	d
Braceborough	Lincolnshire	11	13	4	–			1 to OSL	6	8
Feltham	Middlesex	11 appropriated to OSL	12	0	8 8	0 0	0 0	4 4	0 0	0 0
Gaulby	Leicestershire	22	0	0	–			3 to OSL	6	8
Lowesby	Leicestershire	16 appropriated to OSL	0	0	7	1	4	6 13 4 to vicar by OSL		
Spondon	Derbyshire	30 appropriated to OSL	0	0	6	14	5	–		
Chaddesden [chapelry]	Derbyshire	–			12 [chantry] 2 [curacy]	0 11	0 8	–		
Threckingham	Lincolnshire	2 appropriated to OSL	6	8	6	18	10	–		

Source: *Valor*, 1, p. 434; 3, pp. 159, 162; 4, pp. 106, 110, 152–3, 162, 164.
The *Valor* provides no information about St Giles's, Holborn, Holy Innocents', Lincoln, and Spondon's chapelry at Stanley. The income of the chantry at Chaddesden was made up of £2 0s 0d and a payment of £10 0s 0d from Launde abbey. According to the Chantry Certificate of 1546 the value of the chantry was £36 13s 4d. PRO, E 301/13/51; P. Cholerton, *The Church of St Mary the Virgin, Chaddesden: a guide and history* (Chaddesden, 1997), p. 50.

in 1535. No specific valuation was noted for St Giles's, which as a peculiar might have been deemed to have some special status, though in 1548 William Rowlandson was being paid £8 as 'vicar'.[127] It is not always clear how the vicars who served these cures were remunerated. In the 1526 survey, for example, it appears that the vicars of Lowesby and Threckingham were stipendiaries in the pay of Burton Lazars (receiving £6 13s 4d and £2 13s 4d respectively), yet in the *Valor* the vicar of Lowesby continues to receive his stipend and Threckingham becomes an endowed vicarage with a ludicrously small rectorial income returned to the order.[128] Table 8 illustrates the position as it was in 1535.

It is therefore not always clear how these figures are to be interpreted, and for Spondon some evidence survives that seems to confirm the view that the 'official' valuations are considerable underestimates. The first is the pension of £80 assigned to Hugh de Vienne, compared with the £40 stated to be the value of the rectory *and* vicarage in 1291. Even if Vienne was commanding a margin of profit for the inconvenience of resignation, it would be difficult to resist the conclusion that his living, in reality, was worth much less than £70. Similarly, in the early sixteenth century the order was able to lease the tithes of Chaddesden –

127 *Taxatio*, pp. 61, 63, 66, 245, 246; Kitching, *London Chantry Certificate*, pp. xxxi, 67.
128 Salter, *Lincoln Subsidy*, pp. 57, 108; *Valor*, 4, p. 152.

only a small part of Spondon parish – for £16 *per annum*.[129] Nevertheless, this was more than half the value of the full rectorial tithe of the parish returned in the *Valor*. According to the *Taxatio*, overall spiritual revenue brought in £69 6s 8d in 1291; according to the *Valor* that figure had fallen to £64 12s by 1535, despite the fact that Feltham and St Giles's had been added to the endowment in the meantime – without Feltham the figure was only £53.[130] Though some of these sums may well reflect the erosion of the value of tithes in the fourteenth and fifteenth centuries because of demographic and economic factors, it is clear that spiritual revenue was, nevertheless, an essential part of the economic well-being of the order.[131] Indeed, according to the *Valor Ecclesiasticus*, 19 per cent of gross income was derived from spiritualities. So profitable was this source that the Lazarites were prepared to become lessees and managers of tithes, as is indicated by their farm of the rectory of Melton Mowbray taken from Lewes Priory in 1523.[132]

The provision of clergy

With regard to the implementation of its rights of advowson, the order was not normally able to present its own members to its parochial cures since a dispensation was required even if a brother was in priest's orders. The exception to this rule was the parish church of St Giles, Holborn, which shared the same building as the hospital chapel, separated only by a wall. Since the church was exempt from episcopal jurisdiction no presentation of an incumbent has survived, and it is likely that the cure was served by one of the chaplains of the house. Though, like all religious orders, the Lazarites were happy to provide titles permitting the issue of letters dimissory for ordination, the deacons and priests thus admitted did not necessarily go on to serve their churches.[133] Sometimes the order was able to exploit contacts made by virtue of its landholding network. In the thirteenth century, for example, Ernald the Fleming, a patron in Leicestershire, had two sons who became priests, Michael and Thomas. Michael was a chaplain at Kirby and from there seems to have been promoted to the vicarage of Spondon. His brother-in-law was Roger Beler, indicating that his promotion may well have been assisted by the fact that he had friends in high places.[134] Likewise, it is notable how, prior to 1341, a David de Spondon was vicar of Lowesby, suggesting a similar peregrination around the territories of the order.[135]

In general terms, however, the Lazarites were obliged to look to the pool of clerical talent available in the diocese to fulfil their pastoral obligations.[136]

129 Jeayes, *Derbyshire Charters*, pp. 613–14.
130 *Taxatio*, pp. 60, 61, 63, 64, 66, 245, 246; *Valor*, 4, p. 152.
131 Orme and Webster, *English Hospital*, p. 129.
132 Harley, *Hastings Mss*, 1, p. 90. The lease was taken for 24 years at £30 13s 4d *per annum*: the master and brethren had to maintain the chancel and pay the vicar of Melton £11 *per annum*. See also PRO, C 1/808/24 for a sixteenth-century case involving the parsonage; and E 134/27 and 28 Eliz 1/Mich 26.
133 LAO, Dalderby Memoranda, pp. 148, 393, 581, 744, 750, 864.
134 BL, Cart, ff. 137, 141.
135 Bennett, *Registers of Berghersh*, 1, p. 148.
136 Men were often presented in minor orders and then progressed rapidly to the priesthood once in

Though they appear to have been efficient in finding clergy – no presentations by lapse have been encountered – there is a predictable and possibly qualitative difference between the sort of men who occupied the rectories of Braceborough and Gaulby and those in the less well-endowed vicarages. Indeed, one of the advantages for a small order in preserving at least some of its rectories was the possibility of using them as a source of patronage for friends or relatives of the master or those who by their skills could provide necessary help or support. When the question of the Braceborough advowson was resolved in 1331 the person presented to the living was none other than Hugh Beler, possibly a relative of Roger Beler, chief baron of the Exchequer, and a major patron of the order.[137]

Gaulby, the more valuable of the two rectories and also the more convenient because of its proximity to Burton, was especially jealously guarded as a source of patronage. During the legal difficulties of the mid-fourteenth century, for example, the incumbent of Gaulby was Thomas de Rippeley, a Cambridge graduate and canon lawyer, and in 1527 another lawyer, Thomas Hickman, succeeded to the living.[138] Fifteenth-century rectors included Richard Lynton and William Sutton, who look suspiciously like relatives of masters of the same name. Sutton, in particular, had a distinguished academic career at Oxford where he had a reputation as a preacher and was Junior Proctor (1467–68) and Chancellor's Commissary (1481 and 1483). He is likely to have been resident at Gaulby in the 1470s when, no doubt, he worked in close harmony with his presumed kinsman, Sir William Sutton.[139] Another rector of Gaulby, Gervase Croft, had been a fellow of Corpus Christi College, Cambridge, before he was appointed to the living in 1534.[140] At Braceborough too, university-trained clergy crop up from time to time, such as Master Ralph Brun, presented in 1268, and John de Trickingham, who was sent away for a year of study by Bishop Oliver Sutton after having been excommunicated for non-payment of the clerical tenth in 1296.[141]

Clerics of this type were perhaps more likely to be non-resident than their less privileged colleagues, yet the clerical poll-tax for the Lincoln diocese points to an adequate number of supplementary clergy to serve local needs in the event of an absence. At Gaulby and Lowesby in 1377 the incumbent was supported by two parochial chaplains, and at Braceborough and Threckingham in 1381 he had one.[142] In 1526 the rectors of Gaulby and Braceborough were still both supporting curates, paid £5 and £4 5s respectively, though the second chaplain at Gaulby had by this time vanished.[143] In the vicarages the clergy tend to be more

office. For example, John de Trickingham was appointed to Braceborough as subdeacon (March 1291); he was a deacon (June 1291); and a priest (December 1291). Hill, *Registers of Sutton*, 7, pp. 11, 16, 24.

137 Bennett, *Registers of Berghersh*, 1, p. 41.
138 A.B. Emden, *A Biographical Register of the University of Cambridge to 1500* (Cambridge, 1963), p. 482; J. Foster, *Alumni Oxonienses, 1500–1700*, 2 (Oxford, 1891), p. 704.
139 A.B. Emden, *A Biographical Register of the University of Oxford to AD 1500*, 3 (Oxford, 1959), pp. 1826–7.
140 J. and J.A. Venn, *Alumni Cantabrigienses, pt 1, to 1751*, 1 (Cambridge, 1922), p. 420.
141 Davis, *Register of Gravesend*, p. 27; Hill, *Registers of Sutton*, 5, p. 154.
142 McHardy, *Lincoln Poll-Taxes*, pp. 23, 26, 107, 110.
143 Thomas Hill at Braceborough and William Monke at Gaulby. Salter, *Lincoln Subsidy*, pp. 59, 119.

anonymous, but bishops' registers occasionally provide a glimpse that enables us to put some flesh on the bare bones – Geoffrey de Scrafield resigning Threckingham after seven years in 1293 because he had decided to become a Dominican friar; Thomas Croke working in association with his brother John at Threckingham in 1381; or John de Hale exchanging Feltham after less than a year in 1370 for a more congenial living in Surrey in the gift of the Black Prince.[144] Perhaps one of the most compelling portraits is of William Potter, vicar of Spondon, who died in 1534. With goods valued at £16 13s listed in his inventory he comes over as a small farmer possessing 20 quarters of corn, 45 sheep, 3 pigs and some hives of bees. He must have been sharing a house at the time of his death because his household furnishings totalled only 3s and did not include even basic items such as a bed, bedding or table.[145] Such were the varying shifts and fortunes of the lesser clergy in medieval England.

Parochial life

With regard to the quality of parochial ministration offered by the Lazarites and their dependent clergy, evidence is very slight. At St Giles's brothers provided a measure of ale, traditionally known as 'St Giles's bowl', for condemned prisoners as they made their way towards Tyburn for execution 'as their last refreshing of this life'.[146] Orme suggests that this compassionate gesture may have been inspired by the drink of wine and gall given to Christ on the way to his crucifixion and mentioned in St Matthew's gospel.[147] The inventory taken in 1371 notes 'a mazer called *Pardon*', bound with silver, which was possibly the vessel used for this purpose.[148] A similar charitable obligation existed at Holy Innocents' Hospital, Lincoln, where the order was expected to bury all persons hanged on the city gallows at Canwick Hill and inscribe their names in the book of the confraternity of St John the Baptist.[149]

For one of the order's churches, possibly Gaulby, a 49 page book of Homilies drawn up in 1529 still survives. Headed 'An instruction for Christian people to be read on Sundays and holidays by diverse portions', it comprises 12 discourses, in the first of which the preacher exhorts the congregation to pray for the Pope and cardinals, 'especially my Lord Cardinal of England', the bishop of Lincoln 'and the master and brethren of Burton Lazar, patrons of this church'. The discourses comprise conventional instructional rhetoric such as might have been directed by a conscientious non-resident parson to his curate. In one passage, for example, the preacher is expected to say to his audience:

---

144 Hill, *Registers of Sutton*, 1, p. 87; McHardy, *Lincoln Poll-Taxes*, p. 110; R.C. Fowler (ed.), London Diocese, *Register of Simon of Sudbury*, 1, CYS, 34 (1927), pp. 271, 273. Hale moved to Wisley, Surrey.

145 LJRO, B/C/11 (William Potter, 1534).

146 Stow, *Survey of London*, p. 364; J.S. Davies (ed.), *An English Chronicle of the Reigns of Richard II, Henry IV, Henry V and Henry VI*, CS, 64 (1856), pp. 39, 46.

147 Orme and Webster, *English Hospital*, pp. 63–4; Matthew 27: 33–4.

148 PRO, E 326/12434.

149 Holy Innocents' received a payment for this service from the Hospitallers of Maltby, Lincolnshire. In 1284 the hospital had been the site of an alleged miracle when a condemned criminal, Margaret, wife of Alan Everard of Burgh-by-Wainfleet, had revived after execution and was permitted to live out her remaining years as a sister in the Malandry. *CPR, 1281–92*, p. 113; Brooks, 'Holy Innocents', p. 163.

But first you shall understand that upon Thursday next you shall have the feast of the holy apostles Simon and Jude [28 October] which is commanded to be kept holiday and double feast in Holy Church and all that be twelve year old or more shall fast the even on Wednesday to dispose themselves to serve God and those holy apostles the better and the more devoutly on the morrow. We must fast also on Saturday next in the honour of God and All Saints, whose day shall be on Monday after.[150]

The volume may have been the work of Thomas Hickman, rector of Gaulby, with marginal notes by Wolsey's intruded incumbent, John Allen. It indicates, at least, that parishioners of livings in the gift of the Lazarites were not devoid of spiritual instruction of a relatively high standard. Nor were they deprived of fun and games, it seems. When the parishioners of All Saints', Derby, were saving up to build their impressive church tower in the early sixteenth century, two entrepreneurial individuals, Thomas Parker and Thomas Hornby, took to organising church ales in local parishes. In 1532 they returned a clear profit of £23 13s 8d from such an event at Chaddesden, suggesting that the people of this relatively small chapelry had few inhibitions about enjoying themselves.[151]

Parish church architecture

The final piece of evidence concerns the attention paid by the order to the fabric of the churches in its care, especially the appropriated vicarages where it had a legal obligation to support the chancel and a moral duty that arguably went further than that in times of crisis. The inventories of 1371 and 1391 indicate that St Giles's, Holborn, was appropriately equipped for liturgical worship, with adequate supplies of service books, vestments and altar plate on both occasions.[152] Five 'copes for the choir' in 1371 suggest a choral tradition, though these vestments were not noted in 1391 when, indeed, the number of items in the church had generally decreased. In the absence of documents we are thrown back on architectural evidence, and, sadly, some churches have vanished completely in their original form, notably St Giles's, which was pulled down, along with its extraordinary tower, in 1624. However, enough has survived to provide some useful insights. Of the 8,000 or so surviving medieval churches, about 75 per cent were rebuilt or extended during the late Middle Ages, providing ample evidence of religious enthusiasm both on the part of patrons and the laity.[153] This 'architectural revolution', most evident at Burton Lazars itself, was also reflected in many of the order's churches.

Despite its missing spire, the charming little church of Lowesby, with its polychrome stonework, still exudes the character of a well-maintained late-medieval building, at least from external appearance (Plate 34).[154] Though

150 PRO, SP 6/4; *LP, Addenda, 1 pt 1, 1509–37*, p. 657.
151 Cholerton, *Chaddesden*, p. 52.
152 PRO, E 326/12434 (1371); E 315/38 (1391).
153 Harper-Bill, 'English Church', p. 121.
154 N. Pevsner (revised by E. Williamson with G.K. Brandwood), *The Buildings of England: Leicestershire and Rutland* (Harmondsworth, 1960, 2nd edition 1984), p. 296.

Plate 34: All Saints, Lowesby, Leicestershire. A small, attractive church with some good late medieval detail.

some work dates from *c*.1300, an extensive overhaul was undertaken in about 1500 under the auspices of the order. In view of this it is surprising that it was presented to the archdeacon twice in the early sixteenth century for being in decay.[155] The most outstanding feature of this restoration is a remarkable series of gargoyles and a frieze of grotesques running around the outside of the nave and chancel beneath a crenellated parapet. The frieze contains a wide variety of plant, animal and humanoid forms, including what Nichols modestly describes as 'a man in a very indecent situation and posture'. As with all medieval imagery interpretation is difficult, but that this subject matter cannot be ascribed directly to the Lazarites is indicated by the survival of a virtually identical frieze – and exhibitionist male – at Tilton-on-the-Hill, Leicestershire, where the patrons were the monks of Launde Abbey. Quite clearly the same craftsmen were engaged for both commissions.[156]

Threckingham is an impressive church by any standard with a massive broached spire built in the thirteenth century (Plate 35).[157] The chancel dates from around 1170 but was deliberately narrowed by the Lazarites in about 1325 by the removal of a chapel on the north side. However, a substantial leaded

[155] M. Bowker, *The Secular Clergy in the Diocese of Lincoln, 1495–1520* (Cambridge, 1968), p. 132. Defects were reported at Lowesby in 1509 and again ten years later.

[156] Nichols, *Leicestershire*, 3 pt 1, p. 341. In the print of Lowesby reproduced by Nichols the chancel is shown without a roof. The author of *A Brief History and Guide: the church of St Peter, Tilton-on-the-Hill* (nd), comments that 'the bizarre gargoyles are supposed to represent the devil and the seven deadly sins'.

[157] N. Pevsner, *The Buildings of England: Lincolnshire* (Harmondsworth, 1978), pp. 695–6; *The Church of St Peter-in-Chains, Threekingham: a walk round guide* (nd).

Plate 35: St Peter, Threckingham, Lincolnshire. Twelfth-century east windows; thirteenth-century nave arcade; and sixteenth-century timber roof.

timber roof was added in the early sixteenth century, about the same time as the improvements were being made at Lowesby. It has been suggested that an unusual thirteenth-century cross *patonce* in stone, discovered in 1962, may have been part of a monument to a member of the order, but this is unlikely in view of the survival of a very similar cross at the Augustinian nunnery of White Ladies, Shropshire.[158] The Lazarites maintained some sort of hospital establishment at Threckingham and it is possible that it may have taken over, briefly, from Carlton-le-Moorland as the focus of operations in Lincolnshire. If this was so, it ties in well with the close relationship between the order and the wealthy local family of Trickingham, but it also raises the question of whether it was the order or the Trickinghams who initiated the changes and alterations to the church fabric, particularly the building of the spire. The secular family is perhaps the more likely patron in view of the chantry chapel they established in the church and their massive monuments that still adorn it, particularly the formidable stone effigy believed to be that of Sir Lambert de Trickingham who died in 1280 (Plate 30 above).

The most remarkable instance of support is at Spondon, where a disastrous fire swept through the village in 1340 destroying the parish church and virtually all of the houses. The cost of the damage was said to exceed £2,000 and the inhabitants successfully petitioned the king for relief from their subsidy payments.[159] The order was put under immediate pressure to assist with the rebuilding and when it explained its financial plight to the Pope in 1355 fire damage was a point that was forcefully made. There is little doubt that the case · referred to was that of Spondon, since the supposed fire at Burton Lazars has now been proved to be based on an error. As a result of the fire, Spondon church was completely rebuilt in the mid-fourteenth century in the Decorated style, and though it was the victim of an over-zealous restoration in 1826, some fine fragments still remain in the form of a sedilia, piscina, book corbel and traceried windows.[160] By the 1530s Spondon had a Lady Chapel with its own image of the Virgin, which the parish was collecting money to have gilded.[161] Cox described Spondon as 'the most melancholy instance in Derbyshire of a good church spoilt', and in that statement he inadvertently paid tribute to the order, which must have played an important part in its rebuilding. Profits drawn from appropriated tithes clearly carried obligations and when the hand of God struck, as it did at Spondon, it could take many years to recoup the outlay caused by a single day of conflagration.

Spondon parish contained two chapelries at Stanley and Chaddesden. Stanley

---

158 The master John de Horbling has been suggested, it seems for no other reason than the fact that Horbling, his presumed place of origin, is near Threckingham. A member of the Trickingham family is more likely, for whom see above, p. 187. UNCLH, Letter from Canon F.R. Money to Revd P. E. Hunt, 23 July 1965.

159 Cox, *Derbyshire Churches*, 3, p. 297.

160 *Ibid*; T. Bourne and J. Smithers, 'The Burning of Burton Lazars Hospital: the pitfalls of antiquarianism', *Bulletin of Local History, East Midlands Region*, 19 (1984), pp. 60–1; N. Pevsner, *The Buildings of England. Derbyshire* (Harmondsworth, 1986), p. 195; J.R. Hughes and S.T. Lusted, *Parish Church of St Werburgh, Spondon, Derby* (Spondon, 1999), pp. 3, 5–6.

161 LJRO, B/C/11 (John Butler, 1534); (William Widdowson, 1534); (William Drakeloe, 1535); (William Lockey, 1536). All leave legacies 'to the gilding of our Lady ... if the parish will gild her'.

Plate 36: St Mary, Chaddesden, Derbyshire. The decorated fifteenth-century rood screen, restored in 1900.

was the older of the two and is the one noted in the *Taxatio* of 1291. This is deduced from the fact that, of the two, only Stanley has architectural features which pre-date the fourteenth century.[162] Chaddesden was probably new at this time, and it came to be dominated by the substantial and well-endowed chantry of Henry de Chaddesden.[163] In the mid-fifteenth century building works were going on again, this time involving the construction of a tower and the extension of the north and south aisle walls to meet up with its west face.[164] It is likely that these improvements necessitated the removal of the house of an anchoress, possibly built up against the south wall of the chapel and getting in the way of one of the aisle extensions. Nothing is known of this woman, though she may have been a sister of St Lazarus who had adopted the contemplative life.[165] Certainly the order claimed rights of ownership over her house and felt so strongly about its removal that the master, Sir Geoffrey Shriggley, commenced litigation in

---

162 Pevsner, *Derbyshire*, p. 324. Stanley has a Norman doorway, a thirteenth-century lancet window and an east window which is early fourteenth century.
163 See Chapter 3, pp. 78–80; Pevsner, *Derbyshire*, p. 191.
164 Cholerton, *Chaddesden*, p. 5.
165 For hermits and anchorites, see Orme and Webster, *English Hospital*, pp. 66–7.

Chancery against the local chaplain, John Ive, and his supporters who had carried the house away.[166] Despite this loss, Chaddesden has preserved some fine medieval features. There is much evidence of fourteenth- and fifteenth-century work in the church (including a book corbel similar to the one at Spondon), and a wooden rood screen, which is probably contemporary with the construction of the tower (Plate 36). Though it was heavily restored in 1900 it still retains much of its original carved decoration.[167]

The order of St Lazarus cared for the spiritual and material well being of the parishes under its supervision in a responsible and conscientious fashion, and up to a point, at least, justified the considerable amounts of tithe income that were directed away from the localities in terms of appropriations. If this appropriation of parochial tithe was shared with other religious orders, the privileged position of the Lazarites with regard to clerical taxation, alms gathering and the sale of indulgences was less common and in the end much more controversial. It was not unreasonable to expect some special contribution to society in return for such unusual and generous concessions. The organisation of the confraternity, of course, was a major achievement, which moved the order closer to the preoccupations of late-medieval spirituality, but such initiatives were to be regarded with growing doubt in the changing religious climate of the early sixteenth century. By the time that Bowyer was writing in the 1560s this vibrant late-medieval piety was dismissed as mere superstition and hypocrisy, divorced from the preaching and teaching that Protestants believed to be all important. If the Lazarites had managed to undertake a successful transformation from old-style preceptory to new-style collegiate church in the fifteenth century, the pace of change took them by surprise and left them stranded and vulnerable in the age of the Tudors. The reformers who regarded their limited charitable provision as a justifiable cause for reformation could look to their religious activities and draw precisely the same conclusion.

166 PRO, C 1/45/33.
167 Cholerton, *Chaddesden*, pp. 13–19, 21.

7

Dissolution and Dispersal

Alas, what pity it were that such a vicious man shall have the governance of that honest house.

(Letter of Thomas Howard, duke of Norfolk, 1537)

The order under the Tudors, 1485–1526

During the fifteenth century the order of St Lazarus successfully reorganised itself by adding to its charitable provision a new sense of purpose based on spiritual aspects of its work, such as its confraternity and intercessionary function. But all of this was to be put in the balance and eventually swept away by the circumstances of Henry VIII's Reformation, which regarded with grave suspicion both masses for the dead and charity ineffectively distributed by suspect religious orders.[1] Yet, even before these traumatic events, the order was not in as strong a position as it might have been to weather the storm because of the political alignment of its leaders and the attitude of the Tudor kings.

Sir William Sutton, master for over thirty years, was a formative influence on these late-medieval developments and also a stalwart supporter of the house of York, reflecting in this the views of his Mowbray and Howard patrons. During his long period in office he broke with many well-established traditions, having been married and being the father of at least two sons.[2] Under Sutton's leadership the order became something akin to a family business, a trend possibly reflected in France with the ascendency of the Mareuil family at about the same time.[3] When his eldest son, John, died in 1473, the master procured a licence from the Pope to enable a Robert Sutton, possibly a younger son and then aged twenty-six, to govern any Lazarite house.[4] This never came about, possibly through Robert's premature death, and Sir William eventually resigned in about 1483 in favour of another relative, George Sutton. Sir William lived on in retire-

---

1 Orme and Webster, *English Hospital*, pp. 147–55.
2 Rylands, *Visitation of Cheshire, 1580*, p. 220.
3 See Appendix 1.
4 Sir John Sutton of Disley was probably born before 1450 and Robert (if a son of Sir William) was born in 1447. For Sir Richard Sutton, Sir William's second son, see below. The statutes said that the master had to be at least thirty. *CPapR, Letters* 13 pt 1, *1471–84*, pp. 369–70.

ment until 1491, long enough to witness the collapse of the Yorkist monarchy and the death of Richard III at Bosworth in 1485.[5]

Sir George Sutton came to be trusted enough by Henry VII to serve on the commission of the peace for Leicestershire in 1500 and 1501, but the wider affinities of the Sutton clan were still ambivalent to say the least.[6] The younger son of Sir William, Sir Richard Sutton, enjoyed a distinguished career under the first Tudor as a lawyer and privy councillor. Along with William Smith, bishop of Lincoln (1495–1514), he founded Brasenose College, Oxford, in 1512, yet when he died in 1524 he used part of his very considerable wealth to endow a chantry to pray for the souls of a whole galaxy of Yorkist *alumni*: Edward IV, Queen Elizabeth Woodville, Lord Rivers and the marquis of Dorset, among others.[7] Dr William Sutton, erstwhile rector of Gaulby, underlined an even closer relationship with the Yorkist cause by being named as one of the executors of the will of Queen Elizabeth Woodville in 1492. He may even have been privy to delicate family secrets, because in 1495 he was condemned to death along with Sir William Stanley for apparently upholding the notion that Perkin Warbeck was indeed Richard, duke of York, younger son of Edward IV.[8] The affair is an exceptionally perplexing one, and although Stanley paid for his disloyalty with his life, Sutton was reprieved and died peacefully in his bed in 1503, leaving legacies to the college of Burton Lazars in his will.

In this difficult situation Sir Richard Sutton possibly used his influence to the benefit of his relative, but Henry VII, a ruler who did not forgive past indiscretions easily, may well have felt that the order harboured Yorkist sympathies, which justified a limited curtailment of its privileges.[9] In 1489 the king granted the mastership of the hospital of Holy Innocents', Lincoln, to Henry ap John despite previous assurances in favour of Burton Lazars, and in 1491 the order was obliged to pay an unaccustomed tenth to the crown on its properties in the archdeaconries of Leicester and Northampton.[10] Sutton managed to obtain a fresh grant of the mastership of Holy Innocents' in 1504, but at about this time some of the St Giles's lands were lost, without immediate compensation, because of the king's expansion of his favoured residence at Hanworth Park, Middlesex.[11] The fact that both Henry VII and his mother had once been members of the confraternity did not result in any particular favours being shown to the order

---

5 Sir John Sutton of Disley had a son George, but he would have been too young to become master without a dispensation in 1483. The new master might therefore have been another son of Sir William, possibly the 'Robert' misnamed (?) in the dispensation of 1473. Ormerod, *History of Chester*, 3, p. 759.

6 *CPR, 1494–1509*, p. 646.

7 PRO, PROB 11/21, ff. 209–10 (Sir Richard Sutton, 1524); *DNB*, 19, pp. 181–2; R. Churton, *The Lives of William Smyth, bishop of Lincoln, and Sir Richard Sutton, Knight, founders of Brasen Nose College* (London, 1800), p. 411. There are doubts about the Sutton genealogy, for which see Ormerod, *History of Chester*, 3, p. 759. William Smith, bishop of Lincoln, 'is said to have peopled Lincoln Cathedral with William Smiths, probably his kinsmen'. For one of this name who was a brother of Burton Lazars, see below, p. 233.

8 R.F. Flenley (ed.), *Six Town Chronicles of England* (Oxford, 1911), p. 165; A.H. Thomas and I.D. Thornley (eds), *The Great Chronicle of London* (London, 1938), pp. 256, 441; I. Arthurson, *The Perkin Warbeck Conspiracy 1491–1499* (Stroud, 1997), pp. 85, 90.

9 Emden, *Biographical Register of Oxford*, 3, pp. 1826–7.

10 *CPR, 1485–94*, p. 274; BL, Add Chart, 44698.

11 *CPR, 1494–1509*, p. 391; *LP, 4 pt 1, 1524–26*, p. 332.

once he became king, or, indeed, to hospitals in general, which found their rights and privileges under attack during his reign. The only exception was the Savoy Hospital, constructed between 1512 and 1519 as a result of the provisions of the king's will.[12]

Sir George Sutton was replaced as master in about 1505 by Sir Thomas Norton. Norton's ancestry has not been traced, but there were several families of gentle blood bearing that name and spanning the country from Yorkshire to Middlesex.[13] Although in 1524 Norton eventually received some remuneration for the earlier loss of the St Giles's property, his mastership was marked by the same petty encroachments with which his predecessor had had to contend.[14] In defiance of long-standing immunities, Wolsey's new tax assessments of the clergy during the 1520s included the properties of the order, and tenths continued to be paid despite the traditional exemptions.[15] Moreover, following the death of Richard Woodroff, rector of Gaulby, in 1523, Wolsey used his legatine authority to confer the living on John Allen, one of his agents in the suppression of the minor religious houses.[16] Allen resigned in 1527, but the incident created a stir and it was one of the charges brought against the cardinal when he fell from power in 1529.[17] Norton's attitude to Wolsey's usurpation of his patronage is not clear, but the incident may not be unconnected with the grant of compensation noted above. It was certainly another step in what appears to have been a concerted attack by the crown on the order's privileged position after 1485.

Sir Thomas Ratcliffe, 1526–1537

Norton was succeeded in 1526 by Sir Thomas Ratcliffe, under whose mastership the trends already in evidence were to reach a dramatic climax. Like his immediate predecessors his background was unimpeachable, socially if not politically. The new master may have been a relative of John Ratcliffe, sixth Lord Fitzwalter, who, along with Dr William Sutton and a Robert Ratcliffe, was implicated in the Perkin Warbeck conspiracy. Despite the executions of Robert Ratcliffe in 1495 and Lord Fitzwalter in 1496, the family had managed to rehabilitate itself, and Fitzwalter's son, another Robert Ratcliffe, was created earl of Sussex by Henry VIII in 1529.[18] Whatever his connections, it is likely that Ratcliffe's immediate antecedents were in the west country. In 1538 Elizabeth Speke of East Dawlish, Somerset, widow of Sir George Speke, left 6s 8d to 'the lazar-houses' of Burton,

12 Orme and Webster, *English Hospital*, p. 148.

13 See, for example, G.J. Armytage (ed.), *Middlesex Pedigrees*, HS, 65 (1914), pp. 114–16; *VCH, Yorkshire. North Riding*, 1 (London, 1914), p. 393; *LP, 1 pt 1, 1509–13*, p. 222. Norton received the king's protection in 1523, *LP, 3 pt 2, 1519–23*, p. 1204; and was recorded in the pardon roll in 1510, *LP, 1 pt 1, 1509–13*, p. 221.

14 He received lands in Feltham where St Giles's already owned estates. *LP, 4 pt 1, 1524–26*, p. 332.

15 Salter, *Lincoln Subsidy*, p. 120; LRO, 10D41/12/3, p. 53.

16 Allen became archbishop of Dublin and chancellor of Ireland in 1528 but was murdered by the followers of Sir Thomas Fitzgerald. *DNB*, 1, pp. 305–7.

17 *LP, 4 pt 3, 1529–30*, p. 2686; *DNB*, 21, pp. 796–814.

18 J.R. Lander, *The Wars of the Roses* (1990, reprinted Stroud 1992), pp. 210–11; V. Gibbs and H.A. Doubleday (eds), *The Complete Peerage*, 5 (London, 1926), pp. 486–7; G.H. White (ed.), *The Complete Peerage*, 12 (London, 1953), pp. 517–20; *DNB*, 16, pp. 571–2.

Langport, Bridport and Taunton. Sir George Speke had earlier bought lands in Up-Ottery, near Axminster, Devon, which were bequeathed to an Anne Ratcliffe, widow, and the heirs of Thomas Ratcliffe. Anne, and other members of the Ratcliffe family, also received additional generous legacies.[19]

The link between the Ratcliffes and Burton Lazars is further strengthened by the fact that an Ottewell Ratcliffe was joined with Sir Richard Sutton in a land transaction involving Burton and Melton Mowbray as early as 1514 and another, involving Sir Thomas Norton, concerning Barkestone-le-Vale, Wycomb and Chadwell in 1516.[20] That Suttons, Nortons and Ratcliffes were brought together in these land sales is highly significant and points to a relatively small, occasionally suspect, group of families dominating the affairs of the order during its last years. In any event, the new master was among those summoned to the meeting of the Convocation of Canterbury in 1529 to discuss, among other things, Henry VIII's impending divorce from Katherine of Aragon.[21]

Wolsey's fall from power, and the ascendancy of Thomas Cromwell after 1530, opened the way for the breach with Rome, and, eventually, the reform of the English church along Protestant lines. In 1534 Henry was proclaimed Supreme Head of the Church in England, and this was followed up by a close investigation of the religious houses to determine their wealth and the standard of morality and morale within them. The English Reformation did not demonstrate a keen interest in hospital foundations, but the larger ones were considered out of step with the times because of their quasi-monastic organisation and prayers for the dead. As Orme has stated, 'their pastoral works would not always atone for this'.[22] In the first inquiry, which resulted in the *Valor Ecclesiasticus* of 1535, Burton Lazars (along with the hospitals of St Giles and Holy Innocents) received a gross valuation of £336 6s 0½d, or £265 10s 2½d after deductions (Appendix 3).[23] The combined totals of temporalities and spiritualities for the entire estate are presented in Graph 3.

A major difficulty with the *Valor* is that it represents a bare minimum, and the entry relating to 'Burton Lazars' does not take account of payments that various individuals and institutions claimed to be making to the order and that are registered elsewhere in the survey. Some of these were quite considerable. The archdeaconry of Stow provided an annual pension of £13, though this may be the same sum accounted from the manor of Nettleham in the *Valor*.[24] As late as 1672 a dispute broke out over this payment between the bishop of Lincoln and the archdeacon of Stow during which it emerged that a former bishop had allocated £13 *per annum*, payable by the archdeacon out of the profits of the episcopal manor of Nettleham to Holy Innocents' Hospital, Lincoln.[25] Further pensions of

---

19 F.W. Weaver (ed.), *Somerset Medieval Wills, 1531–1558*, Somerset Record Society, 21 (1905), pp. 38–9.

20 Farnham, 1, pp. 263–4; A.H. Thompson (ed.), *A Calendar of Charters and other Documents belonging to the Hospital of William Wyggeston at Leicester* (Leicester, 1933), pp. xxxii, 139–42, 566–7.

21 *LP, 4 pt 3, 1529–30*, p. 2698.

22 Orme and Webster, *English Hospital*, p. 147.

23 *Valor*, 4, pp. 152–3.

24 *Ibid*, p. 27. This pension was still being paid to the successors of the order as late as 1699. LAO, Dean and Chapter Patent Book, Bii.2.13, ff. 197–8.

25 PRO, E 134/24 Chas 2/Trin 8. The payment was already established in 1417 when one deponent claimed to have seen it in the *Novum Registrum* of the Dean and Chapter.

Graph 3: Temporalities and Spiritualities according to the *Valor Ecclesiasticus*

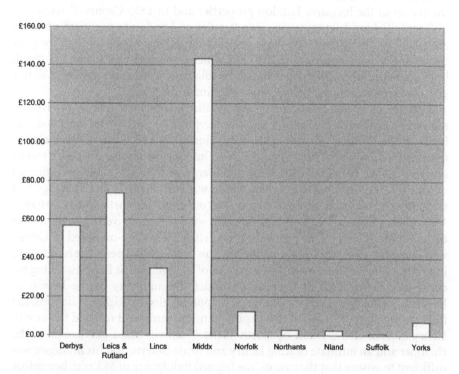

Source: *Valor*, 4, pp. 152–3.

£1 6s 8d each were provided by the Lincolnshire priories of Sempringham and Newstead, near Stamford. Conversely, Burton Lazars was obliged to make certain payments that are similarly unrecorded in the *Valor* – for example, the 1s noted as due to St James's Priory, Derby, in 1532.[26] However, there is less evidence of unrecorded money going out than coming in, and, even if the Stow pension is discounted, it is possible that the order could anticipate an extra £5 *per annum* from these miscellaneous sources – though the remuneration the order received from alms gathering and the sale of indulgences, which make no mark in the *Valor* at all, must remain a moot point.[27]

Since Burton Lazars did not fall within the remit of the 1536 Suppression Act (it was not a monastery, neither was its net income less than £200 *per annum*) it did not qualify for closure. Nevertheless, even allowing for the shortfalls and inaccuracies of the survey, it is interesting to reflect that had the house been monastic, and had it not been for the benevolence of the crown after 1299, with the gifts of the hospitals of St Giles and Holy Innocents, Burton Lazars may well have vanished as one of 'the lesser houses of religion' in the wake of the *Valor*.

---

[26] BL, Add Mss, 6672, f. 119. St James's was, in fact, a small hospital for the poor.

[27] *Valor*, 4, pp. 103, 110. See also, *Valor*, 1, pp. 399, 401; 3, pp. 152, 162, 366, 387; 4, pp. 29, 106, 149, 152, 162, 322. See also Chapter 6, pp. 178–86.

Some hospitals did indeed perish as a result of the 1536 Act, but usually those associated with monasteries.[28] As it was, the valuation reawakened the interest of the crown in the lucrative London properties and in 1535 Cromwell requested his agent, Richard Layton, to summon Ratcliffe to London to negotiate a further exchange. Evidently there was some fear that the master would forestall the plan by making a direct approach to the king, which Cromwell was anxious to avoid, but Layton prevailed upon him 'to put his sole trust in you and that he shall not go to the king in anywise before you bring him to his grace'.[29]

Early in 1536 the arrangement was finalised. The king was to receive the manors of Feltham and Heston (with the exception of Feltham rectory) and also lands in the parishes of St Martin, Westminster, and St Giles which included three inns, *The White Hart*, *The Rose* and *The Vine*. In return, the order was to obtain a licence to hold Burton Grange under lease from the abbot and convent of Vaudey, 'the dissolution of which house was imminent'.[30] The exchange was undoubtedly hastened by an incident that occurred in North Wales at Easter 1535 when Cromwell, Layton and Ratcliffe were still in active negotiation over the question of lands. This may have been deliberately stage-managed by Cromwell's supporters to put additional pressure on Ratcliffe and persuade him to give in to the wishes of the crown. The pardoner of the order of St Lazarus, selling his customary indulgences at Caernarvon under the authority of the bishop of Bangor's commissary, Robert Okinge, was apprehended by Richard Gibbons, the bishop's registrar, who seized the 'papistical muniments' and referred the case to Henry Norris, chamberlain of North Wales.[31] Norris was a gentleman of the chamber and an intimate of King Henry and Anne Boleyn, and his influence was sufficient to ensure that the case of 'the feigned indulgence of St Lazar, heretofore granted by the Popes' was not easily forgotten.[32] Significantly, when the licence to acquire the Vaudey lands was issued in January 1536, there was an additional clause pardoning the order for all violations of praemunire as enacted by the Parliament of 1529. The grant was sealed with the common seal of the order on 2 June 1536 and enrolled on the Close Rolls.[33]

Richard Layton was active with Thomas Legh and John Price in the visitation of the monasteries in 1535 and 1536, which resulted in the drawing up of the *Compendium Compertorum*. Kirby Bellars Priory, the closest monastic neighbour of Burton Lazars, received the visitors in 1536, and the state of the house was reported to be satisfactory.[34] However, no report has survived for Burton, though it is clear that Legh visited the house and apparently discovered some

---

28 Orme and Webster, *English Hospital*, p. 156.

29 *LP*, 8, *1535*, p. 188. The fact that Ratcliffe even considered a direct approach to the king suggests his relatively high social position.

30 J. Parton, *Some Account of the Hospital and Parish of St Giles-in-the-Fields, Middlesex*, (London, 1822), pp. 29–32; Honeybourne, 'Leper Hospitals', p. 25: *Statutes of the Realm, 3 pt 2*, 28 Hen VIII c.42, pp. 701–3; *LP*, 10, *1536*, p. 81. This represented the culmination of a long and ongoing contest with Vaudey Abbey, for which see Chapter 4, p. 110.

31 *LP*, 8, *1535*, pp. 242–3.

32 Norris was executed in 1536 for alleged adultery with Anne Boleyn. *DNB*, 14, pp. 566–7.

33 PRO, C 54/408, no.34. See also, SC 6/Hen VIII/2006, m.9 for a survey dated September 1536. Ratcliffe had held Burton Grange on lease, presumably from Vaudey, since 10 August 1529.

34 *VCH, Leicestershire*, 2, p. 26.

information about Ratcliffe that could have led to his deprivation.[35] In August 1536 Legh wrote to Cromwell from Darley Abbey, Derbyshire, making reference to a plan by which he hoped to secure control of Burton Lazars for himself, the precedent having been set by his collation to the mastership of Sherburn Hospital, Durham, in September 1535. Ratcliffe already had the reputation of 'a papist', potentially hostile to government policy, and if the house could not be closed lawfully under the terms of the Suppression Act, the next best thing might be to secure an amenable head.[36] But before Cromwell and Legh could act further, Lincolnshire and the north of England erupted into rebellion as Catholic insurgents converged on Doncaster under the banner of the Five Wounds of Christ. Thomas Howard, eighth duke of Norfolk, with some sense of embarrassment, was sent north to confront them, and by Christmas, as a result of his astute negotiations, the Pilgrimage of Grace had dissolved in a mixture of acrimony and false promises.

It is improbable that the Lazarites played an active part in these happenings, unlike some of the monks of Lincolnshire and Yorkshire, but the suppression of the rebellion merely hardened the attitude of the government to the religious orders. In March 1537 Cromwell wrote to Ratcliffe requesting him to travel to London to discuss his resignation, but though in the first instance the master was 'fully minded' to go he was persuaded to change his mind at the last minute because of the intervention of William Faunt. Faunt was an 'attorney at law and fellow of the Inner Temple . . . one who ever carried himself just and upright, a learned man'.[37] As the order's bailiff of Melton, Spondon and Kedington, Ratcliffe knew that he could rely on his opinion. Moreover, though a Catholic by persuasion, Faunt had built bridges with Cromwell, which in this situation might be considered particularly useful. Having been sent for by the master 'to have his counsel', Faunt's advice was clear.[38] He urged Ratcliffe:

> in no wise to appear, and comforted him that he could make means and friends for the discharge of his appearance . . . For this counsel is given by them and other persons which do say to the master by these words 'stick to it and do not resign, we doubt not but this world will turn and not ever continue at this point'.[39]

In the hope that the world would indeed turn, Faunt suggested a direct approach to Norfolk, the patron of the house and a known opponent of Cromwell, and on the morning after the meeting with Ratcliffe he rode post-haste to meet the duke at Newcastle to procure letters to the king 'to accomplish their desires'.[40]

Cromwell and Legh were well informed about these goings on because the counsels of the order had been infiltrated by John Port, probably the son of Sir John Port who was made a judge of King's Bench in 1525. The Ports came from

35 PRO, SP 1/127, p. 180.
36 LP, 12 pt 2, 1537, p. 192.
37 Burton, Leicestershire, p. 105.
38 Valor, 4, p. 153; Bindoff, House of Commons, 2, pp. 121–2; Jack, 'Monastic Lands', p. 17. Faunt became MP for Leicester (1553) and Leicestershire (1555). See also, Fetherston, Visitation of Leicester, 1619, p. 28. Faunt had an elder brother, John, who was a monk of Ramsey Abbey.
39 J.H. Baker (ed.), The Notebook of Sir John Port, SS, 102 (1986), p. lii.
40 Ibid, pp. lii–iii. For Norfolk, see DNB, 10, pp. 64–71.

Plate 37: Thomas Howard, eighth duke of Norfolk. Norfolk resisted the appointment of Dr Thomas Legh to the mastership, but his influence was insufficient to save the house.

Derbyshire and had connections with Sir Richard Sutton's Oxford foundation at Brasenose.[41] John Port Jnr, described as a gentleman, was already established at Burton Lazars as a landholder in 1537 and it was Port's influence that proved strong enough with Ratcliffe to convince him, eventually, of the need to resign.[42] In a letter, probably to Thomas Legh, he informed the prospective master of a meeting with Ratcliffe during which 'he answered me that he cared not though he did resign if the house might do well and he to have a poor living, for he was but old. But now this Faunt and other hath given such counsel that he is of another mind.'[43] Port's solution was that Cromwell should write a 'quick and sharp' letter 'that he do appear immediately upon the sight of the same'. If, on appearance, he still proved to be recalcitrant, Port suggested that two charges might productively be levelled against him. First, that 'he keepeth one Webster's wife and maintaineth her husband to pick quarrels against gentlemen and other'. Second, that a bull had been published by him in St Margaret's chapel, Burton, 'out of his parish and jurisdiction' and against praemunire, 'and if my lord privy seal did know what a papist he is I think he would so inform the king's grace that he should not be more head of such house as knows Jesu'.[44] Despite the circumstantial nature of these complaints, on 10 March (two days after Port's letter to Legh) the reversion of the mastership was granted to Legh by the crown, the revival of a precedent set with the nomination of Richard Clifford in 1389.[45]

Meanwhile, in the far north, Faunt had obtained an audience with Norfolk, who immediately wrote to Cromwell (on 11 March) pointing out that Legh's wedded status should preclude him from holding the mastership (Plate 37). Filled with righteous indignation about these happenings, 'now being in the king's service and not present to speak for mine own affairs', he went on:

> This matter doth touch mine inheritance and if such one as Dr Legh shall for ambitiousness go about to pluck the same from me and to go about to destroy that honest, poor house I trust your good lordship will impeach his malicious purposes and surely for my part I shall show him no less displeasure if it be in my power than if he would pluck from me Framlingham castle. Alas, what pity it were that such a vicious man shall have the governance of that honest house![46]

Even if Norfolk's sense of outrage at upstarts such as Cromwell and Legh lacked a grounding in history (he had failed to take on board that there were precedents not only for royal appointments but also for a married master), it was a heartfelt

---

41 John Port Jnr was knighted in 1549 and founded Repton School under the terms of his will (1557). *DNB*, 16, p. 165. John Port Snr. was an executor of the will of Sir Richard Sutton in 1524. PRO PROB 11/21, ff. 209–10 (Sir Richard Sutton, 1524).

42 PRO, CP 40/1094, m.237d (Farnham, 1, p. 265).

43 Baker, *Notebook*, p. liii. Baker identifies the addressee, 'Mr Doctor Leigh at Austin Friars in London', as Dr Roland Lee, subsequently bishop of Coventry and Lichfield. Considering the context of the letter, it is more likely to be Dr Thomas Legh.

44 *Ibid.* 'Webster' can be identified as the Robert Webster who later appears as a servant of Dr Legh in the Military Survey of the Framland Hundred, 18 March 1539. He was classed as an archer. PRO, SP 1/145, f. 26d.

45 *LP, 12 pt 1, 1537*, p. 351.

46 PRO, SP 1/116, f. 249.

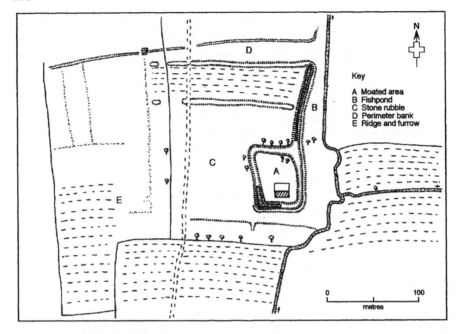

Plan 9: Vaudey Grange, Burton Lazars.

plea from a man who felt marginalised and was obliged to seek help from the individual who was himself the architect of the situation he sought to redress.[47]

Predictably, Cromwell did nothing. Later in the same year, or possibly 1538, Ratcliffe eventually agreed to resign and as his 'poor living' received a personal grant of Vaudey Grange and the other properties acquired by lease in 1536, Vaudey Abbey having been dissolved in the meantime (Plan 9).[48] It is likely that the promise that the house would 'do well' – in other words, perhaps, that it would be spared dissolution – was a vital factor in persuading Ratcliffe to act as he did. The incident has many parallels with the surrenders being enforced on the larger religious houses at about this time, for example Lenton Priory near Nottingham, demonstrating how Cromwell and local agents such as Legh and Port worked in close harmony, using a combination of threats and promises to achieve their ends.[49] The only difference with the case of Lenton was that Burton Lazars did not disappear, at least over the short term. It continued its life, for a while, under a master the like of whom it had never experienced before.

---

[47] Sir William Sutton is the obvious comparison, though his wife may have been dead by the time he attained the mastership. Legh's wife, Joan, was still alive.

[48] PRO, C 54/408, no. 34 (Farnham, 1, p. 265). Ratcliffe may have been the same 'Thomas Ratcliff' noted as deceased in July 1539 and owning lands in Lancashire. If so he had a son, William, who became a ward of the crown, a fact that makes the identification less likely since the master was said to be 'old'. *LP, 14 pt 1, 1539*, p. 588.

[49] D. Marcombe, 'The Last Days of Lenton Priory', in D. Wood (ed.), *Life and Thought in the Northern Church, c.1100–c.1700: essays in honour of Claire Cross* (Woodbridge, 1999); G.R. Elton, *Policy and Police* (London, 1972), p. 354; Baker, *Notebook*, pp. lii–iii.

Sir Thomas Legh, 1537–1544

Dr Thomas Legh was of a Cumbrian family and was trained in law at Cambridge. He was almost certainly less alien to the order of St Lazarus than Norfolk believed. The Leghs were prolific in Cheshire and his arms indicate that he was descended from the Leghs of Adlington who were related to the Leghs of Ridge Hall, near Macclesfield, connected, by marriage, to the Suttons.[50] Indeed, Roger Legh of Ridge Hall, along with John Port, was an executor of the will of Sir Richard Sutton, suggesting that Legh may have been part of a London-based legal *clique* closely watching the fortunes of Burton Lazars because of family connections and the traditional propertied interests of the house close to the inns of court.[51] This group of lawyers may well have lodged and drank in the Holborn taverns owned by the order, and picked up there the inevitable gossip about the scale of its land holdings, not to mention other matters less palatable to Protestants.

Legh first came to prominence in the service of his cousin, Roland Lee (or Legh), Cromwell's confidant and bishop of Coventry and Lichfield (1533–43). He took a major part in the visitation of the monasteries, and after 1540 served the government on various diplomatic missions to the Netherlands and the Scottish borders.[52] Like most of his contemporaries during this period of rare opportunity, Legh used his positions of influence to enrich himself with grants of monastic lands as well as important hospital masterships at Sherburn and Burton Lazars. Certainly at Sherburn there is evidence that he was the beneficiary of hospital leases, and many contemporaries shared Norfolk's view that he was indeed a 'vicious man'. Even his companion on the visitation commission, John Price, complained to Cromwell that he was 'very insolent and pompatique', 'excessive in taking' and of a 'satrapic countenance'. Along with Roland Lee, Richard Layton and Cromwell himself, he was one of those the rebels of 1536 wished to see punished and removed from positions of power.[53] The exact date of Ratcliffe's resignation and Legh's succession to the mastership is not known, but the first reference to him being in office comes in 1537.[54]

How did Legh compare to his predecessors as master of Burton? Such were the uncertainties of the period that it cannot be said whether he regarded himself as the long-term successor of Ratcliffe or merely involved in a holding operation until the inevitable collapse of the institution. His governmental duties meant that he was largely non-resident, but John Port continued to live at Burton and probably acted as his agent. One of the most controversial agrarian practices of the period was enclosure, by which landlords aspired to achieve consolidated holdings, often in the hope of exploiting the profits available from the rearing of cattle and sheep. The smaller farmers were fiercely opposed to the

---

50 B. Burke, *The General Armory of England, Scotland, Ireland and Wales* (London, 1884), p. 596; Ormerod, *History of Chester*, 3, pp. 762, 765–6.
51 PRO, PROB 11/21, ff. 209–10 (Sir Richard Sutton, 1524).
52 *DNB*, 11, pp. 861–2; Bindoff, *House of Commons*, 2, pp. 513–14.
53 Bindoff, *House of Commons*, 2, p. 514; Surtees, *History of Durham*, 1, pp. 130, 131, 140.
54 BL, Harl Mss, 80, f. 26.

impact that this was likely to have on their livelihoods and the traditional infra-structure of their villages, and in this they received the support of the government, which saw enclosure as a principal cause of unemployment, vagrancy and social unrest. As Brown has shown, enclosure began early at Burton Lazars, but Port was anxious to extend the practice and at least one new enclosure was created in the parish under the orders of Legh.[55]

But, controversial though this might have been, this was not to be the initial cause of conflict between the order and the local farmers. By 1539 Port had obtained an interest in a lease of the tithes of Burton from the vicar of Melton Mowbray, an acquisition that soon provoked a confrontation with the community's principal yeoman, Thomas Hartopp. When he attempted to collect his tithe, Port alleged that Hartopp was moving sheep to pastures in another parish to avoid payment. Moreover, being summoned before the ecclesiastical court to make answer, he pulled the citation out of the hands of William Smith, one of the priests of the college, prompting Port to complain to Star Chamber, accusing his rival of riot and disloyalty to the crown.[56] Although these charges were extremely flimsy and were strongly denied by Hartopp, it did not prevent Port from making further recourse to the London courts to try to overawe his opponents and stem the growing feeling in the village against him.

In 1542 further Star Chamber indictments were procured against Thomas Hartopp, William Allen, Bartholomew Coke, Henry Cley and others, accusing them of conspiracy, assault and depasturing Port's portion of the common land.[57] Although the details of the issues dividing the parties are sketchy, it would appear that a more aggressive style of agrarian management on the part of Legh's agents was the underlying issue. Certainly Hartopp was emphatic that over the matter of tithe he had not broken with traditional practice, having offered his payments 'according to the custom of the country then and before this time'. Significantly, the dispute was being fought out between the two leading land-holders of the parish. According to the Lay Subsidy of 1543, Hartopp's goods were valued at £20 and those of Port at £12. This put them head and shoulders above the rest of the Burton farmers, all of whose goods were assessed at under £5.[58]

As the first and only post-Reformation master of the Lazarites, it was probably Legh who ordered that all reference to the Pope be expunged from Innocent III's charter of confirmation in the Cartulary, yet in other matters he proved himself to be more conservative and was unusually active in protecting the interests of the house.[59] When the advowson of Spondon had been granted by William de Ferrers, fifth earl of Derby, in 1250 he had reserved for the chaplain of St Peter in Tutbury Castle 'two parts of the tithe corn arising from his demesnes in Spondon, which the same chapel had from ancient time been accus-

55 CPR, 1554–55, pp. 318–19; Farnham, 1, pp. 264–5. For the history of enclosures at Burton Lazars and on other estates of the order, see Chapter 4, pp. 105, 119–20, 131.
56 PRO, STAC 2/24/122; Farnham, 1, pp. 264–6. In all Richard Hartopp, yeoman, possessed £30 in goods.
57 PRO, STAC 2/28/9B; 2/19/295; 2/19/327; 2/19/340; 2/26/429.
58 PRO, STAC, 2/24/122; Farnham, 1, p. 266.
59 BL, Cart, f. 205.

tomed freely and quietly to receive'.[60] Before long this was commuted to a payment of £2 13s 4d, often given to an Exchequer clerk appointed by the crown in lieu of a chantry priest serving in the chapel. In 1532 this customary pension was granted to one Thurstan Curtenall, but Legh refused to pay it, not because he felt that no payment was due, but because he claimed to have no idea how the sum had been arrived at.[61] Accordingly, in 1540/41 Legh petitioned the chancellor of the Duchy of Lancaster 'that some order or decree may be made . . . for the assurance of the said tithes to him and to his successors and he will be contented . . . to pay to the said chaplain and his successors yearly the said annuity of £2 13s 4d'.[62] What Legh really feared, perhaps, was that the old commutation would be overthrown and that Curtenall would sue for an increased payment based on the Ferrers grant: certainly the Chancellor's award specifically stated that the rights of the tenant of the rectory, John Brownell, were in no way to be prejudiced.

In addition to this, Legh commenced three suits in Chancery: against Geoffrey Ratcliffe, executor of the former master, for detaining money and goods belonging to the house;[63] Richard Byrde for a close in Locko;[64] and William Asheby for encroachment on rights of pasture at Lowesby and Cold Newton.[65] In this litigation it was alleged that he was abusing his position as a master in Chancery to put his opponents to unreasonable charges for the resolution of matters that could have been determined, locally, by the common law. And there is a deep sense of irony in the Lowesby case, since here Legh was on the receiving end of exactly the same sort of treatment he was meting out at Burton Lazars.

The cases were largely academic because Burton Lazars hospital was not destined to last much longer. The years of Legh's mastership were, indeed, a dangerous period for the hospitals, colleges and chantries. Since 1536 their numbers had been gradually eroded and the 'creeping process' of surrenders affected them as much as it did the larger monasteries. St Thomas of Acre surrendered in 1538, St Mark's, Bristol, in 1539 and St Leonard's, York, in 1540. These were major foundations, by hospital standards, and the retrospective Act of 1539 significantly included colleges and hospitals within its provisions.[66] Between 1540 and 1545 the process of what Kreider has termed 'anticipatory dissolutions' was stepped up prior to the Chantries Acts of 1545 and 1547. 1543 was a quiet year, but 1544 saw the suppression of six colleges and two hospitals – plus Burton Lazars, which Kreider does not include in his totals – the whole

60 Mosley, *Tutbury*, p. 235.
61 The payment 'to the Honour of Tutbury' is noted in Wolsey's valuation of 1526 but not in the *Valor*. Therefore it might have been Sir Thomas Ratcliffe who actually suspended it. Salter, *Lincoln Subsidy*, p. 120; *Valor*, 4, pp. 152–3.
62 Mosley, *Tutbury*, p. 238; S. Armitage-Smith (ed.), *John of Gaunt's Register*, 1, CS, 3rd series, 20 (1911), pp. 172–3.
63 PRO, C 1/1094/26.
64 PRO, C 1/1094/24; 1/1094/25.
65 PRO, C 1/1022/40. See also C 1/986/6 for a similar case (trespass on glebe at Lowesby) between William Faunt, tenant of Burton Lazars, and Everard, son and executor of William Asheby. For other cases, where Legh was named as a defendant, see C 1/750/15; 1/808/24.
66 Orme and Webster, *English Hospital*, pp. 156–7; A. Kreider, *English Chantries: the road to dissolution* (Cambridge, Massachusetts and London, 1979), p. 160.

business being carried out with a lack of documentation typical of this shadowy aspect of the Reformation.[67]

Sir Thomas Legh's will, drawn up on 9 March 1544, makes it clear that his mastership gave him no interest in the property of the order beyond that enjoyed by earlier masters.[68] As at Sherburn his only long-term interest in the house was probably by way of a manipulation of its leases to his own benefit, though because of poor documentary survival, and leases already made by the Lazarites, no direct evidence of this practice exists at Burton.[69] Soon after making his will Legh departed for Scotland with Edward Seymour, earl of Hertford, and during his absence, on 7 April 1544, an Inquisition was held at Loughborough before George Vincent, king's escheator for Leicestershire, which curtly declared that Burton Lazars Hospital was wholly extinct and dissolved and that it had reverted to the crown.[70] The legal basis for this pronouncement is not at all clear, in line with other closures effected at about this time. As stated above, Burton did not fall within the provisions of the Suppression Act nor had the first Chantry Act, under which the institution might have been earmarked for closure, yet been passed.[71] It was unlikely to have been voluntarily surrendered (as some others were during this period), and 'There is certainly no evidence that dissolution was an especially severe retribution for the lax discipline or cold spirituality of an institution.'[72]

The most likely explanation is that when Ratcliffe resigned and Legh's reversion came into effect in 1537, the house was taken to be 'surrendered' into the king's hands. The traditional mode of appointing masters had been successfully interrupted for the first time in the order's history. Yet no formal deed of surrender has survived and it is unlikely that Legh, once in power, would have agreed to one. Hence the business of dissolution was executed while he was absent in Scotland. Since Cromwell's fall in 1540 the government had been less sensitive about the interests of his immediate followers, though it is significant that it was on 11 May 1544 that Legh received his knighthood from Hertford, possibly an attempt to salve his injured pride. A little earlier, on 3 May, the entire properties of Burton Lazars and St Giles's had been granted to John Dudley, Viscount Lisle, 'for his services', a man currently riding high in the king's favour as commander of the English forces at the siege of Boulogne.[73] Norfolk, who was lieutenant-general of the army in France, probably acquiesced in the arrange-

---

67 Kreider, *English Chantries*, pp. 160–4.

68 PRO, PROB 11/30, ff. 348–50 (Sir Thomas Legh, 1544). Although the relevant Lists and Index volume suggests a date of 1545 for Legh's will, the will itself is dated 9 March 1544 and 35 Hen. VIII, confirming the date of 1544.

69 The grant of the Braceborough advowson to William and Richard Layton looks suspicious; see below, p. 233. Also between 1547 and 1600 there was a measure of litigation over Burton Lazars property, suggesting conflicting interests between crown grantees and holders of leases from the house. See below and Farnham, 1, p. 267.

70 PRO, C 78/1/1. For Seymour, see *DNB*, 17, pp. 1237–48.

71 *SR*, 3 pt 2, 37 Hen. VIII c.4, pp. 988–93. Dissolution might lawfully have been justified under this statute.

72 Kreider, *English Chantries*, p. 163.

73 *LP, 19 pt 1, 1544*, p. 371. The Chancery Decree Roll stated 6 May for the grant to Dudley. D. Loades, *John Dudley, Duke of Northumberland, 1504–1553* (Oxford, 1996), pp. 73, 291. This provides the best account of Dudley's political career.

ment out of dislike of Legh, and Dudley may well have had peripheral contacts with the house in any case because of the links between his family and the Berkeleys, Suttons and Ratcliffes, thus making the pill marginally easier for Norfolk to swallow.[74] In Kreider's view the driving force behind these dissolutions, which on the surface appear quite random, was that some influential person coveted the endowments of the institution, and in this instance the culprit seems to be clear. The suppression of Burton Lazars came in the same year as that of St Mary's, Dover, and St Bartholomew's, London, and only a few more hospitals and colleges were to follow before the king's death in 1547.[75]

That this sequence of events may not be the whole story is hinted at by two pieces of evidence that suggest an even more complicated scenario. On 19 July 1539, when Legh was indisputably installed as master, the Court of Augmentations granted a substantial lease of some of the St Giles's property to George Sutton and Ralph Martin, fishmonger of London, suggesting that, at that time, the property of the order was at the disposal of the crown.[76] This provides some confirmation for the theory, expressed above, that the house was considered to be surrendered into the king's hands following the resignation of Ratcliffe in 1537. This would have enabled Legh to be appointed without impediment and the Court of Augmentations to dip into the resources of the institution during the interregnum. Yet, in view of the fact that the grant to Sutton and Martin was made in 1539, the Court of Augmentations was clearly still interfering well after Legh was installed as master. It may be, of course, that this grant was part of the St Giles's property exchanged with the crown in 1536, though on balance it seems more likely to have been part of a fresh assault on the coveted London properties. Then, at an Inquisition taken at Market Harborough on 7 August 1544, four months after the escheator's pronouncement at Loughborough, the property of the hospital of Burton St Lazarus of Jerusalem in England was stated to be part of the possessions of William Fitzwilliam, earl of Southampton – and this in spite of the grant made to Dudley on 3 May of the same year.[77]

How is Southampton's interest in the Burton Lazars property, not confirmed by any surviving documentation, to be explained? Southampton was a personal friend of the king and had led an active military career in the service of his sovereign on land and sea. He had been the recipient of many grants of monastic land and died at Newcastle-upon-Tyne in December 1542 while leading the vanguard

---

[74] Ormerod, History of Chester, 3, p. 758. Dudley's great-grandmother was Elizabeth, daughter of Sir John Berkeley of Beverstone, Gloucestershire. He was also descended from the Sutton, Lords Dudley, whose arms Or, a lion rampant vert appear in a slightly adapted form as a quartering used by Sir William Sutton and Sir Richard Sutton. Indeed, it appears that the names Dudley and Sutton were interchangeable. B.L. Beer, Northumberland: the political career of John Dudley, Earl of Warwick and Duke of Northumberland (Kent, Ohio, 1973), pp. 5–7; H.S. Grazebrook, 'The Barons of Dudley', Collections for a History of Staffordshire, 9 (1888), pp. 1, 65–91; Rylands, Visitation of Cheshire, 1580, p. 220; CA, L Series, Ms 10, f. 92v.

[75] Orme and Webster, English Hospital, p. 157; Kreider, English Chantries, p. 164.

[76] LP, 14 pt 1, 1539, p. 605; CPR, 1553–54, p. 198. The lease was regranted for 21 years in 1554, following the death of Sutton, for £14 19s 2d per annum.

[77] BL, Harl Mss, 760, f. 1. The source is a book of Inquisitions of the Court of Wards collected by Thomas Cole. It is quoted in Nichols, Leicestershire, 2 pt 1, p. 267.

of the English army into Scotland under the duke of Norfolk.[78] He left no immediate heirs, and it was during a series of Inquisitions, taken by the Court of
Wards in 1544 and 1545, to attempt to define the extent of his estate, that his
interest in the Lazarite property first comes to light. The best explanation that
can be arrived at is that Southampton may have had a verbal promise of these
lands from the king to take effect after the suppression of the house or Legh's
death. Norfolk may have been instrumental in the arrangement out of dislike of
Legh and suspicion of the ambitions of Dudley. Wheeling and dealing such as
this was not uncommon in the Tudor court, and in 1542 Lord Maltravers was
trying to persuade Henry VIII to give him the property of Arundel College even
before it had been surrendered.[79] In the end, Dudley succeeded in being the first
to get the promise written down, though what might have happened had
Southampton lived longer is anyone's guess. It is interesting to recall that the
recipient and potential recipient of these lands, and also Norfolk who had
contacts with both of them, were all part of Henry VIII's military establishment.
Did the king see some poetic justice in these lands, given for the endowment of a
military order, going, via his cronies, to the defence of the Tudor state? It is clear
that by the time of the suppression of the house the military faction of the 1540s
was taking precedence over the legal interests that had dictated the fortunes of
the order in the 1530s.

Legh had been effectively outmanoeuvred, and given the strength of the forces
ranged against him there was very little he could do but use his knowledge of the
law to save what he could from a swift and largely unexpected wreck. He clearly
believed that he needed to be compensated for his loss of the mastership, but at
the same time he could see that a protracted conflict was in no one's interests and
that, legally, he was on shaky ground. Accordingly, he once more used his
position as a master in Chancery to refer the matter to the arbitration of Sir
Thomas Wriothesley, Lord Chancellor, whose judgment both parties agreed to
accept. On 8 September Wriothesley's decision was duly recorded on the Chancery Decree Roll.[80] Legh was to receive all of the St Giles's property, somewhat
depleted owing to recent transactions with the crown and the activities of the
Court of Augmentations, and the outlying estates in Norfolk, Yorkshire,
Northumberland and Northamptonshire. Dudley obtained the Leicestershire
estates including 'the manor and grange in Burton Lazars . . . given or exchanged
by the late abbot of Valle Dei [Vaudey] with Sir Thomas Ratcliffe', the properties
in Derbyshire, Lincolnshire, Rutland and Suffolk and also the rectory of Feltham.
Legh was given until 1 November to vacate the preceptory at Burton and all
other properties to which he had no entitlement under the arbitration, and the
parties were ordered to co-operate with one another over the exchange of
conveyances. What is not immediately clear from the Decree Roll is whether
Legh's interest in his portion of the property was absolute or merely for life, with
reversion to Dudley, but, since Legh was obliged to hand over all title deeds to

[78] White, *Complete Peerage*, 12 pt 1, pp. 121–2; *DNB*, 7, pp. 230–2. Southampton was described as 'one of
      the best captains in England'
[79] Kreider, *English Chantries*, p. 161.
[80] PRO, C 78/1/1.

Viscountess Lisle and Dudley was charged with the payment of pensions and annuities, the latter seems more likely. Indeed, Legh did not even bother to make a new will (which he surely would have done in the event of a freehold windfall of this size), and he only survived for a year to enjoy the rents that had been given to him.

Sir Thomas Legh died on 25 November 1545 and was buried at the church of St Leonard, Shoreditch, where a monument bearing a brass was erected to his memory (Plate 38).[81] It displayed a fulsome epitaph, which exalted his perceived virtues and service to the crown:

> Here under lie the ashes and the bones
> of Sir Thomas Legh that good and learned knight
> Whose hasty death, alas, the Godly still bemoans
> though his soul always rejoice in God's sight.
> Great was his wisdom and greater was his wit
> his visage comely with no sad change dismayed.
> A man in all affairs, a King to serve most fit
> had not death so soon his mortal life betrayed.
> He died the 25 day of November Anno Domini 1545.[82]

Legh's religious convictions are not known. Despite the fact that this memorial and much of his career points to a man of possible Protestant sympathies – why else should the godly have bemoaned his passing? – the matrix for a small brass above the central figure seems to suggest the shape of a *Pietà*. This piece of Catholic imagery looks out of place on the tomb of the man who was such a leading light in the suppression of the monasteries, but perhaps as the last master of Burton Lazars he began to rediscover a sympathy for the old ways in the more conservative religious environment of the early 1540s. A degree of spiritual uncertainty, at the very least, might be expected from anyone who lived through these particularly difficult times.

On 8 March 1546 Sir Thomas Legh's daughter, Katherine, obtained a further Chancery Decree, yet Dudley was soon selling off portions of land granted to her father in the arbitration.[83] Wriothesley's settlement was chiefly concerned with the property rights of the two main contenders for the Lazarite estate and it said little about the individuals who were dependent on the order as clergy, almsmen or secular servants. Nevertheless, Dudley was obliged to pay 'all yearly fees . . . so that the discharge thereof does not exceed £20 in any one year'.[84] This clause would appear to be directed principally at the secular officers of the house, such as William Faunt, the payments to whom came to £9 3s 4d in 1535. Certainly

---

81 The medieval church was demolished and replaced by a new building, designed by George Dance, in the eighteenth century. Prior to demolition the monuments, including that of Legh, were drawn and recorded. E. and W. Young, *London's Churches* (London, 1986), pp. 134–6.

82 BL, Add Mss, 27348 (Drawings of English churches, monuments, etc. by Sir Charles Frederick). Other, less reliable, versions of the inscription are to be found in BL, Harl Mss 1096 and H. Ellis, *The Parish of Saint Leonard, Shoreditch, and the Liberty of Norton Folgate* (London, 1798).

83 PRO C 78/3/108; S.K. Land, *Kett's Rebellion; the Norfolk Rising of 1549* (Ipswich, 1977), p. 23.

84 PRO, C 78/1/1.

Plate 38: Sir Thomas Legh, last master of Burton Lazars (1537–1544).
An eighteenth-century drawing of his monument once in the church of
St Leonard, Shoreditch.

such a sum would not have covered the £47 2s 11d paid out to the almsmen in the same year.[85]

Legh, for his part, was bound to pay 'all fees, annuities, rents etc' chargeable on his portion of the estate, and, since he obtained most of the St Giles's property, that could be interpreted as an obligation to support its 14 almsmen, many of whom appear to have been receiving out-relief in any case. But, if that was the intention, it seems strange that the Lord Chancellor did not enunciate it more clearly, since provision for the sick and elderly was, arguably, the main duty of the house. One explanation for this lack of a clear directive is the possibility that few or no almsmen were left by 1544. Ten years had elapsed since the making of the *Valor Ecclesiasticus* and Legh might well have followed a less than enthusiastic policy of attracting replacements as the old incumbents died. This policy would certainly have been in line with what was happening elsewhere, where patrons and masters were taking it into their own hands to lop off inconvenient parts of the foundation.[86] In any event, the whole question of charitable provision was left extremely ill defined, to say the least.[87]

With regard to the regular members of the order, the arbitration was more precise, stating that Dudley was to pay 'any yearly pensions to the brethren of the late hospital as the Lord Chancellor should think requisite'.[88] Leaving pensions up to the good will of the Lord Chancellor epitomised the hit-and-miss attitude to severance pay that characterised the dissolutions of the early 1540s. In fact, Burton Lazars probably did better than most because 'for the majority of the collegiate clergy . . . the government seems to have provided no pensions whatever'.[89] On 1 January 1544, as one of the last acts of the old corporation, Legh and five brethren, meeting in the chapter house at Burton, granted the next advowson of Braceborough to William and Richard Layton. Those involved were William Frankis, Thomas Bitchfield, Robert Coke, William Smith and John Capper, and this comparatively small number might be further evidence of a 'running down' policy pursued by Legh after 1538.[90] Certainly, like the king, his attitude to the work of chantry priests was probably ambivalent.

Of the brethren in 1544, all except Capper have been identified as priests, and Bitchfield was a brother of the house as early as 1524.[91] For Bitchfield, Capper and Smith no pensions have been discovered, which suggests that they were overlooked, died or enjoyed other preferments. William Smith might be the same man who was incumbent of the Tattershall chantry in St Benedict's church, Lincoln, and subsequently curate of North Hykeham, but it is a common name and no certain identification can be made.[92] Robert Coke remained at Burton

---

85 *Valor,* 4, pp. 152–3.

86 Orme and Webster, *English Hospital,* p. 163.

87 The question is complicated by separating obligations of individual houses (principally St Giles's and Holy Innocents') and those of the order.

88 PRO, C 78/1/1.

89 Kreider, *English Chantries,* p. 163.

90 LAO, PD 1545/42.

91 Taylor, *Berkeleys of Wymondham,* p. 35.

92 Hodgett, *Chantry Priests,* pp. 18, 50, 66, 123, 149. Smith witnessed several wills at Burton Lazars between 1533 and 1540 and cited Thomas Hartopp in a tithe dispute *c.*1540. If he was indeed related

Lazars and in 1553, at the start of Mary's reign, was still described as 'chaplain', presumably serving the parochial chapel there.[93] In 1547 he had been in receipt of a pension of £5, but when it was granted and when it terminated is not clear.[94]

Indeed, the only clearly documented case is that of William Frankis, 'formerly a fellow of the house at Burton St Lazars', who is stated to have been awarded a pension of £4 on 6 March 1540, though the date is probably an error since the Chancery Decree makes it clear that no pensions had been awarded before September 1544. Frankis, who never married and never obtained any other preferment, went to live in Melton Mowbray and died there on 9 May 1555.[95] As late as 1574 a Derek Dreson was still claiming a pension of £2 13s 4d out of 'Burton Lazars abbey', but he was clearly not a brother of the house and must have been either a lay officer or a speculator who had bought out the pension rights of one of the last brethren.[96] So ended the 'valiant brotherhood', under the mastership of a heretic and far removed from the crusade against the Ottomans, which had revived in ferocity and intensity in the sixteenth century. As Frankis eked out his pension in Melton one wonders what he made of all this, possibly the last man in England in the long and illustrious tradition of the order of St Lazarus. In the archives of Melbourne Hall, Derbyshire, some sixteenth-century rentals for Melton Mowbray are bound with fragments of pre-Reformation printed religious texts of continental origin. These may just be the last physical remnants of the world of Frankis and his colleagues, denied the brief respite granted to the order of St John by Queen Mary.[97]

Redistribution of property

Following the death of Legh, Dudley seems to have been in full control of the estate, but he was not to enjoy it without difficulties. As early as 1545 he was selling off lands in Norfolk to the brothers Robert and William Kett and in 1546 he was obliged to return lands in Derbyshire and Lincolnshire to the king 'in payment of certain debts'.[98] Beer regarded the Lazarite inheritance as 'a diverse assortment of lands' and commented that 'A grant of such scope as this extended the Dudley influence into corners of England never before penetrated.'[99] But the main focus of Dudley's attention was the consolidated Leicestershire estate, a regional presence that was to be further underlined by the marriage of his son,

to the late bishop of Lincoln (see n. 7), he may well have had contacts in the cathedral city enabling him to obtain chantries and work in the courts.

93 PRO, LR 2/87, f. 290. Coke was tenant of a croft, formerly part of the possessions of Burton Lazars, at a rent of 7s.

94 Hodgett, *Chantry Priests*, pp. 47, 63.

95 *Ibid*, pp. 86, 137, 143.

96 *Ibid*, p. 145. William Proudlove, a clerk of Dieulacres Abbey, Staffordshire, retired to the village of Burton Lazars and drew his pension there but he was not a brother of the house.

97 For a similar instance concerning St Giles's, Norwich, see Rawcliffe, *Medicine for the Soul*, Pl. 42. I am grateful to Julian Roberts for his observations on these fragments.

98 Land, *Kett's Rebellion*, pp. 23, 144; *LP, 21 pt 1, 1545, p. 561; Addenda, 1 pt 2, 1538–47*, p. 582. In 1552 the Derbyshire property was regranted to the duke of Suffolk for services to Henry VIII. The subsequent history of the estate is traced in Marcombe, 'Locko', pp. 55–60. See also *CPR, 1550–53*, p. 241; *1553–54*, p. 350; UNMD, Dr D 33.

99 Beer, *Northumberland*, p. 176.

Guilford, to Lady Jane Grey from nearby Bradgate House. Indeed, the fact that Dudley at once changed the traditional designation of Burton Lazars to Burton Lisle indicates the importance with which he regarded it and also his desire to dissociate himself from the traditions of the past. But, before he could exercise unfettered control over his new acquisition, there was the problem of tenants who held land by virtue of leases from the dissolved college, principally John Beaumont of Grace Dieu and Robert Packenham of Tooting-Bec, Surrey, who had married the widow of Maurice Berkeley of Wymondham.[100]

In Northumberland and Yorkshire Dudley carried out 'a complicated series of exchanges which defies logical analysis' and this degree of complexity was also the hallmark of what went on in Leicestershire.[101] As a result of a series of transactions in 1547 and 1548 involving Dudley, Beaumont and Packenham, Dudley was able to buy out the interest of his rivals and in 1548 lease 'the site of the manor and mansion house of Burton Lisle', including stables, gardens and a dovecote, to one Henry Alicock for five years at a rent of £120.[102] On 27 December 1552 Alicock converted his five-year lease into one for 30 years at a rent of £160, it being specified that Dudley could either accept cash or 500 fat sheep and 30 fat oxen 'of the greatest and best sort feeding upon the premises'. If the latter option was chosen the animals were 'to be paid and delivered at Alicock's costs at such place as the duke's household should be maintained', a reflection of the position Dudley then enjoyed as the most powerful man in the land.[103] As his Leicestershire dealings suggest, he was less a traditional landed magnate than a man who viewed property as a marketable commodity, something which, by means of the raising of revenue, could consolidate his position in the king's service.

By 1552 Dudley was certainly too preoccupied with affairs of state to pay much personal attention to Burton, because as earl of Warwick and later duke of Northumberland he came to dominate the government of Edward VI.[104] Even so, by June 1552 he owed the crown £74 16s in arrears of rent on his Burton property and when he fell from power and was executed for treason in the following year his estates were forfeited. A rental taken by the crown at the beginning of Mary's reign put the value of the Leicestershire estate at £215 11s 10d, with Henry Alicock making up the lion's share of that as tenant of the manor of 'Burton Lisle'.[105] In these circumstances Alicock took the precaution of surrendering his lease to Chancery and accepting a new one from the crown, but at the same time Thomas Hartopp attempted to purchase the estate from two obscure characters, George Cotton and William Manne of London, in July 1554.[106] Why

100 PRO, E 326/11965; 326/10661. According to a published genealogy, Robert Packenham was married to Elizabeth, *daughter* of Maurice Berkeley of Wymondham. Taylor, *Berkeleys of Wymondham*, opposite p. 58.

101 Beer, *Northumberland*, p. 181.

102 PRO, E 326/10554; E 328/154. For other conveyances involving Dudley and Alicock, see Farnham, 1, pp. 266–7.

103 *CPR, 1554–55*, pp. 318–19.

104 For Dudley's ascendancy and economic fortunes, see Beer, *Northumberland*, pp. 92–123, 167–198.

105 PRO, LR 2/182, ff. 291–2. Alicock's rent for the manor was £120 *per annum*.

106 PRO, E 328/328; *CPR, 1553–54*, p. 474; *1554–55*, pp 318–19; LRO, Hartopp Mss, 8D39/1811. Smaller

Cotton and Manne felt able to sell these lands is not clear, unless they had gained an interest in Southampton's claim, but, whatever the reason, the transaction failed in its objective of transferring freehold ownership to the Hartopps.

In 1561, as part of a grant comprising lands in Yorkshire and Kent, Queen Elizabeth granted 'Burton Lazar manor or hospital' to her favourite, Lord Robert Dudley, son of the disgraced duke of Northumberland.[107] However, Dudley's grant was at once challenged by Sir William Cecil and Sir Richard Sackville, who had inherited Southampton's claim to the property. This difficulty, which had been rumbling on for twenty years, was finally settled amicably before the Exchequer in 1563, the same year in which Dudley had a comprehensive rental of his estates, including the Leicestershire possessions, drawn up.[108] The survey makes it clear that, despite his aspiration to own the lands, Hartopp was still merely a tenant, but a very important one, paying rent of £40 for a portion of the old hospital demesne and £3 13s 8d for a tenement.[109] In 1599 a further lease from Elizabeth I granted the Burton estate to the bishop of Ely, who sublet 'a messuage or tenement called "Pauntons or Berkeleys" . . . late parcel of the possessions of John, late duke of Northumberland, and before that, parcel of the possessions of the late hospital of Burton Lazars, now dissolved' to the Hartopps for three lives.[110] William Hartopp set about improving his new estate with some enthusiasm. In 1601, for example, he requested permission from Martin Heton, bishop of Ely (1600–9), 'to take down a [ruined] barn in the abbey yard a distance from the mansion house'.[111]

Although this ambitious and upwardly mobile family came to have its main seat at Little Dalby, it also occupied the 'mansion house' at Burton Lazars 'situated at the top of a hill, in an open and bleak location'.[112] The origins of this building are unknown, but, if it was close to the barn in the abbey yard, it was probably somewhere among the buildings of the college, possibly improvised from one of them – perhaps even the master's house. In 1648 the complex was described as a half-timbered house with associated gardens, orchards and outbuildings. The house does not appear to have been on a grand scale, comprising a hall (16' × 18') and a dining room of similar size. In addition, there was a buttery, kitchen 'and other rooms below stairs . . . and divers small lodging rooms above stairs'. Ominously, the Parliamentary commissioners who undertook the survey reported that the roof timbers were in decay. All of this suggests that the house at Burton Lazars may have been the home of the Hartopps before

parcels of land were granted to a number of recipients by the crown in 1554 and 1555. *CPR, 1553–54*, pp. 125, 154, 163; *1554–55*, p. 243; *1555–57*, p. 178.

107 *CPR, 1560–63*, pp. 189–91; LH, marquis of Bath Mss, Dudley Papers, III/23. For Robert Dudley, see *DNB*, 6, pp. 112–22.

108 PRO, E 326/12927; LH, marquis of Bath Mss, Dudley Papers, III/33, ff. 130–2. The dispute between Dudley and Cecil and Sackville only involved the Leicestershire property of Burton Lazars.

109 LH, marquis of Bath Mss, Dudley Papers, III/33, ff. 130, 132.

110 PRO E 371/601, ff. 1–27; Farnham, 1, p. 267. For the pattern of land holding as it had established itself at Burton Lazars by the nineteenth century, see the Tithe Award map (*c.*1845), LRO, DE746/5.

111 LRO, Clayton Mss, 35'29/155.

112 LRO, 8D39/2179. For the Hartopps, see Fetherston, *Visitation of Leicestershire, 1619*, p. 8, and for a Hartopp family dispute over the Burton Lazars lands, see PRO E 134/37 Eliz 1/Trin 10; 37 and 38 Eliz 1/Mich 54.

they obtained their knighthood and aspired to more gracious living in the early seventeenth century, abandoning Burton in favour of Little Dalby Hall.

Though the house has long since vanished, even today the most prominent landscape feature is a terraced walkway in the shape of a 'T', which probably dates from a reworking of the gardens in the sixteenth or seventeenth century and was placed to command the best possible view of the rolling landscape to the south.[113] Somewhere close to the house the old collegiate church still stood abandoned and neglected. By 1648 it was in urgent need of repair and 15 of the best oaks were thought necessary to consolidate the roof alone, suggesting a building of considerable size.[114] Decayed roofs seem to have been a persistent problem at Burton Lazars, and failure to carry out repairs may help to explain Nichols's statement that 'The mansion-house . . . was blown down in an extraordinary high wind in 1705.'[115] For such an event to be recalled almost a hundred years later it must have made a lasting impression in the locality and since then the site has remained uninhabited.

The archaeology of Burton Lazars

It is not known when the church and other preceptory buildings disappeared, but over the years there have been persistent suggestions of migration of materials from the site. In the early seventeenth century the antiquary William Burton and William Wyrley, Rouge Croix, noted heraldic glass in the chapel at Eye Kettleby 'that was removed from Burton Lazars' (Plate 39).[116] There was similar glass in the chapelries of Freeby and Welby, though neither Burton, Wyrley nor Nichols ascribe this directly to Burton Lazars.[117] Eye Kettleby had already vanished when Nichols was writing in the late eighteenth century, but it is possible that some of the glass was saved and ended up in the parish church of Melton Mowbray, of which both Burton Lazars and Eye Kettleby were chapelries.[118] Dr Thomas Ford, vicar of Melton Mowbray (1773–1820), was a clergyman of keen antiquarian interests who gathered together old glass from a number of different sources. Wing and Ward, writing in the nineteenth century, stated that some of his collection came from Burton Lazars and that the fragments were reassembled by William Wailes of Newcastle in 1869 to create a new window in the parish church.[119]

---

113 LRO, 8D39/2179; Brown, 'Burton Lazars', pp. 32–3. A comparable feature exists at the deserted manor house site at Cotes, near Loughborough. See Hartley, *Central Leicestershire*, pp. 8–9, 19.

114 A. Dryden (ed.), *Memorials of Old Leicestershire* (London, 1911), p. 151; LRO, 8D39/2179.

115 Nichols, *Leicestershire*, 2 pt 1, p. 268.

116 CA, Vincent Mss, 197, f. 30. Only Wyrley mentioned the fact that the glass had come from Burton Lazars. Burton misdescribed the Mowbray arms as Beler, and was followed in this by Nichols (see n.119). Burton, *Leicestershire*, p. 145.

117 Burton, *Leicestershire*, pp. 108–9, 300–1; Nichols, *Leicestershire*, 2 pt 1, pp. 281, 285.

118 Nichols, *Leicestershire*, 2 pt 1, p. 278. Nichols used Wyrley's notebook and mentioned the migration of glass to Eye Kettleby. However, out of seven coats of arms, he ignores one and misdescribes two.

119 V. Wing, *Reminiscences of the Revd Thomas Ford LLD, formerly Vicar of Melton Mowbray* (Melton Mowbray, 1864), p. 12; V. Wing, 'An Enquiry Concerning the Founders and Ancient Monuments of Melton Mowbray Church', *Transactions of the Leicestershire Archaeological Society*, 3 (1874), p. 24; J. Ward, *Chronological Events in the History of Melton Mowbray together with sketches of the hamlets*

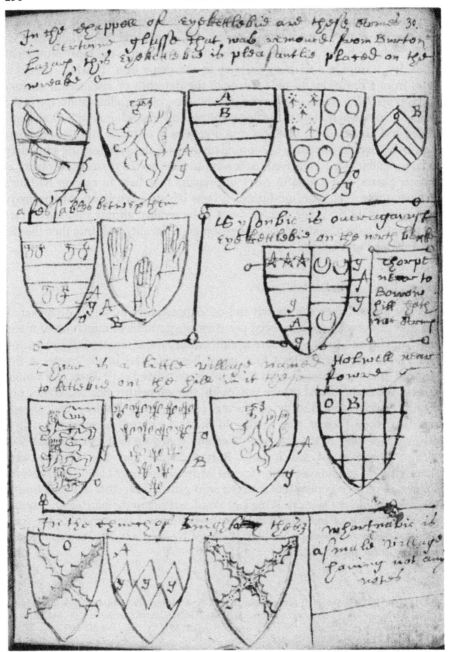

Plate 39: The first seven coats of arms were represented on stained glass removed from the church at Burton Lazars to the chapel at Eye Kettleby, Leicestershire. From the notebook of William Wyrley, Rouge Croix, c.1600.

From the subject matter of Ford's glass, now located in the south aisle at Melton Mowbray, there is little to associate it beyond doubt with Burton Lazars, except, perhaps, the splendid representation of the Mowbray arms. Among the seven coats of arms at Eye Kettleby, that of the Mowbrays would have been readily recognisable, and for that reason, and its local associations, would have been the first to be saved when the chapel was abandoned.[120] It is possible, therefore, that the Mowbray arms now in Melton church did, indeed, originate from Burton Lazars, as Wing and Ward suggest. Wing, writing in 1864, was in no doubt: 'A part of the glass was brought from Burton . . . whereby are preserved some interesting pieces showing the Mowbray arms'.[121] Nichols also records the tradition that a 'great bell' was salvaged from Burton Lazars and made its way to Melton Mowbray; and that a vestry on the north side of the church 'was built of stones from the ruins of Burton hospital', which, though it might seem likely, is impossible to verify.[122]

The fact that the preceptory was used as a secular dwelling for about 150 years after the Dissolution has caused considerable difficulties in the interpretation of the earthworks which, in the long run, can only be unpicked by archaeological excavation. Indeed, on the strength of our present knowledge it is impossible to say if identifiable features, such as stock pens, were the result of activity before or after the suppression. Given the volume of activity that we know to have taken place in the sixteenth century, many are perhaps not so early as is sometimes believed. On at least two occasions since 1705 archaeological discoveries have been made, but, because of poor recording, on neither occasion have the findings added much to our knowledge. In the late nineteenth century, while a workman was digging a drain, a substantial quantity of animal bones was uncovered, and at about the same time it was established that the broad trackways were 'paved with pebbles'. Moreover, 'beneath this road he found some old coins, but of their value or date we can say nothing, neither do we know in whose possession they are'.[123]

A more substantial and better documented discovery was made in 1913 when a telegraph pole was being erected close to the farmhouse of one Thomas Hack. On this occasion the workman uncovered some old tiles, and realising their significance summoned the marquis of Granby and Captain Charles Lindsay, who carried out an impromptu excavation, with the assistance of Bertell Hubert

---

affiliated thereto (Melton Mowbray, 1889), p. 115; J. Ward, *Melton Mowbray in Olden Times* (Melton Mowbray, 1879), p. 166. For a more recent assessment of the medieval glass at Melton Mowbray, see P. Newton, 'Schools of Glass Painting in the Midlands', 2, University of London, Ph.D. thesis (1961), pp. 202–10.

120 CA, Vincent Mss, 197, f. 30v; Nichols, *Leicestershire*, 2 pt 1, p. 278. The Mowbray arms is one of the two coats misdescribed by Nichols (see n. 116). He gives it as *Party per pale, gules and sable, a lion rampant argent* (Beler). In fact, it is *Gules, a lion rampant argent* (Mowbray).

121 Wing, *Reminiscences*, p. 12. Nichols noted a representation of the Mowbray arms at Melton as early as 1583. However, he states that these were charged with a fleur-de-lis on the shoulder of the lion. Nichols, *Leicestershire*, 2 pt 1, p. 252.

122 Nichols, *Leicestershire*, 2 pt 1, pp. 250–1. See also, Ward, *Chronological Events*, p. 115. In 1876 the peal at Melton Mowbray included two medieval bells, one of them bearing a dedication to St Mary, though there is nothing that might link either of them with Burton Lazars. T. North, *The Church Bells of Leicestershire* (Leicester, 1876), p. 246.

123 Twowell, *Burton Lazars*, pp. 98–9.

Smith, curate of Melton Mowbray.[124] The gentleman-archaeologists went on to uncover:

> at a depth of a few feet a considerable number of complete tiles and fragments loose in the soil, also a portion of a pavement *in situ* and undisturbed, measuring 6ft 9in by 3ft composed of nearly a hundred similar tiles in good preservation. Close by was found a nest of round ovens: it is, however, doubtful whether these are contemporary.[125]

Some of the tiles were similar to examples in the church at Melton Mowbray, suggesting that the two buildings had been supplied by the same manufacturers or that some of the Burton Lazars tiles had been taken to Melton after the Reformation.[126] Smith, in response to a postal enquiry in 1915, recorded that the team 'also unearthed a stone trough two feet in length with a shallow depression at the head'.[127] Lindsay took a photograph of the ovens, the precise location of the tiles was recorded and the complete 'pavement' was moved to the British Museum where it is now on display.

The excavation raises more questions than it solves, and the situation is not helped by the failure of the archaeologists to write up their findings in anything more than a very cursory fashion. Nevertheless, some tentative conclusions are possible. First, the discovery was made on the margins of the site close to the possible location of the Hartopp house. Second, the 'pavement' was laid in a haphazard fashion with little attempt to achieve a symmetrical alignment of the tiles. Third, and very important, the tiles were almost certainly wasters, the surfaces being warped, 'rough and bubbled' and glazed in 'violent green or khaki yellow'. Moreover, the wooden stamps from which they were made were often cracked or split.[128] The designs incorporated some standard religious motifs, such as the sacred heart and IHS monogram, but a proportion of the tiles bore heraldic designs that have not been encountered elsewhere, suggesting that they were specially commissioned for Burton Lazars. Smith particularly highlighted the arms of the Aubignys, and felt that Lord Granby, who in 1915 was serving in the Great War, might have identified others had he not been distracted by military service. Certainly the arms of the Ferrers family were also represented.[129] The date suggested for the majority of the tiles is mid-fifteenth century.

From this assemblage of facts certain possibilities suggest themselves, the most likely being that there was a major commission under way coinciding with the mastership of Sir William Sutton and incorporating the heraldry of important patrons of the house. The only such commission that is likely, necessitating the presence of itinerant tilers on site, would be the rebuilding of the church, a circumstance that fits conveniently with the move towards collegiate status in the

124 BM, Rutland Catalogue. The involvement of Smith is indicated by a letter dated 23 March 1915 in MUOL, 7527. See also, *Crockford's Clerical Directory* (London, 1910), p. 1347.
125 BM, Rutland Catalogue. The 'excavation report' is no more than a series of random manuscript notes.
126 Nichols, *Leicestershire*, 2 pt 1, Plate 46, opposite p. 240.
127 MUOL, 7527.
128 Whitcomb, *Medieval Floor Tiles*, p 13.
129 MUOL, 7527. Others remain unidentified.

Plate 40: Fragment of a late-medieval octagonal column, decorated with trailing maple leaves on flat scrolls, recovered from the garden of Burton House, Burton Lazars, in 2000.

late Middle Ages, Leland's 'very fair' church and a sizeable chapel, which required renovation some two hundred years later. If the best of the tiles did indeed go into a new church, the residue may well have been used to construct 'low status' surfaces in some of the more peripheral buildings of the college, such as bakehouses and brewhouses. An alternative suggestion would be that the tiles were removed, possibly from the church, and relaid in a different context after the Reformation, precedents for this sort of activity being provided by the migration of materials from Ulvescroft Priory to Bradgate House at about the same time.[130] But if this was so, it raises the question of why such poor-quality tiles had been in use where they were most likely to be seen (i.e. in the church) and why sixteenth-century Protestants were prepared to tolerate such blatant popish imagery even in the outbuildings of a manor house. On balance the first suggestion seems the more likely.

The most exciting archaeological discovery to date, however, was made as a result of investigations undertaken by Mary Hatton, archaeological warden for

[130] Whitcomb, *Medieval Floor Tiles*, p. 24.

the parish of Burton Lazars, in March 2000. In the garden of Burton House, just a short distance from the preceptory, Hatton came across a large quantity of worked stone concealed in a rockery and called in members of the Burton Lazars Research Group to assess the importance of the find. Two distinct types of stone were in evidence. First, some decorated items, which were medieval in style and must have come from an ecclesiastical building of some importance (Plate 40). Second, some plainer pieces, probably of sixteenth- or seventeenth-century date, which are more likely to have been part of a secular building. The owners of Burton House gave permission for the stones to be recorded, and in March 2001 a project was embarked upon involving Dr Jenny Alexander and student volunteers from the University of Nottingham. During two days of frenetic activity at Burton Lazars village hall, the stones were raised, moved, washed, photographed, recorded and returned to their original locations at Burton House. The significance of the medieval stones, in particular, soon became apparent. Worked in 'coarse-grained and highly fossiliferous limestone' from the area of Ketton, Barnack or Raunds, the fragments comprised late-medieval architectural details, many of them richly decorated with leaf or floral motifs.[131] The collection consisted almost exclusively of hollow-backed decorative stone, of little value in terms of reuse but invaluable as architectural evidence. Since the stones were discovered a short distance from the preceptory site, it is necessary to look closely at their provenance to eliminate the possibility that they might have been imported from elsewhere.[132]

Burton House was built by Captain James Burns-Hartopp and opened in 1912 for 'hunt lettings'. It was therefore a speculative piece of building made 'from a hotch potch of gathered materials'.[133] Some of these certainly came from Little Dalby Hall, the main seat of the family, either when Burton House was built or when the Burns-Hartopps took up residence there after Little Dalby was sold in 1938. Little Dalby Hall was Elizabethan, and extensive works were carried out there in 1951 when the old house was rebuilt on a smaller scale.[134] It is possible, therefore, that some of the 'secular' stone may be provenanced to Little Dalby, but the medieval material is too old and of the wrong style for such a house.[135] If it came from a church, which is virtually indisputable, it is unlikely to have been the parish churches at Burton Lazars or Little Dalby, which are relatively complete and constructed in a different architectural style.[136] Nor is it likely to have been from the eighteenth-century spa at Burton, which, if it was built from new, was probably mock-gothic. If, on the other hand, the spa made use of materials reclaimed from the preceptory site (as suggested in Chapter 5), it

131 Alexander, 'Loose Stones'.
132 UNCLH, J.M. Allsop and M. Hatton, 'Notes on the possible provenance of the carved stone in fragments at Burton Lazars near the site of the medieval hospital', MFR 00/4 (2000).
133 Rothery, Burton Lazars, p. 36.
134 Ibid.
135 It is possible, of course, that the sixteenth- and seventeenth-century 'secular' stone also originated from the preceptory. Though the Hartopps' manor house at Burton was said to be of timber construction, there may have been a sixteenth-century building on site from which the stone was taken.
136 Pevsner, Leicestershire and Rutland, pp. 119, 275.

is just possible that the decorative fragments became available following the demolition of the bath-house in 1849.[137] However, they provide no evidence of later mortar residue, which would tend to go against this suggestion.

Assuming that the stone did not come to Burton House via the spa, there are some interesting clues as to how and when it might have arrived there. Burton Hall, which was built in 1881 by Captain Samuel Tudor Ashton, was occupied in the 1930s by Captain William Higson, who was said to have had a collection of worked stone from the hospital site.[138] How he acquired it is not clear, nor is it known how it was dispersed, except that one of his pieces, the 'leper head', ended up in the Bede House Museum at Melton Mowbray.[139] It must be said that the 'leper head' is different in style, date and type of stone from the Burton House assemblage, but that does not discount the possibility that the majority of Higson's collection came from the preceptory and found its way to the rockery as garden ornaments. Another possibility is that after the collapse or demolition of the collegiate church (which presumably took place some time after the storm of 1705), fragments that could not be sold or reused were simply discarded in the quarry that separates the hospital site from Burton House. From here they may have been recovered by the Burns-Hartopps or other keen gardeners as ornaments. It does not appear that the stones were in the garden of Burton House much before the 1960s. Weathering, staining and the development of a tree root around one of them, would seem to confirm that they had lain undisturbed for thirty or forty years, at least, prior to Hatton's investigations in 2000. Suffice to say that, on the basis of our present knowledge, a migration from the collegiate church seems the most likely explanation of their presence.

A detailed analysis of the Burton House stones will be the subject of a forthcoming publication, but some preliminary observations are possible following the work of Alexander and Martin.[140] It is likely that the medieval stones represent parts of an impressive ecclesiastical building constructed in the fifteenth century in Perpendicular style. Though some of the stylistic forms pre-date this, originating as early as the late thirteenth century in some instances, they are features that had a long life and are nevertheless compatible with a late-medieval date. Three architectural details are outstanding. First, a number of portions of a substantial octagonal structure, which has been cut away on one face so as to fit within a confined space. It is not clear what this structure was. It seems too small to have been a font or well-head, but it may have been the stem of a large font or the base of a pulpit. A possible clue to its use is provided by its decoration, which is made up of foliate roundels on all of the faces of the octagon with the exception of the 'cut away' side. The foliage is naturalistic, comparable to that in Southwell Minster chapter house, and depicts an unexpected mix of plants, all of them possessing medicinal qualities and included in the herbal. The plants represented are *Hedera helix* (common ivy); *Acer campestre* (field maple);

137 See Chapter 5, p. 144.
138 Rothery, *Burton Lazars*, pp. 35, 47; Marcombe and Manchester, 'Leper Head', p. 87.
139 Marcombe and Manchester, 'Leper Head', p. 88; Hunt, *Melton Mowbray*, p. 78.
140 Alexander, 'Loose Stones'. I am grateful to Bernard Martin, RIBA, for examining the stones from a structural point of view.

Bryonia dioica (white bryony); *Atropa bella-donna* (deadly nightshade); and *Sinapis arvensis* or *alba* (charlock or white mustard).[141] Second, some substantial portions of a Perpendicular window with grooves for glass and recesses for supporting bars. These features provide the best dating evidence, firmly placing the building in the fifteenth century.

The third detail comprises a series of fragments which, when reassembled, have been demonstrated to make up octagonal Perpendicular columns with a common diameter of 630 mm at the capitals and 480 mm in the piers. Two varieties of capital survive, though there is no evidence of any bases. The piers are decorated and unusually ornate for the period, harking back to earlier English styles or contemporary developments in Spain and particularly Portugal.[142] The last comparison is not as unlikely as it might seem, because in the fifteenth century the Iberian peninsula was the last bastion of the Crusade and English pilgrim traffic to the shrine of St James at Compostela was on the increase. It is not impossible that ideas, and inspiration, filtered back.

The piers were constructed with a thin outer face of decorated, curved stone and an inner core probably made up of rubble and mortar. Staggered jointing was effected to ensure structural stability and so as not to detract from the carved detail. Three types of column have been reconstructed by Martin out of the four groups of stone identified by Alexander (see Plate 15). Two of them have eight narrow vertical roll mouldings connecting the capital and base. On these examples the faces between the roll mouldings are filled with fleurons or trailing maple leaves on flat scrolls.[143] However, it is the third variety (Alexander's Group 3) that is the most spectacular. Here, the eight roll mouldings depart from their vertical alignment and adopt a breathtaking spiralling twist, the faces between them being filled with stems of trailing white bryony interdispersed with berries. These contrasting columns, when arranged in an arcade, would have made an striking visual impact, such a combination being most unusual, if not unique, in terms of late-medieval English architecture. According to Alexander, this quality of decorative detail 'demonstrates a considerable degree of wealth on the part of the patron', and it opens up a wide range of questions about the aims and aspirations of the order in its late-medieval reincarnation.[144]

In this context the significance of the leaves should not be underestimated. On one level they had a practical relevance in terms of the order's declared hospitaller vocation and on another a spiritual significance which, arguably, went well beyond that. Maple was beneficial to the liver and spleen; ivy was used in the treatment of dysentery and jaundice; white mustard cured digestive complaints, bronchitis and rheumatism; and deadly nightshade was a sleep-

141 C.F. Leyel (ed.), *Mrs M. Grieve, A Modern Herbal* (1931, reprinted Harmondsworth, 1982), pp. 132–3, 570, 583–9, 440–2 .

142 W. Swaan, *Art and Architecture of the late Middle Ages* (London, 1988), pp. 188, 195, 199–202. For an example of spiralling columns from Germany, see p. 150.

143 The type not reconstructed by Martin is very similar, having maple leaves connected by stems rather than scrolls (Alexander, Group 2). However, there are doubts about this category because of the poor state of preservation of the stone.

144 Alexander, 'Loose Stones'.

inducing anaesthetic that was also useful for eye disorders.[145] But it was white bryony which, above all, seems to have been the enduring hallmark of the order. This unpretentious plant, common in hedgerows and woodland, was 'a favourite medicine with the older herbalists' and was recommended by Bartholomew Anglicus, John Gerard and Nicholas Culpeper.[146] Among its many beneficial uses, 'under the name of wild nep it was known in the fourteenth century as an antidote to leprosy'.[147] In common with deadly nightshade, white bryony was poisonous if not used correctly. Could it have become, almost, a badge of the medieval Lazarites? Like them, it professed the utmost humility; like them, it exuded messages of life and death, inextricably intermingled amongst its tangled stems. It was clearly a plant of some considerable significance to the order, triumphantly proclaimed to visitors in the architecture of the new collegiate church. Here was a world in which the small were made great and the rejected weed spiralled up to heaven, in line with the enduring parable of Lazarus the beggar and a set of ideals rooted in twelfth-century Jerusalem.

Unfortunately, Henry VIII did not see it quite like this or, if he did, he chose to ignore it. In 'On the Hypocrite Brother', William Bowyer glorified the changes of the Reformation period as a well deserved judgement on the depraved order of St Lazarus. The king was very much the hero of the moment, God's instrument of retribution on an organisation that had run its course:

> But Almighty God destroyed our abominable crimes
> When our impiety was flourishing in the highest degree.
> He sent a king from heaven to strike the structure down,
> A king adorned in pure reverence.
> Through his help our deceits have been exposed,
> Our false superstition made known to the world.
> Yet lest the faithful actors lack their reward,
> He gave our estates to noble men.[148]

The reality was more prosaic and had its roots in changes initiated by Henry VII. The order did not adapt well to the Tudor regime, and despite its naturalisation in the fifteenth century remained an object of suspicion. Since it adhered to so few traditional codes of practice it was extremely difficult for administrators to categorise, and Sir Thomas Legh's appointment as master, following the deliberate removal of his predecessor, was a means both of rewarding a loyal servant of the crown and monitoring the behaviour of a fairly marginal organisation. Certainly government policy towards the hospitals was highly inconsistent and 'The question of what survived and what did not is a complicated one.'[149] Once the government had embarked upon its policy of random dissolutions in the early 1540s, it was only a matter of time before some ambitious speculator cast covetous eyes on the properties of the Lazarites. Much depended on the power

---

[145] *Culpeper's Complete Herbal* (Ware, 1995), p. 159; Leyel, *Modern Herbal*, pp. 442, 567, 570, 588–9.
[146] Leyel, *Modern Herbal*, pp. 132–3; *Complete Herbal*, pp. 42–3.
[147] Leyel, *Modern Herbal*, p. 132.
[148] HL, HM 160, f. 129.
[149] Orme and Webster, *English Hospital*, p. 161.

struggles at court and the never-ending ebb and flow of the factions tugging at the king, a series of political complexities that ensured that fortunes could just as easily be lost as made on the monastic land market.

The fragility of Legh's position, dependent as it was on Cromwell, became evident in 1544 when the order was unexpectedly dissolved and its properties granted to the current court favourite, Lord Lisle. In all of this Norfolk's protection proved to be ineffective, and by 1550 he was languishing in the Tower while the Lazarite estate was enjoyed by the most powerful man in England, John Dudley, earl of Warwick, apparently a committed Protestant and reformer. For all his Protestantism, the transparency of which was to be proved on the accession of Mary, Dudley did nothing with his new lands to further the cause of religion or the gospel. If the order was doing a little in the way of charitable provision in 1530, its properties generated nothing by 1550. The dissolution of the order in England therefore can hardly be viewed as a positive act of reform, unless the uprooting of Bowyer's pernicious weed defacing Christ's garden is seen as justification enough. Over the long term the only beneficiaries of the disappearance of the order of St Lazarus were aspiring families of secular gentry such as the Hartopps at Burton or the Drury-Lowes at Locko who, eventually, came to be the tenants or owners of the sequestered estates.

Conclusion

Almost twenty years on from the start of our research project, the allegorical figure depicted by Sibert looks almost comical in the light of the development of the order of St Lazarus in medieval England. Yet it still has a relevance in a wider context. The order grew up in a twelfth-century leper hospital in Jerusalem with a quasi-monastic way of life. Because it catered principally for members of the knightly class, and because lepers were believed to have some special religious vocation, by the thirteenth century it became militarised as a response to the reverses the Christians were suffering in the Latin kingdom. This was the age of the leper knight who was to be such an influential figure in terms of the order's sense of identity and later development. The military operation, which was never very extensive or successful in conventional terms, was backed by a growing network of estates in western Europe and privileges granted by successive Popes. In this the order differed from the Templars and Hospitallers only in degree, and these similarities became even more marked after the mid-thirteenth century when leper brothers (and leper knights) ceased to be a regular feature of its activities. The fall of Acre in 1291 forced the Lazarites back on to their European properties and the French preceptory at Boigny claimed leadership of the order.

The fourteenth century was a period of acute difficulties, characterised by a growing resentment against the domination of the French, not to mention more generalised social and economic problems. The result was schism and the disintegration of the truly international religious order that had existed in the thirteenth century. England went its own way after a bitter dispute over the mastership, and in the fifteenth century the battered remnants of the brotherhood began to regroup around a new set of values – or rather, values that had come through from the past but which were subtly reinterpreted. Falling back on the traditions of the order, and particularly the papal privileges granted in the thirteenth century, the Lazarites skillfully played on the changing climate of late-medieval spirituality by establishing a large and successful confraternity and directing their attentions to the recital of masses for the dead. The climax of this reorientation came with the building of the new collegiate church at Burton Lazars in the fifteenth century, just when the order was receiving confirmations of national autonomy from the Pope. If the early years in Jerusalem had represented the pristine values of the order, Yorkist England provided it with a second spring, a chance to show off its new nationalistic, chivalric and liturgical credentials. For the first time the master of Burton Lazars was invariably a knight, not a leper knight of the old crusading *genre*, but a reflection of the new, Arthurian concepts of romantic chivalry that were then fashionable.

This transformation was achieved, in part, by the exploitation of three potent and long-enduring myths that stemmed from the founding ideologies of the order – the notions that it was knightly, leprous and poor. All of this was true, up to a point, in the early years, but as time went on these ideals faded and had to be kept alive by an ever-active public relations onslaught and changing interpretations of key values. After 1291 there is no evidence that the Lazarites ever took part in a crusade; they spent more time closing down leper hospitals than developing them; and it is unlikely that their poverty would have been upheld by anyone who had a chance to look closely at their balance sheets. This last point is important, because the relative wealth of the order had widespread ramifications. The endowment of Burton Lazars rested on generous gifts of land and tithes in the twelfth and thirteenth centuries, on tax immunities and on papal privileges permitting alms gathering and the sale of indulgences. It is probable that, in reality, the income of the order exceeded the sums suggested in either the *Taxatio* or the *Valor*, and in the fifteenth century (or even before) the obligation to send a third of this to the mother house in the Holy Land or France lapsed. Further enhanced by the grant of St Giles's Hospital, Holborn, by Edward I in 1299, bringing with it some lucrative properties in the capital, the order in England was relatively well off by the fifteenth century. This enabled it not only to weather the economic storms of the period with some comfort, but also to maintain its dependant parish churches in a good state of repair and, most important, to embark on the ambitious scheme of building the collegiate church. Though this has now completely disappeared, sufficient archaeological evidence has survived to begin to piece together a picture of what appears to have been a spectacular undertaking. This mismatch between what the Lazarites *claimed* and what they *did* was picked up by William Bowyer in the sixteenth century in his stinging satirical attack on the 'hypocrite brother'. It was very much a barometer of changing times.

As might be expected, the national identity of the order of St Lazarus was not enough to save it in the climate of the new Tudor polity of the sixteenth century. Not only was its religious ethos out of step with the growing body of Protestant thought, its estates offered a tempting target too – especially the London properties, which had been enhanced by a policy of expansion in the fifteenth century. The faltering charitable role of the order barely compensated for these factors and though it struggled on longer than most, it was finally suppressed in 1544, its lands being granted to John Dudley, earl of Warwick. But even then the myth lingered on, proving how enduring the medieval image-building had been. In the seventeenth century, concluding the Leicestershire section of his *Worthies*, Thomas Fuller requested in his 'Farewell' 'that the lands may also . . . return to the hospital of Burton Lazars in this shire, if not entire, yet in such a proportion as may comfortably maintain the lepers therein'.[1] He appears to have missed the point that Burton Lazars never supported lepers in any number, and subsequent generations of antiquaries, including Nichols, fell into the same trap. When the order of St Lazarus was revived in the twentieth century in England and overseas,

---

1   R. Barber (ed.), *Fuller's Worthies. Selected from* The Worthies of England *by Thomas Fuller* (London, 1987), p. 299.

it is hardly surprising, therefore, that it harked back to the old ideals of chivalry, leprosy and poverty as its defining values. In that context the allegorical engraving of the eighteenth century begins to make some sense. The fact that the reality is a good deal more complicated than the myth underlines not only the importance of detailed and objective historical research, but also the adaptable qualities of this most versatile and enduring of medieval institutions.

Appendix 1: Masters-General of the Order of St Lazarus, Masters of Burton Lazars and its Daughter Houses

Masters-General of the Order of St Lazarus[1]

Masters-General in the Holy Land
Bartholomew occurs in 1153[2]
Hector occurs in 1154[3]
Hugh de St Paul occurs in 1155[4]
Lambert occurs in 1164[5]
Gerard de Montclar occurs in 1169[6]
Bernard occurs between 1185 and 1186[7]
Walter de Novo Castro occurs between 1228 and 1234[8]
Reynald de Fleury occurs between 1234 and 1235[9]
Miles occurs in 1256[10]
Thomas de Sainville occurs between 1277 and 1304[11]

Masters-General in France
Adam de Veau occurs in 1327[12]
John de Paris occurs between 1332 and 1348[13]
John de Comti occurs between 1357 and 1371[14]
James de Besnes occurs between 1382 and 1384[15]
Peter des Ruaulx occurs between 1431 and 1453[16]
John le Cornu occurs between 1478 and 1485[17]

---

[1] The list relies on the research of Hyacinthe and Jankrift and omits several masters, who may or may not be spurious, listed by other historians of the order. See, for example, Bagdonas, *St Lazarus*, p. 55; http://www.kwtelecom.com/chivalry/lazarus, 'The Order of St Lazarus. The Heraldry of the Order'.
[2] Marsy, 'Fragment d'un Cartulaire', p. 131.
[3] *Ibid*, p. 133.
[4] *Ibid*, pp. 133–4.
[5] *Ibid*, p. 139.
[6] Jankrift, *Leprose*, p. 206.
[7] Marsy, 'Fragment d'un Cartulaire', pp. 147, 149.
[8] *Ibid*, pp. 151–2; AN, S 4841/B, doc. 16.
[9] Marsy, 'Fragment d'un Cartulaire', pp. 154, 155.
[10] *Close Rolls, 1256–59*, p. 130.
[11] AN, S 4866; S 4891.
[12] AN, S 4884, doc. 9.
[13] Jankrift, *Leprose*, p. 206; AN, S 4884, doc. 9.
[14] AN, S 4884, doc. 9: *CPapR, Letters 4, 1362–1404*, p. 84.
[15] AN, S 4894/B; S 4849, doc. 2.
[16] AN, S 4866.
[17] AN, S 4884; S 4866.

Francis d'Ambroise occurs in 1498[18]
Agnan de Mareuil occurs from 1501 to 1511[19]
Claude de Mareuil occurs from 1536 to 1550[20]
Michael de Seurre occurs from 1565 to 1571[21]
Francis de Salviati occurs from 1571 to 1585[22]
Charles de Gayon occurs in 1604[23]

Master-General (without precise date)
William Desmares occurs late-fifteenth century[24]

Masters of Burton Lazars

William occurs in 1204 and 1208 (prior) [25]
Michael occurs in 1212[26]
Hervey occurs in 1222[27]
Terry de Alemanius occurs in 1235[28]
Roger de Reresby occurs in 1246[29]
Philip de Insula occurs in 1250 and 1251[30]
Robert de Talington occurs between 1252 and 1254 and again in 1267[31]
Richard Bustard occurs in 1264[32]
Sir Richard de Sulegrave occurs in 1271–72[33]
John de Horbling occurs between 1277 and 1281[34]
Robert de Dalby occurs between 1284 and 1289[35]
Richard de Leighton occurs in 1299 and 1319[36]

---

[18] AN, S 4885.

[19] AN, S 4892; S 4866.

[20] AN, S 4866.

[21] *Ibid.*

[22] *Ibid.*

[23] T. de St Luc, *Mémoires en forme d'abrégé historique de l'institution de l'ordre royal des chevaliers hospitaliers de Notre-Dame du Mont-Carmel et de St Lazare de Jérusalem*, pt 2 (Paris, 1666), p. 161.

[24] Inscription in the chapel at Grattemont, Département of Seine-Maritime, France.

[25] Described as Prior William. *Feet of Fines, Lincolnshire*, p. 92; PRO, CP 25/1/121/6 (Farnham, 1, p. 252).

[26] BL, Cotton Mss, Vespasian E xxiii, f. 145. Possibly the same Michael mentioned in BL, Cotton Mss, Claudius A xiii, ff. 22–3.

[27] PRO, CP 25/1/121/9. Hervicius, described incorrectly as Heincius in Farnham, 1, p. 269; 2, p. 270.

[28] Holmes, *Cartulary of St John of Pontefract*, 1, pp. 199–200.

[29] Described as Brother Roger de Rearsby in *CLR, 1245–51*, p. 44; but as master in BL, Cart, f. 141.

[30] BL, Harl Mss, 3868, ff. 15b, 16a.

[31] PRO, CP 25/1/122/22 (Farnham, 6, p. 115); PRO, KB 26/154, m.20d (Farnham, 1, p. 254); Davis, *Register of Richard Gravesend*, p. 27. Probably the same Robert mentioned in BL, Cart, f. 135.

[32] BL, Cart, f. 61. Probably the same Richard who is described as master in an agreement dated 1256. Foster, *Final Concords*, 2, p. 122.

[33] Parkin, *Norfolk*, 8, p. 493. This date assumes that James de Belvaco, in whose mayoralty Sulegrave is placed, did not serve as mayor, again, between 1273 and 1278. At any rate, Sulegrave can be no later than 1278–79. H. le Strange, *Norfolk Official Lists* (Norwich, 1890), p. 188.

[34] PRO, KB 27/33, m.7, 8d (Farnham, 3, p. 109). Described as Master John, keeper (*custodem*) of the hospital of St Lazarus of Burton in PRO, CP 40/39, m.15 (Farnham, 1, p. 255).

[35] PRO, JUST 1/462, m.5. Described as Brother Robert in PRO, KB 27/118, m.15 (Farnham, 2, p. 51). See also, PRO, SC 8/302/15081.

[36] PRO, E 315/35, no. 8. Also appears as general attorney of the master and brethren of the house of St Lazarus of Jerusalem in 1311, 1313, 1316 and 1321. *CPR, 1307–13*, p. 344; *1313–17*, pp. 1, 394; *1317–21*, pp. 394, 571.

Sir Adam de Veau occurs in 1308[37]
John Crispin occurs in 1316[38]
William de Aumenyl occurs in 1321[39]
William de Tye occurs in 1324 and 1327[40]
Hugh Michel occurs between 1331 and 1347[41]
Richard occurs in 1345[42]
Thomas de Kirkeby occurs in 1347[43]
Robert Haliday occurs between 1350 and 1358[44]
Geoffrey de Chaddesden occurs in 1354[45]
Nicholas de Dover occurs between 1364 and 1389[46]
Richard de Clifford occurs in 1389 (appointed by the king)[47]
Walter de Lynton occurs between 1401 and 1421[48]
Sir Geoffrey Shriggley occurs between 1421 and 1446[49]
Sir William Sutton occurs between 1450 and 1485[50]
Sir George Sutton occurs between 1484 and 1504[51]
Sir Thomas Norton occurs between 1504/5and 1526[52]
Sir Thomas Ratcliffe occurs between 1526 and 1537[53]
Sir Thomas Legh occurs between 1537 and 1543/4[54]

Masters of Burton Lazars (without precise dates or titles)
Roger occurs mid-twelfth century[55]
Robert son of Hugh occurs mid- to late twelfth century (prior)[56]
Arnald occurs mid- to late twelfth century (prior)[57]

---

37 GRO, Berkeley Castle Muniments, J7/67/02/001/00/00 (MF 1354).
38 BL, Cart, f. 107. Described as Brother John Crispin, but titled master in PRO, JUST 1/633, m.85d.
39 *CCR, 1318–23*, p. 498.
40 BL, Cartulary, f. 97. Also appears as general attorney of the master and brethren of the house of St Lazarus of Jerusalem in 1325 and 1328. *CPR, 1324–27*, p. 126; *1327–30*, p. 238; PRO, CP 40/271 m.9d (Farnham, 1, p. 258).
41 Bennett, *Registers of Berghersh*, 1, no. 1172; *CCR, 1346–49*, p.382. See also PRO, SC 8/302/15081.
42 PRO, CP 40/342, m.290 (Farnham, 1, pp. 258–9).
43 *CPR, 1345–48*, p. 414.
44 BL, Cotton Mss, Claudius A xiii, f. 25. Was probably master in all but name in 1349. See f. 69; *CCR, 1354–60*, p. 498. See also PRO, SC 8/302/15081.
45 *CPR, 1354–58*, p. 43. Also appears as *confrère* and proctor of the master of the hospital of St Lazarus of Jerusalem in 1355 and 1356. *CPR, 1354–58*, pp. 284, 352.
46 PRO, KB 27/416, m.36 (Farnham, 1, p. 259); E 315/35, no. 8. See also SC 8/302/15081.
47 *CPR, 1388–92*, pp. 117, 120.
48 PRO, E 315/42, no. 156; *CPapR, Letters 7, 1417–31*, p. 181.
49 *CPapR, Letters 7, 1417–31*, p. 181; LRO, Gretton (Sherard) Mss, DG40/481.
50 Hardy, '*Rymer's Foedera*', 11, p. 262; SRO, Sutherland Collection, D 593/A/1/32/2.
51 PRO, CP 40/890, m.226d (Farnham, 1, p. 263); *CPR, 1494–1509*, p. 391.
52 PRO, E 326/6015; BL, Add Chart, 53710.
53 PRO, CP 40/1050, m.7d (Farnham, 1, p. 265); *LP, 12 pt 1, 1537*, p. 351.
54 BL, Harl Mss, Charter 80 F 26. Described as master of St Giles's, but undoubtedly master of Burton as well. Williams, *Early Holborn*, 2, no. 1673.
55 Described as Roger of St Lazarus. J. Hunter (ed.), *Great Rolls of the Pipe, AD 1155–58* (London, 1844) p. 184.
56 Described as prior of the hospital of St Lazarus in LRO, DE2242/5. The charter is undated, but probably mid-twelfth century.
57 Appears as a witness to the charter of William Burdet granting Tilton Hospital to the infirm brethren of St Lazarus and described as prior of the infirm. BL, Cart, f. 203. Burdet's gifts were confirmed by Henry II and were therefore made before 1189.

Walter de Novo Castro occurs late twelfth to early thirteenth centuries[58]
Matthew de Crembre occurs late twelfth to early thirteenth centuries (preceptor)[59]
Robert occurs in 1201[60]
Henry de Cadeby occurs early thirteenth century[61]
Richard Gernin occurs early to mid-thirteenth century[62]
Osbert de Stanford occurs early to mid-thirteenth century[63]
Philip occurs early thirteenth century[64]
William de Thame occurs early fourteenth century[65]

Masters of Daughter Houses

Carlton-le-Moorland, Lincolnshire
No record found

Choseley, Norfolk
Richard occurs in 1378 (preceptor)[66]

Foulsnape, Pontefract
No record found

Harehope, Northumberland
Walter de Novo Castro occurs in 1189[67]
Thomas occurs in 1236[68]
John de Horbling occurs in 1291[69]
Robert de Horpol occurs in 1307[70]
Roger de Robeby occurs in 1308[71]
William de Thame occurs in 1331[72]

---

[58] BL, Cart, ff. 5, 67. Only titled master on f. 67. However, this charter was not contemporary with Walter.
[59] Described as preceptor and custodian of all alms of St Lazarus on this side of the sea and the other brethren dwelling in England. BL, Cart, f. 91.
[60] Described as Brother Robert of the hospital of St Lazarus. *Curia Regis Roll, 1196–1201*, p. 411. Probably the same Robert who appears as Robert son of William in *Curia Regis Roll, 1196–1201*, p. 203.
[61] PRO, SC 8/302/15081.
[62] BL, Cart, f. 125. There is a possibility that this is the same person as Terry de Alemanius who occurs during the same period.
[63] BL, Cotton Mss, Vespasian E xxiii, f. 108.
[64] Foster, *Registrum Antiquissimum*, 3, pp. 258–9. The charter is undated but is considered to be c.1210–20. However, there must be a possibility that this is Philip de Insula.
[65] Appears as a brother of Burton Lazars in 1327. PRO, CP 40/271, m.9d (Farnham, 1, p. 258). Appears in 1332 as general attorney of the master and brethren of the house of God and St Lazarus, Jerusalem. *CPR, 1330–34*, p. 242. Also master of Harehope in 1331, see n. 64.
[66] NRO, Norwich Consistory Court, Will Register, 1370–83, Heydon, f. 155 (MF 22).
[67] Boutflower, *Fasti Dunelmensis*, p. 195. Also appears as master of Burton Lazars, but the dates are uncertain.
[68] *Curia Regis Roll, 15, 1233–37*, p. 443. A.H. Thompson, *Northumberland Pleas*, Newcastle-upon-Tyne Records Committee, 2 (1922), p. 115, mentions an Osbert being a predecessor of Thomas. There is a possibility that this is Osbert de Stanford.
[69] PRO, KB 27/129, m.69; AC, Archives of the duke of Northumberland, Northumberland Collections, 23, p. 428. He also appears as master of Burton Lazars between 1277 and 1281.
[70] PRO, KB 27/129, m.69; AC, Archives of the duke of Northumberland, Northumberland Collections, 23, p. 1021.
[71] GRO, Berkeley Castle Muniments, J7/67/02/001/00/00 (MF 1354).
[72] *CPR, 1330–34*, p. 75. Also appears as master of Burton Lazars, see n. 58.

Harting, Sussex
No record found

Holy Innocents', Lincoln
Gilbert Thimbleby occurs in 1534 (warden)[73]

Locko, Derbyshire
Hugh Michel occurs in 1347[74]

Tilton, Leicestershire
No record found

Threckingham, Lincolnshire
James occurs in 1319[75]

St Giles's, Holborn

Following the grant of St Giles's by Edward I in 1299, the master of Burton Lazars became master or warden/keeper of St Giles's as well. However, there were exceptions to this and these are listed below:

Walter Christmas[76]
John Crispin occurs between 1303 and 1305[77]
Thomas occurs in 1341[78]
Geoffrey de Birston occurs between 1367 and 1371 (appointed by the king)[79]
William Croxton occurs between 1371 and 1384[80]
John Macclesfield occurs between 1389 and 1391 (appointed by the king)[81]
Richard Crowelegh occurs in 1390 (appointed by the king)[82]
Abbot of St Mary Graces occurs between 1391 and 1402 (following a grant by the king)[83]
Thomas Harringwold occurs in 1493[84]
Robert Barker occurs in 1542[85]

Westwade, Norfolk
No record found

---

[73] *Valor*, 4, p. 29.
[74] PRO, SC 8/210/10456; 8/210/10457. However, it is clear that Hugh was not under the obedience of the master of Burton Lazars, but of the master-general in France. He was previously master of Burton Lazars and in *CCR, 1346–49*, p. 382 is described as preceptor of 'La Maudeleyne' and master of Burton Lazars.
[75] *CPR, 1317–21*, p. 378.
[76] Williams, *Early Holborn*, 2, no. 1622 (but no original source is given).
[77] *CPR, 1301–07*, pp. 189, 357. Appears as master of Burton Lazars in 1316.
[78] BL, Harl Mss, 4015, f. 10. Probably Thomas de Kirkeby who appears as master of Burton Lazars in 1347.
[79] *CPR, 1364–67*, p. 388; PRO, E 326/12434.
[80] *CPR, 1370–74*, p. 418; *1381–85*, p. 463; *1381–85*, p. 463.
[81] *CPR, 1388–92*, pp. 115, 458.
[82] *Ibid*, p. 288.
[83] *CPR, 1396–99*, pp. 47–8; *1401–05*, p. 120.
[84] Parton, *St Giles*, p. 49 (but no original source is given).
[85] Williams, *Early Holborn*, 2, no. 1622 (but no original source is given).

Appendix 2:
Letters of Confraternity and Indulgence

1455   Unidentified[1]
1463   Parishioners of East and West Hagbourne, Oxfordshire[2]
1465   Sir Henry Stafford, Margaret his wife and Henry, Lord Richmond[3]
1466   William Daniel, Alice his wife[4]
1470   Jacob Leveson, Elizabeth his wife[5]
1473   Robert Bostock, Joan his wife, Agnes and Alice their daughters and Alice the
        mother (of Robert?)[6]
1474   Jacob Leveson, Elizabeth his wife (Indulgence)[7]
1475   William of Barrytam[8]
1479   Dame Elizabeth Hesilrige[9]
1481   John Dod, Matilda his wife and all their children[10]
1484   Robert Oldver, Agnes his wife and all their children[11]
1484   John Cherche, Jane his wife[12]
1485   John Becket, Juliana his wife (Indulgence)[13]
1486–1504   Unidentified[14]
1486   Blank (Indulgence)[15]
1486   James Layton, Eleanor his wife[16]
1487   John Lane, Joan his wife[17]
1491   Thomas de Winington, Ellen his wife[18]
1492   Edward Knivet, Elizabeth his daughter[19]
1497   Blank[20]

1   LRO, DE2242/6/7.
2   PRO, C 270/32/5.
3   WAM, 6660.
4   BL, Add Chart, 19864.
5   SRO, Sutherland Collection, D 593/A/1/32/14.
6   LRO, BR 11/19/2.
7   SRO, Sutherland Collection, D 593/A/1/32/1.
8   Bod Lib, Ms Ch Leicester, a 1, f. 21.
9   BL, Add Chart, 47555.
10 Beaumont, 'Original Documents', p. 265. Original not found.
11 DRO, D 2977/2/37.
12 SRO, Sutherland Collection, D 593/A/1/32/15.
13 SRO, Sutherland Collection, D 593/A/1/33/2.
14 BL, Add Chart, 66397.
15 BL, Wolley Mss, Charter viii 13.
16 CRO, Shakerley Collection, DSS 3991, Drawer 2/1, ex Bundle 2.
17 Bod Lib, Top Gen C 23, f. 22.
18 BL, Harl Mss, 2077, f. 33r. Calendar version only, original not found.
19 BL, Harl Mss, Charter 43, A 13.
20 BL, Add Chart, 53492.

1497 Margaret Bowis[21]
1497 John Snaw, Agnes his wife (Indulgence)[22]
1504 Parishioners of Tredington, Gloucestershire[23]
1506 Edward White[24]
1507 Reynold Trethereff[25]
1507 Blank (Indulgence)[26]
1510 Thomas West, Joan his wife[27]
1512 Elizabeth Vachell[28]
1513 Dom Simon Morell[29]
1514? Lawrence Tremane, Elizabeth[30]
1526 Thomas Gamont and his wife[31]

[21] MUOL, 7527.
[22] SRRS, 6000/2623.
[23] Bod Lib, Ms Barlow 1, pp. v–vi.
[24] UNMD, Middleton Mss, MiF 1/6.
[25] PRO, E 135/21/72.
[26] BL, Add Chart, 37362.
[27] BL, c18, e2 (7).
[28] BL, Stowe Mss, Charter 619.
[29] BL, Stowe Mss, Charter 620.
[30] PRO, E 135/21/73.
[31] BL, Add Chart, 53710.

Appendix 3:
The *Valor Ecclesiasticus* (1535)[1]

HOSPITAL OF BURTON SAINT LAZARUS

Demesnes, Manors, Lands, Tenements and other possessions both spiritual and temporal of the Hospital of Burton Saint Lazarus of Jerusalem in England pertaining to Thomas Ratcliffe master therein, that is

VALUE
IN SPIRITUALITIES
COUNTY OF LEICESTER

Profits resulting from the various rectories appropriated to the aforesaid hospital, that is	£	s	d			
Lowesby Rectory	16	0	0			
Spondon Rectory	30	0	0			
Threckingham Rectory	2	6	8			
and Feltham Rectory	11	12	0			
				£	s	d
				59	18	8

As shown by the declaration, having been made in the presence of the Lord King's commissioners in this matter and has been examined and approved by them.

Pensions annually paid to the aforesaid hospital, that is	£	s	d			
from Gaulby church	3	6	8			
and from Braceborough church	1	6	8			
				£	s	d
As per the aforesaid declaration				4	13	4

Offerings in the presence of the image of Saint Lazarus within the hospital of Burton in normal years	£	s	d
		3	4

---

[1] *Valor*, 4, pp. 152–3. Place names have been modernised and, where found, the OS grid reference has been included.

	£	s	d
	64	15	4

IN TEMPORALITIES
COUNTY OF LEICESTER

Rents and fixed payments from tenants
in various demesnes, manors, towns
and hamlets in the county therein,

that is	£	s	d				
In Burton Saint Lazarus (SK 7716)	16	8	2				
Melton Mowbray (SK 7518)	12	7	6				
Kirby Bellars (SK 7117)	2	7	5				
Thorpe Satchville (SK 7311)		4	0				
Twyford (SK 7210)		3	0				
Great Dalby (SK 7414)	2	15	0				
Little Dalby (SK 7714)		14	0				
Stapleford (SK 8018)		14	0				
Buckminster (SK 8722)		11	0		£	s	d
Kimcote (SP 5886)		6	8		50	4	9
Stonesby (SK 8224)		10	0				
Edmondthorpe (SK 8517)		1	0				
Cold Newton (SK 7117)	7	19	7				
Queniborough (SK 6412)	1	14	9				
Pickwell (SK 7811)		1	0				
Leesthorpe (SK 7913)		12	0				
Leicester (SK 5904)		12	0				
Wycomb (SK 7724)	1	8	4				
Stathern (SK 7731)		15	4				

As shown by the declaration,
having been made, examined
and approved

Profits resulting from pleas and	£	s	d
perquisites from the court of			
Burton Saint Lazarus in normal years		2	0

COUNTY OF RUTLAND

Rents and fixed payments from tenants
in various demesnes and manors in the

county therein, that is	£	s	d				
In Belton (SK 8101)		1	0				
Whitwell (SK 9208)		1	0				
and Ashwell (SK 8613)	4	0	0		£	s	d
					4	2	0

As shown in the aforesaid
declaration

COUNTY OF DERBY

Rents and fixed payments from tenants
in various demesnes and manors in the
county therein, that is

	£	s	d		£	s	d
In Spondon (SK 3935)	14	9	4				
Borrowash (SK 4134)	4	9	4				
Chaddesden (SK 3737)		11	3		£	s	d
and Locko (SK 4138)	7	5	0		26	14	11

As shown in the aforesaid
declaration

COUNTY OF NORFOLK

Rents and fixed payments from tenants
in various demesnes and manors in the
county therein, that is

	£	s	d		£	s	d
In the town of Wymondham (TG 1101)	3	11	5½				
King's Lynn (TF 6220)		15	3				
Briston (TG 0632)	1	8	8¼				
Hunworth (TG 0635)		2	9				
Burgh Parva (TG 0433)		1	11½				
Stody (TG 0535)		1	2				
Briningham (TG 0334)		8	2		£	s	d
Brinton (TG 0335)		4	8½		12	10	5¼
Holkham (TF 8944)		7	3½				
Burnham Sutton (TF 8341)		9	0				
and Choseley (TF 7641)	5	0	0				

As per the aforesaid declaration,
having been made, examined and
approved

COUNTY OF LINCOLN

Rents and fixed payments from tenants
in various demesnes and manors in the
county therein, that is

	£	s	d
In the Malandry of Lincoln (SK 9771)	3	9	4
The manor of Nettleham (TF 0075)	13	0	0
The town of Lincoln (SK 9771)	2	0	8
Stainby (SK 9022)		2	4
Owston Ferry (SK 8000)		6	0
Gunby (SK 9021)		1	0
Ashby Puerorum (TF 3271)	2	13	5¾
Edenham (TF 0621)		3	4
Fulletby (TF 2973)		18	0

Woodborough (SK 6347)[2]	6	6
Oxcombe (TF 3177)		7
Gainsborough (SK 8189)		6
Ketsby (TF 3676)		6
Brinkhill (TF 3773)		4
Bag Enderby (TF 3572)	2	4
Somersby (TF 3472)		6
Tetford (TF 3374)		8
Kirkby Underwood (TF 0727)	2	0
Langton (TF 2368 or TF 3970)		6
Branston (TF 0167)	6	8
Carlton-le-Moorland (SK 9058)	2	11	4
Greatford (TF 0811)		6
Witham-on-the-Hill (TF 0516)	1	8
and Threckingham (TK 0836)	4	12	7

	£	s	d
	31	1	3¾

As shown in the aforesaid
declaration

COUNTY OF SUFFOLK

Rents and fixed payments from tenants
in various demesnes and manors in the
county therein, that is

			£	s	d
In Kedington (TL 7046)	14	8			
and Stambourne (TL 7238)[3]	2	0½		16	8½

As shown in the aforesaid
declaration

COUNTY OF HUNTINGDON

	£	s	d
Rents and fixed payments in Upton (SP 7160) in the county therein per year		4	0

As shown in the aforesaid
declaration

COUNTY OF NORTHAMPTON

Rents and fixed payments from tenants
in various demesnes and manors in the
county therein, that is

---

2 Nottinghamshire, not Lincolnshire.
3 Essex, not Suffolk.

In the town of Northampton (SP 7561)	2	1	8			
Thenford (SP 5141)		10	0	£	s	d
Steeple Morden (TL 2842)[4]		4	0	2	18	8
and Steppington Hill, Catesby (SP 5159)		3	0			

As shown in the aforesaid
declaration

COUNTY OF YORK

Rents and fixed payments from tenants
in various demesnes, that is

In Pontefract (SE 4522)	7	0	0			
Muskham (SK 7956 or SK 7957)[5]		1	4	£	s	d
				7	1	4

As shown in the aforesaid
declaration

COUNTY OF NORTHUMBERLAND

Rents and fixed payments in Harehope (NU 0920)	£	s	d
in the county therein per year	2	13	4

As in the aforesaid declaration

COUNTY OF MIDDLESEX

Rents and fixed payments from tenants
in the county therein, that is

In the parish of Saint Giles (TQ 3181)	68	12	8			
Holborn (TQ 3181)	5	8	0			
Feltham (TQ 1072)	5	8	9			
Heston (TQ 1277)	2	1	4	£	s	d
Edmonton (TQ 3493)		13	4	131	13	11
and London (TQ 3079)	49	9	10			

As shown in the aforesaid
declaration, having been made,
examined and approved

COUNTY OF ESSEX

Rents and fixed payments from tenants
in various demesnes and manors in the
county therein, that is

---

4   Cambridgeshire, not Northamptonshire.
5   Nottinghamshire, not Yorkshire. This could be North or South Muskham.

				£	s	d
In Goldenwik	14	0				
Witterys	5	4				
and Sheckwell[6]	8	0		1	7	4

As shown in the aforesaid
declaration

DEDUCTIONS ACCORDING TO THE MEANING,
FORM AND PURPOSE AS ARRANGED THAT IS

IN SPIRITUALITIES
SYNODALS AND PROCURATIONS

	£	s	d
Money payment to the archdeacon of Leicester for the synodals and procurations of Lowesby church		9	1

As shown in the aforesaid
declaration

PENSIONS

	£	s	d		£	s	d
Money payments to various persons for pensions, that is							
Gilbert Sturges, vicar of Lowesby	6	13	4				
and William, vicar of Feltham	4	0	0		10	13	4

	£	s	d
As shown in the aforesaid Declaration	11	2	5

IN TEMPORALITIES

RENTS RELEASED

Rents released to the various persons
listed below, that is

				£	s	d
Prior of Kirby Bellars for land in Little Dalby	3	0				
Aforesaid prior for land in Buckminster	5	4				
The Lord King for land in Spondon	18	6				
Pilkington, gent, for aiding matters in Locko	6	8		3	6	10
The master of Saint John of Northampton for land in the town of Northampton	13	4				
and the abbot of Westminster for land in London	1	0	0			

---

6   None of these places has been located.

As shown in the aforesaid
declaration

FEES

Fees to various persons listed below,
that is

				£	s	d
Fees to William Faunt, bailiff of Melton Mowbray		6	8			
Hugh Walker, bailiff of Cold Newton		10	0			
Aforesaid William, bailiff of Spondon		6	8			
John Langwith, bailiff of Choseley and				£	s	d
the lordship of Wymondham		6	8	9	3	8
John Taylor, bailiff of the manor of Nettleham and Ashby Puerorum with others		13	4			
Aforesaid William Faunt, bailiff of Kedington		1	0			
John Newton, bailiff of the town of Northampton		1	0			
William Kerver, bailiff of Pontefract		5	0			
John Borrowe, bailiff of Derby and certain lands and tenements in the parish of Saint Giles, near London,	2	13	4			
and Thomas Butler, receiver therein per year	4	0	0			

ALMS

Yearly money payments and the
distribution to various paupers, that is

	£	s	d		£	s	d
One pauper existing in the hospital of Burton Saint Lazarus at 3d per day	4	11	3				
from an old foundation,					£	s	d
and fourteen paupers existing in the hospital					47	2	11
of Saint Giles in the Field without the bar, London, according to the meaning and purpose of the foundation, namely	42	11	8				
to every pauper 2d per day							

	£	s	d
	59	13	5

£	s	d
70	15	10

		£	s	d
and it leaves behind clear per year		265	10	2½

	£	s	d
Thereby the tenth	26	11	0¼

Bibliography

The Bibliography is divided into four sections: manuscript sources; printed primary sources; secondary sources; and unpublished secondary sources. In the last section locations have been provided where appropriate.

Manuscript sources

Alnwick Castle, Northumberland
Archives of the Duke of Northumberland, Northumberland Collections, 23

Archives Nationales, Paris
Engraving N.III. Loiret 77
S 4841/B; S 4849; S 4866; S 4884; S 4885; S 4891; S 4892; S 4894/B

Archivio Segreto Vaticano, Rome
Register Avinioni 171

Bibliothèque Nationale, Paris
Mss Francais 203

Bodleian Library, Oxford
Ms Ch Leicester a 1
Ms Barlow 1
Ms Eng Hist a 2
Ms Top Gen C 23
Ms Top Northants C 18

Brasenose College, Oxford
Missal, *c.*1520

British Library, London
Add Chart, 19864; 33635; 37362; 41536; 44698; 47555; 53492; 53710; 63677; 66397
Add Mss, 6672; 27348
Cotton Mss, Claudius A xiii; Claudius D xi; Nero C xii; Vespasian E xxiii
Harleian Mss, 760; 1096; 2077; 3868; 4015; Charters, 43 A 13; 44 B 18, 23–37; 44 R 30–34, 36; 80 F 26
Lansdowne Mss, Charter, ccvii (e)
Seals, D.CH. 37; xxxv 169; lxvi 47, 48a, 48b; lxix 43
c18 e2 (7)
Stowe Mss, Charters, 619, 620
Wolley Mss, Charter, viii 13

British Museum, London
Rutland Catalogue

Burton Lazars Church, Leicestershire
Burton Lazars Spa near to Melton Mowbray, Leicestershire

Canterbury Cathedral Archives
Dcc, Register F

Cheshire Record Office
Shakerley collection, DSS 3991, Drawer 2/1 ex Bundle 2

College of Arms, London
L Series Ms 10
Vincent Mss, 197

Corpus Christi College, Cambridge
Ms 26

Derbyshire Record Office
Clyde Surveys Ltd, Derbyshire County Survey, 1:10,000. 6-inch 23/10/1971, 10 649/7145,
    D/2977/2/37

Fitzwilliam Museum, Cambridge, Department of Coins and Medals
Seals, Waldon 37; A Way 54.1890–01

Gloucestershire Record Office
Berkeley Castle Muniments J7/67/02/001/00/00 (MF 1354); J7/67/02/002/00/00 (MF
    1297)

Huntingdon Library, San Marino, California, USA
HM 160

Leicestershire County Council
SMR, ID M9912 (Sandy Lane, MM SK756)

Leicestershire Record Office
10D 34/123; 41/11/2; 41/12/3; 41/13/2
PR, Register I (1515–26); PR, Register II (1526–33)
5D33; 24D55
BR11/19/2
DE746/5; 2242/5; 2242/6/7
Clayton Mss, 35'29/85–229
Gretton (Sherard) Mss, DG40/12; 40/189; 40/226; 40/283; 40/481
Hartopp Mss, 8D39/1811–2194 (particularly 8D39/2064–66; 39/2179–2194)
Pochin Mss, DG27 Box 688a
Wyggeston Hospital Records, 10D34/123

Library of the Order of St John of Jerusalem, Clerkenwell, London
*Arrest de la Chambre Royale portant union a l'Ordre de Notre-Dame du Mont-Carmel et de
    S Lazare de Jerusalem* (1674)

Arrest du Grand Conseil du Roy concernant les privileges de l'Ordre de Notre-Dame de Mont-Carmel et St Lazare de Jerusalem (1716)
Edit du Roy, donne en faveur de L'Ordre de Notre-Dame du Mont-Carmel et de St Lazare de Jerusalem (1672)
Extrait des Registres du Conseil d'Etat (1738)
Ms K 5/70; K 27/7

Lichfield Joint Record Office
B/C/10; B/C/11

Lincoln City and County Museum, Lincoln
Burton Lazars Confraternity Seal

Lincolnshire Archives Office
PD 1545/42
Dii 90/2/9; Dii 90/2/10
Dalderby Memoranda
Bii 2/13

Longleat House Archives, Wiltshire
Marquis of Bath Mss, Dudley Papers, III/23; III/33; XVI

McGill University, Osler Library, Montreal
7527

Melbourne Hall, Derbyshire
Lothian Mss, Boxes, 21, 23, 24, 25, 34, 35

Norfolk Landscape Archaeology
SMR, 8923; 21554

Norfolk Record Office
Norwich Consistory Court, Will Register 1370–1383, Heydon, f. 155 (MF 22)
Rye Mss, 4

Northamptonshire Record Office
Private Charters, II 27

Northumberland County Council
SMR, ID 3618

Nottinghamshire Archives Office
DDP/CD 28

Österreichischen Staatsarchivs, Vienna
Smitmer-Löschner Collection (seal of James de Besnes)

Public Record Office, Kew, London
C 1/45/33; 1/750/15; 1/808/24; 1/986/6; 1/1022/40; 1/1094/24–26; 1/1288/115–116, 117
C 49/2/23
C 54/182; 54/408C 66/666;C 78/1/1; 78/3/108C 81/616/3376; 81/616/3377

C 82/706

C 143/89/5; 143/318/13; 143/343/7; 143/346/14; 143/356/18; 143/385/8; 143/398/8; 143/399/10

C 270/26/17; 270/32/5

CP 25/1/36/9; 25/1/37/18; 25/1/121/6; 25/1/121/9; 25/1/122/22

CP 40/5; 40/17; 40/39; 40/76; 40/82; 40/247; 40/271; 40/308; 40/342; 40/489; 40/574; 40/626; 40/629; 40/663; 40/675; 40/759; 40/839; 40/882; 40/890; 40/1000; 40/1011; 40/1050; 40/1094

DL 27/121

E 40/11147

E 118/1/62

E 134/27 and 28 Eliz 1/Mich 26; 134/31 Eliz 1/East 6; 134/37 Eliz 1/Trin 10; 134/37 and 38 Eliz 1/Mich 54; 134/42 Eliz 1/Hil 17; 134/3 Chas 1/Mich 11; 134/24 Chas 2/Trin 8; 134/1655/East 21

E 135/21/72, 135/21/73, 135/22/37

E 159/109

E 179/133/34

E 210/1108; 210/1192; 210/3453

E 315/35; 315/38; 315/39; 315/42; 315/47

E 321/43/162

E 326/2388; 326/4417; 326/5712; 326/6015; 326/6759; 326/7229; 326/8075; 326/8796(1); 326/8796(2); 326/9030; 326/9303; 326/10554; 326/10661; 326/11965; 326/12063; 326/12431; 326/12432; 326/12433; 326/12434; 326/12435; 326/12602; 326/12754; 326/12927

E 327/50; 327/53

E 328/154; 328/328

E 329/334

E 344/19/5

E 359/3; 359/14

E 371/601

E 372/151

E 377/50

E 403/45

JUST 1/460; 1/462; 1/633; 1/948; 1/1279

KB 26/154

KB 27/33, 27/114; 27/118; 27/129; 27/189; 27/416

LR 2/87; 2/182

PROB 11/2B; 11/21; 11/30

SC 6/Hen VIII/2006

SC 8/3/110; 8/3/113; 8/49/2448; 8/54/2654; 8/57/2818; 8/97/4812; 8/97/4831; 8/114/5671; 8/155/7723; 8/163/8103; 8/190/9458; 8/198/9870; 8/202/10055; 8/210/10456; 8/210/10457; 8/219/10908; 8/226/11267; 8/266/13294; 8/302/15081; 8/318/E321; 8/318/E322; 8/324/E617A; 8/324/E617B; 8/325/E677

SC 9/2

SP 1/91; 1/116; 1/124; 1/127; 1/145

SP 6/4

STAC 2/19/295; 2/19/327; 2/19/340; 2/24/122; 2/26/429; 2/28/9B

Shropshire Records and Research Service
6000/2623

Staffordshire Record Office
Sutherland Collection, D 593/A/1/32/1; D593/A/1/33/2; D593/A/1/32/14; D593/A/1/132/15

University of Nottingham, Centre for Local History
Letter from Canon F.R. Money to Revd P.E. Hunt, 23 July 1965
Letter from R.A. Monkhouse, British Geological Survey, to J.M. Allsop, 8 December 1986

University of Nottingham, Manuscripts Department
Drury-Lowe Manuscripts, Dr D 33; 33/1; 33/2; 33/3; 33/4; 38/2; 39/4; 58
Dr E 1/2
Dr S 4; 4a; 5
Dr P 5; 68; 81; 82; 85; 86; 87
Middleton Mss, MiF 1/6

Westminster Abbey Muniment Room and Library
6660

Printed primary sources

A. Adams (ed.), *Cheshire Visitation Pedigrees, 1663*, HS, 93 (1941)

S. Armitage-Smith (ed.), *John of Gaunt's Register*, 1, 2, CS, 3rd series, 20, 21 (1911)

G.J. Armytage and J.P. Rylands (eds), *The Visitation of Cheshire, 1613*, HS, 59 (1909)

L. Auvray (ed.), *Les Registres de Grégoire IX*, 1, BÉFAR, series 2 (Paris, 1896)

S. Ayscough and J. Caley (eds), *Taxatio Ecclesiastica Angliae et Walliae, auctoritate Nicholai IV, 1291* (London, 1802)

J. Bain (ed.), *Calendar of Documents relating to Scotland*, 1 (Edinburgh, 1881)

J.H. Baker (ed.), *The Notebook of Sir John Port*, SS, 102 (1986)

B. Bandinel, *Collectanea Topographica et Geneologica*, 1 (London, 1834)

A.T. Bannister (ed.), Hereford Diocese, *Register of Thomas Myllyng*, CYS, 26 (1920)

——— (ed.), Hereford Diocese, *Register of Richard Mayew*, CYS, 27 (1921)

——— (ed.), Hereford Diocese, *Registers of Bothe, Foxe and Boner*, CYS, 28 (1921)

R. Barber (ed.), *Fuller's Worthies. Selected from* The Worthies of England *by Thomas Fuller* (London, 1987)

G.W.S. Barrow (ed.), *Regesta Regum Scottorum*, 2 (Edinburgh, 1971)

M. Bateson (ed.), *Records of the Borough of Leicester, 1327–1509*, 2 (London, 1901)

W. Beaumont, 'Original Documents', *Archaeological Journal*, 24 (1867)

N. Bennett (ed.), *The Registers of Bishop Henry Berghersh, 1320–1342*, 1, LRS, 87 (1999)

E. Berger (ed.), *Les Registres d'Innocent IV*, 1, BÉFAR, series 2 (Paris, 1884)

V.G. Berry (ed.), *Odo de Deuil, De Profectione Ludovici VII in orientem* (New York, 1948)

A.A. Beugnot (ed.), Assises de la Haute Cour, *Recueil des Historiens des Croisades, Lois*, 1 (Paris, 1841)

——— (ed.), Assises de la Cour de Bourgeois, *Recueil des Historiens des Croisades, Lois*, 2 (Paris, 1843)

W. de G. Birch, *Catalogue of Seals in the Department of Manuscripts in the British Museum*, 6 vols (London, 1887–1900)

Black Prince's Register, 3, 1351–65 (London, 1932)

T. Blount, *A Law Dictionary and Glossary* (London, 1717)

The Book of Fees (Testa de Nevill), 1198–1242; 1242–93 (London, 1920–31)

C. Bourel, J. de Loye, P. de Cenival, A. Coulon (eds), *Les Registres d'Alexandre IV*, 1, 2, BÉFAR, series 2 (Paris, 1902)

T. Bourne and D. Marcombe, *The Burton Lazars Cartulary: a Medieval Leicestershire Estate*, UNCLH, Record Series, 6 (Nottingham, 1987)

D.S. Boutflower, *Fasti Dunelmensis*, SurS, 139 (1926)

M. Bowker (ed.), *An Episcopal Court Book, 1514–1520*, LRS, 61 (1967)

W. Brown (ed.), *Register of Walter Giffard*, SurS, 109 (1904)

H.F. Burke, 'Some Cheshire Deeds', *The Ancestor*, 2, 6 (July 1902, July 1903)

Calendar of Chancery Rolls, 1277–1326 (London, 1912)

Calendar of Charter Rolls, 1226–57; 1327–41; 1341–1417 (London, 1903–16)

Calendar of Close Rolls, 1272–79; 1279–88; 1288–96; 1296–1302; 1302–07; 1307–13; 1313–18; 1318–23; 1327–30; 1330–33; 1333–37; 1337–39; 1339–41; 1343–46; 1346–49; 1354–60; 1369–74; 1381–85; 1385–89; 1389–92; 1392–96; 1399–1402; 1402–05; 1413–19; 1419–22; 1422–29; 1435–41; 1441–47; 1447–54; 1454–61; 1468–76; 1476–85 (London, 1892–1954)

Calendar of Fine Rolls, 1272–1307; 1347–56; 1356–68; 1377–83; 1383–91; 1391–99; 1413–22; 1430–37; 1452–61 (London, 1911–39)

Calendar of Inquisitions, 3, 4, 6, 9, 11, 12, 15, 16 (1910–1974); *Henry VII, 1, 3* (1898–1955); *Misc 1, 1219–1307* (London, 1916)

Calendar of Liberate Rolls, 1226–40; 1240–45; 1245–51; 1251–60; 1260–67; 1267–72 (London, 1916–64)

Calendar of Papal Registers, Petitions 1, 1342–1419. Letters 1, 1198–1304; 4, 1362–1404; 5, 1396–1404; 6, 1404–1415; 7, 1417–31; 8, 1427–47; 10, 1447–55; 11, 1455–64; 13, pt 1, pt 2, 1471–84; 15, 1484–1492 (London, 1893–1978)

Calendar of Patent Rolls, 1216–25; 1225–32; 1232–47; 1247–58; 1258–66; 1266–72; 1272–81; 1281–92; 1292–1301; 1301–07; 1307–13; 1313–17; 1317–21; 1321–24; 1324–27; 1327–30; 1330–34; 1334–38; 1343–45; 1345–48; 1348–50; 1350–54; 1354–58; 1361–64; 1364–67; 1367–70; 1370–74; 1377–81; 1381–85; 1385–1389; 1388–92; 1391–96; 1396–99; 1399–1401; 1401–05; 1408–13; 1413–16; 1416–22; 1422–29; 1429–36; 1436–41; 1441–46; 1446–52; 1452–61; 1461–67; 1467–77; 1476–85; 1485–94; 1494–1509; 1549–51; 1550–53; 1553; 1553–54; 1554–55; 1555–57; 1557–58; 1558–60; 1560–63; 1563–66; 1566–69; 1569–72; 1572–75; 1575–78 (London, 1891–1982)

Calendar of Plea and Memoranda Rolls of the City of London, 1323–64; 1381–1412; 1413–1437 (Cambridge, 1926–43)

Calendar of State Papers, Ireland, 1509–73 (London, 1860)

J. Caley and J. Hunter (eds), *Valor Ecclesiasticus, 1535*, 1, 3, 4 (London, 1810–21)

H.M. Cam (ed.), *Eyre of London, 14 Edward II*, SS, 86 (1969)

W. Campbell (ed.), *Materials for a History of the Reign of Henry VII*, 2, Rolls Series, 60 (London, 1877)

L. Campbell and F. Steer, *A Catalogue of Manuscripts in the College of Arms Collections*, 1 (London, 1988)

M. de Capella (ed.), Gilbertus Anglicus, *Compendium Medicinae* (Lugdunum, 1510)

D.S. Chambers, *Faculty Office Registers* (Oxford, 1966)

Chancery Decree Rolls, 36 Henry VIII – 5 and 6 Philip and Mary, List and Index, List and Index Society, PRO Lists and Indexes, 160 (London, 1979)

Chancery Miscellaneous, 2, Bundles 15–21, List and Index Society, PRO Lists and Indexes, 15 (London, 1966)

G. Chaucer, *The Canterbury Tales*, translated into modern English by N. Coghill (1951, reprinted Harmondsworth, 1972)

C.R. Cheney and M.G. Cheney, *The Letters of Innocent III (1198–1216) concerning England and Wales* (Oxford, 1967)

H.M. Chew (ed.), *London Possessory Assizes. A Calendar*, LonRS, 1 (1965)

G.A. Chinnery (ed.), *The Oakham Survey, 1305*, Rutland Record Society (1988)

A. Clarke and F. Holbrooke (eds), T. Rymer's *Foedera*, 1, pt 1 (London, 1816)

Class List of Records of the Exchequer, Lord Treasurer's Remembrancer, List and Index Society, PRO Lists and Indexes, 82, (London, 1972)

Close Rolls, 1231–32; 1234–37; 1237–42; 1242–47; 1247–51; 1251–53; 1254–56; 1256–59; 1261–64; 1268–72 (London, 1905–38)

C. Cocquelines (ed.), *Bullarium Privilegiorum et Diplomatum Romanorum Pontificum Amplissimus Collectio*, 3 pt 1 (Rome, 1740)

Codice Diplomatico Barese, 8 (Bari, 1914)

Codice Diplomatico Pugliese, 21 (Bari, 1976)

R.E.G. Cole (ed.), *Chapter Acts of the Cathedral Church of St Mary of Lincoln, 1520–1536*, LRS, 12 (1915)

—— (ed.), *Chapter Acts of the Cathedral Church of St Mary of Lincoln, 1536–1547*, LRS, 13 (1917)

J. Cornwall (ed.), *The County Community under Henry VIII*, Rutland Record Society (1980)

J.M. Cowper (ed.), *Henry Brinklow's Complaynt of Roderyck Mors*, EETS, extra series, 22 (1874)

J.C. Cox, *The Records of the Borough of Northampton*, 2 (Northampton, 1898)

——, 'A Budget from Repton', *JDANHS*, 36 (1914)

—— (ed.), 'Calendar of Fines for the County of Derby', *JDANHS*, 13 (1891)

A. Crawford, *The Household Books of John Howard, Duke of Norfolk,1462–1471, 1481–1483* (Stroud, 1993)

Culpeper's Complete Herbal (Ware, 1995)

Curia Regis Rolls,1, 1196–1201; 2, 1201–03; 3, 1203–05; 7, 1213–15; 8, 1219–20; 9, 1220; 11, 1223–24; 12, 1225–26; 13, 1227–30; 14, 1230–32; 15, 1233–37 (London, 1922–72)

H. de Curzon (ed.), *Le Règle du Temple*, Société de l'Histoire de France (Paris, 1886)

I. Darlington (ed.), *London Consistory Court Wills, 1492–1547*, LonRS, 3 (1967)

R.R. Darlington (ed.), *Darley Cartulary*, 1 (Kendal, 1945)

J.S. Davies (ed.), *An English Chronicle of the Reigns of Richard II, Henry IV, Henry V and Henry VI*, CS, 64 (1856)

F.N. Davis (ed.), Lincoln Diocese, *Register of Richard Gravesend*, CYS, 31 (1925)

—— (ed.), *Rotuli Hugonis de Welles*, 3, LRS, 9 (1914)

—— (ed.), *Rotuli Roberti Grosseteste*, LRS, 11 (1914)

—— (ed.), *Rotuli Ricardi Gravesend*, LRS, 20 (1925)

G.R.C. Davis, *Medieval Cartularies of Great Britain – a short catalogue* (London, 1958)

H.F. Delaborde, *Chartres de Terre Sainte Provenant de l'Abbaye de Notre-Dame de Josaphat* (Paris, 1880)

Descriptive Catalogue of Ancient Deeds, 2, 3, 4, 5, 6 (London, 1894–1915)

F. Devon (ed.), *Issues of the Exchequer, Henry III–Henry VI* (London, 1837)

J.F. Dimock (ed.), *Magna Vita S. Hugonis Episcopi Lincolniensis* (London, 1864)

D.L. Douie and D.H. Farmer (eds), *Magna Vita Sancti Hugonis. The Life of St Hugh of Lincoln*, 2 vols (Edinburgh, 1961–62)

C.W. Dutschke, *Guide to Medieval and Renaissance Manuscripts in the Huntington Library*, 1 (San Marino, California, 1989)

An Edition of the Cartulary of Burscough Priory, Chetham Society, 3rd Series, 18 (1970)

R.H. Ellis, *Catalogue of Seals in the Public Record Office, Monastic Seals*, 1 (London, 1986)

B. English (ed.), *Yorkshire Hundred and Quo Warranto Rolls*, YAS, Record Series, 151 (1993 and 1994)

Exchequer Augmentation Office, Calendar of Ancient Deeds, Series B, pts 1, 2 ,3, 4, List and Index Society, PRO Lists and Indexes, 95, 101,113, 124 (London, 1973–76)

Exchequer, Augmentation Office, Ancient Deeds, Series BB, Calendar and Index, List and Index Society, PRO Lists and Indexes, 137 (London, 1977)

Exchequer KR Ecclesiastical Documents, List and Index Society, PRO Lists and Indexes, 2 (London, 1965)

R.W. Eyton, *Court, Household and Itinerary of King Henry II* (London, 1878)

C.E. Fenwick (ed.), *The Poll Taxes of 1377, 1379 and 1381, pt 1, Bedfordshire-Lincolnshire*, Records of Social and Economic History, new series, 27 (Oxford, 1998)

J. Fetherston (ed.), *The Visitation of the County of Leicester in the year 1619*, HS, 2 (1870)

Feudal Aids, 1284–1431, 1, 3, 5, 6 (London, 1899–1920)

R. Filangieri (ed.), *I Regestri della Cancellaria Angioina*, 2, 7, 8, 9 (Naples, 1951–58)

C.T. Flower (ed.), *Public Works in Mediaeval Law*, 2, SS, 40 (1923)

Fontes Rerum Bernensium, 3 (Bern, 1880)

C.W. Foster (ed.), *Lincoln Wills*, 2, LRS, 10 (1918)

———— (ed.), *Final Concords of the County of Lincoln*, 2, LRS, 17 (1920)

———— (ed.), *Registrum Antiquissimum*, 3, LRS, 29 (1935)

———— (ed.), London Diocese, *Register of Ralph Baldock*, CYS, 7 (1911)

———— (ed.), London Diocese, *Register of Simon of Sudbury*, 1, CYS, 34 (1927)

T. Foulds, *The Thurgarton Cartulary* (Stamford, 1994)

S. Franco *et al.* (eds), *Bullarium Diplomatum et Privilegiorum Sanctorum Romanorum Pontificum Taurinensis Editio*, 3 (Turin, 1858)

G. Frisk (ed.), *A Middle English Translation of Macer Floridus de Viribus Herbarum* (Uppsala, 1949)

F.J. Furnivall (ed.), *Simon Fish, A Supplicacyon for the Beggers*, EETS, extra series, 13 (1871)

C. Garton (ed.), *The Metrical Life of St Hugh of Lincoln* (Lincoln, 1986)

Gascon Rolls, 1307–17 (London, 1962)

M. Gervers (ed.), *The Cartulary of the Knights of St John of Jerusalem in England: prima and secunda camera, Essex*, Records of Social and Economic History, new series, 6, 23 (Oxford, 1982, 1986)

C. Glover and P. Riden (eds), W. Wooley's *History of Derbyshire*, Derbyshire Record Society, 6 (1981)

H. Gough (ed.), *Itinerary of King Edward I, throughout his reign, AD 1272–1307*, 2 (Paisley, 1900)

J. Guiraud (ed.), *Les Registres d'Urbain IV*, 2, BÉFAR, series 2 (Paris, 1901)

Handlist of Records of Leicester Archdeaconry, Leicester Museum and Art Gallery, Department of Archives (Leicester, 1954)

T.D. Hardy, 'Itinarium Johannis Regis Anglicie', *Archaeologia*, 22 pt 1 (1828)

———— (ed.), *Rotuli Chartarum*, 1 pt 1, 1199–1216 (London, 1837)

———— (ed.), *Syllabus in English of the documents relating to England and other kingdoms contained in the collection known as 'Rymers Foedera'*, 3 vols (London, 1869–85)

J. Harley, F.M. Stenton and F. Bickley (eds), *Hastings Mss*, 1, HMC (London, 1928)

C. Harper-Bill (ed.), *Register of John Morton*, 2, CYS, 78 (1991)

H. Harrod, 'Extracts from early Norfolk wills', *Norfolk Archaeology*, 1 (1847)

————, *Report on the Deeds and Records of the Borough of Kings Lynn* (Kings Lynn,1874)

W.H. Hart, 'Calendar of the Fines for the County of Derby', *JDANHS*, 8,13 (1886–91)

M. Hayez and A.-M. Hayez (eds), *Lettres Communes des Papes du XIV siècle: Urbain V (1362–1370)*, 9, BÉFAR, series 3 (Rome, 1983)

R.M.T. Hill (ed.), *Rolls and Registers of Bishop Oliver Sutton*, 1, LRS, 39 (1948)

———— (ed.), *Rolls and Registers of Bishop Oliver Sutton*, 2, LRS, 43 (1950)

—— (ed.), *Rolls and Registers of Bishop Oliver Sutton*, 4, LRS, 52 (1958)

—— (ed.), *Rolls and Registers of Bishop Oliver Sutton*, 5, LRS, 60 (1965)

—— (ed.), *Rolls and Registers of Bishop Oliver Sutton*, 6, LRS, 64 (1969)

—— (ed.), *Rolls and Registers of Bishop Oliver Sutton*, 7, LRS, 69 (1975)

—— (ed.), *Rolls and Registers of Bishop Oliver Sutton*, 8, LRS, 76 (1986)

G.A.J. Hodgett, *The State of the Ex-Religious and former Chantry Priests in the Diocese of Lincoln, 1547–1574*, LRS, 53 (1959)

R. Holmes (ed.), *The Chartulary of St John of Pontefract* 1, 2, Yorkshire Archaeological Society, Record Series, 25, 30 (1899–1902)

J.M. Horn (ed.), John Le Neve, *Fasti Ecclesiae Anglicanae, 1300–1541*, 5, *St Paul's London* (London, 1963)

M.P. Howden (ed.), *The Register of Richard Fox, 1494–1507*, SurS, 147 (1932)

W. Hudson (ed.), 'The Norwich Taxation of 1254', *Norfolk Archaeology*, 17 (1910)

—— and J.C. Tingey (eds), *A Revised Catalogue of the Records of the City of Norwich* (Norwich, 1898)

J. Hunter (ed.), *Great Rolls of the Pipe, AD 1155–1158* (London, 1844)

W. Illingworth and J. Caley (eds), *Rotuli Hundredorum*, 2 vols, Record Commission (London, 1812–18)

—— (eds), *Placita de Quo Waranto* (London, 1818)

Index Library, *PCC Wills*, 2, *1383–1558*; 3, *1558–83*; 4, *1584–1604*; 5, *1605–19*; 6, *1620–29*; 7,*1653–56*; 8, *1657–60*; 9, *1671–75. Leicestershire Wills, 1495–1649*; *1660–1750. Lincoln Wills, 1601–52* (London, 1895–1942)

Index of Ancient Petitions of the Chancery and the Exchequer, PRO Lists and Indexes 1 (London, 1892, reprinted New York, 1966)

Index of Manuscripts in the British Library, 2, 5 (Cambridge, 1984–5)

Inquisitions Ad Quod Damnum, pts 1 and 2, PRO Lists and Indexes, 17, 22 (1904, reprinted New York, 1963)

Institute of Geological Sciences, 1976 (First surveyed 1906), Melton Mowbray Sheet 142, Drift Edition. 1:50,000. Ordnance Survey, Southampton

Itinerary of Edward I, pt 2, *1291–1307*, List and Index Society, 132 (1976)

I.H. Jeayes (ed.), *Descriptive Catalogue of the Charters and Muniments in the possession of the Rt Hon Lord Fitz-Hardinge at Berkeley Castle* (Bristol, 1892)

——, *Descriptive Catalogue of Derbyshire Charters* (London and Derby, 1906)

B. Jones (ed.), John Le Neve, *Fasti Ecclesiae Anglicanae, 1300–1541*, 6, *Northern Province* (London, 1963)

—— (ed.), John Le Neve, *Fasti Ecclesiae Anglicanae, 1300–1541*, 8, *Bath and Wells Diocese* (London, 1964)

—— (ed.), John Le Neve, *Fasti Ecclesiae Anglicanae, 1300–1541*, 10, *Coventry and Lichfield Diocese* (London, 1964)

—— (ed.), *Index to Records called the Originali and Memoranda*, 2 (London, 1795)

M. Jordan (ed.), *Les Registres de Clement IV*, 1, BÉFAR, series 2 (Paris, 1893)

B.Z. Kedar (ed.), Gerard of Nazareth, *De Conversatione Servatorum Dei*, in 'Gerard of Nazareth. A Neglected Twelfth-Century Writer in the Latin East', *Dumbarton Oaks Papers*, 37 (1983)

E.J. King, *The Early Statutes of the Knights Hospitallers* (London, 1932)

——, *The Thirteenth Century Statutes of the Knights Hospitallers* (London, 1933)

H.P.F. King (ed.), John Le Neve, *Fasti Ecclesiae Anglicanae, 1300–1541*, 1, *Lincoln Diocese* (London, 1962)

C.J. Kitching (ed.), *London and Middlesex Chantry Certificate, 1548*, LonRS, 16 (1980)

L.B. Larking (ed.), *The Knights Hospitallers in England*, CS, 65 (1857)

I.S. Leadam, 'The Inquisition of 1517, Inclosures and Evictions', 2, *TRHS*, new series, 7 (1893)

A.-M. Legras, *L'Enquéte Pontificale de 1373 sur L'Ordre Des Hospitaliers de Saint-Jean de Jérusalem*, 1 (Paris, 1987)

J. Leland, *De Rebus Britannicis Collectanea*, 1 (London, 1774)

Letters and Papers Foreign and Domestic of Henry VIII, 1 pt 1, 1509–13; 1 pt 2, 1513–14; 3 pt 2, 1519–1523; 4 pt 1, 1524–26; 4 pt 2, 1526–28; 4 pt 3, 1529–30; 8, 1535; 10, 1536; 11, 1536; 12 pt 1, 1537; 12 pt 2, 1537; 14 pt 1, 1539; 19 pt 1, 1544; 20 pt 1, 1545; 20 pt 2, 1545; 21 pt 1, 1546; Addenda 1 pt 1, 1509–1537; 1 pt 2, 1538–1547 (London, 1870–1932)

List of Early Chancery Proceedings, 2, 6, 7, 8, PRO Lists and Indexes, 16, 48, 50, 51 (London, 1903–29)

H.R. Luard, *Annales Monastici*, 5 vols, Rolls Series, 36 (London, 1864–9)

—— (ed.), 'Matthaei Parisiensis', *Chronica Majora*, 5, Rolls Series, 57 (London, 1880)

A. Luders *et al.* (eds), *Statutes of the Realm*, 3 pt 2, 27–37 Henry VIII (London, 1817)

J.R. Lumby, *Chronicon Henrici Knighton*, 1, Rolls Series, 92 (London, 1889)

W.E. Lunt and E.B. Graves, *Accounts Rendered by Papal Collectors in England, 1317–78* (Philadelphia, 1968)

A.K. McHardy (ed.), *Clerical Poll-Taxes of the Diocese of Lincoln, 1377–1381*, LRS, 81 (1992)

—— (ed.), *The Church in London, 1375–1392*, LonRS, 13 (1977)

W.D. Macray *et al.* (eds), *Various Collections*, 2, HMC (London, 1903)

F. Madan, H. Crasser and N.D. Young, *A Summary Catalogue of Western Manuscripts in the Bodleian Library at Oxford*, 2, 5, 6 (Oxford, 1905–37)

T. Madox, *Formulare Anglicanum* (London, 1702)

K. Major, *A Handlist of the Records of the Bishop of Lincoln and the Archdeacons of Lincoln and Stow* (London, 1953)

—— (ed.), *Registrum Antiquissimum*, 7, LRS, 46 (1953)

—— (ed.), *Registrum Antiquissimum*, 8, LRS, 51 (1958)

—— (ed.), *Registrum Antiquissimum*, 9, LRS, 62 (1968)

'A Map drawn in 1585 to illustrate a lawsuit concerning Geldings Close', *London Topographical Society, Publication* 54 (1825)

P. Marchegay, *Cartulaires du Bas-Poitou* (Les Roches-Barituad, 1877)

A. de Marsy (ed.), 'Fragment d'un Cartulaire de l'Ordre de Saint Lazare en Terre Sainte', in *Archives de L'Orient Latin*, 2 (Paris, 1884, reprinted New York, 1978)

M.T. Martin (ed.), *The Percy Chartulary*, SurS, 117 (1909)

H. Maxwell, *The Chronicle of Lanercost, 1272–1346* (Glasgow, 1913)

Memoires, Regles et Statuts, Ceremonies et Privileges des Ordres Militaires de Nostre Dame du Mont-Carmel et de S. Lazare de Ierusalem (Lyons, 1649). Reprinted by Les Éditions du Prieuré as *Ordre Militaire de Notre-Dame et de Saint-Lazare: mémoires, statuts, rituels, 1649* (Rouvray, 1992)

H.V. Michelant and G. Raynaud, *Itinéraires à Jerusalem*, Société de l'Histoire de France (Paris, 1882)

C. Moor (ed.), *Knights of Edward I*, 4, HS, 83 (1931)

A.P. Moore (ed.), 'The Metropolitical Visitation of Archdeacon Laud', Leicestershire Architectural and Archaeological Society, *AASRP*, 29 pt 1 (1907–8)

P. Morgan (ed.), *Domesday Book. No. 22, Leicestershire* (Chichester, 1979)

A.S. Napier and W.H. Stevenson, *The Crawford Collection of Early Charters and Documents now in the Bodleian Library* (Anecdota Oxoniensa, pt 7) (Oxford, 1895)

R. Nares *et al.*, *A Catalogue of the Harleian Manuscripts in the British Museum*, 3 (London, 1808)

J. Nasmith (ed.), T. Tanner, *Notitia Monastica* (Cambridge, 1787)

M.S. Ogden (ed.), *The Cyrurgie of Guy de Chauliac*, EETS, 265 (1971)

Ordnance Survey

County Series Sheet XX NW, Leicestershire, 1:10,560

2nd edition, 1904 (surveyed 1883/4, revised 1902), reprint 100/06, Provisional edition 1947 (relevelled 1928)

County Series Sheet XX NE, Leicestershire, 1:10,560

Edition of 1931 (surveyed 1883/4, revised 1928, relevelled 1929), reprint 150/41

County Series Sheet XX SW, Leicestershire, 1:10,560

1st edition, 1890 (surveyed 1883), reprint 50/99

2nd edition, 1904 (revised 1902), reprint 100/29

Provisional edition, 1947 (relevelled 1929)

County Series Sheet XX SE, Leicestershire, 1:10,560

Edition of 1931 (surveyed 1883/4, revised 1928, relevelled 1929), reprint 150/41

County Series Sheet XXVII NW, Leicestershire, 1:10,560

2nd edition, 1904 (surveyed 1883, revised 1902), reprints 50/13 & 150/41

County Series sheet XXVII NE, Leicestershire, 1:10,560

2nd edition, 1904 (surveyed 1883, revised 1902), reprints 50/09 & 150/41

Sheet 7718, 1:2,500, 1972

Sheet SK 71 NE, 1:10,000, 1978

Sheet SK 71 (Melton Mowbray), 1:25,000, 1st series, 1959

Sheet SK 61/71 (Rearsby and Melton Mowbray), 1:25,000, Pathfinder series, 1981

Sheet SK 72 (Scalford), 1:25,000, 1st series, 1959

Sheet SK 62/72 (Scalford and Nether Broughton), 1:25,000, Pathfinder series, 1981

G.D. Owen (ed.), *Marquess of Bath Mss*, 5 (Talbot, Dudley and Devereux Papers, 1533–1659), HMC (London, 1980)

F. Palgrave (ed.), *Rotuli Curia Regis*, 1, 2 (London, 1835)

W.P.W. Phillimore (ed.), *Rotuli Hugonis de Welles*, 1, LRS, 3 (1912)

———— (ed.), *Rotuli Hugonis de Welles*, 2, LRS, 6 (1913)

Pipe Roll Society, old series, 38 vols (London, 1884–1925)

Pipe Roll Society, new series, 1 (1190); 2 (1191–2); 3 (1193);13 (Itinerary of Richard I, 1189–1199); 16 (1203); 24 (1209); 26 (1210); 29 (Feet of Fines, Lincoln, 1199–1216); 44 (Roll of Divers Accounts, 1219–34) (London, 1925–1982)

A. Potthast (ed.), *Regesta Pontificum Romanorum*, 2 vols (Berolini, 1873–75)

Proceedings in the Court of Star Chamber, 1, AD 1485–1558, PRO Lists and Indexes, 13 (London, 1901)

Proceedings in the Court of Star Chamber, 1, AD 1485–1558, Indexes to Lists and Indexes, no. 13, PRO Lists and Indexes, supplementary series, 4 (New York, 1966)

E.K. Purnell (ed.), *Pepys Mss*, HMC (London, 1911)

J. Raine (ed.), *Testamenta Eboracensia*, 1, SurS, 4 (1836)

———— (ed.), *The Priory of Coldingham*, SurS, 12 (1841)

4th Report, pt 1, HMC (London, 1874)

S. de Ricci and W.J. Wilson, *Census of Medieval and Renaissance Manuscripts in the United States and Canada*, 2 (New York, 1937)

H.G. Richardson and G. Sayles (eds), *Rotuli Parliamentorum Anglie Hactenus Inediti MCCLXXIX–MCCCLXXIII*, CS, 3rd series, 51 (1935)

H.T. Riley (ed.), Gesta Abbatum Monasterii Sancti Albani, 1, *Chronico Monasterii S. Albani*, Rolls Series, 28 (1867)

Rotuli Parliamentorum, 6 vols (London, 1767–77)

J.D. Le Roulx, *Cartulaire Général des Hospitaliers de Saint-Jean de Jérusalem, 1100–1310*, 3 (Paris, 1899)

J.H. Round (ed.), *Rutland Mss*, 4, HMC (London, 1905)

E. and P. Rutledge, 'Kings Lynn and Great Yarmouth. Two Thirteenth-Century Surveys', *Norfolk Archaeology*, 37 pt 1 (1978)

G. Ryan and H. Ripperger (eds), *The Golden Legend of Jacobus de Voragine* (New York, 1969)

J.P. Rylands (ed.), *The Visitation of Cheshire in the year 1580*, HS, 18 (1882)

T. Rymer (ed.), *Foedera*, 10, 11 (London, 1710)

H. Salter (ed.), *A Subsidy Collected in the Diocese of Lincoln in 1526*, Oxford Historical Society, 58 (1909)

A. Saltman (ed.), *The Cartulary of Tutbury Priory*, HMC (1965)

E. Sauer, *Der Lazariter-Orden und das Statutenbuch von Seedorf* (Freiburg, 1930)

J.E. Sayers, *Original Papal Documents in England and Wales from the Accession of Pope Innocent III to the Death of Pope Benedict XI (1198–1304)* (Oxford, 1999)

G. Scalia (ed.), Salimbene de Adam, *Cronica*, 1 (Bari, 1966)

M. Secousse, *Ordonnances des Roys de France*, 3 (Paris, 1782)

R.R. Sharpe (ed.), *Calendar of Letter Books of the City of London, C; G; H; I; K; L* (London, 1901–12)

L.T. Smith (ed.), *Leland's Itinerary in England, 1535–43*, 4 (London, 1909)

T. Stapleton (ed.), *De Antiquis Legibus Liber: Chronica Maiorum et Vicecomitium Londoniorum*, CS, 34 (1846)

D.M. Stenton (ed.), *Rolls of the Justices in Eyre*, SS, 59 (1940)

W.H. Stevenson (ed.), *Middleton Mss*, HMC (London, 1911)

R.L. Storey (ed.), 'Clergy and Common Law in the Reign of Henry IV', in R.F. Hunnisett and J.B. Post (eds), *Medieval Legal Records* (London, 1978)

J. Stow, *A Survey of London* (London, 1598)

H. le Strange, *Norfolk Official Lists* (Norwich, 1890)

J. Strype (ed.), J. Stow, *A Survey of the Cities of London and Westminster*, 2 (London, 1755)

D.W. Sutherland (ed.), *Eyre of Northamptonshire, 3–4 Edward III*, SS, 98 (1983)

J. Tait (ed.), *Cartulary or Register of the Abbey of St Werburgh, Chester*, Chetham Society, new series 79 (1920)

J. Tanner (ed.), T. Tanner, *Notitia Monastica* (London, 1744)

A.H. Thomas (ed.), *Calendar of Early Mayors' Court Rolls of the City of London, 1298–1307* (Cambridge, 1924)

———— (ed.), *Calendar of Plea and Memoranda Rolls of the City of London, AD 1413–1437* (Cambridge, 1953)

———— (ed.), *Calendar of Select Pleas and Memoranda of the City of London, AD 1381–1412* (Cambridge, 1932)

———— (ed.), *Visitations of Religious Houses*, 1, LRS, 7 (1914)

———— (ed.), *Northumberland Pleas, 1198–1272*, Newcastle-upon-Tyne Records Committee, 2 (1922)

———— (ed.), *Visitations in the Diocese of Lincoln, 1517–1531*, 1, LRS, 33 (1940)

———— (ed.), *A Calendar of the Charters and other Documents belonging to the Hospital of William Wyggeston at Leicester* (Leicester, 1933)

J.M. Thomson (ed.), *Registrum Magni Sigilli Regum Scottorum, 1306–1424* (Edinburgh, 1912)

A.B. Tonnochy, *Catalogue of British Seal-Dies in the British Museum* (London, 1952)

J. Trevisa (ed.), *On the Properties of Things*, translation of Bartholomaeus Anglicus, De Proprietatibus Rerum, 1 (Oxford, 1975)

W.H. Turner (ed.), *Calendar of Charters and Rolls Preserved in the Bodleian Library* (Oxford, 1878)

F.W. Weaver (ed.), *Somerset Medieval Wills, 1531–1558,* Somerset Record Society, 21 (1905)

J.D. Welding, *Leicestershire in 1777: an edition of John Prior's map of Leicestershire* (Leicester, 1984)

J. Wilkinson, J. Hill and W.F. Ryan (eds), *Jerusalem Pilgrimage, 1099–1185,* Hakluyt Society, 167 (London, 1988)

M. Woodward (ed.), *Gerard's Herbal* (London, 1994)

Secondary sources

E.A. Abbott, *St Thomas of Canterbury,* 1 (London, 1898)

F.A. Aberg, *Medieval Moated Sites,* Council for British Archaeology, Research Report, 17 (London, 1978)

I.H. Adams, *Agrarian Landscape Terms: a glossary for historical geography* (London, 1976)

E. Acheson, A Gentry Community. *Leicestershire in the Fifteenth Century, c.1422–c.1485* (Cambridge)

J.G. Andersen, *Studies in the Medieval Diagnosis of Leprosy in Denmark* (Copenhagen, 1969)

G.J. Armytage (ed.), *Middlesex Pedigrees,* HS, 65 (1914)

I. Arthurson, *The Perkin Warbeck Conspiracy, 1491–1499* (Stroud, 1997)

N. Ashton, *Leicestershire Water Mills* (Wymondham, Melton Mowbray, 1977)

M. Aston, *Interpreting the Landscape: landscape archaeology in Local Studies* (London, 1985)

———, *Know the Landscape. Monasteries* (London, 1993)

———, *Monasteries in the Landscape* (Stroud, 2000)

R. Bagdonas, *The Military and Hospitaller Order of St Lazarus of Jerusalem: its history and work* (nd)

C.O. Banks, *The Romances of Finchley Manor* (North Finchley, 1929)

M. Barber, 'Lepers, Jews and Moslems: the plot to overthrow Christendom in 1321', *History,* 66 (1981)

———, 'The Order of Saint Lazarus and the Crusades', *The Catholic Historical Review,* 80, no. 3 (July 1994)

———, *The New Knighthood: a history of the Order of the Temple* (Cambridge, 1994)

———, *The Trial of the Templars* (Cambridge, 1978)

T.G. Barber, *How the Church came to Spondon and her Chapelries, Stanley and Chaddesden* (Belper, 1950)

F. Barker and P. Jackson, *London. 2000 years of a City and its People* (London, 1974)

B.L. Beer, *Northumberland: the political career of John Dudley, Earl of Warwick and Duke of Northumberland* (Kent, Ohio, 1973)

L. Bellosi, *The Complete Works of Giotto* (Florence, 1981)

P. Bertrand, 'Ordre de St-Lazare de Jérusalem en Orient', *La Science Historique* (June 1927)

P. Bertrand de la Grassière, *L'Ordre Militaire et Hospitalier de Saint-Lazare de Jérusalem* (Paris, 1960)

S.T. Bindoff, *The House of Commons, 1509–1558,* 2 (London, 1982)

R. Bird, *The Turbulent London of Richard II* (London, 1949)

W.H. Blaauw, 'Dureford Abbey. Its fortunes and misfortunes', *Sussex Archaeological Collection,* 8 (1856)

G. de Blasiis, *Della Vita e delle opere di Pietro della Vigna* (Naples, 1860)

F. Blomefield, *History of Norfolk,* 2 (1732, 2nd edition London, 1805)

W. Bonser, *The Medical Background of Anglo-Saxon England* (London, 1963)

The Book of Saints, compiled by the Benedictine Monks of St Augustine's Abbey, Ramsgate (London, 1994)

S. Bottari, 'I Lebbrosari di Messina' in *Lazzaretti dell'Italia meridionale e della Sicilia*, Societa messinese di storia patria (Messina, 1989)

D.J.D. Boulton, *Knights of the Crown: The Monarchical Orders of Knighthood in later Medieval Europe, 1325–1520* (Woodbridge, 1987)

T. Bourne and J. Smithers, 'The Burning of Burton Lazars Hospital: the pitfalls of antiquarianism', *Bulletin of Local History, East Midlands Region*, 19 (1984)

M. Bowker, *The Secular Clergy in the Diocese of Lincoln, 1495–1520* (Cambridge, 1968)

J.R. Boyle, *The County of Durham* (London, 1892)

J.R. Branson, 'Report on Fieldwork, Cold Newton', *TLAHS*, 50 (1974–5)

W. Braunfels, *Monasteries of Western Europe: the architecture of the Orders* (London, 1972)

L. Bemness, *The Complete Book of Herbs* (London, 1988)

A Brief History and Guide: the church of St Peter, Tilton-on-the-Hill (nd)

H.D. Briggs, E. Cambridge and R.N. Bailey, 'A New Approach to Church Archaeology: excavation and documentary work at Woodhorn, Ponteland and the pre-Norman Cathedral at Durham', *AA*, 5th Series, 11 (1983)

———, 'A New Approach to Church Archaeology, II: dowsing and excavations at Ponteland and St Oswald's, Durham', *AA*, 5th Series, 13 (1985)

S.N. Brody, *The Disease of the Soul. Leprosy in Medieval Literature* (New York, 1974)

F.W. Brooks, 'The Hospital of Holy Innocents without Lincoln', Lincolnshire Architectural and Archaeological Society, *AASRP*, 42, pt 2 (1934–5)

D.R. Brothwell, *Digging Up Bones* (London, 1981)

A.E. Brown, 'Burton Lazars, Leicestershire: a planned medieval landscape?', *Landscape History*, 18 (1996)

———, *Fieldwork for Archaeologists and Local Historians* (London, 1987)

——— (ed.), *Garden Archaeology*, Council for British Archaeology, Research Report, 78 (London, 1991)

R. Brown, 'Achievement of Thomas Mowbray, Duke of Norfolk', *Archaeologia*, 29 (1842)

J.A. Brundage, *Medieval Canon Law and the Crusader* (Madison, Wisconsin, Milwaukee and London, 1969)

———, *Law, Sex and Christian Society in Medieval Europe* (Chicago, 1987)

B. Burke, *The General Armory of England, Scotland, Ireland and Wales* (London, 1884)

J. Burton, 'The Knights Templar in Yorkshire in the twelfth century: a reassessment', *Northern History*, 27 (1991)

W. Burton, *The Description of Leicestershire* (London, 1622)

A. Butler, *Lives of the Saints*, 1, 4 (1926, reprinted London, 1956)

K. Cameron, *The Place-names of Derbyshire*, pt 3 (London, 1959)

L.M. Cantor, 'Castles, Fortified Houses, Moated Homesteads and Monastic Settlements', in L.M. Cantor (ed.), *The English Medieval Landscape* (London, 1982)

———, 'The Medieval Parks of Leicestershire', *TLAHS*, 46, 52 (1970–71 and 1976–77)

———, 'The Medieval Castles of Leicestershire', *TLAHS*, 53 (1977–78)

M. Carlin, 'Medieval English Hospitals', in L. Granshaw and R. Porter (eds), *The Hospital in History* (London, 1989)

C. Carpenter, 'Sir Thomas Malory and Fifteen-century Local Politics', *Bulletin of the Institute of Historical Research*, 53 (1980)

E. Casciani, 'Today's Knights', *The Scots Magazine* (July 1985)

G. Chalmers, *Caledonia*, 4 (Paisley, 1889)

J. Cherry, 'The Silver Seal Matrix of the Peculiar Jurisdiction of the Prebend of St Margaret, Leicester', *TLAHS*, 67 (1993)

P. Cholerton, *The Church of St Mary the Virgin, Chaddesden: a guide and history* (Chaddesden, 1997)

The Church of St-Peter-in-Chains, Threekingham: a walk round guide (nd)

R. Churton, *The Lives of William Smyth, Bishop of Lincoln, and Sir Richard Sutton, Knight, founders of Brasen Nose College* (London, 1800)

G.A.L. Cibrario, *Precis historique des ordres religieux et militaires de Saint-Lazare et de Saint-Maurice, traduit par M. Ferrand* (Lyon, 1860)

A. Clarke, 'Digging for Lepers' and 'Search for the Lawrence St Lepers', *Interim*, Newsletter of the York Archaeological Trust, 19(a) (1994)

Revd Clark-Maxwell, 'Some Letters of Confraternity', *Archaeologia*, 75 (1924–25)

———, 'Some Further Letters of Fraternity', *Archaeologia*, 79 (1929)

C.T. Clay, 'The Family of Amundeville', *LAASRP*, 3, new series, pt 2 (1939–44)

———, 'Notes on the Family of Amundeville', *AA*, 4th series, 24 (1946)

R.M. Clay, *The Medieval Hospitals of England* (1909, reprinted London, 1966)

G. Clinch, *Bloomsbury and St Giles's* (London, 1890)

M. Clive, *This Sun of York: a biography of Edward IV* (1973, reprinted London, 1975)

J.S. Cockburn, H.P.F. King and K.G.T. McDonnell (eds), *VCH, Middlesex*, 1 (reprinted London, 1969)

H.M. Colvin, 'Dale Abbey: granges, mills and other buildings', *JDANHS*, 60, new series, 13 (1939)

C.R. Conder, *The Latin Kingdom of Jerusalem, 1099–1291* (1897, reprinted London, 1973)

G.H. Cook, *English Monasteries in the Middle Ages* (London, 1961)

———, *Medieval Chantries and Chantry Chapels* (1947, revised London, 1963)

W.D. Cookson, 'On the Hospital of the Holy Innocents, called *Le Malardri*, at Lincoln: with some account of ancient customs and usages touching leprosy', in *A Selection of Papers relative to the County of Lincoln, read before the Lincolnshire Topographical Society, 1841, 1842* (Lincoln, 1843)

P. Courtney, 'The Monastic Granges of Leicestershire', *TLAHS*, 56 (1980–81)

J. Cowen (ed.), *Sir Thomas Malory, Le Morte D'Arthur*, 2 vols (1969, reprinted Harmondsworth, 1986)

E. Cownie, *Religious Patronage in Anglo-Norman England, 1066–1135* (London, 1998)

J.C. Cox, *Notes on the Churches of Derbyshire*, 3, 4 (Chesterfield, 1877, 1879)

H.H.E. Craster (ed.), *A History of Northumberland*, 10 (Newcastle-upon-Tyne, 1914)

C. Creighton, *A History of Epidemics in Britain*, 1 (London, 1965)

Crockford's Clerical Directory (London, 1910)

F.L. Cross, *The Oxford Dictionary of the Christian Church* (1957, 2nd edition London, 1974)

J. Cule, 'The Diagnosis, Care and Treatment of Leprosy in Wales and the Border in the Middle Ages', *Transactions of the British Society for the History of Pharmacy*, 1, no. 1 (1970)

P.H. Cullum, *Cremetts and Corrodies: care of the poor and sick in St Leonard's Hospital, York, in the Middle Ages*, Borthwick Paper, 79 (York, 1991)

———, 'Leperhouses and Borough Status in the Thirteenth Century', in P.R. Coss and S.D. Lloyd (eds), *Thirteenth Century England*, 3, Proceedings of the Newcastle-upon-Tyne Conference, 1989 (Woodbridge, 1991)

J. Cumming (ed.), *A New Dictionary of Saints* (Tunbridge Wells, 1993)

J. Curtis, *History of Leicestershire* (London, 1831)

H. de Curzon (ed.), *Le Règle du Temple*, Société de l'Histoire de France (Paris, 1886)

G.R.C. Davis, *Medieval Cartularies of Great Britain – a short catalogue* (London, 1958)

L. Demaitre, 'The Description and Diagnosis of Leprosy by Fourteenth-Century Physicians', *Bulletin of the History of Medicine*, 59 (1985)

B. Dichter, *The Maps of Acre, an Historical Cartography* (Acre, 1973)

J.C. Dickinson, *Monastic Life in Medieval England* (London, 1961)

Dictionary of National Biography, 1, 4, 6, 7, 10, 11, 13, 14, 16, 17, 19, 21 (London, 1921–2)

M.H. Dodds (ed.), *A History of Northumberland,* 14 (Newcastle-upon-Tyne, 1935)

M.W. Dols, 'The Leper in Medieval Islamic Society', *Speculum,* 58 (1983)

H.A. Doubleday, V. Gibbs, D. Warrand, H. de Walden and G.H. White (eds), *The Complete Peerage,* 2, 5, 6, 7, 9, 12 (London, 1912–53)

A. Dryden (ed.), *Memorials of Old Leicestershire* (London, 1911)

G. Duby (ed.), *A History of Private Life, 2, Revelations of the Medieval World,* translated by A. Goldhammer (Cambridge, Massachusetts and London, 1988)

E. Duffy, *The Stripping of the Altars: traditional religion in England, c.1400–1580* (Yale, 1992)

W. Dugdale (revised by J. Caley, H. Ellis and B. Bandinel), *Monasticon Anglicanum,* 6 pt 2 (London, 1830)

A.A.M. Duncan, *Scotland. The Making of the Kingdom,* 1 (Edinburgh, 1975)

E. Eames, *Catalogue of Medieval Lead Glazed Earthenware Tiles in the British Museum* (London, 1980)

———, *English Medieval Tiles* (London, 1985)

D.E. Easson, *Medieval Religious Houses. Scotland* (1957, 2nd edition, I.B. Cowan and D.E. Easson, London, 1976)

E.H. Edmunds and K.P. Oakley, *British Regional Geology: the Central England District* (1936, 2nd edition London, 1947)

L.E. Elliott-Binns, *Medieval Cornwall* (London, 1955)

A.S. Ellis, 'Biographical Notes on the Yorkshire Tenants', *The Yorkshire Archaeological and Topographical Journal,* 4 (1877)

H. Ellis, *The Parish of Saint Leonard, Shoreditch, and Liberty of Norton Folgate* (London, 1798)

G.R. Elton, *Policy and Police* (London, 1972)

A.B. Emden, *A Biographical Register of the University of Cambridge to 1500* (Cambridge, 1963)

———, *A Biographical Register of the University of Oxford to AD 1500,* 3 vols (Oxford, 1957–59)

J. Escher and P. Schweizer (eds), *Urkundenbuch der Stadt und Landschaft Zurich* (Zurich, 1901)

M. Farley and K. Manchester, 'The Cemetery of the Leper Hospital of St Margaret, High Wycombe, Buckinghamshire', *Medieval Archaeology,* 33 (1989)

D.H. Farmer, *Saint Hugh of Lincoln* (London, 1985)

———, *The Oxford Dictionary of Saints* (Oxford, 1992)

R.L. Farmer, 'Stydd Preceptory and the Military Religious Orders', *JDANHS,* 33 (1911)

G.F. Farnham, *Leicestershire Medieval Pedigrees* (Leicester, 1925)

———, *Leicestershire: Medieval Village Notes,* 6 vols (Leicester, 1929–33)

———, 'Quenby, the Manor and Hall', *TLAHS,* 16 pt 1 (1929–31)

P.J.C. Field, *The Life and Times of Sir Thomas Malory* (Cambridge, 1993)

R.C. Finucane, *Miracles and Pilgrims: popular beliefs in medieval England* (London, 1977)

J.B. Firth, *Highways and Byways in Leicestershire* (London, 1926)

R. Flenley (ed.), *Six Town Chronicles of England* (Oxford, 1911)

A. Forey, 'The Militarisation of the Hospital of St John', in A. Forey, *Military Orders and Crusades* (Aldershot, 1994)

———, 'The Military Order of St Thomas of Acre', *English Historical Review,* 92 (1997)

G.T. Forrest (ed.), *The Parish of St Leonard, Shoreditch,* Survey of London, 8 (London, 1922)

J. Foster, *Alumni Oxonienses, 1500–1714*, 4 vols (Oxford, 1887–92)

——, *Some Feudal Coats of Arms* (1901, reprinted Bristol, 1984)

——, *The Dictionary of Heraldry. Feudal Coats of Arms and Pedigrees* (London, 1992)

A.W. Fox, *Kirby Bellars: a parish history* (Kirby Bellars, 1997)

A.C. Fox-Davies, *A Complete Guide to Heraldry* (1929, reprinted London, 1993)

—— (ed.), *Armorial Families: a directory of gentleman of coat-armour* (London, 1910)

E.B. Fryde, *Studies in Medieval Trade and Finance* (London, 1983)

T. Fuller, *The History of the Worthies of England* (London, 1662)

D. Gardiner, *The Hospital of St Nicholas, Harbledown* (1950, reprinted Canterbury, 1956)

F.A. Gasquet, *English Monastic Life* (London, 1904)

M. Gervers, 'The Medieval Cartulary Tradition and the Survival of Archival Material as reflected in the English Hospitaller Cartulary of 1442', *Medieval Studies*, 37 (1975)

Der Geschichtesfreund, 12 (1856)

Gibson, *The History of the Monastery founded at Tynemouth in the Diocese of Durham*, 1 (London, 1846)

R. Gilchrist, 'Christian Bodies and Souls: the archaeology of life and death in later medieval hospitals', in S. Bassett (ed.), *Death in Towns: urban responses to the dying and the dead, 1000–1600* (London, 1992)

——, *Contemplation and Action: the other monasticism* (London, 1995)

W.H. Godfrey, *The English Almshouse* (London, 1955)

E. Gooder, *Temple Balsall: the Warwickshire preceptory of the Templars and their fate* (Chichester, 1995)

L. Gordon, *A Country Herbal* (Exeter, 1980)

M. Gray, *The Trinitarian Order in England: excavations at Thelsford Priory* (ed L. Watts and P. Rahtz), BAR, British Series, 226 (1993)

H.S. Grazebrook, 'The Barons of Dudley', *Collections for a History of Staffordshire*, 9 (1888)

J.P. Greene, *Norton Priory: the archaeology of a medieval religious house* (Cambridge, 1989)

D.E. Greenway, *Charters of the Honour of Mowbray, 1107–1191* (London, 1972)

K. Gron, 'Leprosy in Literature and Art', *International Journal of Leprosy*, 41, 2 (1973)

A Guide to Gaulby Church and Village (nd)

A. Gwynn and R.N. Hadcock, *Medieval Religious Houses. Ireland* (London, 1970)

R.N. Hadcock, 'A Map of Medieval Northumberland and Durham', *AA*, 4th series, 16 (1939)

J.H. Hadwin, 'Deflating Philanthropy', *Economic History Review*, 2nd series, 31 (1978)

B. Hamilton, *The Leper King and his Heirs* (New York, 2000)

C. Harnett, *Monasteries and Monks* (London, 1963)

C. Harper-Bill, 'The English Church and English Religion after the Black Death', in M. Ormrod and P. Lindley (eds), *The Black Death in England* (Stamford, 1996)

C. Harrison, 'The *Valor Ecclesiasticus*: a re-appraisal based on the Staffordshire returns', *StS*, 11 (1999)

S. Hart (ed.), *One in Specyal: immortalizers of King Arthur* (Presteigne, 1985)

R.F. Hartley, *The Medieval Earthworks of North-East Leicestershire*, Leicestershire Museums Archaeological Reports Series, no. 88 (Leicester, 1987)

——, *The Medieval Earthworks of Central Leicestershire*, Leicestershire Museums Publication, no. 103 (Leicester, 1989)

J. Harvey, *Medieval Gardens* (London, 1981)

P.D.A. Harvey and A. McGuiness, *A Guide to British Medieval Seals* (London, 1996)

H. Hazard, *A History of the Crusades*, 4 (Madison, 1977)

P. Helyot, *Histoire des Ordres Monastiques Religieux et Militaires*, 2, 3, 6 (Paris, 1714–21)

C.G. Herbermann *et al.* (eds), *The Catholic Encyclopedia*, 9 (London, 1910)

D.I. Hill, *St John Baptist, Northgate*, Medieval Hospitals in Canterbury (Canterbury, nd)

————, *St Nicholas Harbledown*, Medieval Hospitals in Canterbury (Canterbury, nd)

R.H. Hilton, *The Decline of Serfdom in Medieval England* (London, 1969)

A.B. Hinds (ed.), *A History of Northumberland*, 3 (Newcastle-upon-Tyne, 1896)

F. Hitchins, *History of Cornwall*, 2 vols (Helston, 1824)

J.C. Hodgson (ed.), *A History of Northumberland*, 7 (Newcastle-upon-Tyne, 1904)

————, 'The Hospital of St Lazarus and the Manor of Harehope', *AA*, 3rd Series, 19 (1922)

R. Holmes, 'The Hospital of Foulsnape in the West Riding', *Yorkshire Archaeological and Topographical Journal*, 10 (1889)

S. Holmes, 'Trough on Harehope Moor, Northumberland', *Proceedings of the Society of Antiquaries of Newcastle-upon-Tyne*, 2nd series, 9 (1901)

W. Holtzmann (ed.), *Papsturkunden in England (Abhandlungen der Gesellschaft der Wissenschaften zu Gottingen)*, 3 vols (Berlin, 1930–52)

M.B. Honeybourne, 'The Leper Hospitals of the London Area', *Transactions of the London and Middlesex Archaeological Society*, 21 (1967)

W.W. St John Hope, 'The Round Church of the Knights Templars at Temple Bruer, Lincolnshire', *Archaeologia*, 61, pt 1 (1908)

R. Horrox, *The Black Death*, Manchester Medieval Sources Series (Manchester and New York, 1994)

W.G. Hoskins, *The Making of the English Landscape* (1955, reprinted London, 1988)

———— (ed.), *VCH, Leicestershire*, 2 (London, 1954)

P. Hoste, 'Leper Baths', *Gentleman's Magazine* (pt 2, 1866)

B.P. Hudle, *Medieval Roads* (1982, reprinted Aylesbury, 1989)

J. Hughes, *The Religious Life of Richard III. Piety and Prayer in the North of England* (Stroud, 1997)

J.R. Hughes and S.T. Lusted, *Parish Church of St Werburgh, Spondon, Derby* (Spondon, 1999)

E. Hull, 'A Scheme of Water Supply for Villages, and Hamlets and County Parishes of the Central and Eastern Counties', *Quarterly Journal of Science*, 6 (1876)

P.E. Hunt, *Notes on Medieval Melton Mowbray, 1077–1507* (Grantham, 1965)

————, *The Story of Melton Mowbray* (1957, 2nd edition Grantham, 1979)

R. Hyacinthe, 'L'Ordre militaire et hospitalier de Saint-Lazare de Jérusalem aux douzième et treizième siècles', in *Utilis est Lapis in Structura: mélanges offerts à Leon Pressouyre*, Comité de Travaux Historiques et Scientifiques (Paris, 2000)

P. Imms and H. Imms, *The Holy Well*, In search of Spondon series, 1 (Derby, 1996)

S. Jack, 'Monastic Lands in Leicestershire and their Administration on the Eve of the Dissolution', *TLAHS*, 41 (1965–6)

D. Jacoby, 'Montmusard, Suburb of Crusader Acre: the first stage of its development', in B.Z. Kedar, H.E. Mayer and R.C. Smale (eds), *Outremer. Studies in the History of the Crusading Kingdom of Jerusalem presented to Joshua Prawer* (Jerusalem, 1982)

K.P. Jankrift, 'Die Leprosenbruderschaft des Heiligen Lazarus zu Jerusalem und ihre Ältesien Statuten', in G. Melville (ed.), *De Ordine Vitae: zu Normvorstellungen, Organisationsformen und Schriftgebrauch im mittelalterlichen Ordenswesen*, Vita Regularis, 1 (Münster, 1996)

————, *Leprose als Streiter Gottes: institutionalisierung und organisation des ordens vom Heiligen Lazarus zu Jerusalem von seinen anfängen bis zum jahre 1350*, Vita Regularis, 4 (Münster, 1996)

W.J. Jopling, *Handbook of Leprosy* (London, 1984)

W.K. Jordan, *Philanthropy in England, 1480–1660: a study of the changing patterns of English social aspirations* (London, 1959)

J.W. Judd, *The Geology of Rutland and the parts of Lincoln, Leicester, Northampton, Huntingdon and Cambridge included in sheet 64 of the one inch map of the Geological Survey,* Memoir of the Geological Survey (London, 1875)

A.J. Jukes-Browne and W.H. Dalton, *The Geology of the South West parts of Leicestershire and Nottinghamshire* (Sheet 70), Memoirs of the Geological Survey (London, 1885)

M. Keen, *Chivalry* (Yale, 1984)

Kelly's Directory of Lincolnshire, 1905 (London, 1905)

J.N.D. Kelly, *The Oxford Dictionary of Popes* (Oxford, 1988)

P.M. Kendall, *Richard the Third* (1955, reprinted London, 1961)

D.J.C. King, *Castellarium Anglicanum,* 1, 2 (New York, 1983)

E.J. King, *The Grand Priory of the Order of the Hospitallers of St John of Jerusalem in England. A Short History* (London, 1924)

———, *The Knights Hospitallers in the Holy Land* (London, 1931)

G.M. King, *St Mary's Parish Church, Melton Mowbray: a miscellany* (Melton Mowbray, nd)

C.L. Kingsford, *The Early History of Piccadilly, Leicester Square and Soho* (Cambridge, 1925)

N. Knauz, *Magyar Sion,* 2 (Esztergom, 1870)

———, *Monumenta Ecclesia Strigoniensis,* 1 (Esztergom, 1874)

The Knights Templars of Temple Bruer and Aslackby, Lincolnshire Museums Information Sheet, Archaeology Series, 25 (nd)

D. Knowles, *The Monastic Order in England* (1940, 2nd edition Cambridge, 1966)

——— and R.N. Hadcock, *Medieval Religious Houses in England and Wales* (1953, 2nd edition London, 1971)

A. Kreider, *English Chantries: the road to dissolution* (Cambridge, Massachusetts and London, 1979)

G.W. Lamplugh *et al., The Geology of the Melton Mowbray District and South-east Nottinghamshire (Sheet 142),* Memoirs of the Geological Survey (1909)

S.K. Land, *Kett's Rebellion: the Norfolk Rising of 1549* (Ipswich, 1977)

J.R. Lander, *The Wars of the Roses* (1990, reprinted Stroud, 1992)

The St Lazarus Gazette: the Newsletter of the Grand Priory of Canada, 8, no. 1 (February 1994)

G.A. Lee, *Leper Hospitals in Medieval Ireland: with a short account of the military and hospitaller order of St Lazarus of Jerusalem* (Blackrock, Co. Dublin, 1996)

———, 'Leper Houses of Munster', *North Munster Archaeological Journal,* 10, 1 (1966)

The Leicester and Nottingham Journal, 10 May 1760

C. Lewis *et al., Village, Hamlet and Field: changing medieval settlements in Central England* (Manchester and New York, 1997)

C.F. Leyel (ed.), *Mrs M. Grieve, A Modern Herbal* (1931, reprinted Harmondsworth, 1982)

G. Lipscombe, *History of the County of Buckinghamshire,* 4 vols (London, 1847)

A.G. Little, 'The Corrodies of the Carmelite Friary of Lynn', *Journal of Ecclesiastical History,* 9 (1958)

D. Loades, *John Dudley, Duke of Northumberland, 1504–1553* (Oxford, 1996)

T. de St Luc, *Mémoires en forme d'abrégé historique de l'insitution de l'order royal des chevaliers hospitaliers de Notre-Dame du Mont-Carmel et de St Lazare de Jérusalem,* pt 2 (Paris, 1666)

W.E. Lunt, *Financial Relations of the Papacy with England,* 1, *to 1327* (1939); 2, *1327–1534* (Cambridge, Massachusetts, 1962)

————, *The Valuation of Norwich* (Oxford, 1926)

D. and S. Lysons, *Magna Britannia, 5, Derbyshire* (London, 1817)

R. Mabey (ed.), *The Complete New Herbal* (London, 1988)

F. Madan (ed.), *Brasenose College Quatercentenary Monographs*, Oxford Historical Society, 52 (1909)

J.R. Magilton and F. Lee, 'The Cemetery of the Hospital of St James and St Mary Magdalene, Chichester – a case study', *World Archaeology*, 21 (1989)

————, 'The Leper-house of St James and St Mary Magdalene, Chichester', in C.A. Roberts *et al.* (eds), *Burial Archaeology: current research methods and development*, BAR, British Series, 211 (1989)

K. Manchester, 'A Leprous Skeleton of the 7th Century from Eccles, Kent, and the present evidence for Leprosy in early Britain', *Journal of Archaeological Science*, 8 (1981)

————, 'Leprosy', *Current Archaeology*, 81 (March, 1981)

————, 'Tuberculosis and Leprosy in Antiquity: an interpretation', *MH*, 28 (1984)

———— and C. Knüssel, 'A Medieval Sculpture of Leprosy in the Cistercian Abbaye de Cadouin', *MH*, 38 (1974)

O. Manning and W. Bray, *The History and Antiquities of the County of Surrey*, 3 vols (1804–14, reprinted Wakefield, 1974)

D. Marcombe, 'Burton Lazars and the Knights of St Lazarus', *St John Historical Society Newsletter*, 6 (1986)

————, 'The Last Days of Lenton Priory', in D. Wood (ed.), *Life and Thought in the Northern Church c.1100–c.1700: essays in honour of Claire Cross* (Woodbridge, 1999)

————, 'The Preceptory of the Knights of St Lazarus at Locko', *DAJ*, 111 (1991)

———— and K. Manchester, 'The Melton Mowbray "Leper Head": an historical and medical investigation', *MH*, 34 (1990)

————, 'The Confraternity Seals of Burton Lazars Hospital and a newly discovered Matrix from Robertsbridge, Sussex', *TLAHS*, 76 (2002)

H.E. Mayer, *The Crusades* (Oxford, 1972)

T. McLean, *Medieval English Gardens* (1981, reprinted London, 1989)

A. Mee, *Lincolnshire* (London, 1949)

Melton Mowbray Parish Church (Gloucester, nd)

C.A. Mercier, *Leper Houses and Medieval Hospitals* (London, 1915)

T.S. Miller, 'The Knights of St John and the Hospitals of the Latin West', *Speculum*, 53 (1978)

B. Moffat *et al.* (eds), *Sharp Practice, Reports on Researches into the Medieval Hospital at Soutra, Lothian Region*, Sharp-Soutra Hospital Archaeoethnopharmacological Research Project, 1 (Edinburgh, 1986)

V. Möller-Christensen, 'Evidence of Leprosy in Earlier Peoples', in D. Brothwell and A.T. Sandison (eds), *Diseases in Antiquity* (Springfield, Illinois, 1967)

————, *Leprosy Changes of the Skull* (Odense, 1978)

A.R.H. Moncreiff, *Romance and Legend of Chivalry* (London, nd)

J.L. La Monte, *Feudal Monarchy in the Latin Kingdom of Jerusalem, 1100–1291* (Cambridge, Massachusetts, 1932)

N. Moore, *The History of St Bartholomew's Hospital*, 1, 2 (London, 1918)

R.I. Moore, *The Formation of a Persecuting Society* (Oxford, 1987)

P. Morris, *Agricultural Buildings in Roman Britain*, BAR, British Series, 70 (1979)

R. Morris, *Churches in the Landscape* (London, 1989)

O. Mosley, *History of the Castle, Priory and Town of Tutbury* (London, 1832)

A. Mutel, 'Recherches sur l'Ordre de Saint-Lazare de Jérusalem en Normandie', *Annales de Normandie*, 33, no. 2 (June 1983)

A.R. Myers, *London in the Age of Chaucer* (London, 1972)

G. Newman, *Prize Essays in Leprosy,* New Sydenham Society (London, 1895)

J.G. Nichols, *History and Antiquities of Leicestershire,* 2 pt 1 (London, 1795); 2 pt 2 (London, 1798); 3 pt 1 (London, 1800)

———, 'The Armorial Windows in Woodhouse Chapel, Leicestershire', *Transactions of the Leicestershire Architectural, Archaeological and Historical Society,* 1 pt 3 (1864)

———, 'The Family of Wauncy', *The Herald and Genealogist,* 4 (1867)

H. Nicholson, *Templars, Hospitallers and Teutonic Knights: images of the military orders, 1128–1291* (Leicester, 1993)

S.K. Noordeen, 'The Epidemiology of Leprosy', in R.C. Hastings (ed.), *Leprosy* (Edinburgh, 1994)

T. North, 'The Mowbrays, Lords of Melton', *Transactions of the Leicestershire Architectural and Archaeological Society,* 1 pt 3 (1864)

———, *The Church Bells of Leicestershire* (Leicester, 1876)

W.B. Ober, 'Can the Leper Change his Spots? The Iconography of Leprosy', *American Journal of Dermatopathology,* 5 (1983)

N. Orme and O. Padel, 'The Medieval Leper-House at "Lamford", Cornwall', *Historical Research,* 69, no. 168 (February, 1996)

N. Orme and M. Webster, *The English Hospital, 1070–1570* (New Haven, London, 1995)

G. Ormerod, *The History of the County Palatine and City of Chester,* 3 vols (London, 1819)

D.M. Owen, *Church and Society in Medieval Lincolnshire,* History of Lincolnshire, 5 (Lincoln, 1971)

———, *The Making of Kings Lynn,* Records of Social and Economic History, new series, 9 (Oxford, 1984)

W. Page (ed.), *VCH, Derbyshire,* 2 (1907, reprinted London, 1970)

———, *VCH, Leicestershire,* 1 (1907, reprinted London, 1969)

———, *VCH, Lincolnshire,* 2 (London, 1906)

———, *VCH, Middlesex,* 2 (London, 1911)

———, *VCH, Norfolk,* 2 (1906, reprinted London, 1975)

———, *VCH, Nottinghamshire,* 2 (London, 1910)

———, *VCH, Sussex,* 2 (1907, reprinted London, 1973)

———, *VCH, Yorkshire,* 2, 3 (London, 1912–13)

———, *VCH, Yorkshire, North Riding,* 1 (London, 1914)

R. Parker, *Men of Dunwich* (London, 1980)

C. Parkin, *History of Norfolk,* 8, 9, 10 (London, 1808–9)

J. Parton, *Some Account of the Hospital and Parish of St Giles-in-the-Fields, Middlesex* (London, 1822)

M.P. Pearson and R.T. Schadla-Hall (eds), *Looking at the Land: archaeological landscapes in eastern England,* Leicestershire Museums, Arts and Record Service (Leicester, 1994)

C. Pendrill, *London Life in the 14th Century* (1925, reprinted London, 1971)

R. Pétiet, *Contribution à l'Histoire de l'Ordre de Saint-Lazare de Jérusalem en France* (Paris, 1914)

N. Pevsner, *The Buildings of England. Derbyshire* (Harmondsworth, 1953)

———, *The Buildings of England. Leicestershire and Rutland* (Harmondsworth, 1960)

——— (revised by E. Williamson with G.K Brandwood), *The Buildings of England. Lincolnshire* (Harmondsworth, 1964, 2nd edition 1984)

———, *The Buildings of England. Yorkshire. The West Riding* (Harmondsworth, 1959)

——— and E. Hubbard, *The Buildings of England. Cheshire* (Harmondsworth, 1971)

R. Phillips and N. Foy, *Herbs* (1990, reprinted London, 1992)

A.J. Pickering, 'A Spa – the mineral baths and holy wells', *The Guardian and South Leicestershire Advertiser* (22 and 28 March 1924)

M. de Pierredon, *L'Ordre Militaire de Hospitaliers de Saint-Lazare de Jérusalem* (Paris, 1930)

C. Platt, *The Monastic Grange in Medieval England: a reassessment* (London, 1969)

A.W. Pollard and G.R. Redgrave, *A Short Title Catalogue of Books printed in England, 1475–1640*, 1, 2 (1926, 2nd edition, London, 1976–86)

J.M. Powell, *Anatomy of a Crusade, 1213–1221* (Philadelphia, 1986)

F.M. Powicke, *King Henry III and the Lord Edward* (Oxford, 1966)

P. Pradel, *Sculptures Romanes des Musées de France* (Paris, 1958)

J. Prawer, *Crusader Institutions* (Oxford, 1980)

———, *The Latin Kingdom of Jerusalem* (London, 1972)

H.E. Quilter, 'The Lower Lias of Leicestershire', *Geological Magazine*, 3 (1886)

J. Raine, *History of Blyth* (Westminster, 1860)

A. Ransome, 'Extracts from the Milroy Lectures on the Pathology and Prevention of Phthisis', *British Medical Journal* (1 March 1890)

C. Rawcliffe, 'The Hospitals of Later Medieval London', *MH*, 28 (1984)

———, *Medicine and Society in Later Medieval England* (Stroud, 1995)

———, *Medicine for the Soul: the life, death and resurrection of an English medieval hospital, St Giles, Norwich, c.1249–1550* (Stroud, 1999)

———, 'Learning to love the Leper: aspects of institutional charity in Anglo-Norman England', *Anglo-Norman Studies*, 23 (2001)

R. Reader, 'New Evidence for the Antiquity of Leprosy in early Britain', *Journal of Archaeological Science*, 1 (1974)

W. Rees, *A History of the Order of St John of Jerusalem in Wales and on the Welsh Border* (Cardiff, 1947)

S. Reynolds (ed.), *VCH, Middlesex*, 3 (London, 1962)

J. Richard, *The Latin Kingdom of Jerusalem* (Amsterdam, 1979)

———, *The Crusades, c.1071–c.1291* (Cambridge, 1999)

P. Richards, *The Medieval Leper and his Northern Heirs* (Cambridge, 1977, reprinted 2000)

L. Richardson, *Wells and Springs of Leicestershire*, Memoirs of the Geological Survey (1931)

S. Riches, *St George: hero, martyr and myth* (Stroud, 2000)

S.H. Rigby, *English Society in the later Middle Ages: class, status and gender* (Basingstoke, 1995)

W.E. Riley (ed.), *The Parish of St Giles-in-the-Fields*, pts 1 and 2, Survey of London, 3, 5 (London, 1912–14)

J. Riley-Smith, *The Knights of St John in Jerusalem and Cyprus* (London, 1967)

———, *Hospitallers. The History of the Order of St John* (London, 1999)

C. Roberts, 'Leprosy and Leprosaria in Medieval Britain', *MASCA Journal*, 4 (1986)

——— and K. Manchester, *The Archaeology of Disease* (Ithaca, 1996)

D.M. Robinson, *The Geography of Augustinian Settlement in Medieval England and Wales*, BAR, British Series, 80 (1980)

———, 'The Site Changes of Augustinian Communities in Medieval England and Wales', *Medieval Studies*, 43 (1981)

R. Rose, *Hale Magna Church: brief notes on the church and its registers* (1976)

C. Ross, *Edward IV* (1974, reprinted London, 1997)

C.D. Rothery, *Burton Lazars: story of a village* (1980, 2nd edition Burton Lazars, 1984)

M. Rubin, *Charity and Community in Medieval Cambridge* (Cambridge, 1987)

———, 'Development and Change in English Hospitals, 1100–1500', in L. Granshaw and R. Porter (eds), *The Hospital in History* (London, 1989)

S. Rubin, *Medieval English Medicine* (Newton Abbot, 1974)

S. Runciman, *A History of the Crusades*, 2 (Cambridge, 1952)

J.C. Russell, 'Population in Europe 500–1500', in C.M. Cipolla (ed.), *The Fontana Economic History of Europe: the Middle Ages* (London, 1972)

C. Sagittarius, *Historia Gothana Plenior* (Jena, 1700)

'The Sale by Auction of a Very Valuable Freehold Estate (tithe free) in Burton Lazars', *Leicester Journal*, 26 January 1815

N. Salmon, *Roman Stations in Britain* (London, 1726)

L.F. Salzmann, *English Life in the Middle Ages* (London, 1926)

—— (ed.), *VCH, Sussex*, 4 (London, 1953)

N. Saul, *Richard II* (1997, reprinted New Haven and London, 1999)

M.J. Sayer, 'Twyford of Kirk Langley and Spondon: problems in the history of a medieval Derbyshire family', *DAJ*, 94 (1974)

——, 'Twyford of Kirk Langley and Spondon: some problems resolved', *DAJ*, 97 (1977)

W.S. Scott, 'The Story of the Magistral House of the Order of St Lazarus in England at Burton Lazars', *Armorial*, 4 (1964)

——, 'A Burton Lazars Seal', *Archaeological Journal*, 10 (1853)

——, 'An Inedited Seal of the Hospital of Burton Lazars', *Archaeologia*, 18 (1817)

V. Sekules, 'A Lost Tomb from Sawley', in A. Borg and A. Martindale (eds), *The Vanishing Past: studies of mediaeval art, liturgy and metrology*, BAR, International Series, 111 (1981)

D. Selwood, *Knights of the Cloister: Templars and Hospitallers in Central-Southern Occitania, 1100–1300* (Woodbridge, 1999)

R.M. Serjeantson and W.R.D. Adkins (eds), *VCH, Northamptonshire*, 2 (1906, reprinted London, 1970)

D. Seward, *The Monks of War; the military religious orders* (London, 1972)

S. Shahar, 'Des lépreux pas comme les autres. L'Ordre de Saint-Lazare dans le royaume latin de Jérusalem', *Revue Historique*, 541 (January–March, 1982)

M.R.B. Shaw (ed.), 'Joinville and Villehardouin', in *Chronicles of the Crusades* (Harmondsworth, 1963)

F. Sheppard, *London. A History* (Oxford, 1998)

G. de Sibert, *Histoire des Orders Royaux, Hospitaliers-Militaires de Notre Dame du Mont Carmel et de Saint Lazare de Jerusalem* (Paris, 1772)

J.Y. Simpson, 'Antiquarian Notices of Leprosy and Leper Houses in Scotland and England', *Edinburgh Medical and Surgical Journal*, 56 (1841)

F.E. Skillington, 'Enclosed in Clay: a study of Leicester wills', *TLAHS*, 42 (1966–7)

O.K. Skinsnes, 'Travelogue of Leprosy Related Art', *International Journal of Leprosy*, 40 (4) (1922)

R. Somerville, *History of the Duchy of Lancaster, 1, 1265–1603* (London, 1953)

A.F. Sopp, *Pictures in Glass: notes on twelve coloured windows in Saint Mary's Church, Melton Mowbray* (Melton Mowbray, nd)

'South Witham', *Current Archaeology*, 9 (July 1968)

B. Spencer, 'Two Leaden Ampullae from Leicestershire', in 'Archaeology in Leicestershire and Rutland', *TLAHS*, 55 (1979/80)

J. Spottiswoode, *An Account of all the Religious Houses that were in Scotland at the time of the Reformation*, included in R. Keith, *An Historical Catalogue of the Scottish Bishops* (Edinburgh, 1824)

S.P.H. Statham, 'Ralph Fitz-Nicholas', *JDANHS*, 59, new series, 11 (1937)

W. Stevenson and A. Stapelton, *Some Account of the Religious Institutions of Old Nottingham* (Nottingham, 1895)

R. Le Strange, *Monasteries of Norfolk* (Kings Lynn, 1973)

R. Studd, 'From Preceptor to Prisoner of the Church: Ralph Tanet of Keele and the last of the Templars', *Staffordshire Studies*, 8 (1996)

A.I. Suckling, *History of Suffolk*, 1, 2 (London, 1846–48)

R. Surtees, *The History and Antiquities of the County Palatine of Durham*, 1, 2 (1816–20, reprinted Wakefield, 1972)

W. Swaan, *Art and Architecture in the late Middle Ages* (London, 1988)

T.H. Swales, 'The Redistribution of the Monastic Lands in Norfolk at the Dissolution', *Norfolk Archaeology*, 34 (1969)

R.N. Swanson, *Church and Society in Late Medieval England* (Oxford, 1989)

J. Taaffe, *History of the Order of St John of Jerusalem*, 4 vols (London, 1852)

C.H. Talbot, *Medicine in Medieval England* (London, 1967)

C. Taylor, *The Archaeology of Gardens* (Princes Risborough, 1983)

R. Taylor, *Index Monasticus: abbeys and other monasteries . . . formerly established in the Diocese of Norwich and the ancient Kingdom of East Anglia* (London, 1821)

R.P. Taylor, *The Berkeleys of Wymondham* (Wymondham, 1980)

W.E. Tentzel, *Supplementum Historiae Gothanae* (Jena, 1702)

A.H. Thomas and I.D. Thornley (eds), *The Great Chronicle of London* (London, 1938)

A.H. Thompson, *The Abbey of St Mary of the Meadows, Leicester* (Leicester, 1949)

———, 'The Chapel of St Peter at Kirby-upon-Wreake (Kirby Bellars)', *TLAHS*, 16 (1929–31)

———, *The History of the Hospital and the New College of the Annunciation of St Mary in the Newarke, Leicester* (Leicester, 1937)

———, 'Notes on the History of Bardney Abbey', Lincolnshire Architectural and Archaeological Society, *AASRP*, 32, pt 1 (1913)

B. Thompson, 'Monasteries and their Patrons at Foundation and Dissolution', *TRHS*, 6th series, 4 (1994)

J. Thirsk, *The English Rural Landscape* (Oxford, 2000)

J. Throsby, *The Supplementary volume to the Leicestershire Views: containing a series of excursions in the year 1790, to the villages and places of note in the county* (Leicester, 1790)

S. Tibble, *Monarchy and Lordships in the Latin Kingdom of Jerusalem, 1099–1291* (Oxford, 1989)

J. Tilley, *The Old Halls, Manors and Families of Derbyshire*, 2 (London, 1893)

F.-O. Touati, *Maladie et société au moyen âge. La lépre, les lépreux et les léproseries dans la province ecclésiastique de Sens jusqu'au milieu de XIVe siècle*, Bibliothèque du moyen âge, 11 (Paris, 1998)

G. Turbutt, *A History of Derbyshire*, 2 (Cardiff, 1999)

S. Turnbull, *The Book of the Medieval Knight* (London, 1985)

T. Turner, *English Garden Design: history and styles since 1650* (Woodbridge, 1986)

W.B. Twowell, *Leicestershire Village History, Past and Present, 1, Burton Lazars* (Melton Mowbray, 1882)

R. Twysden, *Historiae Anglicanae Scriptores X* (London, 1652)

J.M. Upton-Ward, *The Rule of the Templars* (Woodbridge, 1992)

R. Vaughan, *Matthew Paris* (Cambridge, 1958)

——— (ed.), *The Illustrated Chronicle of Matthew Paris: observations of thirteenth century life* (Stroud, 1993)

J. and J.A. Venn, *Alumni Cantabrigienses, pt 1, to 1751*, 4 vols (Cambridge, 1922–27)

E. Vignat, *Les Lépreux et les Chevaliers de Saint-Lazare de Jérusalem et de Notre Dame du Mont-Carmel* (Orléans, 1884)

G.W.J. Wagner, *Die Vormaligen Geistlichen Stifte im Gross Herzogthum Hessen* (Darmstadt, 1873)

W.S. Walford, 'A Discussion Paper on Seals', *Proceedings of the Society of Antiquaries*, 1st series, 4 (1859)

J. Walker, 'The Motives of Patrons of the Order of St Lazarus in England in the Twelfth and Thirteenth Centuries', in J. Loades (ed.), *Monastic Studies: the continuity of tradition* (Bangor, 1990)

J. Ward, *Chronological Events in the History of Melton Mowbray together with sketches of the hamlets affiliated thereto* (Melton Mowbray, 1889)

———, *Melton Mowbray in Olden Times* (Melton Mowbray, 1879)

C. Wells, *Bones, Bodies and Disease* (London, 1964)

———, 'A Leper Cemetery at South Acre, Norfolk', *Medieval Archaeology*, 11 (1967)

J. West, *Village Records* (1962, reprinted Chichester, 1982)

P. Whalley (ed.), J. Bridges, *The History and Antiquities of Northamptonshire*, 2 vols (Oxford, 1791)

N.R. Whitcomb, *The Medieval Floor-Tiles of Leicestershire* (Leicester, 1956)

A. White, *Stow Green Fair*, Lincolnshire Museums Information Sheet, Archaeology Series, no. 16 (1979)

W. White, *History, Gazetteer and Directory of Leicestershire* (Sheffield, 1846)

W.E. Wightman, *The Lacy Family in England and Normandy, 1066–1194* (Oxford, 1966)

E. Williams, *Early Holborn and the Legal Quarter of London*, 2 (London, 1927)

V. Wing, 'Melton Church', *TLAAS*, 1, pt 1 (1862)

———, *Reminiscences of the Revd Thomas Ford LLD, formerly vicar of Melton Mowbray* (Melton Mowbray, 1864)

———, 'An Enquiry Concerning the Founders and Ancient Monuments of Melton Mowbray church' *Transactions of the Leicestershire Archaeological Society*, 3 (1874)

J. Woodward, *A Treatise on Ecclesiastical Heraldry* (Edinburgh and London, 1894)

J. Wright, *The History and Antiquities of the County of Rutland* (London, 1684–1714, with additions, printed 1788, reprinted Wakefield, 1973)

J.P. Yeatman, 'Pedigree of the Albinis', *The Feudal History of the County of Derby*, 4 sect 8 (London, 1905)

E. and W. Young, *Old London Churches* (London, 1956)

———, *London's Churches* (London, 1986)

Unpublished secondary sources

UNCLH, J. Alexander, 'Burton Lazars Loose Stones Project: preliminary report on the medieval stonework' (September 2001)

UNCLH, J.M. Allsop, 'Burton Lazars – an earthwork survey of the leper hospital', MFR, 88/8 (1988)

UNCLH, J.M. Allsop, 'Earthwork survey of the "Mount" at Melton Mowbray', MFR, 88/11 (1988)

UNCLH, J.M. Allsop, 'Earthwork survey and stereo-aerial photo analysis of the Tilton hospital site', MFR, 95/20 (1995)

UNCLH, J.M. Allsop, 'Preliminary notes on Tilton Hospital', MFR (2001)

UNCLH, J.M. Allsop, 'Site notes and interpretation of the earthwork of Harehope Hospital in the parish of Eglingham, Northumberland', MFR, 01/02 (2001)

UNCLH, J.M. Allsop, 'The interpretation of the earthwork site of the order of St Lazarus at Burton Lazars', MFR, 01/10 (2001)

UNCLH, J.M. Allsop and M.J. Allsop, 'Analysis of the possessions of the order of St Lazarus in Burton Lazars', MFR, 87/11 (1987)

UNCLH, J.M. Allsop, M.J. Allsop and M. Hatton, 'Service trenches adjacent to and SE of the hospital site at Burton Lazars', MFR 99/7 (1999)

UNCLH, J.M. Allsop and M. Hatton, 'Ground survey of crop (parch) marks on the earthwork site of the medieval order of St Lazarus at Burton Lazars', MFR, 96/8 (1996)

UNCLH, J.M. Allsop and M. Hatton, 'Earthwork survey of Man Mill (Mannemilne), possession of the medieval order of St Lazarus on the River Eye at Burton Lazars', MFR 98/5 (1998) updated MFR, 00/01 (2000)

UNCLH, J.M. Allsop and M. Hatton, 'Notes on the possible provenance of carved stone fragments at Burton Lazars, near to the site of the medieval hospital', MFR, 00/4 (2000)

UNCLH, J.M. Allsop and M. Hatton, 'Description and sketches of the Ham Bridge, Burton Lazars', MFR, 00/06 (2000)

UNCLH, K.D. Baird, *An address delivered on 23 May 1984 in the Collegiate Church of St Vincent, Edinburgh* (nd)

LRO, M. Best, *Arms in Leicestershire Churches* (1969)

UNCLH, Burton Lazars Research Group, University of Nottingham, *The Preceptory of the Order of St Lazarus at Choseley* (Nottingham, 2000)

P.H. Cullum, 'Hospitals and Charitable Provision in Medieval Yorkshire, 936–1547', University of York, D.Phil. thesis (1989)

M. Evans, 'The Crusades and Society in the English Midlands, c.1160–1307', University of Nottingham, Ph.D. thesis (1997)

T. Foulds, 'Thurgarton Priory and its benefactors, with an edition of the Cartulary', University of Nottingham, Ph.D. thesis (1984)

R. Hyacinthe, 'L'Ordre militaire et hospitalier de Saint-Lazare de Jérusalem en Occident: histoire – iconographie – archéologie', University of Paris (Sorbonne), Ph.D. thesis (2000)

LOSJ, J.R. Lawrence-Owen, 'The Military and Hospitaller Order of St Lazarus of Jerusalem' (1964)

P. Newton, 'Schools of Glass Painting in the Midlands', University of London, Ph.D. thesis (1961)

M. Satchell, 'The Emergence of Leper-Houses in Medieval England, 1100–1250', University of Oxford, D.Phil. thesis (1998)

J. Walker, 'The Patronage of the Templars and the Order of St Lazarus in England in the Twelfth and Thirteenth Centuries', University of St Andrews, Ph.D. thesis (1990)

Websites:

http://www.kwtelecom.com/chivalry/lazarus   G.S. Sainty, 'The Order of St Lazarus. An alternative viewpoint' and 'The Heraldry of the Order'

http://www.st-lazarus.net/world/history.htm   St Lazarus Net International

http://www.users.globalnet.co.uk/~tyderwen/thegrand.htm   The Grand Priory of England and Wales

Index

The order of St Lazarus in the Holy Land and western Europe is indexed according to the area in which it is to be found (i.e. France, Germany, Holy Land, Hungary, Italy, Scotland and Switzerland). The main body of the index deals principally with the affairs of the order of St Lazarus in England. Generic references are to be found under 'St Lazarus of Jerusalem, order of in England'. Individual hospitals and preceptories are indexed separately (i.e. Burton Lazars; Carlton-le-Moorland; Choseley; Foulsnape; St Giles, Holborn; Harehope; Harting; Holy Innocents', Lincoln; Locko; Tilton; Threckingham and Westwade), as are parishes in the ownership of the order.

Printed and bound by CPI Group (UK) Ltd, Croydon, CR0 4YY

13/04/2025

14656522-0003